NEW PERSPECTIVES ON THE ROMAN
CIVIL WARS OF 49–30 BCE

Also available from Bloomsbury

AFTER THE CRISIS: REMEMBRANCE, RE-ANCHORING AND RECOVERY IN ANCIENT GREECE AND ROME
edited by Jacqueline Klooster and Inger N. I. Kuin

LANDSCAPES OF WAR IN GREEK AND ROMAN LITERATURE
edited by Bettina Reitz-Joosse, Marian W. Makins and C. J. Mackie

LUCAN'S IMPERIAL WORLD
edited by Laura Zientek and Mark Thorne

NEW PERSPECTIVES ON THE ROMAN CIVIL WARS OF 49–30 BCE

Edited by
Richard Westall and Hannah Cornwell

BLOOMSBURY ACADEMIC
LONDON • NEW YORK • OXFORD • NEW DELHI • SYDNEY

BLOOMSBURY ACADEMIC
Bloomsbury Publishing Plc, 50 Bedford Square, London, WC1B 3DP, UK
Bloomsbury Publishing Inc, 1359 Broadway, 12th Floor, New York, NY 10018, USA
Bloomsbury Publishing Ireland, 29 Earlsfort Terrace, Dublin 2, D02 AY28, Ireland

BLOOMSBURY, BLOOMSBURY ACADEMIC and the Diana logo
are trademarks of Bloomsbury Publishing Plc

First published in Great Britain 2024
This paperback edition published 2025

Copyright © Richard Westall, Hannah Cornwell & Contributors, 2024

Richard Westall and Hannah Cornwell have asserted their right under the Copyright,
Designs and Patents Act, 1988, to be identified as Editors of this work.

For legal purposes the Acknowledgements on p. x constitute
an extension of this copyright page.

Cover image: *The death of Julius Caesar*. Painting by Joseph Court (1797–1865), 1827. Fabre Museum, Montpellier, France. Photo by Leemage/Corbis via Getty Images

All rights reserved. No part of this publication may be: i) reproduced or transmitted in any form, electronic or mechanical, including photocopying, recording or by means of any information storage or retrieval system without prior permission in writing from the publishers; or ii) used or reproduced in any way for the training, development or operation of artificial intelligence (AI) technologies, including generative AI technologies. The rights holders expressly reserve this publication from the text and data mining exception as per Article 4(3) of the Digital Single Market Directive (EU) 2019/790.

Bloomsbury Publishing Inc does not have any control over, or responsibility for, any third-party websites referred to or in this book. All internet addresses given in this book were correct at the time of going to press. The author and publisher regret any inconvenience caused if addresses have changed or sites have ceased to exist, but can accept no responsibility for any such changes.

A catalogue record for this book is available from the British Library.

Library of Congress Cataloging-in-Publication Data
Names: Cornwell, Hannah, editor. | Westall, Richard, editor.
Title: New perspectives on the Roman Civil Wars of 49-30 BCE / edited by Hannah Cornwell and Richard Westall.
Description: London ; New York : Bloomsbury Academic, 2024. | Includes bibliographical references and index.
Identifiers: LCCN 2023039090 (print) | LCCN 2023039091 (ebook) | ISBN 9781350272460 (hardback) | ISBN 9781350272477 (paperback) | ISBN 9781350272484 (pdf) | ISBN 9781350272491 (ebook)
Subjects: LCSH: Rome–History–Civil War, 49-45 B.C. | Rome–History–Civil War, 43-31 B.C. | Rome–History–Civil War, 49-45 B.C.–Historiography. | Rome–History–Civil War, 43-31 B.C.–Historiography.
Classification: LCC DG266 .N49 2024 (print) | LCC DG266 (ebook) | DDC 937/.05–dc23/eng/20231130
LC record available at https://lccn.loc.gov/2023039090
LC ebook record available at https://lccn.loc.gov/2023039091

ISBN: HB: 978-1-3502-7246-0
PB: 978-1-3502-7247-7
ePDF: 978-1-3502-7248-4
eBook: 978-1-3502-7249-1

Typeset by RefineCatch Limited, Bungay, Suffolk

For product safety related questions contact productsafety@bloomsbury.com.

To find out more about our authors and books visit www.bloomsbury.com
and sign up for our newsletters.

CONTENTS

List of Figures   vii
List of Tables   viii
List of Contributors   ix
Acknowledgements   x
List of Abbreviations   xi

Introduction   1

1   **Negotiation as a Tool for Legitimacy in the Roman Civil War of 49–48 BCE: 'A New Policy for Achieving Victory' (Cic. Att. 9.7C.1)**
Hannah Cornwell   13

2   **What Is Civil about Civil War? Political Communication and the Construction of 'The People' on the Eve of Civil War (49–48 BCE)**
Emilio Zucchetti   33

3   **The Meaning of ⊥II on Caesar's Civil War Coinage (RRC 452)**
Olga Liubimova   55

4   **Creating Alternative Legitimacy: Octavian, Sextus Pompeius and Divine Filiation**   Laura Kersten   75

5   **Negotiating the Failure of Roman Hegemony: The Experience of Allied Rulers During the Civil Wars (49–30 BCE)**   Bradley Jordan   95

6   **Brothers at the Crossroads: Agrippa and His Brother in Civil War**
Sabina Tariverdieva   117

7   **Ghost Walls and Vanishing Towns: The Case of Caesar's Siege of Corfinium Between Historical Sources and Archaeological-Topographical Data**   Vasco La Salvia and Marco Moderato   127

8   **The Changing Face of the Command Structure During the Civil Wars (49–30 BCE)**   Bertrand Augier   141

9   **The Civil War of 43–42 BCE and Army Finances**   François Gauthier   153

Contents

10 Sallust's Mithridates and the Cultural Trauma of Civil War
   Jennifer Gerrish   167

11 Towards a New Archaeology of the Lost *Histories* of C. Asinius
   Pollio   *Richard Westall*   181

Bibliography   201
Index   227

FIGURES

3.1	*Aureus* of C. Julius Caesar, *RRC* 452/1; Ex Numismatica Ars Classica NAC AG, Auction 46, Lot 416	55
3.2	*Denarius* of C. Julius Caesar, *RRC* 452/2; Barber Institute of Fine Art Coin Collection, R0696	56
3.3	*Denarius* of C. Julius Caesar, *RRC* 452/3; Ex Numismatica Arts Classica NAC AG, Auction 63, Lot 356	56
4.1	*Denarius* of Q. Nasidius, *RRC* 483/1; National Museum of Denmark, RP 651.1 (photograph: Andreas Mogensen)	78
4.2	*Denarius* of Q. Nasidius; *RRC* 483/2; Münzkabinett der Staatlichen Museen zu Berlin, 18213373 (photograph: Dirk Sonnenwald)	79
4.3	*Denarius* of Sextus Pompeius; *RRC* 511/3; Münzkabinett der Staatlichen Museen zu Berlin, 18207996 (photograph: Dirk Sonnenwald)	79
4.4	*Denarius* of Sextus Pompeius (reverse); *RRC* 511/4; Münzkabinett der Staatlichen Museen zu Berlin, 18202271 (photograph: Dirk Sonnenwald)	80
4.5	Coin (bronze) of Octavian; *RRC* 535/1; ANS 1944.100.6017	83
4.6	*Aureus* of Octavian (obverse); *RRC* 490/2; Münzkabinett der Staatlichen Museen zu Berlin, 18202283 (photograph: Dirk Sonnenwald)	83
7.1	Corfinium: in Central Italy; 3D rendering of the valley and aerial photo of the present town (image: Vasco La Salvia)	128
7.2	Corfinium: plan of the Roman town with known archaeological features (image: Vasco La Salvia)	130
7.3	Corfinium: urban fortification system (image: Vasco La Salvia)	131
7.4	Reconstruction of the siege camp adapted from Stoffel 1887's map (image: Vasco La Salvia)	132
7.5	Corfinium, *Campus Militaris*: Plan, aerial photo and drone imagery from the excavation (image: Vasco La Salvia)	134
11.1	Diagram illustrating the use of the prepositions ἀπό and ἐκ, from Hansen and Quinn 1992: 54	185

TABLES

3.1	Contemporary coin issues (49–47 BCE)	58
3.2	Caesar's military successes	65
9.1	Opposing forces at Philippi in 42 BCE	155
9.2	Gifts to soldiers 43–42 BCE	157
9.3	Attested sources of income for Cassius and Brutus	158
9.4	Attested sources of income for Octavian and Antony	160

CONTRIBUTORS

Bertrand Augier is Lecturer, Department of History, History of Art and Archaeology, Université de Nantes.

Hannah Cornwell is Associate Professor, Department of Classics, Ancient History and Archaeology at the University of Birmingham.

François Gauthier is Faculty Lecturer, Department of History and Sociology at the University of British Columbia (Okanagan).

Jennifer Gerrish is Associate Professor, Department of Classics, College of Charleston.

Bradley Jordan is Postdoctoral Fellow, Department of Archaeology, Conservation and History at the University of Oslo.

Laura Kersten is Research Associate in Ancient History at the Friedrich-Meinecke-Institut, Freie Universität Berlin.

Vasco La Salvia is Associate Professor of Archaeology, Università degli Studi 'Gabriele d'Annunzio' Chieti.

Olga Liubimova is an independent researcher, Moscow.

Marco Moderato is Postdoctoral Researcher, Università degli Studi 'Gabriele d'Annunzio' Chieti.

Sabina Tariverdieva is an independent researcher, Moscow.

Richard Westall is Associate Member of the *Sapienza Centre for the Study of the Mediterranean and Near East in Late Antiquity and Early Middle Ages*, Sapienza, Università di Roma.

Emilio Zucchetti is Lecturer in Roman History, Classics Department, Royal Holloway University of London.

ACKNOWLEDGEMENTS

This edited volume is the product of an international workshop, *The Roman Civil Wars of 49–30 BCE: Analysing the Breakdown of Models*, held at the British School at Rome, 22–4 July 2019. We are grateful to both the British School at Rome and the University of Birmingham for their generous support in organizing and hosting the event. We would also like to thank the anonymous peer-reviewers of the book proposal and draft manuscript as well as our editors at Bloomsbury Academic.

ABBREVIATIONS

BMCCR	*British Museum Catalogue of Coins of the Roman Empire*, ed. H. Mattingly et al. (1923–).
BNP	*Brill's New Pauly. Encyclopaedia of the Ancient World: Classical Tradition*, ed. M. Landfester, H. Cancik, H. Schneider (2006–11).
CIL	*Corpus Inscriptionum Latinarum*, ed. T. Mommsen et al. (1863–).
CIRB	*Corpus Inscriptionum Regni Bosporani*, ed. V. V. Struve (1965).
CRR	*The Coinage of the Roman Republic*, ed. E. A. Sydenham (1952).
DNP	*Der Neue Pauly. Enzyklopädie der Antike. Altertum*, ed. H. Cancik, H. Schneider (1996–2008).
FGrHist	*Fragmente der griechischen Historiker*, ed. F. Jacoby (1923–).
FRHist	*The Fragments of the Roman Historians*, ed. T. J. Cornell et al. (2013).
I.Didyma	*Didyma, II. Die Inschriften*, ed. A. Rehm (1958).
IG	*Inscriptiones Graecae* (1873–).
IGR	*Inscriptiones Graecae ad Res Romanas Pertinentes*, ed. R. Cagnat (1906–28).
ILLRP	*Inscriptiones Latinae Liberae Rei Publicae*, ed. A. Degrassi, vol. 1^2 (1965), vol. 2 (1963).
ILS	*Inscriptiones Latinae Selectae*, ed. H. Dessau (1892–1916).
Inscr. Ital.	*Inscriptiones Italiae Academicae Italicae Consociatae ediderunt*, ed. A. Degrassi (1937–67).
IMT	*Inschriften Mysia und Troas*, ed. M. Barth and J. Stauber (1993).
HRR	*Historicorum Romanorum reliquiae*, ed. H. Peter (1870–1914).
MRR	T. R. S. Broughton, *The Magistrates of the Roman Republic* (1951–2); Suppl. (1986: supersedes Suppl. 1960).
OGIS	*Orientis Graeci Inscriptiones Selectae*, ed. W. Dittenberger (1903–5).
OLD	*Oxford Latin Dictionary*, ed. P. G. Glare (1982).
RE	*Real-Encyclopädie der klassischen Altertumswissenschaft*, ed. A. Pauly, G. Wissowa and W. Kroll (1893–).
RIC	*Roman Imperial Coinage*, ed. H. Mattingly et al. (1923–67); rev. edn of vol. 1, ed. C. H. V. Sutherland and R. A. G. Carson (1984).
RPC	*Roman Provincial Coinage*, eds A. Burnett, M. Amandry and P. P. Ripollès (1992–).

Abbreviations

RRC	*Roman Republican Coinage*, ed. M. H. Crawford (1974).
RS	*Roman Statutes*, ed. M. H. Crawford, with contributions by J. D. Cloud et al. (1996).
Samos	*Inscriptions. Texts and List.* 'The Princeton Project on the Inscriptions of Anatolia', The Institute for Advanced Study, Princeton, ed. D. F. McCabe (1986).
SEG	*Supplementum epigraphicum Graecum* (1923–).
StR[3]	Th. Mommsen, *Römisches Staatsrecht*, 3rd edn (1887).
Syll.[3]	W. Dittenberger, *Sylloge Inscriptionum Graecarum*, 3rd edn (1915–24).
TLL	*Thesaurus Linguae Latinae* (1900–).

INTRODUCTION

1. Historiography and the contemporary world

Within the wider world where scholarship intersects with government policy, the topic of civil war has been steadily growing in interest since the invasion of Afghanistan and Iraq by American-led coalitions in the wake of 9/11. That is the context for seminal work such as *The Logic of Violence in Civil War* by Stathis Kalyvas (2006) and *Civil Wars: A History in Ideas* by David Armitage (2017). The paradigm of the Cold War has gradually been replaced by that of a Hobbesian, anarchic system.[1] Needless to say, the triumphalist rhetoric that theorized the possibility of hegemonic monopoly has also been toned down in the wake of American defeats in Iraq and Afghanistan. In a world where autonomy is prized, at least in theory, civil war seems set to become the normal form of conflict.[2] Hence, the above-mentioned publications characterize the response by academia at large.

Within the world of classical studies, where trends are slower and sometimes one has the feeling of observing the consequences of Carsic rivers, scholarly response to the focus of studies expressed by Erich Gruen's *The Last Generation of the Roman Republic* (1974) and Paul Zanker's *Augustus und die Macht der Bilder* (1987)[3] resulted in a new appreciation of authors, texts, iconography, and problems linked to the Roman civil wars constituting the transition from the late Republic to the Principate. So, for instance, fresh work was done resulting in ambitious, programmatic articles by Richard Westall on the Forum Iulium as a civil war monument (1996) and Gregory Bucher on the *Roman History* of Appian (2000). The most successful and influential instance of this work was *Caesar's Legacy: Civil War and the Emergence of the Roman Empire* by Josiah Osgood (2006).

Noteworthy monographs have followed, illuminating our understanding of a particular aspect of this period. So, for instance, just as Jan Felix Gaertner and Bianca Hausburg dedicated a philologically rigorous monograph to the *Bellum Alexandrinum* (2013), monographs by William Batstone and Cynthia Damon (2006), Luca Grillo (2012), Ayelet Peer (2015), and Richard Westall (2017) have explored the literary art and historical reliability of Caesar's *Civil War*. Prosopography and epigraphy have admirably been deployed to provide seminal re-readings of well-known figures and episodes with monographs such as Kathryn Welch's *Magnus Pius: Sextus Pompeius and the Transformation of the Roman Republic* (2012), Josiah Osgood's *Turia: A Roman Woman's Civil War* (2014), Kit Morrell's *Pompey, Cato and the Governance of the Roman Empire* (2017), and Susan Treggiari's *Servilia and her Family* (2019). Of no less significance and interest are the monographs that have re-calibrated our understanding of institutions, concepts, and material culture, as in the respective cases of Carsten Hjort Lange's *Triumphs in the Age of Civil War: The Late Republic and the Adaptability of Triumphal Tradition* (2016), Hannah Cornwell's *Pax and the Politics of Peace: Republic to Principate* (2017), and Dominik Maschek's *Die römischen Bürgerkriege: Archäologie und Geschichte einer Krisenzeit* (2018). The list might easily be expanded; let these serve to illustrate the flourishing health of the field.

The past decade or so has been characterized by an increase in collective volumes drawing together the results of conferences or research groups dedicated to the theme of civil war at Rome or within the Graeco-Roman world. Leading the way is *Citizens of Discord: Rome and Its Civil Wars* edited by Brian Breed, Cynthia Damon, and Andreola Rossi (2010). This elegant volume started the ball rolling nicely with its numerous contributions examining the cultural poetics of civil war at Rome over the course of the Republic and Principate. Then followed a more ambitious and comprehensive survey of the entirety of Graeco-Roman history with *Civil War in Ancient Greece and Rome: Contexts of Disintegration and Reintegration* edited by Henning Börm, Marco Mattheis, and Johannes Wienand (2016). Likewise ambitious in its scope, but limited to the issue of memory and its construction, is the stimulating volume of *After the Crisis: Remembrance, Re-anchoring and Recovery in Ancient Greece and Rome* edited by Jacqueline Klooster and Inger N. I. Kuin (2020).[4] More focused and addressing issues strictly related to Roman civil war and the end of the Republic are the collective volumes of *The Triumviral Period: Civil War, Political Crisis and Socioeconomic Transformations* edited by Francisco Pina Polo (2020) and *Coins of the Roman Revolution 49 BC–AD 14: Evidence Without Hindsight* edited by Anton Powell and Andrew Burnett (2020). The effect produced by these welcome additions to the scholarship is that of an immense photomontage, where minor advances collectively offer a new vision of the transition from Republic to Principate and a sense of the overall context of this complicated historical phenomenon.

Another fundamental strand of research that has created the premises for a radically new understanding of the civil wars of the late Republic is *The Fragments of the Roman Historians* (2013). This critical edition produced by a team of editors led by T. J. Cornell provides comprehensive analytical introductions with bibliographical surveys, editions with facing translations, and detailed historical and philological commentary on the surviving fragments of Roman historians whose writings have not reached us by direct transmission in the manuscript tradition. The culmination of seventeen years' labour (1996–2012), it replaces the formerly indispensable critical edition of Hermann Peter (*HRR*) and offers a reference tool on a par with those of Felix Jacoby (*FGrHist*) and Hans Beck and Uwe Walter (*Die frühen römischen Historiker*). Of similar effect, albeit more modest in appearance and limited to a single author, is the volume of sixteen essays dedicated to the *Roman History* of Appian of Alexandria and edited by Kathryn Welch (2015). The influence of both is evident in subsequent publications. Thought turns, for instance, to the multiple volumes on Cassius Dio in the Brill series 'Historiography of Rome and Its Empire' and the review volume *The Historiography of Late Republican Civil War* edited by Carsten Hjort Lange and Frederik Juliaan Vervaet (2019) in the same series. Scholarship on the fragments has revolutionized our understanding of how the Romans wrote and thought about the civil wars of the late Republic.

No less significant, and equally welcome, are the numerous new critical editions, translations, and commentaries of note that have appeared over the last decade or so. For Caesar there is the work of Cynthia Damon (2015, 2016) and Kurt Raaflaub (2017). For Plutarch there is the work of Christopher Pelling (2011) and John Moles (2017). For Suetonius there is that of David Wardle (2014). For Appian there is that of Paul Goukowsky and colleagues (2008, 2021, 2010, 2022, 2017) and Brian McGing (2020). Last but not least, for Cassius Dio there is ongoing work such as that by Valérie Fromentin and Estelle Bertrand (2008, 2014). All of this philological-historical work likewise facilitates study of the civil wars of the late Republic.

In closing it is to be remarked that the appearance of publications dedicated to analysis of the civil wars that led from the late Republic to the early Principate shows no signs of abating. The monograph that Robert Morstein-Marx (2021) has dedicated to exploring the career of Julius Caesar as a Republican aristocrat competing within a democratic electoral system is a major contribution to debate over the causes of civil war and the disappearance of the Republic. The learned monograph which, in the enticing guise of 'popular history', Giusto Traina (2023) has devoted to narrating the events of 44–30 BCE offers an important revision of perspective, taking into account how Eastern allies in particular experienced the Romans' civil wars. Last but not least, as the present volume goes to press, Henning Börm, Ulrich Gotter, and Wolfgang Havener (2023) have edited a volume of fourteen essays that likewise address the Roman civil wars of the 40s and 30s from a multiplicity of perspectives as regards the fabric and enunciation of Roman culture. Thanks to all of these works and many others, the study of the Roman civil wars of the late Republic has never been more potentially rewarding.

2. New perspectives

Approaching the issue from a wide variety of perspectives, these eleven papers grapple with the problem of the breakdown of Republican forms of government, society and culture during the Roman civil wars of 49–30 BCE. Concentrating upon a specific instance, each paper approaches the phenomenon of the breakdown of Republican forms from a different perspective. One practical consequence of this is that the methodologies deployed vary immensely, ranging from discourse analysis to numismatics and from archaeological fieldwork to trauma theory. Notwithstanding the multiplicity of perspectives, however, the papers complement one another rather than standing in marked contrast. Together they highlight the breakdown of traditional models and the invention of new ones, illustrating the formative process of the Roman civil wars that led from the Republic to the Principate.

These papers can roughly be arranged in three groups, even though other combinations are possible in view of the shared themes under investigation. To the editors, it seems to make sense to talk of these papers as dealing with (1) the arts of government, (2) the interaction of society and government, and (3) the creation of memory for future government.

* * *

The arts of government constitute a pragmatic discourse involving negotiation and representation with a view to constructing consensus. On the one hand, there is the communication and interaction of the elite amongst themselves, which is nicely exemplified by the letters, speeches and informal contacts that were used in an attempt to avoid the rupture occasioned by the emergency decree of the Senate (*SCU*) of 7 January 49 BCE and Caesar's invasion of Italy. A flurry of communication and interaction between the protagonists and their peers preceded the outbreak of war, continuing thick until it had become clear that negotiations were unfeasible. On the other hand, there is the communication and interaction between elites and masses, such as that implied by the readership of the *commentarii* of the *imperator* C. Caesar. As the conflict gained in intensity and became a civil war that was both protracted in time and extended to the whole of the Roman world, emphasis came to be laid upon mobilizing the masses so as to win battles and thereafter secure peace through public opinion. Often calibrated for different audiences, self-representation by means of visual and verbal culture directed at the elite and the masses laid public claim to legitimacy as regards the exercise of control over the government of Rome. Whether letters and speeches, or buildings and statues, or coins and religious ritual, evocative myths were fashioned in the contest for public authority.

Taking her cue from Caesar's epistolary description of his 'new policy for achieving victory' (Cic. *Att.* 9.7C.1), Hannah Cornwell investigates the evolving mechanisms and spaces of Roman diplomacy in time of civil war. Looking at how these were used to construct or deconstruct the legitimacy of the 'other' (viz. one's political opponents), she identifies problems such as that posed by distance, which constituted an impediment to the face-to-face interaction traditionally expected of Roman politics under the Republic, and highlights the new spaces, metaphorical (e.g. letters) as well as literal (e.g. the villa and the commander's tent), where negotiations were undertaken. In so doing, she casts a clear light on the breakdown of traditional forms and the emergence of new forms of elite communication and interaction.

Delving into the 'anarchy' (Plut. *Caes.* 28.4) unleashed by the outbreak of civil war in January 49 BCE, Emilio Zucchetti in his contribution examines Julius Caesar's communicative strategy in 49–48 BCE as a response to the distortion of language and breakdown of consensus. Deploying Laclau's constructionist model, he investigates Caesar's use of the late Republican catchword of *libertas* as a 'floating signifier' useful to fashioning a discourse aimed at reconciliation in the wake of military victory. Drawing upon sociological theory to furnish a critique of the thesis of 'coalition building' that has been advanced by Raaflaub, Zucchetti offers an alternative interpretation of how Caesar's *Bellum Civile* served to secure the support of the masses and legitimize the renegade proconsul.

The breakdown of linguistic models as a consequence of civil war, this time within the realm of numismatics, is likewise addressed by Olga Liubimova in her contribution dedicated to an issue (*RRC* 452) produced in 48 BCE. The absence of any reference to the *IIIviri monetales* is a striking departure from the norms of the last century of numismatic production under the Republic. The appearance of the sole name of the *imperator* C. Caesar, in conjunction with visual motifs commemorating his recent successes in Gaul, is part of the construction of a new grammar of material culture, responding to the necessities of civil war and constituting a transition towards the Principate. Difficulties of interpretation are arguably due to this change in the rules of Roman numismatic grammar.

The breakdown in traditional models of political legitimacy is next analysed by Laura Kersten in her contribution, which examines the contest for legitimacy between Caesar the Younger (Octavian) and Sextus Pompeius. Focusing upon the divine filiation claimed by these two civil war leaders, she explores the creation of an alternative claim to legitimacy that was not contingent upon what happened at Rome. The claim to be the son of a god marked a rupture with the aristocratic tradition of legendary genealogies and effectively undercut Republican models of authority. Intriguingly, as she observes, divine filiation offered a charismatic legitimacy that did not replace the institutional legitimacy conferred by Republican office (e.g. *praefectus orae maritimae* or *consul*), but instead corroborated it, thereby producing the Principate.

Clearly different types of breakdown occurred at different moments in the course of the Roman civil wars of 49–30 BCE. The cessation of normal political discourse prior to the inception of hostilities in early 49 BCE is taken as a given by both Cornwell and Zucchetti, whose contributions together offer a complementary vision of the search for new models and new solutions. On the other hand, their contributions also highlight the growing awareness amongst contemporaries of the irreparable nature of the rupture that had taken place. Such an awareness, it is worth adding *en passant*, seems to lie behind Caesar's eventual decision to leave the *Bellum Civile* incomplete and unpublished. Armed conflict only compounded the fracture, producing further forms of breakdown (e.g. linguistic and cognitive) that invited new solutions heralding the Principate. The contributions of Liubimova and Kersten, likewise complementary, illustrate this process at a later moment in the period under study. While the fact of Roman civil war offers a unifying thread for understanding the period 49–30 BCE, it is important to keep in mind the constantly evolving situation.

* * *

The interaction of society and government, by contrast with the foregoing, represents theory being put into action. Whether it was a matter of disposing of client kingdoms, billetting soldiers or finding the wherewithal for financing armies in the field, the historical accounts and other forms of evidence for the Roman civil wars of the late Republic allow for keen insight into the socialization that accompanied the imperial Republic at work under exceptional circumstances. Generals, officers, and families can be followed in detail as they negotiate visibly changing circumstances, seeking a firm foundation for future prosperity even as they feel the ground shifting beneath their feet. Tensions and compromises are highlighted by experiences such as those of Agrippa and his older brother or the populace of Rhodes when faced with a demand to furnish money for the army of C. Cassius and M. Brutus. As was made evident by things such as the Ptolemaic attempt to eliminate C. Caesar as well as Cn. Pompeius in 48–47 BCE and the military adventurism of the Pontic monarch Pharnaces in 47–46 BCE, Roman civil war called the Roman imperial project into question. Through attention to the pragmatic performance of government and familial relations, it is possible to perceive how the crises provoked by civil war were overcome and the re-affirmation of Roman hegemony was effected.

In a contribution dedicated to the allied rulers, Bradley Jordan explores what effect the breakdown of the Roman state in time of civil war had upon the governance of the Empire. All diplomacy had a personal basis in the Graeco-Roman world, but depended upon public institutions and impersonal forms for its validity. With the advent of Roman civil war and doubt as to who was a legitimate representative of the Roman state, this system was upended. Personal *amicitia* (and its opposite, *inimicitia*) can repeatedly be shown to have determined allied rulers' alignment during the years 49–30 BCE. Conversely, Roman leaders increasingly privileged personal relations. Hence, Herod became the king of Judaea, supplanting the Hasmonean dynasty, and the children of Cleopatra VII were handsomely outfitted with realms. Civil war catalyzed the process resulting in an autocratic form of empire.

The divided family loyalties that manifested themselves as a fundamental aspect of the societal breakdown associated with civil war constitute the focus of the following contribution by Sabina Tariverdieva. Concentrating on the sphinx-like character of Marcus Agrippa, she explores the familial history and early career of this longstanding companion and close collaborator of Caesar the Younger (Octavian). The fact that the family of Agrippa took opposing political stances in the early 40s BCE is of no little interest. Marcus attached himself to Caesar the Elder, whereas his brother (Lucius?) followed Cato the Younger. The household of L. Marcius Philippus (*cos.* 56) emerges as a site of transverse political and social interaction in the late 50s, and the factor of friendship (*amicitia*) can be seen to have affected political choices.

Dealing next with the large-scale, practical consequences of political alignment in time of civil war, Vasco La Salvia and Marco Moderato present the results of recent archaeological work at the site of ancient Corfinium. Strategically situated in central Italy, this Paelignian city had been chosen by the Italian allies as their capital in their war with Rome in 91 BCE, and the same rationale informed L. Domitius Ahenobarbus' decision to take up position there and await the arrival of Julius Caesar's invading army in early 49 BCE. Where were Ahenobarbus' roughly 13,000 soldiers deployed? Conceivably they camped within the open space of an immense structure (*c.* 33,000 m²) occupying an estimated one-sixth of the city's overall surface area of *c.* 20 ha. Dating to the middle of the first century BCE, this structure symbolizes Corfinium's integration with the emerging identity of a unified Italy that identified with the Roman state.

Exploring the sociology of the traditional command structure of the Roman army as it operated under the stresses of civil war, Bertrand Augier illustrates the breakdown in hierarchical order that derived from the perceived need for generals to accommodate soldiers and officers. Officers played a key role in the creation of consent within the Roman army. Owing their legitimacy to their acquaintance with soldiers as well as the *auctoritas* attributed to their position and the *virtus* that they personally displayed, officers directed the men on the battlefield and mediated for them with the general and vice versa in the camp. With Roman civil war armies often resembling autonomous political entities, officers had in effect become *senatores caligati*. Hence, punishment (*ignominia*) in time of civil war became rare for them just as it (corporal) did for the *miles gregarius*.

Next, taking as the object of his investigation the evidence for the finances relating to the years 43–42 and the campaign of Philippi, François Gauthier explores how the breakdown in the normal functioning of state finances stimulated the rise of imperatorial finances. A fundamental problem of civil war was the possession of Rome and hence of the financial resources at the disposal of the Senate (viz. the *aerarium* and the taxes that were owed to it). The precedents of Sulla and Pompeius in the 80s and 70s respectively nicely illustrate the issues faced by the protagonists of the Philippi campaign (C. Cassius and M. Brutus on the one hand, and M. Antonius and Caesar the Younger on the other). Detailing amounts, sources, and expenditures, Gauthier demonstrates the applicability of the term 'war economy' to the *ad hoc* measures of these years.

There are perceptible similarities in the types of breakdown discussed by these papers. Accepted socio-economic forms were called into question or simply set aside *tout court*. As emerges from the papers of Jordan and Tariverdieva, within the context of Roman civil war one-to-one personal relationships often prevailed over the usual considerations of corporate governance and decision-making by entities such as the family or Senate. The predominance of the figure of the *imperator* was accompanied by an eclipse of the multiple poles of elite power that had been characteristic of the oligarchy of the middle and late Republic. In like fashion, the premium placed upon the allegiance of soldiers and their willingness to fight meant that the usual concerns for proper behaviour *vis-à-vis* their superiors or a friendly civilian population might readily be forgotten, as can be seen from the papers of La Salvia and Moderato, Augier, and Gauthier. The opposition between soldier and civilian now witnessed Roman civilian society at the mercy of the legionaries, with the unsettling possibility that, in the manner of a latter-day Coriolanus, a Roman commander might in fact unleash foreign troops upon his fellow-citizens.

* * *

With historiography and representations of the past, we abandon the realm of action or language meant to encourage immediate action and enter into the field of philosophic discourse and the art of self-care. M. Tullius Cicero (*cos*. 63) is perhaps best remembered today for his political and forensic speeches. However, by his activity as an author of treatises of a philosophical nature during his withdrawal from public life in the mid-40s, Cicero offered contemporaries an alternative model to the feckless, self-destructive model of obstinate resistance furnished by Cn. Pompeius, Scipio Metellus and Cato the Younger. Rather than resort to arms yet again, he sublimated conflict by directing his creative energies elsewhere. In the end, as we know, the siren-call of political life proved too strong, and Cicero returned to active engagement in the hope of liberating the Republic from Caesar's heirs. However, his writings survived the Proscriptions of 43 BCE, thanks to the care of Atticus and Tiro, and his alternative model for senatorial comportment was taken up by a significant number of his younger contemporaries. Historiography, as Sallust and Pollio appear to have realized, was the prosecution of civil war by other means, more pacific and constructive. The historian of Roman civil war had the power to instruct future generations, offering guidance no less valuable than that furnished by Cicero in the *De officiis*.

The *Historiae* of Sallust remain an abiding monument to their time of composition (in all likelihood 39–35 BCE) in spite of their extremely fragmentary nature, and Jennifer Gerrish examines them with a view to what they tell us about the breakdown of contemporary society in the midst of civil war. Focusing on the letters attributed by the historian to Pompeius Magnus during the war against Spartacus and Mithridates the Great in his perennial conflict with the Romans, she highlights the absence of normative inversion that we might have expected. Rather than Pompeius and Mithridates being depicted as outstanding examples of the Roman and the barbarian respectively, there is a conscious confusion of categories that implies criticism of the Triumvirs and the impossibility of healing the trauma that their rule has inflicted upon the community.

No less noteworthy for their impact upon posterity were the *Historiae* of C. Asinius Pollio, which Richard Westall seeks to illustrate as a self-referential narrative of the breakdown of political and social norms during the 40s BCE. Reviewing the contemporary testimony of the poet Horace, he pinpoints the beginning and the end of Pollio's historical narrative. This results in a revision of the standard view of Pollio as the principal, immediate source for Plutarch and Appian for the late Republic. Instead, there emerges an image of a more circumscribed work that covered the years 49–40 BCE, wherein events such as the brutal firing of the besieged city of Perusia were evocatively described by a consul who chose to leave a written record. Ardent Caesarian and self-declared defender of the Republic, Pollio offered a partisan, but critical account.

Authors who had participated in the Roman civil wars of 49–30 BCE, in supporting roles of no little significance, Sallust and Pollio both had firsthand experience of the multiple forms of breakdown that had led to civil war and resulted from it. On the one hand, they had derived immense personal benefit from the breakdown of traditional political forms at Rome. On the other hand, their careers had, to varying degrees and in different ways, fractured upon the shoals of conflict exacerbated by civil war. As the contributions of Gerrish and Westall illustrate, these two senators responded to the challenge of Roman civil war by reflecting aloud and elaborating the communal sense of loss through a revisitation (direct or indirect) of the trauma of those years. The loss of innocence had produced a heightened self-awareness in Romans from all walks of life. Standing at the pinnacle of Roman society, the *novi homines* Sallust and Pollio are merely the tip of the figurative iceberg. Their lower-class analogues are to be found in the funeral monuments of former slaves who proudly represented themselves wearing togas and slaves who punctiliously noted their precise position in the housholds of the mighty and powerful.

3. Looking to the future

On a closing note, it seems appropriate to point out some of the new perspectives and questions raised by these contributions that may serve to define future investigation in the coming years. Each contribution, in its own way, adds something new to the ongoing discussion of the history and/or historiography of the Roman civil wars of 49–30 BCE.

As regards the area of pragmatic discourse, the contributions grapple with and raise fundamental questions concerning collective and individual decisions and destinies. How do we imagine consensus as being constructed and maintained? The respective camps of Cn. Pompeius and C. Caesar at Dyrrachium, for instance, were assuredly quite different in terms of the consensus that existed within them, and this consensus is likely to have differed from that normally to be expected within the Senate when it met at Rome. Different spaces (at different moments) generate different forms of socialization. To take another example: what forms of communication or other social and economic interaction are privileged by what parts of society when faced with the *guillotine* of civil war? For instance, drama and *historiae* appealed to rather diverse audiences. Indeed, it is worth adding, Cornelius Balbus the Younger cannot have been completely mad when he staged at Gades a *fabula praetexta* evoking his own part in the civil war of 49–48. Let a final example suffice: why did some individuals prevail and others fade away? The disappearance of an affirmed leader such as M. Lepidus raises a whole host of sociological questions no less than does the eventual success of the much loathed *Divi Filius*. Whether one is focusing on a particular individual or analysing an intermediate group or large-scale collectivity, these questions raised by various contributions – explicitly or implicitly – seem particularly promising for future work. The historical analysis of society and politics in the crucible of civil war is far from exhausted, even if D. R. Shackleton Bailey once famously likened the search for causes to 'reading in the sand where a scorpion has wandered'.[5]

As for what we have labelled pragmatics, the contributions raise significant questions regarding structural issues *vis-à-vis* cultural identity and institutions. What impact did the civil wars have upon the Romanization of the provincials? Arguably, the provincials' involvement in the trauma of civil war, whether willing or not, accelerated their identification with the Romans and their social, economic and political integration within the Roman empire. Herod and Plutarch, like C. Iulius Zoilos, were the products of Roman civil war.[6] Turning to Rome and the city's government, we might ask a related question. Was the Principate a solution without alternative? Could any form of government other than a Hellenistic monarchy, reliant upon a solid oligarchical consensus, have come out of the crucible of Roman civil war? The Vipsanii brothers ended up on opposing sides of the battlefield, but both were ultimately fighting for a *dux* who claimed to represent the state, but relied upon the military might of the legions and a senatorial consensus to exercise his authority. Notwithstanding the strictures of Erich Gruen regarding the need for the historian to avoid writing with hindsight, the path leading from C. Marius and L. Sulla to Magnus Pius, M. Antonius, and the *Princeps* does seem ineluctable, especially when hindsight is applied to discern underlying causes as Michael Crawford advised.[7] Thinking too of the Roman army, that quintessential institution of the Roman civil wars, we would do well to ask yet another question. Was the army itself the crucible of Roman society and economy? Arguably, the relations established between soldiers and officers in the context of civil war endured and left a visible impact upon Roman society and economy in the wake of the resolution of the civil wars. Obviously, there are the colonies in which the veterans of the civil wars were settled, from Philippi to Lyons and from Carthage to Corinth. However, there is much more. The experience of the Roman civil wars of 49–30 determined how an aspiring member of the civic elite might represent himself in a community such as Pompeii as well as how taxation was altered in fundamental fashion so as to accommodate for the phenomenon of the regular, peaceful settlement of veterans. The contributions relating to pragmatic concerns shed light upon these issues and point the way for future progress in research.

As regards the art of self-care, the contributions offer new ways of understanding the historiography associated with the Roman civil wars of 49–30 and invite us to consider new questions, or old questions in a new light. For instance, why was there a flowering of historiography under the sole rule of Caesar the Younger? In view of his bloody past (e.g. proscriptions and the alleged sacrifice of 300 prisoners-of-war after the capture of Perusia) and the celebrated repartee of Asinius Pollio that it is difficult to write against someone who proscribes, it might have been thought that silence regarding the recent past would be golden under the newly established monarchy. To offer another example, what were the social aims of the authors who revisited the trauma of Roman civil war? It might be objected that the aims were as many and varied as the authors who dealt with this theme, but certain common strands of thought seem fairly clear. In spite of the public festivities and the fine words regarding Caesar the Younger as a new founder of Rome, there was a widespread sense of lost innocence and collective guilt. Writing of the past is not merely an exercise in anatomical pathology, but also arguably a utopian endeavour to fashion a better future. To round off with yet a third suggestion for future research, who were the readers of these works and what were their reactions? Addressing their peers and proposing a non-Ciceronian model for Roman historiography, Sallust and Asinius Pollio were *novi homines* who defined what it meant to be a member of the elite under the new, Caesarian dispensation. Corporate behaviour for the reformed Senate was arguably determined as much by their historical works as it was by the exercise of censorial powers by Augustus.

Many other questions might be posed, and these are merely examples of what seem meaningful. Nonetheless, it is to be hoped that the present collection of contributions will provide guidance and stimulation as the discussion continues.

Notes

1. For example, Toni Ñaco del Hoyo and Fernando López Sánchez's 2018 edited volume *War, Warlords, and Interstate Relations in the Ancient Mediterranean* takes as its starting point a 'post 9/11 world', stressing that 'the end of the Cold War gave way to a multipolar, unstable and more insecure world' (2018: 2). They further draw parallels between the world views of Polybius and other Hellenistic writers and the unstable, multipolar world we now inhabit.

Introduction

2. Although in what are traditionally designated as 'third-world countries', such as Sudan, Ethiopia or Libya, civil war is a phenomenon markedly on the increase. Indeed, there are signs that it may not be limited to nations in the making but has the potential to extend to 'superpowers' such as Russia, the United States, and China. For a recent, trenchant analysis of the systemic risk that exists in contemporary polities, see Walter 2022.
3. This promptly appeared in an English translation by Alan Shapiro: *The Power of Images in the Age of Augustus* (1988).
4. We add that we very much look forward to the publication in 2024 of an ambitious collective volume edited by Johannes Wienand, Henning Börm, and Carsten Hjort Lange, which has the provisory title of *Ancient Cultures of Civil War: Polarization, Conflict, and Reconciliation*.
5. Shackleton Bailey 1960b: 267.
6. For Herod, see the comprehensive, detailed assessment of Roller 1998. For Plutarch, still fundamental is the discussion of Jones 1971: 5–9. For Zoilos, see Osgood 2006: 274–6.
7. The refusal to write a narrative based on hindsight is the guiding principle of Gruen 1974. For example, he writes: 'Hindsight deceives and distorts.' (1–2); 'An effort will be made to understand the Ciceronian era in its own terms, without the categories imposed by retrospective judgment' (2); 'The basic aim of this study [...] has been, not to explain the Republic's fall, but rather to explore the age of Cicero without the deceptive hindsight that stems from that fall' (505). In a forceful rebuttal, M. H. Crawford likened the undertaking to writing 'Hamlet without the prince': Crawford 1976: 214–17. The debate continues. For salutary observations, see now Morstein-Marx 2021: 14–21.

CHAPTER 1
NEGOTIATION AS A TOOL FOR LEGITIMACY IN THE ROMAN CIVIL WAR OF 49–48 BCE: 'A NEW POLICY FOR ACHIEVING VICTORY' (CIC. *ATT.* 9.7C.1)[*]

Hannah Cornwell

In a letter written in early March 49 BCE to two of his trusted equestrian friends at Rome, Gaius Oppius and Lucius Cornelius Balbus, Caesar set out what he referred to as his *nova ratio vincendi*, through which he intended to secure his position within (or indeed over) the state (Cic. *Att.* 9.7C.1). While Shackleton Bailey translates *nova ratio vincendi* as 'a new style for conquest' and Roller as 'a new means for conquering', this does not seem to capture the rhetorical intention and argument of the letter. As the title to this chapter indicates, my preferred translation is: 'a new policy for achieving victory'.[1] Caesar's strategy for success in the current conflict sought to use channels of negotiation and reconciliation to achieve a position of legitimacy and permanence, as I will outline below. Caesar would further emphasize this strategy in his commentaries justifying his position in 49–48: his *Civil War*.

The opening of Caesar's *Civil War* (at least as it survives to us) outlines his attempts, through written communications and the efforts of allied tribunes of the *plebs*, to present his requests to the Senate, in order to ensure a peaceful settlement at the start of the new consular year. In the first six chapters, Caesar outlines the attacks and objections raised by his *inimici* (personal opponents); the rejection of any moderate suggestions of mediation through official envoys (*legati*), or even senior magistrates offering independently to appraise him of the Senate's wishes (1.3-4); and the passing of 'that extreme and final decree of the Senate' (*illud extremum atque ultimum senatus consultum*, 1.5.3) on 7 January 49. This last was a clear rejection of any negotiation or reconciliation whatsoever, culminating in the preparation in Italy for war (1.6).[2] At the time of the passing of the so-called *senatus consultum ultimum* (*SCU*), Caesar was also judged to be an enemy of the state (*hostis iudicatus est*), although he merely alludes to the possibility (if he did not disarm his army) of appearing to be *adversus rem republicam* and avoids the use of the term *hostis*.[3] Stressing the gravity and harsh nature of the measures passed by the Senate against both his continued exercise of *imperium* and the tribunes of the *plebs* (1.5.4), Caesar juxtaposes the aggressive stance of Pompeius Magnus, urged on by Caesar's opponents: 'he was keen that the matter be settled by fighting' (*rem ad arma deduci studebat*, 1.4.5), with his own position: '[that] the matter could be brought to peace' (*res ad otium deduci posset*, 1.5.5), characterizing his own demands as 'most lenient' (*lenissima*).[4]

These demands, as he presently clarifies, were that all parties step away from their armies (*omnes ab exercitibus discederent,* 1.9.3), a modification of the earlier grant of retaining his command and standing for the consulship *in absentia*.[5] Caesar presents himself as always open to and insistent on negotiation as a means of resolution; his opponents act against the interests of the state by rejecting his offers or undertaking disingenuous forms of negotiation. In this way, Caesar frames the *Civil War* in terms of diplomatic endeavours on his part. Indeed, according to Batstone and Damon, the structure of book one serves as an allegory of the whole war, with Caesar bringing peace in the wake of Ilerda.[6] Here the Pompeian legates, who up to this point had proved feeble (Afranius) and deceitful (Petreius) models of diplomatic exchange, finally request a conference (*colloquium petunt*, 1.81.1). As a response to the failed public negotiations, which he pushed for at the opening of the book, Caesar rejects their request for a private meeting (*semoto a militibus loco*), creating a very public display before the soldiers and including Afranius' son as a hostage and pledge of negotiations (*obses*, 1.84.2). Similarly, the **extremum** *atque ultimum senatus consultum*, which allegedly forced Caesar's hand in early January (1.5.3) is balanced by Caesar's *una atque* **extrema** *pacis condicio* ('the one and final condition for peace'), which restores order and terminates at least this section of the war, with the discharge of the army (1.87.4-5).

None of this is to say that Caesar's presentation of negotiations prior to and during the civil wars of 49–48 is in fact straightforward or that it should not be questioned.[7] Indeed, reading Caesar's account alongside the Ciceronian corpus of letters reveals a far more complicated and confusing picture of diplomatic exchange between the various Roman political players of the time. Not only do we see the complexities of the mechanisms and the nature of these exchanges, but also varied perspectives on the role of negotiation as a means of conflict resolution. In a world where domestic opponents had become the 'other', diplomacy (or its refusal) assumed paramount importance in the political discourse of the 40s.

In this chapter, I examine the negotiation of legitimacy through an ideological framework of *crudelitas* and *clementia*, and the role Caesar's *nova ratio vincendi* assigns to the art of diplomatic negotiation. An examination of such diplomatic interactions in the early 40s emphasizes the importance of letter-writing as a tool for communication, due to both the physical and social distances between the key political players, something Caesar, through his long absence from the central political spaces of Rome in the 50s, understood well. Yet even when the physical distances were closed, the affirmation or rejection of social interactions was a means through which to legitimize oneself diplomatically. Finally, I examine the social mechanisms of interpersonal relations and *amicitia*, through which spaces for diplomacy in civil war were constructed.

1. A framework of diplomacy

Before turning to examine the mechanisms of negotiation during civil war, I should briefly outline the applicability of a framework of diplomacy for such domestic conflicts.

Traditional state diplomacy can be understood as a system of communication between strangers, as the articulation, through external relations with other political entities, of a sovereign state's self-identity.[8] Understandably, diplomacy has been viewed, first and foremost, as a mechanism for regulating external interactions and relations, as something between distinct communities, not internal concerns of a single political entity.[9] We could, of course, argue that in civil war the rules change and certainly the hostile, external nature of opponents within Roman politics is stressed at least rhetorically, if not legally.[10] As Costas Constantinou states in his work *On the Way to Diplomacy*:

> [D]iplomacy is the enacted regulation of relations between self and other(s). It is impossible to communicate with what is already one, with an undivided unity. There is neither a reason nor a need to mediate what is same. Furthermore, knowledge of the other is essential for knowledge and construction of the self … Diplomacy's *raison d'être* is … established only when there are boundaries for identity and when those boundaries of identity are crossed. Diplomacy's condition of possibility lies in identity/difference, but in the radical alterity of the other also lies diplomacy's impossibility of mediating final identities.[11]

In the turbulent, internal conflicts of the Republic, the state was not an 'undivided unity'. The 'othering' of politically active members of the Roman state and the justification of violence against them as necessary for the safety of the *res publica* are evident from at least the end of the second century BCE, with the implementation of various mechanisms for internal crisis management, notably the so-called *SCU* and the action of *iudicare hostes* mentioned above.[12] These processes both normalized and formalized the use of the language of external war within domestic politics.[13] This normalization can be seen, for example, in Cicero's use of *hostis* rhetoric against political opponents such as the so-called Catilinarian conspirators or Marcus Antonius, both of whom had not (ever or yet) been declared public enemies of the *res publica*. Cicero clearly made distinction between himself and his audience, who shared a collective interest in the state, and the Roman 'other', who were both the root of domestic and civil strife but also *hostes*, and so characterized (whether rhetorically or legally) as separated from the citizen body.[14] The mediation of 'self' and 'other' among the political actors of the late Republic provide suitable grounds for a framework of diplomacy as a political tool.

2. Negotiating between *crudelitas* and *clementia*

In his *Civil War*, Caesar uses the capture of his opponents (Pompeian senators, their sons, military tribunes, and knights) at Corfinium, followed by their safe dismissal (*dimittit omnes incolumes*),[15] as a means to articulate his adherence to a particular *institutum* (custom or habit), which he referred to in his letter to Oppius and Balbus (*Att.* 9.7C.2) as proof of his compliance with their *consilium* (that he 'should negotiate a reconciliation between himself and Pompeius'[16]). This practice of dismissal appears eight times in the work, underlining its significance as a Caesarian trait of negotiation.[17] It is this lenient treatment of his opponents which he emphasizes as the policy he intends to apply to Pompeius himself:

> that I should present myself as most lenient (*quam lenissimum*) and I should make an effort to reconcile Pompeius (*Pompeium darem operam ut reconciliarem*). Let us see, by this method, if we can recover the consent of everyone (*omnium voluntates*) and make use of a lasting victory (*diuturna victoria*), since others have not been able, by their cruelty (*crudelitate*), to escape hatred nor to hold on to victory for any length of time (*victoriam diutius*) except one man, Lucius Sulla, whom I am not going to copy. Let this be a new policy for achieving victory (*haec nova sit ratio vincendi*), that we fortify our position by compassion and generosity (*misericordia et liberalitate*).[18]

To further articulate this stance, Caesar goes on to outline his most recent actions: the capture (*en route* to Brundisium) and immediate release of N. Magius, who is the second of Pompeius' prefects of engineers to be treated in this way.[19] This, Caesar stresses, is his *institutum* and he elaborates on the reasons for this practice:[20]

> If they wish to show their gratitude, they ought to urge Pompeius to prefer to be my friend (*amicus*) rather than that of those men, who have always been most hostile (*inimicissimi*) to both him and to me; the effect of their artifice has brought the commonwealth to this current situation.[21]

Not only is Caesar distancing himself from charges of *crudelitas*, but he is also demonstrating how he hopes to secure reconciliation with Pompeius and so renew their *amicitia* (friendship). In fact, Balbus forwarded the above letter to Cicero to demonstrate Caesar's desire for 'agreement' (*concordia*) and reconciliation with Pompeius and 'how removed he is from all cruelty (*crudelitas*)'.[22] Earlier arguments had been made to Cicero on 24 February by young Balbus (who was *en route* from Caesar to the consul Lentulus with letters, verbal instructions, *mandata*,[23] and promises of a province, if Lentulus came to Rome) of Caesar's desire to show goodwill (*Att.* 8.9a.2). Moreover, the elder Balbus, writing to Cicero from at least mid-February, was likewise trying to persuade Cicero of Caesar's intention to live 'without fear, with Pompeius as leader'.[24] Cicero, however, was not convinced, choosing rather to link any notion of Caesar's *clementia* to the feared *crudelitas* (*metuo, ne omnis haec clementia ad illam crudelitatem colligatur*) and referring to Caesar as a τέρας (monstrosity).[25]

Here, as in his *Civil War*, Caesar demonstrates that he champions the quality of leniency (*quam lenissimum*), which enables him to dispel any Sullan associations. Caesar's initial demands were *lenissima* (*BCiv.* 1.5.5), which he further emphasizes through his practice of leniency towards opponents: Caesar's *lenitas* is noted by Afranius' soldiers at Ilerda (1.74.7), while he affirmed his own *lenitas* to the Pompeians at Pharsalus (3.98.2).[26] As Josiah Osgood has recently noted, Caesar's *Civil War* served to promote this *nova ratio vincendi*, highlighting numerous instances of Caesar's leniency in contrast to his opponents' *crudelitas*.[27]

While Caesar does not explicitly associate Pompeius with *crudelitas* in this letter, he did ascribe it to his *inimici* in his *Civil War*, including the Senate circumscribing the rights of the tribunes of the *plebs* (1.32.6) and the death that Petreius inflicts on Caesarian soldiers found within his camp (1.76.5, 1.85.3).[28] Caesar also associates such acts with oral communication (1.2.8). Petreius performed a fraudulent act of negotiation against Caesar's soldiers: 'to kill most cruelly (*crudelissime*) men ... deceived through (the show of) a conference (*colloquium*)' (1.85.3). Otacilius' cruel massacre (*crudelissime interficiuntur*) of members of Caesar's navy was a violation of the sanctity of the oaths of surrender he had exchanged (3.28.4-5). Not only did Otacilius violate his promise to accept *deditio* (surrender), but his actions were also an inversion of Caesar's own leniency through his reneging on the promise of safe dismissal (3.28.2: *incolumitatem deditis pollicebatur*).[29]

Caesar thus depicts his opponents' *crudelitas* as a consequence of fraudulent or even illegitimate acts, where speech has not been used to create consensus and harmony within the state, but rather as a rejection of correct practices of debate and negotiation. In this respect he is using the institutional structures of the *res publica* to imply something about his opponents' legitimacy, and by extension his own. As Altay Coşkun has stressed, we should 'look more closely at how legitimacy of rule, or alternatively, of the use of violence is constituted, denied or negotiated, and how partisan interests ... manipulate the representation of legitimacy'.[30] In the narratives of the late Republican civil wars, the themes of *crudelitas* and *clementia* served as tools for such manipulation of legitimacy.[31]

Caesar's agents and supporters, such as the Balbi and Curio, worked to emphasize Caesar's rejection of *crudelitas*.[32] Such activity may plausibly be understood as attempts to address charges of insincere clemency (*insidiosa clementia*, Cic. *Att.* 8.16.2) and as a tactic for securing popular support through displays of leniency (as a *conservator inimicorum*, *Att.* 8.9a.1). In short, this was a response to the use of *clementia/crudelitas* by individuals such as Cicero, whose initial reaction was to frame Caesar as a latter-day Sulla, or even a Hannibal (*Att.* 7.11.1) or Phalaris (*Att.* 7.12.2),[33] and to fear a repeat of Cinnan slaughter (*Att.* 7.7.7).[34] Cicero also states that the Claudii Marcelli, consuls in 51 and 50, fled because they feared 'Caesar's sword' (*Att.* 9.1.4) and implies that Caesar's real intention was to kill Pompeius.[35] That Cicero draws on not just Sulla but also his opponent Cinna to elucidate the fear and expectation of cruelty also reveals something of the blurred lines between the opposing sides in terms of their capacities for *crudelitas* in early 49. Caesar himself presented Sulla (and by comparison/association his opponents, particularly Pompeius) as the embodiment of *crudelitas*, framing himself as the avenger of the victims of Sulla's cruelty exacted by Pompeius: rumours abounded that Pompeius intended a 'Sullan kingdom' (*Sullanum regnum*). Furthermore, it was Pompeius who is conceived of as threatening proscriptions both at Luceria in February, and Brundisium in March.[36] Caesar (and his agents) actively reported and disseminated instances of his clemency to dispel any association with such past *exempla* of *crudelitas*.[37]

While Caesar himself did not explicitly campaign under the banner of *clementia* (using instead concepts such as *lenitas, liberalitas* and *misericordia*),[38] for his contemporaries this was a malleable concept through which to explain, justify and even question his actions.[39] As the letter to Oppius and Balbus illustrates, Caesar's *nova ratio vincendi* comprised a willingness to engage with the practice of negotiation with the opposition, exhibiting leniency, compassion and generosity in diplomatic encounters (such as at Corfinium) as a means of avoiding any association with *crudelitas*.

This was Caesar's *ratio vincendi*. Caesar's practice of diplomacy – his negotiation with and safe dismissal of his opponents – was both a functional tool for securing channels of communication and the gratitude of his opponents to act as envoys on his behalf,[40] and a rhetorical tool to disseminate testimonies of his work to end civil war through a variety of media.[41] Caesar presented himself as a genuine negotiator in the field: not just because it provided him with a rhetorical framework and justification, as his *Civil War* repeatedly articulated, but also because the framework of communication exchange in civil war provided him with a viable means of legitimizing himself within the state, through opening up and maintaining verbal negotiation and an explicit rejection of violence and *crudelitas*.[42]

Caesar's *nova ratio vincendi* with a view to securing a *diuturna victoria* (lasting victory)[43] was realized through a performance of diplomatic negotiation, whether through the sending of envoys with an oral message or letters as tools of communication and persuasion,[44] the spaces constructed for negotiation, or indeed the selection and negotiation of envoys and mediators. It is to these mechanisms of communication that I now turn, to provide an initial examination into how models of negotiation and diplomacy during civil war might serve as a means of constructing and deconstructing legitimacy within the Roman state. By the 40s, the debate and competition in domestic politics were already firmly rooted in the othering of political opponents. In such an environment, the practice of diplomacy (whether its successful negotiation or its refusal) was a vital component in shaping political discourse.

3. Locating civil war envoys within a social framework

Diplomacy, as Der Derian asserts, 'requires and seeks to mediate otherness, through the use of persuasion, and force, promises and threats, codes and symbols'.[45] Indeed, while at first glance diplomacy may appear to focus on verbal exchange (whether oral or written), non-verbal communication and signalling, including the selection of envoys, is equally as important.[46] In examining Caesar's narrative of the civil war as an account of diplomatic communication, its accuracy is less important than reflecting on the use (both actual and rhetorical) he makes of mechanisms of communication between his own self and the otherness of his opponents.[47] Caesar's use of mediation through carefully selected envoys was a deliberate means of legitimacy and constitutionality, reinforcing his position during the events and not merely a way of presenting them afterwards.[48] The importance of *amicitia* and social bonds in the negotiation of power and legitimacy in civil conflict also provided spaces for agents and envoys to advance their own interests. Caesar's agents in Rome, Balbus and Oppius, were well placed to influence and inform politicians and policy while negotiating on Caesar's behalf.[49]

Throughout the *Civil War*, Caesar not only stresses his active negotiation through the sending of envoys with instructions (*mandata*) and letters but also documents the numerous communities sending embassies to him seeking help or to support him, first as proconsul and then as consul.[50] These embassies serve to illustrate not only the support for Caesar's cause, but also an acknowledgement by communities of the viability of diplomatic encounters with Caesar. Furthermore, a number of his opponents are also presented as seeking the benefits, personal or public, of a conference with Caesar.[51] We have already seen how Caesar drew on the gratitude of the Pompeian prefects he captured and released as justification for using them as envoys of his *mandata*.[52] While these men were a direct route to his opponents, other bonds of duty and friendship within the complex nexus of Roman social connections and obligations, encompassed by the concept of *amicitia*, were equally powerful channels of communication.[53] The potency of such associations is illustrated by the case of M. Terentius Varro, Pompeius' legate in Hispania Ulterior.[54] Having learnt of Caesar's successes in Italy, Varro talked of Caesar in most friendly terms (*amicissime*).[55] His reasoning, as Caesar presents it, was that:

> having been preoccupied with his legation he was bound by loyalty (*fide*) to Cn. Pompeius; but also no less a bond of friendship (*necessitudinem*) with Caesar existed, nor was he ignorant of what the duty of a legate (who holds a position of trust (*fiduciariam operam*)) was, what his strengths were, what the will of the whole province towards Caesar was.[56]

Varro's position is one of ambivalence, although he would, ultimately, on receipt of 'reliable messengers and clear authorities' (*certis nuntiis, certis auctoribus*), speak against Caesar (*graves in Caesarem contiones*) and side with Pompeius (2.18.3). Nevertheless, it is the use made in Caesar's presentation of Varro's careful assessment of the complex intimate social ties of friendship (*necessitudo*),[57] that underlines the relevance of such networks of *amicitia* in diplomatic negotiations during civil war.

Both sides exploited common and familial connections with each other. A particular familial relationship used was that of younger male relatives as either envoys or pledges of negotiation: Pompeius sends the son of one of Caesar's legates, Lucius Julius Caesar, as a personal envoy following the *SCU* of 7 January (*BCiv.* 1.8.2),[58] Caesar sent young Balbus, the nephew of his confidante, with *mandata* to the consul Lentulus in Rome (Cic. *Att.* 8.9A), Ser. Sulpicius Rufus sent his son from Caesar's camp to Pompeius, besieged at Brundisium, to press for peace negotiations (Cic. *Att.* 10.1.4),[59] and Afranius' son was offered as a guarantee (*obses*) during negotiations at Ilerda (*BCiv.* 1.84.2), which was a tactic later used by Lepidus and Antonius to facilitate negotiations with Caesar's murderers.[60] The use of young family members as a form of security as well as female relatives used as envoys and mediators would be a prevalent motif in the triumviral period.[61]

Partisans, clients and those intimately bound, as *familiares* and *necessarii*, to those vying for legitimacy and power also played a key diplomatic role.[62] At Brundisium, Caesar sent his legate Caninius Rebilus, a *familiaris <et> necessarius* of Scribonius Libo,[63] to persuade Libo to act as a mediator for the negotiation of peace (1.26.2-6) and likewise sent Aulus Clodius, a *familiaris* of both himself and Scipio and an individual he regarded as one of his *necessarii*, to deliver both letters and *mandata* to Scipio in Macedonia, in order to persuade him to mediate a peace with Pompeius (3.57.1-5).[64] Outside of Caesar's commentaries, the need to assert social ties and the bonds of *amicitia* are clear from Cicero's letters. Writing to Caesar in March 49 (*Att.* 9.11A), Cicero describes himself as on very good terms (*amicissimus*) to both Caesar and Pompeius, as well as a friend of peace:

> But, as I was at that time (*eo tempore*) not only the supporter of your dignity (*ipse fautor dignitatis tuae fui*) but also proposed to others that they ought to assist you, so now (*nunc*) I am greatly agitated for Pompeius' dignity (*dignitas*). For it has been several years, since I chose you two, whom I especially cherish and for whom I was, as I still am, the best of friends (*amicissimus*). On account of this, I seek from you, or rather I beseech and implore you with all prayers, that among all your great concerns (*in tuis maximis curis*) you might bestow some time also to this consideration: how I might be able, by your benefaction (*tuo beneficio*), to be a good man (*bonus vir*), grateful and finally dutiful in the memory of his great benefactions (*in maximi beneficii*). If this only pertained to me myself, I should hope nevertheless that I would achieve my request from you, but, as I see it, this pertains both to your trust (*ad tuam fidem*) and to the state (*ad rem publicam*), that I, a friend of peace and of both of you (*me et pacis et utriusque vestrum amicum*), should, as far as you are concerned, be maintained in a position best calculated to promote harmony between you both and among our fellow citizens (*ad vestram et ad civium concordiam per te quam accomodatissimum conservari*) ... In which, if you perceive me to be grateful (*esse gratum*), take care, I beg you, that I might be able to also be grateful towards Pompeius (*in Pompeium esse possim*).[65]

Such a position of dual friendship, Cicero intimates, positions him as one who could facilitate agreement between Caesar and Pompeius, as well as the citizen body (*ad vestram et ad civium concordiam*), as someone who could experience the generous benefactions of both men.[66] Indeed, the complexities of political friendship and obligations were a useful tool for enabling negotiation during conflict: shared friends and associates between the two sides were a means of accessing channels of communication. They could, however, also be used in attempts to express neutrality (at best) or indecision (at worst). We have already seen how Varro weighed up his commitments and relations to both Caesar and Pompeius, while other individuals attempted to tread the path of neutrality, such as Ser. Sulpicius Rufus, who tried to assert peace by dispatching his son as envoy to Pompeius.[67]

Negotiation as a Tool for Legitimacy in the Roman Civil War of 49–48 BCE

Just as much as *amicitia* served to promote negotiations in civil war, the privation of social contact could also imply or be understood as a breakdown in relations. Caesar accused Pompeius of turning his back on their *amicitia* and reconciling with their common enemies (*cum communibus inimicis in gratiam redierat*, 1.5.4), yet his intimates had already, on Pompeius' understanding, alluded to a separation between the former father- and son-in-law. In early December 50, the imminent threat of war was confirmed for Pompeius in the failure of Hirtius, Caesar's *familiarissimus*, to call on Pompeius or to meet with Scipio, Pompeius' father-in-law. This, Pompeius claimed, was proof of an estrangement: *Hoc illi τεκμηριῶδες videbatur esse alienationis*.[68] Peter White views Pompeius' interpretation of the 'neglect of a courtesy … as proof that civil war was imminent' as extraordinary, but in fact this episode underlines the intense spotlight under which such social expectations were being scrutinized and evaluated.[69]

4. Diplomatic space in civil war

The use of *familiares* and those associated through kinship for communication during civil conflict enabled a construction of diplomatic space within the social framework of *amicitia*.[70] This also allowed for an orientation of space away from public, political space: while *amicitia* was a political concept, the relationships it consisted of also operated within non-public, personal space.[71] Such a distinction may seem artificial and so it is perhaps more useful to think about different registers of space and interaction: for example, Caesar's initial dispatch at the start of the *Civil War* was to the consuls, with the tribunes pushing for the reading aloud of his letter *in senatu* i.e. within an official setting (in terms of being overseen by elected magistrates). Yet as we have already seen, Hirtius' avoidance of both Pompeius and Scipio in a non-official setting (in that the meeting was arranged by Balbus, another *familiaris* of Caesar and Pompeius), was interpreted by Pompeius as an indication of alienation between himself and Caesar. Negotiation could take place between individuals as representatives of the state or in a private capacity. In this final section, I explore some of these capacities in terms of different spaces, places, forms and media in and through which negotiation, and therefore diplomatic space, was constructed. I first examine the different registers of oral communication, including reflecting on diplomatic encounters as spaces for delay, before looking at letter-writing as a form of diplomatic exchange.

Roman political communication and debate was traditionally carried out in the public space of the *comitium*, tribunals or inside temples and the Senate House. The spaces for political negotiation shifted, however, around prominent individuals accumulating power within the state. This is apparent in April 56, when Caesar privately renegotiated a distribution of powers with Crassus and Pompeius at Luca. Several key political figures appear to have gathered around Caesar: Pompeius (proconsul overseeing the *cura annonae*) *en route* to Sardinia and Africa; Crassus, having already been in conference with Caesar at Ravenna (Cic. *Fam.* 1.9.9);[72] Appius Claudius Pulcher (Cic. *QFr.* 2.5.4), likely thinking ahead to his consular campaign in 55; and Q. Caecilius

Metellus Nepos, proconsul of Spain (Plut. *Caes*. 21.3). This movement suggests a dependency of Caesar's position on those able to help him thwart L. Domitius Ahenobarbus' candidacy for consul and of Appius, Crassus and Pompeius' reliance on the support of Caesar's legions for votes.[73] The significance of these private negotiations and Caesar's presence in northern Italy is perceived, only in the later Greek sources, as something akin to a political gravitation pull, with allegedly a substantial public audience of senators, praetors and pro-magistrates travelling from Rome forming a quasi-Senate meeting.[74] In all likelihood the episode rather demonstrates the changing spaces and forms of political debate and negotiation: the private *consilia* of Servilia in 44 and 43 are further examples of this.[75] In autumn 43, the *locus* of negotiating power was further dislocated from both Rome and a public, constitutional space, when Lepidus, Marcus Antonius and Young Caesar met on an island near Bononia, in northern Italy.[76]

At the outbreak of the civil war of 49, however, the distances separating the key players and the subsequent flight of the consuls and Pompeius from Rome, restricted the opportunities for face-to-face interactions.[77] Caesar framed his initial act of war (the second coming of Hannibal crossing into Italy, in Cicero's opinion) as an act of initiating face-to-face negotiation in order to reach resolution, as opposed to the violent conflict initiated by his personal enemies (and perhaps characteristic of many face-to-face political debates at Rome), who rejected such a possibility. When Pompeius was trapped in Brundisium, Caesar, while besieging him, twice sent envoys – firstly the *praefectus fabrum* Magius (captured *en route*), followed by Rebilus to Libo – to prompt some form of an arrangement. In both instances he urged Pompeius to meet him face-to-face (*coram* 1.24.5; *ipse cum Pompeio colloqueretur* 1.26.3). The necessity, in Caesar's account, of having to repeat the request via Rebilus serves to underline the alleged lack of response to the *mandata* he had sent via Magius. Such a repeat demand, following the manifestations of exchange and friendship in Roman letter-writing, could be construed as impolite and indicate a lack of trust in Pompeius' trustworthiness.[78] In fact, Pompeius had sent Magius to Caesar, though only once Caesar had reached Brundisium on 9 March. Caesar himself admits as much in a letter to Oppius and Balbus: 'he sent Numerius Magius to me about peace. I responded as seemed fitting' (Cic. *Att*. 9.13a). Caesar's frustration was that Pompeius had not sent Magius *de pace* sooner (while Caesar was *en route*), perhaps indicating no real desire to agree to a face-to-face meeting at all. Furthermore, the reply he received via Rebilus excused Pompeius from negotiating since no arrangement could be reached, it was claimed, as the consuls were not present, having sailed to Greece. Within Caesar's narrative Pompeius rejects or prevaricates on any negotiation of peace (so confirming his characterization in 1.4.5 as *ad arma* in contrast to Caesar at 1.5.5 as *ad otium*). Nevertheless, if Pompeius was delaying, his argument was made from a position of constitutionality – appropriate for the man who presented himself as having the consuls and Senate on his side – in that the legitimate power to negotiate with Caesar and reach an agreement resided with the two senior magistrates in charge of the *res publica*. Libo would employ a similar tactic of delay at Oricum (Epirus), stressing his own deep desire (*suam summam . . . voluntatem*) for a settlement, while professing a lack of power (*potestatem . . . nullam*) to affect anything 'because by the advice of their council they had committed entire control of the war and everything else to Pompeius'.[79] Though Libo implies that he will refer the whole matter to Pompeius, his refusal either to receive Caesar's *legati* or to give them safe passage reveals his insincerity for a peace settlement. Caesar deconstructs Libo's speech (*oratio*) as a tactical façade professing a desire to negotiate for the sake of a truce (*indutiae*) and as protection from present danger, delaying Caesar's advance without the genuine fulfilment of negotiation.[80]

The apparent unwillingness of the Pompeian leadership to come to the negotiating table in person threw greater emphasis on oral communication through envoys and *mandata*. In the aftermath of the *SCU*, Pompeius sent a kinsman of Caesar, the young L. Julius Caesar, carrying personal, private messages (*privati officii mandata*, *BCiv.* 1.8.2) to Caesar, justifying or excusing his own behaviour in the decisions of the Senate. Although he had also sent the praetor L. Roscius Fabatus in a voluntary capacity, Pompeius appears to have prioritized the familial ties of his chosen messenger as a cover for his personal communication with Caesar, as opposed to Roscius serving in a senatorial embassy.[81] Caesar employed these bearers of private messages to deliver his own in return, further emphasizing personal channels of communication through familial/personal relations, due to the fact that they carried his *mandata* as a favour.[82] Nevertheless, the benefits of using the son of his legate as a go-between in establishing personal pathways of communication were not well received by senatorial members present at Minturnae. Apparently unaware that Pompeius had initiated an exchange with Caesar through the young man, Cicero marvelled at the ridiculousness of this 'loose broom' (*scopas solutas*), believing that either Caesar was making a mockery of the proceedings by sending Lucius as an envoy or that Lucius had passed off a mere conversation (*sermo*) as actual instructions (*mandata*) from Caesar:

> I saw Lucius Caesar at Minturnae on the morning of 23 January with the most absurd instructions (*absurdissimis mandatis*) – he's no man but a loose broom – I think Caesar has sent him for the sake of ridiculing us (*irridendi causa*), to have given instructions (*mandata*) concerning such things to this fellow; unless perhaps he did not give any instructions to him and Lucius has improperly taken up some mere talk they had as instructions (*hic sermone aliquot adrepto pro mandatis abusus est*).[83]

This account clearly frames the *mandata* as orally delivered (as opposed to written) instructions,[84] though Cicero is making an explicit distinction in register between official *mandata* and the casual conversation he assumes Lucius in fact had in Caesar's presence, signalling that *mandata* are perceived to function within an official context, in contrast to the unofficial and personal capacity of Lucius' communication (as *sermo*). Indeed, although Cicero would quickly recognize the legitimacy of Lucius' commission (*Att.* 7.14.1 cf. 7.19 for Curio's reference to Lucius' *legatio*), his initial response indicates that Pompeius' original commission was not a senatorially sanctioned embassy but a private undertaking, potentially intended to renegotiate bonds of *amicitia*. Furthermore, as Shackleton Bailey has convincingly shown, the absence of Roscius from Cicero's initial account and a later reference to 'the proposals of peace conveyed by L. Caesar and <L.> Fabatus' (*Att.* 8.12.2) fail to acknowledge Roscius' official capacity as praetor and Lucius Caesar's superior.[85]

The reception of such personal, private envoys and *mandata* within a political space (constructed by the presence of the consuls and members of the Senate) appears to have prompted the decision to respond in writing and in a form intended for public consumption suggesting that Pompeius was determined to carry out the negotiation in a more open vein:

> You ought to know by now the reply (*responsa*) which Lucius Caesar is carrying back from Pompeius, and what letter (*litteras*) he carries from him to Caesar. For it was written and given so that it might be displayed in public (*scriptae enim et datae ita sunt ut proponerentur in publico*). In which matter I, personally, lay the blame on Pompeius, who, although he is a splendid writer (*scriptor luculentus*), has given to Sestius the task of writing (*scribendas*) such important matters and which will come into every one's hands (*in omnium manus venturae essent*).[86]

Cicero clearly thinks Sestius is not the writer for such a vital public communiqué: 'I have never read anything written that is more Sestian (Σηστιωδέστερον)', no doubt thinking himself a fitting candidate for the role![87] Nevertheless, what is clear from this incident is that not only were letters a diplomatic tool for communication (which was particularly necessary given the distances between addresser and addressee at this time) but also a means for disseminating and publicizing one's ostensible position in negotiation to a public audience. While Caesar was the primary addressee, the letter was also intended as a vehicle for Pompeius to publicly (*in publico*) demonstrate that he was in fact working to de-escalate the threat of war, as Cicero indicates with his remark that Pompeius' reply was said to be pleasing to the *populus* and approved in a *contio*.[88]

Letters were a means of disseminating information but also a form of self-presentation, the promotion and maintenance of relationships, and criticism of one's opponents: a particularly potent tool for negotiating power during civil conflict and physical separation.[89] The letter that Caesar wrote to Oppius and Balbus, so clearly stressing his adherence to reconciliation as his *nova ratio vincendi,* was forwarded to Cicero by Balbus explicitly as evidence of the genuine nature of Caesar's political stance.[90] Cicero likewise used the epistolary practice as a space for negotiation, reiterating himself as a *pacis auctor* and positioning himself as a mediator between the two men (cf. *Att.* 9.11A). Notably, when Caesar had conferred with Cicero in mid-February about his gladiators at Capua, Cicero took the opportunity to write positively to him about Pompeius and to urge Caesar to agreement (*ad concordiam*). Cicero explicitly tells Atticus that he wants Caesar to circulate this letter and to set it up *in publico* (*Att.* 8.2.1).

* * *

Both sides manipulated and adapted the spaces they used for diplomatic exchange. Negotiation with the genuine aim of conflict resolution appears, however, to have been limited. While Cicero and Sulpicius Rufus struggled in articulating either neutrality or as advocates of peace, Caesar, Pompeius and their various legates deployed and manipulated various social connections and communication exchange to strengthen their positions against the other.

For Caesar, a key aspect of his rhetoric was to present his opponents as either dishonest or cruel ambassadors and thereby delegitimize their positions and claims. As we have seen, Caesar presents Libo's actions at Oricum in January 48 – asking to negotiate but not being able to guarantee any terms because he needed to refer everything to Pompeius – as motivated by self-interest rather than any real desire for peace, and so validating Caesar's own decision to recognize the futility of pursuing any hope or agreement of peace (*spem aut condicionem pacis*) and instead to turn his attention to the planning of war (*cogitationem belli*).[91] A short while later, as the two armies are camped on either side of the river Apsus and enjoying a cease-fire of sorts, exchanging conversation across the river,[92] a peace conference was negotiated through Caesar's *legatus* P. Vatinius. When the two delegates met to discuss initial arrangements, the renegade T. Labienus sought an altercation with Vatinius, and when missile fire broke out from all sides, Labienus dismissed the prospect of negotiation: 'Let us, therefore, stop talking about an agreement; for there can be no peace for us unless Caesar's head is handed over.'[93] Moreover, following the soldier-led peace initiative at the river Ebro in the summer of 49, Petreius interrupted the *colloquia* of the soldiers, driving out and killing any Caesarians he found in his camp, whereas Caesar ordered any of his adversaries' soldiers found in his camp to be sent back.[94] Perhaps most striking of all is the portrayal of Otacilius, who tricks Caesarian sailors with promises of safe dismissal under oaths of surrender, only to slaughter them most cruelly (*BCiv.* 3.28).

Caesar's narrative obscures the fact that both sides, plus those attempting the difficult task of political neutrality, heavily employed social relations, modes of communication, and diplomatic exchange to negotiate legitimacy within the state. The different registers of space used in the construction and deconstruction of negotiations offers an initial insight into the collapse and failure of senatorial political legitimacy to manage and contain violence and conflict within the Republican political system.[95] The use of familial and personal relationships in politics was nothing new, but the spaces constructed for communication and exchange in the necessity of civil war throws light onto the personal nature of social contracts and models of negotiation. Beyond merely a structural tool for framing his narrative of the civil war, diplomatic exchange was, for Caesar, a means through which to position himself within the state, to assert his claims to legitimacy and at the same time question those of his opponents, and to distinguish himself from the horrors of the last victory in civil war.

Through this examination of the mechanisms of diplomacy as a means of constructing and deconstructing political legitimacy in civil war, this chapter has demonstrated how the disruption and breakdown of political language and social practices and norms created new spaces of diplomatic interaction. This construction of spaces to mediate legitimacy enables us to re-evaluate the impact of internal crises on power dynamics of the Roman state.

Notes

* My special thanks to Richard Westall and Henriette van der Blom for their insightful comments and suggestions, and also the CAHA Research Reading Group at the University of Birmingham for additional feedback. Any errors are my own.
1. Shackleton Bailey 1968: 157; Roller 2001: 183; Morstein-Marx 2021: 458–62 succinctly discusses the issues with interpreting and translating Caesar's *nova ratio vincendi*, proposing the translation as 'a new style of victory'.
2. On the passing of this decree see also: Cic. *Fam.* 16.11.2; Livy *Per.* 109; Cass. Dio 41.3.3. This so-called *senatus consultum ultimum* is only referred to as such in Caes. *BCiv.* 1.5.3, although a generic formula (*ne quid res publica detrimenti capiat/caperet*) is preserved in accounts of other, earlier enactments: Cic. *Cat.* 1.4; *Phil.* 8.14; Sall. *Cat.* 29.2. See McGushin 1987: 132–3 and 148 for discrepancies in the wording of the *SCU*. On the decree as a response to a perceived threat to the state: Mitchell 1971; Cloud 1994: 494–6; Lintott 1999: 89–93; Golden 2013: 42–3, 104–49, esp. 140–6 for the *SCU* of 49 BCE.
3. Caes. *BCiv.* 1.2.6; for explicit mention of this declaration: App. *BCiv.* 2.31, 2.33, 2.50; Flor. 2.13; Plut. *Caes.* 30.1; Cass. Dio 41.3.4; Allély 2012: 79–81. For the '*hostis* declaration' as an institutionalized practice, see Allély 2012: 18–19, however see also Zucchetti 2022 on the original political (not legal) action of Sulla's introduction of *iudicare hostes*. Cornwell 2014 for the language of *hostis* in the 40s to 30s BCE.
4. Notably Scipio stresses to the Senate that they should not 'hesitate or go softer (*lenius*)' (*BCiv.* 1.1.4), and the gentler (*leniorem*) opinion offered by Marcellus (1.2.1-3) was reprimanded by the consul Lentulus. The quality of leniency is championed by Caesar and rejected by his opponents. See n.26 below.
5. Caes. *BCiv.* 1.9.2; Cic. *Att.* 7.7.6.
6. Batstone and Damon 2006: 75–84. Westall 2017: 271–80 and Osgood 2019: 151–7 examine the incomplete nature of Caesar's *Civil War* and its impact on his purported claims to desire peace and reconciliation; Peer 2015: 177–81 argues that each book was published at different times and served different purposes.
7. Carter 1993: 17, 'Throughout, one has the strong impression that he was willing to settle only on his own terms. The same may have been true of Pompeius, indeed probably was. Of such stuff are civil wars made.'
8. Der Derian 1993: 244.
9. On civil war as occurring 'within the boundaries of a single political community', see Armitage 2017: 50 and 57; Lange 2017: 129–30.
10. See Allély 2012: 45 for the *SCU* and '*hostis* declaration' as independent procedures for deconstructing legitimacy within the state; See also nn.2–3 above.
11. Constantinou 1996: 112–13. See Cornago 2016 for the importance of the domestic pluralism of a 'state', as opposed to understanding a state to exist as 'a perfect, stable and timeless political community' (187), in relation to understanding (para)diplomacy.
12. For a discussion of the naming of the institution introduced by Sulla in 88 BCE, see Zucchetti 2022, esp. for the issues of the modern term '*hostis*-declaration', Sulla's initial creation of such judgement as a political act intended to justify and legitimize civil war after the fact, and the later development of the institution which would legally permit civil war once a declaration had taken place.
13. Rosenblitt 2019; Cornwell 2014; Allély 2012.

14. Cic. *Cat.* 4.15; *Phil.* 4.14.
15. Caesar took Corfinium on 21 February (Cic. *Att.* 8.14.1); for the events at Corfinium: Caes. *BCiv.* 1.17-22; Vell. 2.50.1; Plut. *Caes.* 34.6-8; Suet. *Iul.* 34.1; *Ner.* 2.2; App. *BCiv.* 2.38; Cass. Dio 41.10-11; Liv. *Per.* 109; Oros. 6.15; see also Gelzer 1968: 202.
16. Cic. *Att.* 9.7A.1.
17. Caes. *BCiv.* 1.13.5 (L. Pupius, *primi pili* centurion under the Pompeian P. Attius Varus at Auximum), 1.18.4 (Attius Pelignus) 1.23.3 (Corfinium), 1.34.1 (L. Vibullius Rufus), 2.28.1 (Sextus Quintilius Varus' release after Corfinium, cf. 1.23), 3.10.1-2 (L. Vibullius Rufus, referring to his release at Corfinium and then again in Spain), see also 3.11.3-4 (L. Torquatus' surrender of himself and Oricum: *incolumisque ab eo conservatus est*), 3.27.2 (*quos omnes conservatos Caesar domum remisit*); cf. Liv. *Per.* 109 (Corfinium), 110 (Ilerda): *omnesque incolumes dimisit*.
18. Cic. *Att.* 9.7C.1.
19. The first being L. Vibullius Rufus, captured and released at Corfinium and again in Spain (Caes. *BCiv.* 1.34.1, 3.10.1). For the capture of Magius see also *BCiv.* 1.24.4. Both were given *mandata* by Caesar to take to Pompeius (*BCiv.* 1.24.5, 1.26.2, 3.10.2, 3.18.3).
20. See n.17 for instances of Caesar's *institutum*.
21. Cic. *Att.* 9.7C.2.
22. Cic. *Att.* 9.7B.1.
23. Williams 2000: 161-3.
24. Cic. *Att.* 8.9A.2; see 8.2.1 for the first reference to a letter from Balbus (and Caesar) to Cicero, which he forwarded to Atticus; subsequent letters from Balbus (actual letters in bold): 8.9A.2, **8.15A**, 9.5.3, 9.6.1, 9.7.3, **9.7A, 9.7B**, 9.13.8, **9.13A**, 9.14.1.3.
25. Cic. *Att.* 8.9A.2. τέρας also means 'portent'.
26. See Benferhat 2005: 18-20 for Caesar's *lenitas* as a political tactic. See also n.4 above.
27. Osgood 2019: 139, 140-7 for Caesar's leniency and 147-50 for his opponents' cruelty. See also Rosenblitt 2019: 10-11, 94, 101-2 for Sallust's implicit reference to the *clementia* of Caesar in the opening word of his speech of Lepidus.
28. *Crudelitas/crudelissime* in the *Civil War*: *BCiv.* 1.2.8, 1.32.6, 1.76.5, 1.85.3, 3.28.4, 3.32; Osgood 2019: 147-50; Grillo 2012: 83-4.
29. On the practice of *deditio* in war see *BNP* s.v. 'deditio'; Hölkeskamp 2000: 232-48; Burton 2011: 114-58; Sanz 2015; Burton 2016.
30. Coşkun 2018: 220.
31. Notably at Philippi, M. Antonius is framed as lenient, in contrast to Young Caesar (Octavian): Suet. *Aug.* 13.2; App. *BCiv.* 4.129; Dowling 2006: 8, 195-202, 279; 29-75 for the *crudelitas* of Young Caesar and the *clementia* of Augustus; see also the so-called *Laudatio Turiae* for Lepidus' *crudelitas* and Augustus' *clementia* (CIL 6.41062. ll.19-20).
32. Cic. *Att.* 10.4.8, where Curio outlines Caesar's innate rejection of cruelty, alongside conceptualizing *clementia* as a means of holding and maintaining the favour of the people, which if lost would provoke him to cruelty.
33. A notoriously cruel sixth-century tyrant of Akragas. Cicero also compares the march to *barbarorum adventus* (*Att.* 7.13.3).
34. For Sullan clemency and cruelty: Dowling 2000; Thein 2014. Cicero uses Cinna as a particular model of *crudelitas*: *Att.* 7.7.7, 8.3.6, 9.10.3, see also Cic. *Phil.* 1.34, 2.108; *Brut.* 227;

see Cic. *Cat.* 3.10.[24] for Sullan violence as a reaction to Cinnan slaughter and *crudelitas*; Dowling 2000: 309. For *Cinnae dominatio* (cf. Cic. *Att.* 8.3.6) as a Sullan construction to delegitimize Cinna's regime see Badian 1962; Lovano 2002: 53–78; Rosenblitt 2019: 59 and 133 for the Sallustian notion of cruelty from both sides in the 80s. Caesar was notably associated with Cinna through his marriage to his daughter Cornelia, even refusing to divorce her despite Sulla's demand: Suet. *Caes.* 1.2; Plut. *Caes.* 1.1; Gelzer 1968: 19–21.

35. Cic. *Att.* 7.23.1 and 9.5.3; Gelzer 1968: 201, n.2. See Westall 2017: 16 n.26 for Domitius' contemplation of suicide at Corfinium (Plut. *Caes.* 34.6), suggesting no expectation of mercy.

36. Cic. *Att.* 8.11.2; 9.7.3 for the *Sullanum regnum*; in *Att.* 9.10.6 (18 March 49) Cicero says that Pompeius had been 'eager to play at Sulla (*sullaturit*) and proscriptions (*proscripturit*)', which he reiterates in 9.11.2: *sermones minaces . . . meras proscriptiones, meros Sullos;* Cicero implies that there was talk of proscriptions at Luceria (*Att.* 8.11.4, 11.6.2); for the association of Pompeius with *crudelitas*: Cic. *Att.* 9.6.7, 9.15.3, 10.14.1. Benferhat 2005: 20 sees Cicero's assessment of the barbarity of Pompeian *crudelitas* (*Att.* 11.6.2) as 'reproducing the cliché' sustained by Caesar's narrative. For Pompeius' constitutional position at the end of the 50s, see Vervaet 2014: 216–23, esp. 222–3.

37. Cic. *Att.* 9.14.2; see also 9.7C.1 for the rejection of a Sullan model and the implication of its acceptance by his opponents.

38. On terms related to and nearly synonymous with *clementia* see Konstan 2005, esp. 341–3; Dowling 2006: 6–7; Grillo 2012: 79–80. For *lenitas* as an aspect of *clementia*, see Sen. *Clem.* 2.3.1 and Flamerie de Lachapelle 2011: 150–1. As Richard Westall has reminded me, Caesar's aversion to the word *clementia* may be due to the word's close association with Hellenistic monarchy and philosophy.

39. Cic. *Att.* 8.9a.2; 8.16.2; 9.16.1; 10.4.8; *Fam.* 15.15.2; 15.19.2-4; *Lig.* 6, 10, 15, 19, 29, 30; *Marc.* 1, 9, 12, 18; Caes. *BHis.* 17.2. As Peer 2015: 174 stresses 'Cicero shrewdly and possibly even sarcastically uses [this] loaded word missing from the *Bellum Civile*' multiple times in the *Pro Marcello* and *Pro Ligario*. On Roman *clementia*: Brunt 1990: 314–16; Thome 2000: 77–84; Caesar's *clementia*: Konstan 2005; Dowling 2006: esp. 20–8; Picone 2008; Grillo 2012: 78–105. See Griffin 2003a: 159–63 for extensive Ciceronian use of *clementia* applied to Caesar; Konstan 2005: 337–45 for the lack of contemporary dictatorial implications of the concept; for the temple of Caesarian Clemency (*Clementia Caesaris*): *RRC* 480/21 (44 BCE); App. *BCiv.* 2.106; Cass. Dio 44.6.4; see Konstan 2005: 342–3 for the suggestion that this act helped consolidate *clementia* as the expression of Caesar's generosity.

40. For the role of intermediaries in political communication and the practice of *adlegatio* see Tatum 2017.

41. Wiseman 1998b for recitations of Caesar's *commentarii*; Wiseman 2015: 98–102, esp. 101 for the people 'listening to history'.

42. Osgood 2019: 143 argues that Caesar's 'preferred means of ending civil war truly is verbal negotiation: conversation (*colloquium*) literally is a way for citizens to come back together'.

43. Caesar's reference to a *diuturna victoria* (Cic. *Att.* 9.7C.1) may be addressing and appropriating the language used in early February to assess Caesar's aims and the fear of murder they generated: 'You fear slaughter not without cause, though nothing could procure for Caesar a lasting victory (*ad diuturnitatem victoriae*) and domination (*dominationis*) less' (*Att.* 7.22.1).

44. On the uses of letters: White 2010: 21–9; see also García Riaza 2020 for the methods and mechanisms of information exchange and political communication during the triumviral period.

45. Der Derian 1993: 244.

46. Jönsson and Hall 2003, esp. 201–3.
47. Constantinou 1996: 95–120 for diplomacy and the other.
48. Cf. Cic. *Att.* 9.7C; Westall 2017: 275–80 for the goal informing the composition of the *Civil War*; see also Osgood 2019.
49. See Welch 1990: 62–9, esp. 65 for their positions early in the civil war.
50. Embassies sent to Caesar: towns of Picenum (1.15.1-2); Sulmo (1.18.1); Corfinium (1.20.5); Osca, Calagurris, Tarraco, the Iacetani, Ausetani and Illurgavonenses (1.60.1); communities of Hispania Citerior (2.21.4-5); Salonae (3.9.5); Apollonia, the Byllidenses, Amantini and the whole of Epirus (3.12.4-5); Thessalia and Aetolia (3.34.2); Macedonian communities (3.36.1 embassies to Caesar's legate, Domitius); Gomphi (3.80.1). Several of these communities are presented as 'promising to do whatever he ordered' (*quaeque imperaverit se cupidissime facturos pollicentur* cf. 1.18.1, 1.20.5, 1.60.1, 3.12.5, 3.34.2). Embassies in Books 1–2 would have been to Caesar the proconsul, whereas those in Book 3 were sent to him as consul; see *MRR* 2.262, 272.
51. Lentulus Spinther (1.22.1-2); the soldiers of Petreius and Afranius (1.74.3); Petreius and Afranius (1.84.1-2); Libo Scribonius (3.15.6–17.5); Caesar as notes at 3.61.2 that Pompeius' soldiers were fleeing to his side on nearly a daily basis.
52. See p. 16 and n.19 above.
53. For the meaning and framework of *amicitia*: Williams 2012: 1–62, esp. 40–4; see also Hellegouarc'h 1963; Brunt 1965.
54. *MRR* 2.100, n.7 and 269. For Varro's unsuitability for leadership during the civil war see Westall 2017: 20; Rowe 1967: 404–6.
55. On Varro's effective negotiation of relations with both Pompeius and Caesar over the course of his career, see Spencer 2019: 22–7.
56. Caes. *BCiv.* 2.17.1-2.
57. See Hellegouarc'h 1963: 71–6 for the meaning and application of *necessitudo* as a form of friendship that relies on the intimacy of relations, often associated but not limited to kinship relations and dependent on *fides*.
58. See also Cic. *Att.* 7.13a.1, 7.14.1, 7.16.1, 7.17.2, 7.18.2, 7.19.
59. Cicero appears to upbraid Sulpicius Rufus and Q. Titanius for placing their sons in Caesar's army for the purpose of besieging or capturing Pompeius (*Att.* 9.9.1, 9.18.2, 9.19.2, 10.3A.2), though he does reveal in *Att.* 10.1.4 that Sulpicius' son was sent to treat for peace; see Saunders 1923: 110–11.
60. Liv. *Per.* 116; App. *BCiv.* 2.142; Cass. Dio 44.34.6; Cic. *Phil.* 1.31 just refers to M. Antonius' son, naming him a *pacis obses*; Rohr Vio 2020, esp. 173–9.
61. For kinship diplomacy in the triumviral period, see Cornwell 2020: 164–6. For an earlier instance of a son as envoy in civil conflicts, see Plut. *C. Gracch.* 16.1-3, where Fulvius Flaccus sent his younger son as a herald to negotiate with the Senate. Wiseman 1998a: 52–9 sees Plutarch's ultimate source for activities surrounding Gaius and Fulvius' conflict with Opimius as plausibly a *fabula praetexta* (historical drama), which would frame the role of the son as a conventional dramatic device.
62. Hellegouarc'h 1963: 68–71 for *familiaritas* and the application of *familiaris* to a client; Williams 2012: 40–2, 54. See also n.57.
63. Damon 2015: 18 *familiarem <et> necessarium* (cf. Cic. *Rab. Post.* 32), noting that a later correction of *familiarem necessarium<que>* was made in manuscript **M**. Carter 1991: 179 omits *familiarem* from his edition noting that it appears to be an 'intrusive gloss on *necessarium*'.

64. Caes. *BCiv.* 1.26.2-6.
65. Cic. *Att.* 9.11A.2-3.
66. Significance of acknowledging *beneficia* is also noted by Caesar at Corfinium: *BCiv.* 1.22.3, 1.23.3.
67. Cic. *Att.* 9.9.1, 9.18.2, 9.19.2, 10.3A.2, 10.1.4, 10.14.1; see Saunders 1923 for Sulpicius' political position; Cicero's friend Atticus is perhaps the best example of successful neutrality in civil war, as both his own work *Liber Annalis* and Nepos' biography suggest: Westall 2019: 71–5; Lobur 2019: 91–7.
68. Cic. *Att.* 7.4.2. For *alienatio* as a severing or disconnection (*disiunctio*) as in opposition to ideas of friendship, see Hellegouarc'h 1963: 200–1.
69. White 2010: 18–19.
70. For the social construction of space, see Low 2017, esp. 68–81.
71. See Russell 2016: 25–42 for a discussion of the Roman concepts of *publicus* and *privatus*.
72. For evidence of ongoing communication and correspondence between Caesar and Crassus in this period, see Caes. *BGall.* 3.9.1.
73. Appius (who does not appear to have taken up his proconsulship of Cilicia yet, see Shackleton Bailey 1980: 183) may have been attempting to secure Caesar as a paymaster (cf. Plut. *Caes.* 21.4; App. *BCiv.* 2.17) and the votes of his soldiers. In the context of L. Domitius Ahenobarbus' threats against Caesar should he achieve the consulship of 55 (Suet. *Iul.* 23.1-24.1), much of the interest at Ravenna and then Luca appears to have been focus on securing loyal candidates for the senior political offices for the next few years (Plut. *Pomp.* 51.4, *Crass* 14.6 for Caesar's explicit support in terms of votes for Pompeius and Caesar; Pelling 2011: 246 notes that this is omitted from the account at *Caes.* 21.6). Appius and Domitius would be colleagues in the consulship in 54 (*MRR* 2.221).
74. Plut. *Pomp.* 51.3, *Caes.* 21.5; *Crass.* 14.5; App. *BCiv.* 2.17. Suet. *Iul.* 24.1 and Cic. *Fam.* 1.9.9 just depict a small, private meeting. On the problem of the improbable numbers of 120 lictors and 200 senators in Plutarch and Appian, derived from the same source, see Pelling 2011: 246, particularly for Plutarch's discrepancies in the telling of Luca across his various *Lives*. In *Caes.* 12.5–6 the image is of Caesar as a powerful figure able to convene a Senate outside of Rome. While Pelling 2011: 45–7, 204 identifies Asinius Pollio as the common source for Appian and Plutarch for these events, others have convincingly argued that Livy, rather than Pollio, should be understood as the common source: see, for example, Stevenson 2015: 269–72; Westall 2015b, esp. 146–52, 156–60; see also Westall in this volume, 184–5, 195–6.
75. On the two 'very political *consilia*' (253) in private, family spaces, see Flower 2018, who argues that Servilia seems 'to have been working for reconciliation among various factions and a more stable political future' (263).
76. App. *BCiv.* 4.2; Plut. *Ant.*19-20; Cass. Dio 46.55; Flor. 2.65; Cornwell 2020: 155–8.
77. García Riaza 2020: 293–8 for face-to-face dialogue and neutral spaces in the triumviral period.
78. Roesch 2004: 151 points to *Fam.* 13.75.1, where Cicero apologizes to T. Titius for writing a second time to recommend Avianius Flaccus, due to the latter's demands that Cicero write to Titius *saepissime*. Cicero stresses that this should not be taken as a reflection of his own opinion of Titius' constancy.
79. Caes. *BCiv.* 3.16.4.
80. For Libo's encounter with Caesar's legates and then Caesar at Oricum, see Caes. *BCiv.* 3.15.6-17.6.

81. Caes. *BCiv.* 1.8.2-4 for the two envoys. 1.8.2: '[L. Caesar], once the rest of the talk was concluded, for which reason he had come, shows that he has instructions of a private duty (*eum privati officii mandata*) from Pompeius to him'. Roscius had volunteered along with the censor L. Piso to deliver information to Caesar following the initial meeting of the Senate (1.3.6); Cass. Dio 41.5.1-2 also stresses that Pompeius sent both L. Caesar and Roscius in a voluntary capacity: αὐτεπαγγέλτους. See also Cic. *Att.* 8.12.2.

82. Caes. *BCiv.* 1.9.2-11.4.

83. Cic. *Att.* 7.13A.2.

84. This supports Williams 2000: 161–3 on the uses of *mandata* in late Republican literature as, for the majority of its uses, oral rather than written communication.

85. Shackleton Bailey 1960a.

86. Cic. *Att.* 7.17.2.

87. Cicero's annoyance at the assignment of the task is clear. That Cicero was not as vital as he might have hoped in these negotiations might be suggested by the fact that Caesar seems to have only communicated his wishes to Cicero through Trebatius and did not write directly to Cicero himself (*Att.* 7.17.4). For Sestius' prose style, see also Catull. 44.

88. Cic. *Att.* 7.18.2. See *Att.* 7.14.1 for Cicero's hope of peace following the consuls and Pompeius accepting Caesar's *mandata* sent via L. Caesar, and *Att.* 7.15.2 for the prevailing hope of the senatorial order that Caesar adhere to the arrangement.

89. For the letter-writing tradition in the late Roman Republic, see White 2010.

90. Cic. *Att.* 9.7B and 7C. White 2010: 43–6 for enclosures in the Ciceronian corpus.

91. Caes. *BCiv.* 3.16.3-17.6.

92. For rivers as delineating boundaries, see Whittaker 2004: 6–9; Purcell 2012; as site of negotiation (in the triumviral period), see Cornwell 2020: 155–6 and García Riaza 2020: 294–8.

93. Caes. *BCiv.* 3.19.8.

94. Caes. *BCiv.* 1.75.2-76.5 for Petreius' actions, 1.77 for Caesar's.

95. See Arena 2020 for the failure of institutional management of violence.

CHAPTER 2
WHAT IS CIVIL ABOUT CIVIL WAR? POLITICAL COMMUNICATION AND THE CONSTRUCTION OF 'THE PEOPLE' ON THE EVE OF CIVIL WAR (49–48 BCE)*

Emilio Zucchetti

Pharsalus, 9 August 48 BCE, the eve of the decisive battle between Caesar and Pompey's armies. To test Pompey's willingness to engage in battle, Caesar displayed his army outside the camp in battle formation, boosting his soldiers' confidence:

> So he led the army out and drew up his line, at first in a spot he controlled, some distance from Pompey's camp, but on the following days advancing further from his own camp and setting his line at the foot of the hills controlled by Pompey. This made his army more confident every day.[1]

Rather unsurprisingly, the description exudes military language and reasoning. Romans imagined civil wars as fully-fledged military conflicts between armies in an open field. More than a century later, under Domitian, the poet P. Papinius Statius opened his epic poem about brotherly strife, the *Thebaid*, with the words *fraternas acies* ('fraternal warfare'), where *acies* indicates the army deployed before the fighting begins.[2] The word is regularly associated with external as much as with civil war: limiting the research to Caesar's *commentarii*, one finds that *acies* appears fifty-eight times in the books dedicated to the *Civil War*, and only thirty-six times in those dedicated to the *Gallic Wars*.[3]

An openly military character is often associated with Roman civil wars. Appian stresses the point in his account of Sulla's first march on Rome in 88. He explains that this war marked a break with previous seditions since 'the faction leaders attacked each other with great armies, as if they were at war' (πολέμου νόμῳ), and features of external wars appear in internal conflicts, such as 'trumpets and military standards', the novelty of which is pointed out by Appian.[4] As the historian observes, this went beyond the usual scheme of civic unrest and factional dispute (known to his Greek readers as στάσις).[5] The Greek *stasis* indicates a state of things, a paralysis of political life, whereas Roman civil war was truly different from those dissensions, demonstrations, riots and disturbances that often erupted in the capital. Roman civil war was a matter of armies, even in those rare cases when (e.g. Sulla's first march of Rome) it happened in the city.[6]

By contrast, as is apparent for instance in what is probably the most important theoretical work on the subject in political science, Stathis Kalyvas' *The Logic of Violence in Civil War* (2006), today's image of civil war is linked to irregular wars and militia, and guerrilla techniques, such as occurred during the Greek civil war (1946–9) and the Italian *Resistenza* (1943–5). For this reason, in addressing the question of the role of those who did not bear arms in Roman civil wars, this work on civilians' collaboration and support in twentieth-century civil wars can hardly be used.[7] The specific nature of Roman civil wars must be considered: all able-bodied *cives* living in the *civitates*/communities involved in the conflict were, at least in principle, liable to be called to arms in a levy. However, the large majority of the *populus Romanus* did not partake in the war directly. It can be calculated that no more than 13 per cent of total free population, according to different estimates, bore arms in the war. According to Peter Brunt's calculations, about forty-eight legions were fighting in 49–48: considering an average of 4,800 men in each legion, it would give a total of 230,400 units, mostly of Italian background, to whom allies and auxiliary troops are to be added. Even with the most conservative figures of population, 3 million people in total, including women and males of minor age, this accounts for roughly 13 per cent of the population.[8] If this is true even in general terms, the importance of the section of the population who did not bear arms cannot be underestimated. They still occupied a fully functional political role and were considered politically relevant by the Roman leaders, who continued to engage with them.

According to Plutarch, the city of Rome before the war was in complete anarchy, 'like a ship drifting without a helmsman'.[9] This obvious hyperbole serves to dramatically represent a collapsed political system, in which common people 'gave their support not with their votes, but with their arrows and swords and slings' in exchange for bribes and some 'sensible people' started to consider Pompey as a viable monarch.[10] Appian's account is not much different from that of Plutarch (App. *BCiv.* 2.19.96), suggesting that both authors might depend on Pollio's account for this period.[11] A rather more literal interpretation of Plutarch's use of the word ἀναρχία is available. The same word is used twice in the *Life of Pompey*, at 54.3-4. In this passage, 'anarchy' indicates the conflictual moments when consuls could not be elected. The first time is used in reference to the elections for 53, which failed to elect anyone and only ended with M. Valerius Messalla Rufus and Cn. Domitius Calvinus entering upon their consulship seven months after the regular time. At 54.4, Plutarch writes that 'an anarchy arose again' for the election for the following year. Concluding with Pompey as sole consul, this is arguably the most contested election in the history of the *res publica*. During the disorders, Clodius was killed by the armed bands of Milo, and Pompey brought the army into town for the first time ever to repress civil unrest.[12] The passage in the *Life of Caesar* is either a vague reference to the elections of that period or else a specific reference to those of 51 or 50.[13] However, the consuls of 51 took office on 1 January, and there do not seem to be any other accounts supporting this hypothesis.[14] It appears that Plutarch is offering a blank description of the tense political situation and continuous institutional disruptions in Rome in the late 50s. Be that as it may, the tension was palpable. Appian writes that the *populus* was 'somewhat disgruntled with Pompey because of the bribery trials'.[15]

At the end of the year 50, Caesar was still trying to conduct the campaign in the political sphere, and public opinion must have backed his position since Plutarch notes that his 'claim had the appearance of being strikingly just'.[16] In an unspecified 'popular assembly' (ἐν τῷ δήμῳ), likely on 1 December 50, just before his term as tribune ended, C. Scribonius Curio proposed that both Caesar and Pompey lay down their armies. The proposal seems to have enjoyed the support of the Senate (App. *BCiv.* 2.30) as well as of the 'common' people. He was greeted with loud applause and escorted to his house in a spectacular example of popular support, as though (according to the sources) a victorious athlete.[17] It is clear that the civilian population in Rome was interested in the evolution of the political situation, but what role was played by that enormous part of the population, citizens and non-citizens (women, children, slaves) alike, that did not bear arms?

If one sets out to use Caesar's *Civil War* as a source, many complex problems arise.[18] First, one should question whether Caesar's partisan account can be considered a witness of Caesar's communicative strategy during the war. The problem is tightly linked to the question of composition and publication, which is a debate that is far from settled.[19] Some scholars have argued that Caesar abandoned the project of the *Civil War* after Pompey's death, on 28 September 48, an event that radically transformed the political context.[20] The work would then have only been published in the context of the 'complete Caesar' edited by Hirtius, after Caesar's murder. Discussing in detail the problem of composition and publication would take me far away from the topic of this essay, so that I shall be content in stating that, as Osgood recently acknowledged, 'scholars do tend to agree that Caesar wrote the *Civil War* more or less as it unfolded in 49 and 48, perhaps bringing his work to an end while in Alexandria in 48/47'.[21] For the argument put forward here the publication is relatively unimportant, what matters is the composition. In fact, the point at stake is whether the *Civil War* was, at least at first, intended to play a part in persuading audiences, and thus, public opinion, of the legitimacy of Caesar's actions. Indeed, if the *commentarii* were at least partially circulated as was the *Gallic War*, this would strengthen my interpretation.[22] If, however, the hypothesis of a publication after Caesar's death is correct, then the text would still offer a substantial example of Caesar's communicative strategy during 49 and 48, since it was never revised. It might be inferred that the strikingly limited and localized set of occurrences of LIBERTAS in the *Civil War* reflects the limited use of the concept and its abandonment in Caesar's communication during the war.[23] I shall therefore assume, for the scope of this chapter, that the *Civil War* indeed reflects Caesar's genuine communicative strategy, at least to some extent, and can therefore be used to analyze the discursive construction that supported Caesar's narrative.

As Kurt Raaflaub, Robert Morstein-Marx and Josiah Osgood have already argued, Caesar advanced the claim in the *Civil War* that he was acting legitimately and in the interests of the Republic, of the Senate, and of the *populus Romanus*.[24] Going back to my starting point, just before the beginning of the battle of Pharsalus, I would like to focus on the short direct speech that Caesar attributes to Crastinus.[25]

> There was a reenlisted man, Crastinus, in Caesar's army, who had been his chief centurion in the Tenth Legion the year before, a man of remarkable courage. After

the signal was given, Crastinus said 'Follow me, you who were men of my unit, and give your commander the effort you have resolved on. This one battle remains. Once it is over, he will have his dignity (*dignitatem*) again and we our liberty (*libertatem*).' At the same time, looking at Caesar, he said, 'My actions today, general, will make you thank me either alive or dead.'²⁶

Even though LIBERTAS had long since disappeared from Caesar's communicative strategy, the pairing of LIBERTAS and *dignitas* in the mouth of a soldier must still have seemed to him a strong, emotional narrative technique to mark the beginning of the decisive battle. The construction parallels the more elaborate one at 1.22.5, in an indirect speech reporting Caesar's own words.²⁷ In Crastinus' short speech, this combination of values indicates a community of interests between Caesar and his soldiers, as Caesar had done in his first indirect speech, at Ariminum (*BCiv.* 1.7).²⁸ In *BCiv.* 1.7, asking the soldiers to fight for their commander and the safety of the tribunes of the *plebs*, Caesar appeals to their status both as soldiers and as citizens. In articulating the soldiers' identity as directly linked to his own political project, Caesar attempted to legitimize his position with them and to strengthen his own *popularis* narrative. Crastinus' direct speech recalls that of Caesar directly and, referring to him with the official title of *imperator*, strengthens the perfect unification of Caesar with his army, as well as the legitimacy of Caesar's position, right before the decisive battle. Moreover, Crastinus' words are framed in an almost sacral way. The final sentence seems to allude to a *devotio*, the extreme vow through which a Roman general dedicated himself to the chthonic gods in exchange for victory in the battle.²⁹ Finally, his sacrifice is poignantly described by Caesar, who devotes a few lines to Crastinus, at 3.99.2-3, while considering the losses in battle: he is attributed an *excellentissima virtus*, which elevates the episode to a paradigmatic status and, at once, recalling 3.91.1, where he is defined *vir singulari virtute*. These features, including the later reference, frame this short and relatively humble speech as a crucial narrative turning point, reconnecting the decisive battle to the very beginning of the hostilities. If in a probably incomplete work like the *Civil War* one were to look for a mark of *Ringkomposition*, this would be it. But how did the narrative construction link LIBERTAS and *dignitas*?

To answer this question, I propose to look afresh at Caesar's political strategy with the assistance of Ernesto Laclau's theory of popular subjectivity. Before going into greater detail, I shall first give a compressed account of Laclau's theory of 'The People' as formulated in *On Populist Reason* (2005) and grounded in the work he co-authored with Chantal Mouffe in 1985, *Hegemony and Socialist Strategy*.³⁰ I shall then argue that the three necessary conditions for its application identified in the first part can be found in the political context of 49–48. In turn, looking at Caesar's political strategy through this lens means necessarily arguing against the use of the model of 'coalition-building' advocated by Raaflaub.³¹ Through the model of 'construction of the people', I wish therefore to suggest a fresh angle to look at the complex political phase on the eve and in the early stages of the civil war, starting from (and not in contradiction with) the most recent scholarly debates on the topic.

1. Hegemony and *popularis* strategy: theoretical grounds for a re-reading

To open this reflection, a necessarily brief and compressed account of Laclau's mature theory, as formulated in *On Populist Reason* (2005), is in order. Laclau's views are largely inspired by the work of an Italian Marxist thinker and activist Antonio Gramsci (1891–1937), as his idea of 'The People' relies on what Gramsci called a 'historical bloc'. He defined this concept as a 'historical congruence between material forces, institutions and ideologies, or broadly, an alliance of different class forces politically organized around a set of hegemonic ideas that gives strategic direction and coherence to its constituent elements'.[32] This 'set of hegemonic ideas' is nothing but ideology itself (Q11§12).[33] Ideology is the representation of the reality of a social group, or, in other words, the world-view that concretizes and unifies the 'historical bloc'.[34] It is something that no one 'owns', but rather lives in, and, as such, it affects the choices and behaviours of the subject (whether an individual or a group). Every individual has a worldview that is shared with the groups in which they participate or takes elements from the worldviews of different groups and welds them into an eclectic system.[35] At the same time, the relationship between choices, behaviours and ideology is dialogical: realized only in everyday life, the worldview constitutes the individual as a subject.

The definition of ideology as a 'set of hegemonic ideas' refers to the concept of 'hegemony', a crucial element in Gramsci's thought. This can be understood as a dialectical process between coercion and consent, based on the material socio-economic power relations, or, in Marxist terms, on the 'base'. It is indeed clear that the hegemonic process is not resolved in a top-down transmission of a narrative by the dominant class, but is rather linked to the 'spontaneous' consent conceded by the ruled:

> The intellectuals are the dominant group's 'deputies' exercising the subaltern functions of social hegemony and political government. These comprise:
>
> 1. The 'spontaneous' consent given by the great masses of the population to the general direction imposed on social life by the dominant fundamental group; this consent is 'historically' caused by the prestige (and consequent confidence) which the dominant group enjoys because of its position and function in the world of production.
> 2. The apparatus of state coercive power which 'legally' enforces discipline on those groups who do not 'consent' either actively or passively. This apparatus is, however, constituted for the whole of society in anticipation of moments of crisis of command and direction when spontaneous consent has failed.[36]

Even though Gramsci never defines 'hegemony', this classic locus makes clear that 'social hegemony and political government' concern both consent and coercion. For the mechanism to work, the contribution of the ruled is necessary both at the moment of constructing the hegemonic setup and in reproducing the social norms that are embedded in the system of dominance. Gramsci's conception of hegemony has the masses actively contributing to the creation of any hegemonic setup, either through accommodation or resistance.[37] In the former case, the ruled act as producers of the hegemonic ideology, both in political society (narrowly understood, i.e. governmental and coercive apparatuses) and in civil society. If, however, some of them refuse to comply, coercive powers force them to do so. If this also fails, then the non-compliant groups are turned into negative examples in the hegemonic discourse, as if they were the 'antagonists' in a fairy tale. In other words, any hegemonic construction must include all actors, including the subalterns, whether they decide to cooperate or not.

These two Gramscian ideas ('historical bloc' and 'hegemony') are crucial to the development of Laclau's thought, and it is to this that I now turn. In Laclau and Mouffe's language, hegemony is seen as an articulation of class interests in a wider political and ideological discourse.[38] The hegemonic effort is the basic structure for the construction of a historical bloc that actually exists and is capable of intervening in the history of a given society. While Gramsci's reading is completely organic to Marxist thought, Laclau resorts to the Foucauldian concept of discourse, to escape any form of class essentialism or *economicismo*, the class-reductionist approach to Marxism which Gramsci vigorously contested.[39] In Laclau and Mouffe's theoretical account, hegemony is an 'articulation'. They call '*articulation* any practice establishing a relation among elements such that their identity is modified as a result of the articulatory practice'.[40] In fact, all objects are articulated through discourse, which is the 'structured totality resulting from the articulatory practice'.[41] The aim of discourse is the transformation of 'elements' (in the words of Laclau and Mouffe, 'any difference that is not discursively articulated') into 'moments', where the meaning – read the identity – of each moment is temporarily fixed through the differential relation with all the other moments, as is the case in structural linguistics ('the differential position, insofar as they appear articulated within a discourse'). These identities and meanings are only temporarily fixed, because in Laclau the transformation is never complete, and is limited by the contingent nature of the discourse that produces it. Here comes into play an element of contingency: if discourse is always the result of a contingent articulatory practice, the subject that it generates will have the same characteristics and will only exist in a specific time and place. Since the meanings are never entirely fixed, there is always scope for hegemony, intended as an articulatory practice.

Every object can have a material referent but is nevertheless constructed in the field of discourse:

> The fact that every object is constituted as an object of discourse has nothing to do with whether there is a world external to thought, or with the realism/idealism opposition. An earthquake or the falling of a brick is an event that certainly exists, in the sense that it occurs here and now, independently of my will. But whether their specificity as objects is constructed in terms of 'natural phenomena' or 'expressions of the wrath of God', depends upon the structuring of a discursive field. What is denied is not that such objects exist externally to thought, but the rather different assertion that they could constitute themselves as objects outside any discursive condition of emergence.[42]

In this sense, any external input, the real object, is always lacking something. This absence allowed Laclau to appeal to Lacan's concept of *manque* (lack) in ontological terms. If no discursive object, including the collective subjectivity, ever achieves completeness of identity, as there cannot be any completeness of meaning in any signifier, then any discursive object is haunted by a 'lack', by the elements that it does not have and that cannot be successfully integrated.[43] Any discourse is a construction that aspires to dominate what Laclau and Mouffe call 'the field of discursivity'. As already detailed, every discourse is a contingent articulation, and therefore identities and meanings also are.[44] This contingency is precisely the historical development, how ideas and institutions change over time. For instance, what the current paradigm defines as a 'political culture' can be understood as a discursive field that all linguistic utterances, symbols, practices, and texts (broadly understood) shape and articulate.

Thanks to this condition, discourse always attempts to complete an identity to round off concepts and make them interact in a totality. It can do so only for a limited time, through the institution of 'nodal points' and a 'centre', thereby stopping, at least temporarily, the flow of differences (the basic condition for any identity to be partially fixed).[45] Laclau's mature theory clarifies that these nodal points are constituted by what he calls empty (or floating) signifiers, drawing the concept from semiotics. These have been 'variously defined as a signifier with a vague, highly variable, unspecifiable, or non-existent signified'.[46] They bear different meanings in the understanding of different individuals and 'may stand for many or even any signifieds; they may mean whatever their interpreters want them to mean'.[47] In the field of ancient history, an appropriate example is the use of a concept such as LIBERTAS, the full meaning of which is unattainable, and comes to signify something only in a discursive articulation: think, for instance, of the distinct meanings that LIBERTAS seems to have in Cicero's speeches against Catiline and those attributed to Catiline by Sallust.[48] The fluctuation of the meaning of LIBERTAS, observed as a floating signifier, affects the semantic construction of the entire political discourse, as it is articulated by any given agent.

LIBERTAS is indeed the example discussed by Ronald Syme in chapter 11 of *The Roman Revolution* (1939), 'Political Catchwords', where he reflected upon the relationship between political language and political realities, offering a negative depiction of what he saw as a continuous deception enacted by the Roman politicians to the detriment of the people. In Syme's view, the common political values to which all speeches appeal were no more than vague ideals that assumed a specific meaning only in the partisan view of the speaker: 'Roman politicians, whether they asserted the People's rights or the Senate's, were acting a pretence: they strove for power only'.[49] The study of political catchwords would thus be an attempt to uncover the articulation of ideological positions and their consequences on the dynamics of power.[50] Santangelo has recently traced some parallels between Syme's view and Morstein-Marx's category of 'ideological monotony', the idea that in the *contiones* only one public ideology was displayed by the most different actors in order to ingratiate themselves with the audience.[51] Morstein-Marx complemented that thesis with some remarks on hegemony in a book chapter entitled '"Cultural Hegemony" and the Communicative Power of the Roman Élite' (2013), stressing the importance of the people as co-producers of public ideology. The category of 'floating signifiers' proposed here operates in the Gramscian intellectual tradition but presents two specific differences from Syme and Morstein-Marx. First, it analyses specific, contingent discourses through which the signifiers are organized. This might allow us to appreciate the differences between different moments in the history of a signifier to which historical actors appeal in ideologically relevant contexts. Secondly, the meaning of a certain signifier is not determined by partisanship, but by a differential relationship within a certain discursive hegemony. Its meaning is constructed in a contingent way and inscribed in the aspects of continuity in the history of a concept.

The differential relationship is also crucial to understanding the question of the subject in Laclau and Mouffe. In Marxist theory, including Gramsci, the subject position is always occupied by the fundamental class, the proletariat.[52] In Laclau and Mouffe's theory, there is no aprioristic subject and subjectivity can only be conceived in terms of differential 'subject positions': this refers to the complex and overdetermined aggregate of differential positions.[53] Arguing for this different understanding of the subject, they appeal to the notion of 'overdetermination', imported into Marxist theory by Althusser. This intuition was a means for thinking about the many forces, sometimes opposed, at play in any political situation, without interpreting them as 'contradictory' and, thus, ideological.[54] Inspired by Gramsci's reading of ideology, Althusser argued that 'a revolution in the *structure* does not *ipso facto* modify the existing superstructures and particularly the *ideologies* at one blow (as it would if the economic was the *sole determinant factor*)' and that 'the new society produced by the Revolution may itself *ensure the survival, that is, the reactivation of older elements* through both the forms of its new superstructures and specific (national and international) "circumstances".[55] This concept operates in a social totality, distinguishing structures and superstructure only 'didactically' and not ontologically.[56]

Any subjectivity is thus precarious, and never fulfilled, since the identity occupying the subject position is contingent. To be concretized into a historical bloc, this emerging subjectivity needs a further process to take place: antagonism. In Laclau's theory, the conflict between two subjects becomes antagonistic when it contrasts with an aspect of one's identity outside the relations of production.[57] The antagonistic experience constitutes the object as it sheds light on the limits of the identity of a given social group. This pluralism is what makes possible a re-constitution of the subject, without assuming that it should be constituted around any particular group (the obvious example being the working class).

Laclau and Mouffe offer two relational logics that articulate the process of re-composition of a subject: difference and equivalence.[58] Without going into too many details, in the 'logic of difference', each moment remains differential from each other, and obtains its meaning from the differential relations instituted ($\alpha \neq \beta \neq \gamma \neq \delta \ldots$).[59] To understand this logic, one should think about the heterogeneity of 'the social' in the contemporary world: a variety of social groups exist, each with their own grievances or demands, different from that of other social groups (e.g., trade unions, ethnic/racialized groups, LGBTQIA+ advocacy groups, etc.). They address the centre (i.e., the government or the institutions) to meet their demands on an individual level. The centre is likely to adopt tactics to cope with these demands in different ways. When it does so, the problem is addressed on an institutional level, regular activities resume, and there is no space for hegemonic construction.[60] When it fails to do so, or the social groups involved consider the response insufficient, then the 'logic of difference' can be transformed into a 'logic of equivalence'. The different groups find themselves in the same relationship with the 'centre' and find they have at least one characteristic in common: their rejection. These social groups with their individual unfulfilled demands in society 'discover' an equivalence with one another through their relationship with the centre.[61] The 'logic of equivalence' then is what constitutes two opposed fields ($\alpha \neq$ not-α), something like 'us' against 'them'. That is the relationship of antagonism between the centre and the 'chain of equivalential demands'. Laclau and Mouffe use as an example the relationship between rural and urban population in millenarian movements.[62]

The two logics can exist together. While the logic of equivalence (i.e., the relationship between the chain and the centre) institutes the centre in terms of otherness, the social groups with unfulfilled demands are in differential relation to each other. Through a discursive articulation (that is to say, through hegemony), they can undergo a process of unification and become a historical bloc, with a stable system of signification that keeps their demands together. They only need a name, e.g. 'The People', to become a singularity, i.e. 'an assemblage of heterogeneous moments kept together only by a name'.[63] This historical bloc, this hegemonic subject can finally be defined as a particularity (a part) claiming to be a universality (the whole).[64]

To apply it to the source material, I offer a brief summary of this complex theory in terms of the three fundamental elements that are prerequisites for constituting a formation that can be (but is not necessarily) called 'The People':

1. an equivalential chain of unfulfilled demands, put forward by a variety of social groups dissatisfied with an unresponsive power and coming together into a hegemonic formation, a singularity;
2. an antagonistic line separating *us*, 'The People', from *them*, the Others;
3. floating signifiers: key concepts temporarily fixing their meaning in the hegemonic articulation.

2. People or coalition? Caesar's hegemonic strategy in 49–48 BCE

It is now time to go back to Caesar's strategy and see if these three necessary conditions apply. I shall begin from the equivalential chain. Kurt Raaflaub argued more than once for a precise political strategy put into effect by Caesar, first in 59 and again in 49, which he described as 'the construction of a Grand Coalition of True Roman Citizens'.[65] The concept of Grand Coalition seems to me to have been borrowed from German political vocabulary: *die große Koalition* is the name for a coalition government formed when none of the political parties gains a majority by itself, which is a common feature in proportional multi-polar systems.⁶⁶ This coalition, argues Raaflaub, comprised different groups in society dissatisfied with the *status quo*: the lower *plebs*;⁶⁷ sections of the *equites*, the second property-based census class, notably the *publicani* and the money-lenders (Cic. *Att*. 7.7.5).⁶⁸ Other groups with different material interests may be seen taking their place in the equivalential chain. For instance, Caesar's sarcasm at the beginning of the *Civil War* seems to suggest that a large part of the Senate was ready to occupy a neutral position if they were not forced by Pompey's faction to side against Caesar.⁶⁹ Appian's account shows that most of the senators (370 vs. 22) wanted to find a way to preserve peace, which makes Caesar's narrative more believable.⁷⁰ Moreover, Mark Antony held *contiones* in Rome, during which Caesar's letters from Gaul were read aloud to the crowd in order to mobilize the population against Pompey's faction.⁷¹ Finally, he surely enjoyed the support of the vast majority of his simple soldiers on immediate material grounds, as they would have expected to obtain some material advantage from their choice.⁷² Even a letter of Cicero to Atticus stresses the composite nature of this group, wittily noticing that 'Caesar's side lacks nothing but a cause, all else they have in abundance'.⁷³

The language of the *Civil War* also reflects the wide nature of the groups involved. If the *populus Romanus* unequivocally was the intended audience of the *Gallic War*, with forty-one occurrences of the term in the first book, as remarked already by Wiseman and Marincola, and sixty-three in the whole work, this cannot be said for the *Civil War*, where the formulation appears only nine times in total.⁷⁴ Extending the research to *populus* without specification, one gets twenty-one occurrences. On the assumption that the terminology reflects, at least loosely, that used in different phases of the war, the distribution of these occurrences might also be of interest. Book 2 never refers to the *populus Romanus*, whereas the occurrences are concentrated at the beginning of Book 1 and at the end of Book 3.⁷⁵ Taking a closer look, it becomes apparent that most occurrences appear in official contexts concerning matters of legitimacy: the justification for entering a civil war (1.7.5; 1.9.2; and 1.22.5, in Corfinium); the declaration of neutrality by the Massilienses (1.35.3); the refusal of the Greeks of Oricum to fight *contra imperium populi Romani* (3.11.3); after the death of Pompey, in the context of the failed arbitration between Ptolemy and Cleopatra, legitimizing Caesar's decision to act in an official capacity in the conflict (3.107.2); in the indirect reporting of the will of Ptolemy the father (3.108.5); and, finally, as an antonym to describe the un-Roman habits of Gabinius' former soldiers 'who had become accustomed to the dissolute lifestyle of Alexandria, forgotten the name and discipline of the Roman people, and taken wives', 3.110.2). From this perspective, the distribution of the occurrences suggests two precise moments in which Caesar thought that the institutional argument would help legitimize his own actions after winning the war.

The occurrences of other key terms of Roman politics confirm the picture delineated by this compressed study of *populus Romanus*: *senatus* appears twenty-three times in the *Gallic War*, and thirty-six in the *Civil War*, among which three included in the formula *senatus populusque* (1.9.5; 3.10.8; 3.10.10); *res publica* occurs twenty-seven times in the *Civil War* against a mere six times in the *Gallic War*.⁷⁶ The lexical distribution might then be taken as a reflection of the different political objectives Caesar imagined for his *commentarii*. His self-fashioning as a true Republican, which particularly informs Books 1 and 3, for different reasons, was intended to be a tool of legitimization.[77] If the *populus* was the intended audience of the *Gallic War*, as has been argued by Wiseman, the *Civil War* was meant to address a set of diverse social groups.[78] These constituted the links of the 'equivalential chain', a very composite historical bloc. As I said, they did not share immediate material interests, and therefore their class difference was not that important. They would have been favoured in any case by a change in power configuration.

The next point of our analysis is the construction of otherness, or the moment of antagonism. Caesar constructed the campaign not as a civil war, but as a war against his own enemies, slowly becoming enemies of the *res publica*: *inimici*, but also *hostes*, public enemies, as they are called sixty-five times in the *Civil War*.[79] The strategy of playing down the civil war and blaming his enemies for it was also favoured by Pompey's persistent refusal of peace offers and negotiations.[80] As Andreola Rossi has argued, Pompey and his supporters are constantly depicted as Orientals in the *Civil War*, stressing their vices (and above all *luxuria*), their un-Romanness, and, by contrast, reinforcing Caesar's representation as the archetype of Roman qualities. Caesar's strategy of representation in the *Civil War* 'tends towards a process of de-familiarization of the enemy, of de-romanization'.[81] A suitable example of such a narrative is in the temporary informal truce in Spain. The soldiers do not want to fight the war, and as soon as Pompey's commanders Petreius and Afranius leave the troops alone, they start fraternizing with each other.[82]

> With their departure, the soldiers had a clear opportunity for negotiations, and they came out in a body, each man looking and calling for his acquaintances and townsmen in Caesar's camp. First, they gave collective thanks to everyone for having spared them the previous day, when they were terrified. 'Your kindness kept us alive.' Then they asked about the general's reliability, and whether it would be a good move to entrust themselves to him, lamenting the fact that they had not done so from the beginning and had fought against men who were their friends and relatives. Encouraged by this discussion they asked for the general's promise concerning the future of Petreius and Afranius, so that they would not think that they had incurred guilt or betrayed their own side. Once these matters were settled the men guaranteed that they would transfer their standards immediately and sent to Caesar a peace delegation of chief centurions. Meanwhile, some led friends into their own camp to entertain them, and others were led off by friends, with the result that the two camps seemed to have become one.... Everything was full of joy and thanksgiving on both sides: the one saw themselves as having escaped great danger, the other as having achieved a great success without bloodshed. In everyone's opinion Caesar was winning great credit for his former clemency (*lenitatis*), and his strategy had everyone's approval.

The episode gives Caesar the chance to boast his leniency, one of the cardinal points of his *nova ratio vincendi*, discussed in this volume by Hannah Cornwell.[83] Caesar's vocabulary warmly represents a whole that is reuniting, as is admirably depicted in the unification of the two camps (*adeo ut una castra iam facta ex binis viderentur*). This has a parallel in the fragments of Livy's account of 40 (Liv. *Fr.* 51-53), when a *dissensio* is resolved with the two armies and standards coming together *in una castra*. His language might remind us of the many instances in Livy's first pentad where the focus is on the fear of permanent division of a community.[84] In 1.74-5, Caesar wants to evoke the opposite process, reunification. In this civil war that he claims he did not wish to fight, all that is needed to restore the integrity of the community is the absence of the outcasts, the internal enemies, the *pauci*, here embodied by Petreius and Afranius.[85] When they withdraw, the soldiers have a clear opportunity for negotiation, which is qualified as *libera*, and not by chance. The allusion to the soldiers' LIBERTAS of not fighting this war is all too evident. The reunification is a unanimous desire. The Pompeian soldiers thank all the Caesarians for having spared their lives the day before and lament the fact that they did not entrust themselves to Caesar 'from the beginning and had fought against men who were their friends and relatives' (*cum hominibus necessariis et consanguineis*). In fact, once the commanders return, their reaction is unremittingly severe.[86] They execute all of Caesar's soldiers they can find, even though some are hidden by Pompey's legionaries. By contrast, Caesar shows extreme leniency, and spares the lives of Pompey's soldiers, after his victory, on the one condition that the legions be dismantled, and the soldiers be sent back home (*BCiv.* 1.76.4-7). Caesar favours a political solution, seeing 'civil war' as belonging to the realm of the political and not as a purely military affair, as his opponents do. The *factio paucorum* occupied the Republic for their own interest and deprived the Roman citizens of their power to confer magistracies (*honores*) on those citizens (e.g. Caesar) who served the Republic well (*bene de re publica merere*).[87] This is how the narrative runs. Having the legal framework on his side, after the law of 52 allowing him to run for the consulship *in absentia*, and being impeded by his enemies from standing for office, Caesar can frame the whole war as a personal attack against him and an attack to the principles of the Republic itself, especially after Mark Antony, tribune of the *plebs*, and Curio had to leave the city, at the beginning of January, fearing for their own lives.[88] The antagonism is created between 'The People' and the *factio paucorum*, between the equivalential chain and the centre.

The spectacular scapegoating of the *pauci* is as effective as it is unsurprising. Excluding the polluted part of the community to resolve moments of intense crisis, which operation recalls the *pharmakos*, was not a novelty. Quite the contrary, Sulla did something similar after the first march on Rome in 88, when, needing to resolve the conflict and reconstruct the community, he preferred the invention of the *hostis* declaration.[89] Citizens who were declared *hostes* (the sources consistently use the term *iudicare*) lost all the prerogatives of citizen status, becoming outcasts. In turn, the expulsion of a limited number of clearly defined enemies allowed the new political leader Sulla, to 'pardon' all those citizens who did not side with him in the conflict and achieve reconciliation in the community. Very different, as is well known, was Sulla's policy in 82. His proscriptions became a model of tyrannical domination and Caesar used their spectre to delegitimize Pompey and his other opponents.[90] In so doing, Caesar created an antithesis between his *nova ratio vincendi* and the tyrannical attitude that Pompey and his men could be expected to demonstrate. In a certain sense, it might be said that their strategies of conflict resolution can be viewed as a clash between two Sullan strategies. In any case, it is patent that an antagonism, based on a relationship of pure equivalence (α ≠ non-α), and therefore incompatibility in the same community, was in place.[91]

Once this 'us' vs. 'them' antagonism is delineated and two conditions are fulfilled, the bearers of unfulfilled demands need no more than a discourse articulated in some nodal points to rediscover the fact that they are 'The People', i.e. a singularity. In other words, our equivalential chain needs a way to make sense of the floating signifiers into a coherent narrative. In this context, however, I cannot possibly develop the analysis of this narrative to the extent it would deserve. My attempt here should rather be seen as an argument to apply Critical Discourse Analysis to texts such as the *Civil War* in the future, aiming to further investigate the intratextual discursive construction that articulates the political views expressed, as has already been done in the last few years with a renewed theoretical foundation. I propose here as examples three empty/floating signifiers that assume a distinctive meaning once included in Caesar's discourse: LIBERTAS, *voluntas*, and *dignitas*.[92] After Thucydides's account of the unrest in Corcyra, semantic distortion was a defining feature of this breakdown of consensus.[93] These three words' mutual relationship activates a net of significations that was not already embedded in the nouns themselves. In other words, they are not merely catchwords. In the articulation of Caesar's discourse, as Morstein-Marx has argued, *dignitas* is not only linked to his private status, but is also connected to Republican traditions, and thereby to the powers of the *populus* as an institution.[94] It was their legitimate task to reward deserving citizens with magistracies, reconfirming the 'meritocratic' nature of the Republic. This is the will of the people, the *voluntas*, which in the first book of the *Civil War* stands for the sympathy that the Italian communities show towards Caesar.[95] *Voluntas* is a key concept in this phase, as is shown by a letter (dated 5 March 49) that Caesar sent to his friends Oppius and Balbus after the capture of Corfinium.[96]

> I shall willingly follow your advice, all the more willingly because I had of my own accord decided to show all possible clemency and to do my best to reconcile Pompey. Let us try whether by this means we can win back the good will of all (*omnium voluntates*) and enjoy a lasting victory, seeing that others have not managed by cruelty to escape hatred or to make their victories endure, except only L. Sulla, whom I do not propose to imitate. Let this be the new style of conquest, to make mercy and generosity our shield. [...] If they wish to show themselves grateful they should urge Pompey to prefer my friendship to that of those who have always been his and my bitter enemies, by whose machinations the country has been brought to its present pass.[97]

In this crucial text, which is analysed in greater depth in Hannah Cornwell's contribution to this volume, Caesar lays out the crucial aspect of his *nova ratio vincendi*, a policy in conscious discontinuity with Sulla's proscriptions (*tenere praeter unum L. Sullam, quem imitaturus non sum*).⁹⁸ The stress in this programmatic passage is on *voluntas*, a keyword of no particular importance in traditional civic discourse, but firmly connected with *amicitia*, and through this with the political aspect of CONCORDIA, or harmony within the civic community. Incidentally, it should be noted that Balbus in forwarding this letter of Caesar's to Cicero tells his correspondent that he could see 'how anxious he [*sc.* Caesar] is to restore good relations with Pompey, and how far removed from any sort of cruelty he is' (Cic. *Att.* 9.7B, *ex quibus perspicere poteris quam cupiat concordiam <suam> et Pompei reconciliare et quam remotus sit ab omni crudelitate*).⁹⁹

More importantly, even if excluded from the traditional political discourse, *voluntas* could be linked to an idea of *political will*.¹⁰⁰ According to Hellegouarc'h, *voluntas* is the appropriate term for indicating a political opinion ('*le terme propre à designer la notion d'opinion politique*'); however, as Brunt observed, this definition is too narrow, for *voluntas* signifies the possibility of pursuing one's will and opinions, not only within the political sphere.¹⁰¹ Even if not necessary, however, the political nuance was indeed possible: the fifteen occurrences in the *Commentariolum petitionis* strongly point to this semantic value.¹⁰² In this work, the concept might be translated by the idea of support, backing and goodwill towards a candidate canvassing for a magistracy. By insisting on *voluntas*, Caesar was reactivating the legitimate framework of institutional magistracies. Re-focusing the conflict on individuals' and communities' *voluntates* meant bringing it back from the extraordinary military aspect of the political conflict to its 'ordinary' course.

Caesar communicated his intention to recover the general consensus (*omnium voluntates*) via his *nova ratio vincendi*, probably because he was concerned about the tenability of his position after the war.¹⁰³ In the same letter, Caesar stresses the value of leniency, and the need to keep offering Pompey a way to resolve the conflict without bloodshed.¹⁰⁴ This confirms what Raaflaub argued about LIBERTAS, the most Republican of the floating signifiers here analysed: in this context, its meaning is linked to *dignitas* and the Republican constitution.¹⁰⁵ Within a quasi-meritocratic system, such as that posited by Karl-Joachim Hölkeskamp, the LIBERTAS of the Roman *populus* is realized by distributing *honores* to and rewarding the *dignitas* of the most deserving citizens.¹⁰⁶

LIBERTAS seems important in the early stages of the war and until 48 BCE, but was then dropped in favour of *lenitas* (leniency). Coinage from 48 also shows the legend LIBERTAS.¹⁰⁷ In the *Civil War*, the distribution of LIBERTAS seems to be consistent with this assumption and not dissimilar to the one observed above for the *populus Romanus*.¹⁰⁸ On a closer inspection, however, only two of the occurrences (1.22.5 and 3.91.2, Caesar's indirect and Crastinus' direct speech) refer to the LIBERTAS of the Roman people and are connected to one another through the use of the same vocabulary. *Dignitas* likewise occurs at the beginning of Book 1 (Ariminum) and late in Book 3 (prior to the battle of Pharsalus) in passages dedicated to justifying Caesar's actions.¹⁰⁹ The expression *res publica* occurs in similar contexts for the most part. Indeed, eight of the twenty-seven occurrences are in close proximity to *dignitas*, underlining the official, and thus legitimate, and selfless aspects of Caesar's actions.¹¹⁰ For example, at 1.9.3, Caesar says in indirect speech that he 'accepted the loss of prestige with equanimity for the sake of the republic'.¹¹¹

The whole passage is full of politically relevant terms. He refers first to his *dignitas* (1.9.2), and then complains his *inimici* stripped him of the honour that the Roman people had bestowed on him (1.9.2, *doluisse se quod populi Romani beneficium sibi per contumeliam ab inimicis extorqueretur*). The interconnectedness of these concepts in creating a discourse that supports a political formation ought by now to be clear. The use of *voluntas* rounds it off, with Caesar insisting that the new political formation to support his hegemony after the war depends on the *nova ratio vincendi*, and, therefore, on *voluntas*. The word appears twenty-six times in the *Civil War*, and can mean 'will, goodwill, or support', and indicates an individual's or a group's attitude towards Caesar and Pompey. For instance, at 1.12, *voluntas* is used four times to signify the goodwill of the inhabitants of Iguvium and more generally of the municipalities towards Caesar.[112] It seems clear that this use in the *commentarii* echoes that of the letter, showing a certain discursive unity between the different sources. Both might have been read out to the people performatively in public spaces in the city.

Even from this rapid survey, it is clear that these keywords match the role of floating signifiers in Laclau's theory. They are the fundamental (nodal) points by means of which the audience made sense of Caesar's political communication and then reconfigured its own position, which *mutatis mutandis* would have been different for different social groups or individuals. They clarify what the roles of the *populus*, of the leaders, and of the Italian allies were, and construct the order of Caesar's discourse; through this operation, their own meaning is temporarily fixed and determined by the differential relation between one another.

3. Conclusions

The application of Laclau's theory of popular subjectivity to the analysis of Caesar's political discourse before and during the civil war seems to be justified, as the three necessary conditions are fulfilled. The *populus Romanus* invoked by Caesar with a legitimizing function can thus be described as a discursive political construction, rather than the source of law or the totality of the civic body. This philosophical approach generates new questions and new angles through which to look at the sources. It also opens up the possibility of thinking in depth about the process of collective bodies' formation and its relationship with communicative strategies and social alliances. During the Roman civil wars, most of the population was not directly involved in the fighting and had to be targeted with specific strategies of political communication, partly different from the ones used to gain the allegiance of the soldiers. Roman citizens, both in the city and in Italy, remained the main addressee of the narrative construction of the struggle for legitimacy between Caesar and Pompey, with women, freedmen and slaves indirectly involved in the process through their personal ties. For this reason, civil war was capable of tearing asunder the very fabric of society: it affected the relationships and personal stories of those who did not bear arms as well as the leaders and the soldiers.

This constructionist process seems to better suit Caesar's strategy in the making than Raauflaub's idea of a Grand Coalition.[113] Even if one moves beyond Raaflaub's untechnical conceptualization of 'coalition', the resulting taxonomy appears unlikely. For instance, contemporary sociological theory divides coalition-building between office-seeking and policy-seeking: neither model seems to effectively describe Caesar's strategy.[114] It would not be enough to adopt a broader definition, like the one offered by Ted Caplow, who says that 'in modern social science, the meaning [of coalition] has broadened to include any combination of two or more social actors formed for mutual advantage in contention with other actors in the same social system'. In fact, on this view, one must take the process of becoming subject – and thus, the identity of the groups – for granted. Only stable identities might permit a process of coalition-building, whereas the construction of 'The People' highlights the dynamic and relational constitution of identities. Responding to the *senatus consultum ultimum* and the *hostis* declaration that made Caesar and his soldiers 'public enemies' on 7 January 49, Caesar's strategy seems to have been devised to compose and rearticulate individual identities into a unifying group, aiming for a reconciliation of the whole civic community through the exclusion of a few selected 'enemies'. Indeed, the *pauci* are depicted as nothing other than treasonous internal enemies who are to be cast out of the community so that the true and legitimate *populus Romanus* can reclaim its pristine unity. Thanks to the theoretical shift, the contingent discursive construction on which Caesar's communicative strategy relied stands out as the crucial step for his political objectives. Rather than forging a temporary alliance between pre-existing groups in society, Caesar's communication constructed a new universal entity, 'The People'.

Notes

* This chapter is based on a paper delivered in Rome in July 2019: I wish to thank Richard Westall and Hannah Cornwell for their kind invitation and all the participants in the workshop for their comments during the day. The contribution stems from my PhD project DISCORDIA, *Hegemony, and Popular Subjectivities* (2016–21): my deepest gratitude to the Northern Bridge DTP, the School of History, Classics and Archaeology at Newcastle University, and the Society for the Promotion of Roman Studies for their generous support to my research. Many thanks to Amy Russell, Federico Santangelo, and Jakob Wisse, my supervisors in Newcastle, who gave me precious feedback on an earlier draft of this chapter, and to Richard and Hannah and the reviewer for their invaluable observations; any remaining inaccuracy is my own.

1. Caes. *BCiv.* 11.84.2 (tr. Damon 2016).
2. As is typical of epic poetry, the first line of the proem indicates the poem's subject matter: *Fraternas acies alternaque regna profanes/decertata odiis sontesque evolvere Thebas/Pierius menti calor incidit* (tr. Shackleton Bailey 2003: 'Pierian fire falls upon my soul: to unfold fraternal warfare, and alternate reigns fought for in unnatural hate, and guilty Thebes'); thorough analyses of the themes of civil war in Statius' *Thebaid* can be found, e.g., in Franchet-d'Espèrey 1999. On the proem, see now Briguglio 2017 *ad loc.*

3. Occurrences are calculated through Brepols' *Library of Latin Texts* database. For comparison, Sallust uses it ten times in *Bellum Iugurthinum* and twice in *De Catilinae Coniuratione*, both in relation to the battle of Pistoia (*Cat.* 59.3 and 60.4).
4. App. *BCiv.* 1.55; App. *BCiv.* 1.58.259.
5. App. *BCiv.* 1.58.259.
6. For matters of political communication in the context of 88, see Zucchetti 2022, with the bibliography there cited.
7. See, for instance, the section about 'popular support' or 'civilian collaboration' (Kalyvas 2006: 91–104). However, Lange 2014 attempts to use Kalyvas productively in the study of Roman civil wars, arguing that the locus of violence was not only the battlefield but also civil society, including civil unrest and 'conspiracies' in the count: I remain sceptical of reading the whole late Republican period as one long civil war and would rather stress the ordinary, almost every-day importance of riots and civil unrest as the chief communicative channel of the subalterns in the production of discourse, as I argued in my doctoral thesis; see Zucchetti 2021a.
8. In the well-known debate about Roman demography, the two prevailing sides are labelled *high count* and *low count;* among the latter, see De Ligt 2012, in continuity with Brunt 1971, and also, substantially, with the position held by Beloch 1886. The high-count interpretation, with detailed reference to the population of Republican Rome, can be found in Lo Cascio 1997 and, regarding military mobilization rates, in Lo Cascio 2001. For an overview of the debate, see Scheidel 2008. Brunt's figures for military mobilization in 49–42 are in Brunt 1971: 473–5 and those for the size of post-Marian legions at pp. 687–93. If applied to a high-count extreme scenario, we get an estimate of 5.6 per cent. For precapitalist economies, we tend to assume that the male adults represented roughly a third of the population: this would mean that a percentage comprised between 16.8 per cent and 23.1 per cent of male citizens directly took part in the conflict. It is hard to say anything more specific: it should, however, be considered that mostly cohorts of *iuniores* will have taken arms with the two generals. It is hard to formulate an estimate of how many disabled citizens were exempt from enrolment.
9. Plut. *Caes.* 28.5. Translation that of Pelling 2011 who *ad loc.* comments that 'the idea rests on a traditional insight of political theory, that one-man power often springs from civic disorder' and signals the intertext with Plut. *Cat. Min.* 45.7. The trope of the 'ship of the state' in the storm of civil discord is extremely well-known: the most obvious models are to be found in Alc. F 6a and 326 and Plato, *Rep.* 6.488a-489d. Other obvious parallels in Verg. *Aen.* 50-156 and, with variations, Luc. 5.476-721. On this trope in Latin literature, see Fantham 1972: 125–36.
10. Plut. *Caes.* 28.4.
11. *Pace* Westall in this volume. See Pelling 2011 *ad* 28.4.
12. On these electoral contests of the late 50s, see Gruen 1969 and 1974: 331–2 and 343–7; Evans 1991: 123; Yakobson 1999: 169–79; Steel 2012: 88–90 and 2013: 183–8; and Ramsey 2016.
13. For two different accounts of the events between 51 and December 50, see, e.g., Gruen 1974: 470–90; and Morstein-Marx 2021: 258–320.
14. See Steel 2013: 185–94 on the political issues of 51–50.
15. App. *BCiv.* 2.27.106 (tr. McGing 2020).
16. Plut. *Caes.*30.1-2. The idea of 'appearing' just, presupposes appreciation by the public; see Pelling 2011 commentary *ad loc.*

17. Plut. *Caes.* 30.2; *Pomp.* 58.4-5; App. *BCiv.* 2.106 and 2.27. On the representation as a victorious athlete, see Pelling 2011 *ad* 30.2. On the political interpretation, see now Morstein-Marx 2021: 292–6.

18. Westall 2017 is a positive attempt at addressing all these problems in a fully integrated historical and philological discussion.

19. The date of composition and publication of the *BCiv.* has always been a topic of fervent discussion among scholars; see Klotz 1911; Kalinka 1912; La Penna 1952: 231; Collins 1959: 130; Wiseman 1998b and 2015: 101–2 and 141 (on the *Commentarii* more generally), Rossi 2000: 254 and n.71; Batstone and Damon 2006: 31–2; Raaflaub 2009: 180–2; 2017a; and 2017b; Grillo 2012: 178–80; Peer 2015: 167–82; Raaflaub 2017a: lii–lv; Raaflaub 2017b: 208–9; Westall 2017: 273–80; Osgood 2019: 151–7; and Spielberg 2023: 67–9.

20. Westall 2017: 274–5.

21. Osgood 2019: 152.

22. On the role of writing in consensus-building during civil wars, see Lange 2021, who notes the connection between Caesar's laurelled letters – the military dispatches read publicly to the Senate and, often, to the people *in contione* – and autobiographic writing.

23. Caes. *BCiv.* 1.14.4, 1.22.5, 1.57.3, 2.21.1, 3.91.2, but see *infra*. On Caesar's abandonment of LIBERTAS, see Raaflaub 2003: 56–67 and Raaflaub 2017c: 252 and fn JJ13.b. For the use of small capitals for divine qualities 'to reflect the "indeterminacy" integral to them', see Clark 2007: 20.

24. See Raaflaub 1974; 2003; 2007; 2010a and 2010b; Morstein-Marx 2009; and Osgood 2019. The detail of the analysis proposed in Morstein-Marx 2021, which appeared after this chapter had been written, made it difficult for me to engage here in depth with this important contribution. On the composition of the *Civil War*, see n.18 above.

25. Cf. Luc.7.470-473; Flor. 2.46; Plut. *Caes.* 44 and Pomp. 71; App. *BCiv.* 2.82; see Perrin 1884; Kahn 1973; Lounsbury 1975: 210–11, discussing the possible filiation of Plutarch's and Appian's accounts from that of Pollio; Schuller 1995: 190–2; Brown 1999, with bibliography at n.36 p. 349 and rhetorical analysis at 350–1; Krebs 2018: 37–8; and Spielberg 2023: 88–94. On the function of centurions' speeches in Caesar's writings, see Spielberg 2023, arguing that these independent voices guided the readers' interpretation of important episodes, on which Caesar did not find appropriate comment in his own voice.

26. Caes. *BCiv.* 3.91.2-3 (tr. Damon 2016).

27. *cuius orationem Caesar interpellat: se non malefici causa ex provincia egressum sed uti se a contumeliis inimicorum defenderet, ut tribunos plebis in ea re ex civitate expulsos in suam dignitatem restitueret, ut se et populum Romanum factione paucorum oppressum in libertatem vindicaret* (tr. Damon 2006: 'Caesar interrupted him mid-speech. "I did not leave my province with harmful intent but to defend myself from the insults of my enemies, to restore the tribunes – who have been expelled from Rome in connection with this business – to their proper dignity, and to liberate myself and the Roman people from oppression by a small faction."'). Spielberg 2023: 88–94 notes the differences between the speech pronounced by Caesar's Crastinus and that of Appian and Plutarch's Crassinius, in which there is no mention of *dignitas* or LIBERTAS, and concludes that Caesar composed his account of Pharsalus when statements about the restoration of LIBERTAS after Caesar's victory would not have sound tragically ironic.

28. This text has been discussed often in recent scholarship; see Westall 2017: 49–57, with bibliography there cited.

29. The attribute *evocatus* at the beginning of the paragraph might be a further allusion to the sacral context. Fucecchi 2011: 250 n.80 thinks that the enthusiasm of the *devotus*, with which

Crastinus is depicted in Lucan as well, was a feature of Pollio's account of the scene. The research on *devotio* has largely developed in the last few years, see Ferri 2017; and *Acta Antiqua* 60 (3-4), including contributions by Blomart 2021 and Mastrocinque 2021. Also, see OCD s.v. 'devotio'; Versnel 1976; Sacco 2004; and Rosenblitt 2011 (with a different focus).

30. Laclau and Mouffe 2001 and Laclau 2005, esp. 65–171.
31. See Raaflaub 2010a.
32. The synthesis is in Gill 2003: 58.
33. Gerratana 1975: 1375–95, and Hoare and Nowell-Smith 1971: 323–43.
34. Liguori 2006: 66 (= Liguori 2015: 84).
35. Liguori 2006, *ibid*.
36. Gramsci, Q12§1 (Gerratana 1975: 1519, and Hoare and Nowell-Smith 1971: 12); I discussed Gramsci's hegemony in relation to Classics and Ancient History in Zucchetti 2021b and 2021c.
37. Gramsci talks about 'centralismo democratico' as a means of considering the contribution of the ruled (*governati*) to the hegemonic setup; see e.g. Q9 §68, where he defines democratic centralism as 'una continua adeguazione dell'organizzazione al movimento storico reale ed è organico appunto perché tiene conto del movimento, che è il modo organico di manifestarsi della realtà storica'.
38. Laclau and Mouffe 2001: 120–31.
39. Gramsci was much less 'essentialist' than Laclau and Mouffe wanted to concede. See Laclau/Mouffe 2001: 91–3, on the category of 'discourse' in Foucault.
40. Laclau and Mouffe 2001: 91; see also 120–31.
41. Laclau and Mouffe 2001: 91.
42. Laclau and Mouffe 2001: 94.
43. Laclau and Mouffe 2001: 99 and Laclau 2005: 114–15.
44. Laclau and Mouffe 2001: 112–13.
45. Laclau and Mouffe 2001: 112–14 and Laclau 2005: 103–5.
46. Chandlar and Munday 2011: 124.
47. Chandlar and Munday 2011: 125.
48. On LIBERTAS, see Arena 2012, with reference to the discourses developed in *optimatis* and *popularis* milieu. I discussed the consequences of the two different conceptions of LIBERTAS showcased in Cicero's and Catiline's discourses in Zucchetti 2021a: 181–93.
49. Syme 1939: 156; n.1 refers to Sall. *BC*. 38.3: *bonum publicum simulantes pro sua quisque potentia certabant* (tr. Woodman 2007: 'each of them, despite his pretence of the common good, was competing for his own powerfulness').
50. Santangelo 2020: 60.
51. Morstein-Marx 2004, esp. 230–40; see also Santangelo 2020: 59.
52. Mouffe 1977; cf. e.g. Gramsci, Q13§17 (Gerratana 1975: 1578–89, and Hoare and Nowell-Smith 1971: 177–85).
53. Laclau and Mouffe 2001: 101–8.
54. Althusser 1965: 87–108 (originally published in 1962).
55. Althusser 1965: 107–8 (Eng. tr. Althusser 1969: 115–16). Emphasis in the original.
56. Cf. Q13§17 (Gerratana 1975: 1578–89, and Hoare and Nowell-Smith 1971: 177–85).

57. Laclau and Mouffe 2001: 108–13 and Laclau 2005: 84–5.
58. Laclau and Mouffe 2001: 113–20.
59. Laclau and Mouffe 2001: 116–17 (citing the example of the politics of Disraeli in nineteenth-century Britain).
60. Laclau 2005: 85–6 and 129–30.
61. Laclau 2005: 72–7.
62. Laclau and Mouffe 2001: 115–16 and Laclau 2005: 120–2.
63. Laclau 2005: 100.
64. Laclau 2005: 100.
65. The definition is the title of Raaflaub 2010a; see also Raaflaub 2010b: 153–4.
66. There is no hint that Raaflaub 2010a considered the technical definitions of 'coalition'; see e.g. Caplow 1992 and Lees 2001 for the use of the concept in political studies.
67. See Cic. *Att*. 8.3.5: *multitudo et infimus quisque propensus in alteram partem, multi mutationis rerum cupidi* (tr. Shackleton Bailey 1999, revised: 'whereas the populace and the lower orders sympathized with the other side and many were eager for change').
68. See Raaflaub 2010a: 165–7 and 2010b: 148. More sources for the lower plebs in Raaflaub 1974: 65 n. 260 and Morstein-Marx 2009: 132 n.73; criticism in Riggsby 2006: 12–14 and Jehne 2010: 316 n.19.
69. Caes. *BCiv*. 1.3–4. See Raaflaub 2018: 25–6; on speeches in the *Commentarii*, see Grillo 2018.
70. App. *BCiv*. 2.30; see Raaflaub 2010a: 166.
71. Plut. *Caes*. 30.3 (with Pelling 2011 *ad loc.*); see Raaflaub 2010b: 148 and Krebs 2018: 32–3.
72. Osgood 2019: 138 already observed how important persuasive strategies were in the early stages of a civil war since 'in civil war it is potentially quite easy to lose your supporters, even then soldiers fighting by your side, to your opponents'. Defections, like T. Labienus' spectacular one in 49, seem, however, to have been the exception rather than the rule; a firm distinction between regular soldiers and leaders is typical of Caesar's *BCiv.*, see Osgood 2019: 142–3.
73. Cic. *Att*. 7.3.5 (9 December 50): *causam solum illa causa non habet, ceteris rebus abundat*.
74. Wiseman 1998b: 3.
75. *Populus Romanus*: 1.7.5; 1.9.2; 1.9.5; 1.22.5; 1.35.3; 3.11.4; 3.107.2; 3.108.5; 3.110.2. *Populus*: 1.6.6, 1.7.5, 1.7.6, 1.9.2, 1.32.3, 2.21.3, 3.1.4, 3.1.5 (twice), 3.3.1, 3.10.8. 3.10.10. Among these occurrences, only 2.21.3 and 3.3.1 refer to other people, while the majority of them either implicitly refer to the *populus Romanus* or to popular assemblies; in 1.35.3 *Romanus* is an integration already in the *editio princeps*; 3.12.2 used to read *omnis Italia populus Romanus iudicavisset*, but Damon 2015 prints *omnis Italia praeiudicavisset* and the apparatus reads 'praeiudicavisset Paul test Meusel (u. 2.32.3)' since the manuscripts (μST) have *p.R. iudicavisset per compendia*; therefore, I omitted the latter from the calculations.
76. *Res publica* in *BCiv*: 1.1.1, 1.1.2, 1.1.4, 1.2.6, 1.4.3, 1.5.3, 17.2, 1.7.7, 1.8.2, 1.8.3 (three times), 1.9.3, 1.9.5 (twice), 1.13.1, 1.24.5, 1.32.7 (twice), 2.18.3, 2.18.5, 3.10.6, 3.10.9, 3.21.2, 3.53.5, 3.90.2.
77. On Caesar's Republican characterization in the *BCiv*. see, for instance, Rossi 2000: 241–2 and n.16 with bibliography there cited.
78. A different interpretation in Krebs 2018: 38–41, who claims that 'the frequencies of *populus* and *senatus* therein [scil. in the *BCiv.*] are insignificant because of its content'.
79. See, e.g. Caes. *BCiv*. 1.7 for *inimici*; for the use of *inimicus/hostis*, see Macfarlane 1996; Raaflaub 1974: 192–200 and 2009: 182; Yates 2010: 173 n.21; Grillo 2012: 82 n.14 and

142–3 n.29; Gaertner and Hausburg 2013: 185–8 and cf. Cornwell in this volume. For the strategic use of *hostis* to cast away the internal enemy and reunify the community after serious unrest, see Zucchetti 2022 and *infra*. On the language of *hostis* in the 40s and 30s BCE, see Cornwell 2014.

80. On the strategy and communication of the anti-Caesarians, see Jehne 2017.
81. Rossi 2000: 247; see also Collins 1972: 949–63; Grillo 2012: 106–30 and 142–3; Peer 2015: 19–40; and Johnston 2018: 91–2.
82. Caes. *BCiv*. 1.74-5 (tr. Damon 2016, revised). On the Ilerda episode, see Batstone and Damon 2006: 75–84; Raaflaub 2010a: 159–62; Grillo 2012: 80–5; Westall 2017: 271/80; Osgood 2019: 151–7 and Cornwell in this volume.
83. See Grillo 2012: 78–85, with rich bibliography; Osgood 2019: 140–7; Morstein-Marx 2021: 411–87; also, cf. Cornwell in this volume.
84. Cf. the response of the *legati* from Marseille at Caes. *BCiv*. 1.35.3: *cuius orationem legati domum referunt atque ex auctoritate haec Caesari renuntiant: intellegere se divisum esse populum <Romanum> in partes duas;* [...] (tr. Damon 2006: 'The delegation took his words home and gave him this official response: "We understand that the Roman people is split in two"'). See Livy 2.24.1, 2.44.9, and 4.4.9 (*duas civitates ex una facta*), and, after the fall of Veii, two cities (5.24.8-9).
85. Raaflaub 2010b: 149–50.
86. See Cornwell's contribution to this volume.
87. Cf. Caes. *BCiv*. 1.13. The formulation *factio paucorum* is hapax at *BCiv*. 1.22, but the characterization of Caesar's enemies as *pauci* is often employed in the *Civil War* and takes a political meaning, indicating the personal interests of 'the few' against the collective interests of 'the many'.
88. App. *BCiv*. 2.31. See Raaflaub 1974, esp. 113–52, 2003: 59–61, and 2010b: 150–1; and Westall 2017: 15.
89. See Zucchetti 2022.
90. Cf. Lentulus' claim that he was going to be a second Sulla at *BCiv*. 1.4.2 and, in reference to the political climate in which the events took place, Cic. *Att*. 9.10.2; see Grillo 2012: 151–7 and Osgood 2019: 138–9 and 142.
91. Caes. *BCiv*. 1.5; on the so-called *senatus consultum ultimum*, Buongiorno 2020 includes a set of useful contributions on many aspects of the debate on the topic: see most notably Scevola 2020 and Schettino 2020 with bibliography there cited. On the *hostis* declaration against Caesar, see Allély 2012: 79–91.
92. For studies in this direction but with different theoretical backgrounds see Krebs 2018 and López Barja de Quiroga 2019.
93. Thuc. 3.69-3.85; for the impact of this conception on the Roman world, see, e.g., Sall. *Cat*. 52, Cato's speech, and Batstone 2010, who interprets Cato and Catiline as 'fighting to death about what to call *libertas* and *patria*' (p. 235).
94. See e. g. Caes. *BCiv*. 1.22.5 and 3.91; see Raaflaub 1974; Morstein-Marx 2009 and 2021: 317–20; Grillo 2012: 135–6; and Krebs 2018: 37–41.
95. Caes. *BCiv*. 1.12.2-3.
96. On this text, see Morstein-Marx 2021: 456–65. On Caesar's letters, see Morello 2018.
97. Cic. *Att*. 9.7C (tr. Shackleton Bailey 1999). On this passage, and the translation of *nova ratio vincendi*, see Cornwell in this volume.

98. See Cornwell's contribution to this volume and esp. pp. 15–18.
99. Tr. Shackleton Bailey 1999.
100. Nevertheless, the political use of *voluntas* in rhetoric is not rare: cf. e.g. Cic. *Mur* 1.1, *Sest.* 122, and *Phil.* 5.40 and 7.4. On *voluntas* in the context of civil wars, see Grillo 2012: 131–1; Santangelo 2016: 134 and n.26.
101. See Hellegouarc'h 1963: 183 and Brunt 1965: 4 n.4.
102. Q. Cic. *Comment. Pet.* 4, 16 (twice), 18, 21, 23, 33, 35, 40, 42, 44, 50, 51 (twice), 54. See Tatum 2018: 220
103. This letter and the concept of *crudelitas* are examined in Cornwell's contribution to this volume.
104. On leniency, see Grillo 2012: 78–103; Morstein-Marx 2021: 411–87.
105. Cf. Caes. *BCiv.* 1.22.5; see Raaflaub 2003, 2007 and 2009: 190; and Peer 2015: 53–4.
106. See Morstein-Marx 2009 and Morstein-Marx 2021: 319–20; Hölkeskamp 2013: 14–16. It is not easy to indicate Hölkeskamp's most relevant contributions to the idea of a 'meritocratic' code of behaviour in the Roman Republic: his most recent collection of essays (Hölkeskamp 2020) is an invaluable starting point. A further effective summary in Hölkeskamp 2022 focuses on the 'political culture' paradigm.
107. Crawford 1974 (*RRC*), nos. 449/4 (cf. *RRC* 369, with Crawford's commentary, pp. 387–8, for a similar claim made by Sulla between 82 and 80) and 473/1; pl. LUI, LVI. The dating of *RRC* 449/4 might suggest that the speeches in the *Civil War* also reflect the rhetoric Caesar was using in 48 BCE. On the two coins, see Raaflaub 2003: 56–7, with n.74; Morstein-Marx 2004: 52 and 2021: 522. Crawford 1974: 482–3 dates RRC 473/1, a coinage by a certain Palikanus (presumably the son of M. Lollius Palicanus), to 45 BCE and Weinstock 1971: 131 and 141–3 connect it with the rhetoric of Caesar as liberator after Munda.
108. Caes. *BCiv.* 1.14.4; 1.22.5; 1.57.3; 2.21.1; 3.91.2.
109. Caes. *BCiv.* 1.4.4; 1.7.7; 1.8.3; 1.9.2; 1.22.5; 1.32.4; 3.83.1; 3.91.2.
110. Caes. *BCiv.* 1.4.3, 1.7.7, 1.8.3, 1.9.3, 1.32.7, 3.90.2.
111. Caes. *BCiv.* 1.9.3: *tamen hanc iacturam honoris sui rei publicae causa aequo animo tulisse.*
112. Caes. *BCiv.* 1.12.1-3: *Interea certior factus Iguvium Thermum praetorem cohortibus V tenere, oppidum munire, omniumque* **esse Iguvinorum optimam erga se voluntatem**, *Curionem cum tribus cohortibus quas Pisauri et Arimini habebat mittit. Cuius adventu* **cognito diffisus municipi voluntati** *Thermus cohortes ex urbe reducit et profugit. Milites in itinere ab eo discedunt ac domum revertuntur. Curio* **summa omnium voluntate** *Iguvium recipit. Quibus rebus cognitis* **confisus municipiorum voluntatibus** *Caesar cohortes legionis tertiae decimae ex praesidiis deducit Auximumque proficiscitur* (tr. Damon 2006: 'Meanwhile, having been informed that at Iguvium — a town the praetor Thermus was holding with five cohorts, and fortifying — **the attitude of all the inhabitants toward him was strongly positive**, Caesar sent Curio with the three cohorts he had at Pisaurum and Ariminum. At news of his approach Thermus, **distrusting the community's attitude**, withdrew his cohorts from the city and fled; his soldiers abandoned him on the march and returned home. Curio recovered Iguvium **with great and universal goodwill**. Learning of this, **and confident of goodwill in the towns**, Caesar withdrew the cohorts of the thirteenth legion from garrison duty and set out for Auximum, a town that Attius held with cohorts he had brought in').
113. See again Raaflaub 2010a and 2010b: 153, where it is suggested that the inspiration for this strategy came to Caesar 'from C. Gracchus' and Livius Drusus' failed attempts at basing large-scale and complex reform on broad coalitions.'
114. See Lees 2001.

CHAPTER 3
THE MEANING OF ⊥II ON CAESAR'S CIVIL WAR COINAGE (*RRC* 452)
Olga Liubimova

A coin issue consisting of *aurei*, *denarii* and *quinarii* was minted by Caesar during his civil war with Pompey (*RRC* 452). A goddess is depicted on the obverse (probably Venus on *aurei* and *denarii* and Vesta on *quinarii*)[1] and a trophy with the legend CAESAR on the reverse (the trophy is Gallic on the *aurei* and *denarii* and Spanish[2] on the *quinarii*; a captive Gaul is also depicted on two of the three *denarii* types). On the obverse, there are also three letters ⊥II, which at first glance resemble a control-mark,[3] but remain unchanged on all dies of all the denominations of this issue. As a result, we cannot consider them to be a control-mark.

The majority of scholars agree that these letters signify the age of Caesar – LII equating to fifty-two years – an interpretation suggested for the first time by Borghesi and adopted by various others.[4] The number may indicate that Caesar minted the coins at fifty-two years of age or that he was in his fifty-second year of life.[5] According to this view, Caesar wanted to emphasize that his second consulship in 48 conformed to the *lex annalis*, but there are other interpretations of the letters ⊥II on *RRC* 452. Cavedoni has suggested that the number LII refers to the number of Caesar's victories.[6] Some scholars have argued that it may refer to the number of years that have elapsed since Marius' victory

Figure 3.1 *Aureus* of C. Julius Caesar, *RRC* 452/1; Ex Numismatica Ars Classica NAC AG, Auction 46, Lot 416.

Figure 3.2 *Denarius* of C. Julius Caesar, *RRC* 452/2; Barber Institute of Fine Art Coin Collection, R0696.

Figure 3.3 *Denarius* of C. Julius Caesar, *RRC* 452/3; Ex Numismatica Arts Classica NAC AG, Auction 63, Lot 356.

over the Teutons, or the establishment of the Transalpine province and the final conquest of Gaul.[7] The letters ⊥II have also been read as I(*mperator*) IT(*erum*) or simply IIT, the perfect tense form of the verb *eo*.[8] The clarification of their meaning might shed light on some nuances of Caesar's self-presentation during the civil war. Furthermore, if the letters indeed signify Caesar's age, they might be used as evidence in the long-standing debate on his date of birth.

It is common knowledge that the sources for the latter question contradict each other as well as other evidence for Caesar's career. His birthday fell on 13 July, but as of 42 BCE it was publicly celebrated on 12 July to avoid any clash with the festival of the *ludi Apollinares*.⁹ Suetonius and Appian tell us that on 15 March 44, Caesar – in his fifty-sixth year of age (that is to say, before his fifty-sixth birthday but after his fifty-fifth) – was assassinated, which means that he was born in 100.¹⁰ Their testimony is confirmed by Velleius Paterculus (2.41.2), who states that Caesar was only about eighteen years of age (*habuissetque fere duodeviginti annos*) at the time Sulla took control of Rome in 82. But the evidence of Plutarch – according to which Caesar was fully fifty-six years old at the time of his death – suggests 101 as the year of his birth.¹¹ Eutropius, however, tells us that Caesar was fifty-six (*natus annos sex et quinquaginta*; 6.24) on the day of the battle of Munda (17 March 45), which would mean that he was born in 102,¹² and this latter date is also supported by Caesar's career. Cicero (*Phil.* 5.48) expressly says that the consular age is the forty-third year of life.¹³ Since Caesar was consul in 59, he cannot have been born any later than 102.

Thus, both the meaning of the letters on these coins and the year of Caesar's birth are controversial problems. However, Crawford, in his standard work on the chronology of Roman coinage, confidently interprets the symbol in question as the age of Caesar and claims that the dictator was born in 100, thereby stating that the coinage should be dated between 13 July 48 and 12 July 47.¹⁴ Buttenberg follows him, whereas Woytek slightly modifies Crawford's dating but bases his argumentation on the same questionable premises.¹⁵ Campana is unaware of the full range of problems concerning Caesar's birth, and the evidence he cites in favour of 100 (and, consequently, in favour of 48 for the ⊥II issue) is inconclusive.¹⁶ The same may be said about the argumentation of Amisano, who prefers 101 as Caesar's year of birth and, consequently, 49 as the date of the issue ⊥II.¹⁷ Amela Valverde notes the existence of other hypotheses regarding the year of Caesar's birth and the date of the issue (although he does not mention other interpretations of ⊥II) but also follows Crawford's logic.¹⁸ This is the case for the overwhelming majority of scholars, as is evident from the bibliography cited by Amela Valverde.¹⁹ Therefore, first of all, we ought to date the coinage in question regardless of Caesar's birth year and the mysterious symbol's meaning.

In Crawford's table indicating the composition of representative hoards (that is the large hoards which may be expected to contain all the major contemporary issues)²⁰ between 49 and 46, the issue ⊥II appears for the first time in the Dračevica (Croatia) and Surbo (Italy) hoards buried no earlier than 46; these hoards are closed by the issues *RRC* 463-466 (Rome, 46 BCE).²¹ Notably, the issue ⊥II is absent from large Italian hoards which immediately precede them: Cadriano (49 BCE, 3000 Roman coins), San Cesario (49 BCE, 730 Roman coins), Carbonara (48 BCE, 426 Roman coins) and San Giuliano Vecchio (48 BCE, 1758 Roman coins).

The most numerous coins of this issue are the *denarii RRC* 452/2: Sydenham characterizes them as 'very common';²² Crawford estimates the number of obverse dies at 63 and of reverse dies at 70.²³ Let us examine the appearance of contemporary issues of similar importance in the above-named hoards.

If the issue ⊥II was minted in 49, its absence from the Cadriano and San Cesario hoards may be explained by the assumption that the coins were put into circulation after

Table 3.1 Contemporary coin issues (49–47 BCE)

RRC number	Monetalis/ magistrate	Date (RRC)	Dies number (RRC)	Degree of rarity (CRR)*	Mint (RRC)	Cadriano, Italy, 49 BCE, 3,000 coins	San Cesario, Italy, 49 BCE, 730 coins	Carbonara, Italy, 48 BCE, 426 coins	San Giuliano Vecchio, Italy, 48 BCE, 1,758 coins	Dračevica, Croatia, 46 BCE, 106 coins	Surbo, Italy, 46 BCE, 140 coins
440	Sicinius	49	129/143	3	Rome				+		+
442	Acilius	49	651/723	2	Rome		+		+	+	+
443	Caesar (with elephant)	49	750/833	1	Moving with Caesar	+	+		+	+	+
444	Sicinius, Coponius	49	105/117	3	Moving with Pompey				+	+	
448/1	Saserna	48	99/110	2	Rome			+		+	+
448/2	Saserna	48	57/63	3	Rome			+	+	+	
448/3	Saserna	48	126/140	3	Rome			+	+	+	
449/1	Pansa	48	279/310	2	Rome			+			
449/2	Pansa	48	54/60	1	Rome				+		
449/4	Pansa	48	33/37	2	Rome						
450/1	Albinus	48	69/77	2	Rome				+	+	

450/2	Albinus	48	171/190	2	Rome	+	+
450/3	Albinus	48	51/57	3	Rome	+	
452/2	**Caesar ⊥II**	**48**	**63/70**	**2**	**Moving with Caesar**	**+**	**+**
453	Plautius Plancus	47	195/217	3	Rome	+	
454/1	Nerva	47	66/73	3	Rome	+	
458	Caesar (with Aeneas)	47	390/433	1	Moving with Caesar	+	+
459	Metellus Scipio	47	93/103	3	Africa		

* Degrees of rarity according to *CRR*: 1 – 'extremely common', 2 – 'very common', 3 – 'common'. The composition of the hoards is indicated according to Schiassi 1820 (Cadriano), Cavedoni 1829 (San Cesario), Quagliati 1904 (Carbonara), Crawford 1974: 658–61 (San Giuliano Vecchio), Lockyear 2013: DRA (Dračevica), and Lockyear 2013: SUR (Surbo).

the deposition of these hoards (e.g. in the second half of the year) and/or were minted in Spain where Caesar waged a campaign, so they did not reach Italy until later. Nevertheless, their absence from the Carbonara and San Giuliano Vecchio hoards seems very odd: these hoards contain all the large issues of 49. Even if the issue ⊥II had been minted in Spain, Caesar's soldiers (who received these coins) would have brought them into Italy late in 49. On the contrary, if the issue ⊥II was minted in 48, its absence from the hoards is quite natural in the case of the Cadriano and San Cesario hoards and more comprehensible in that of the Carbonara and San Giuliano Vecchio hoards: these coins could have been issued after the deposition of the hoards and/or not in Italy but in Illyria, Epirus or Thessaly by the mint moving with Caesar. In any case, the Carbonara and San Giuliano Vecchio hoards do not contain other large issues of 48, which were minted in Rome (*RRC* 449/4, *RRC* 450/2-3). The hoard evidence therefore allows us to date the issue ⊥II to 48, 47 or 46.

Besides *denarii*, the issue ⊥II includes *aurei* and *quinarii*. In the late Republic, *aurei* were struck episodically, and their weight steadily diminished. According to Campana, the average weight of Sulla's *aurei* minted in 84–81 (*RRC* 359/1, 367/2, 367/4, 375/1, 381/1) is 10.8 grams or 1/11 of a pound;[24] the average weight of Pompey's *aurei* minted *c*. 71[25] (*RRC* 402/1) is 8.94 grams or 1/12 of a pound;[26] the weight of Metellus Scipio's unique *aureus* minted in 47 or 46 in Africa (*RRC* 460/1) is 8.05 grams or 1/13 of a pound.[27] Turning to Caesar's coinage, besides the *aurei* with ⊥II we find a small series of *aurei* with the legend CAES DICT ITER (*RRC* 456/1), minted in 47; their average weight is 8.02 grams, also equivalent to 1/13 of a pound.[28] From 46 onwards, Caesar began to regularly commission for large quantities of *aurei* to be struck: *RRC* 466/1 (46 BCE), 475/1 (45 BCE), 481/1 (44 BCE); their average weight also ranges from 8.2 to 8.3 grams, that is 1/13 of a pound.[29] But the average weight of Caesar's *aurei* with ⊥II is considerably higher: it is 8.54 grams, or 1/14 of a pound.[30] So, this issue should be dated between the heavier *aurei* of Pompey and the lighter *aurei* of 47–46, and its introduction into the Roman economy should predate not only mass coinage of *aurei* which started in 46, but also the small issue *RRC* 456/1 struck in 47.[31]

Botrè has analysed the chemical composition of the *aurei* with ⊥II and has concluded that they are characterized by an exceptionally high (*c*. 100 per cent) gold content in comparison with previous and subsequent Roman gold coinage. The scholar indicates that such purity is typical for the native gold of some Gallic deposits at that time and concludes that the ⊥II issue was minted by Caesar in Gaul in 50, before he had access to the less pure gold being kept in the Roman treasury.[32] However, in his study Botrè does not take into account the fact that the ⊥II issue included not only *aurei*, but also *denarii* minted in considerable quantities. The absence of those *denarii* from the representative hoards of 49–48 does not permit us to date the issue to 50. Botrè's hypothesis on the Gallic gold as a source for the *aurei* with ⊥II may be correct, but the Gallic bounty still remained in Caesar's disposal after his crossing of the Rubicon and his seizure of the Roman *aerarium*, and it would be quite natural if he decided to start his first gold coinage (and the first one in Rome since 61 at the least) with the purest metal available to him.[33]

As for *quinarii* – small silver coins that were each equivalent to half of a *denarius* in value – they had disappeared in 81 (the last issue was *RRC* 373/1), but Caesar restored

The Meaning of ⊥II on Caesar's Civil War Coinage (RRC 452)

them and issued *quinarii* in every year of his dictatorship (*RRC* 454/3, 455/3 (47 BCE), *RRC* 463/4, 463/4, 463/6, 465/6, 465/7 (46 BCE), 472/3, 473/3, 474/6 (45 BCE), 480/23-25 (44 BCE)). Another small silver coin – the *sestertius* – was a quarter of the *denarius*' value and had fallen out of use even before the *quinarius*: the last coins indisputably identified as *sestertii* before the civil war of Caesar and Pompey were minted in 90 (*RRC* 340/3).[34] Caesar restored the *sestertii* too: from 48 onwards they were minted every year (*RRC* 449/5 (48 BCE), 454/4-5, 455/4-6 (47 BCE), 463/5-6, 464/7-8, 465/8 (46 BCE), 472/4, 473/4, 7-8 (45 BCE), 480/26-28 (44 BCE)). How do the *quinarii RRC* 452/3 with ⊥II fit into this picture? If they were minted in 49, it would mean that in that year Caesar restored the *quinarius*, but in 48 he abandoned it for some reason and began to mint *sestertii*, and it was only from 47 onwards that both small silver denominations entered circulation together. It is far more natural to consider the *quinarii* with ⊥II as a missing element of the coinage of 48. In this case, the renewal of both small silver denominations would fall in the same year.[35]

The evidence of hoards, metrology and denomination analysis shows that the issue *RRC* 452 was minted in 48. This conclusion is drawn regardless of the meaning of the mysterious symbol on the obverse. The analysis of types hardly allows us to add detail to this picture.

De Salis points out that the coins with ⊥II strongly resemble both previous and subsequent issues of the monetary magistrates active at the Roman mint and concludes that these coins were also struck in Rome and probably in Caesar's presence; it follows that they would have been issued in April or December of 49 when Caesar visited Rome.[36] However, it is hard to agree with such reasoning. For example, Venus on the *denarii* of A. Allienus, proconsul of Sicily (*RRC* 457, 47 BCE), looks very similar to Venus on the *denarii* of Man. Cordius, *monetalis* in Rome (*RRC* 463/3, 46 BCE), but Allienus clearly struck his coins in his province. The elephant on Metellus Scipio's coins (*RRC* 459/1, 47–46 BCE) looks like the elephant on Caesar's *denarii* (*RRC* 443/1, 49–48 BCE), but these coins were struck not only on different continents, but also in opposite camps of the civil war. If the coins with ⊥II were issued by the Roman mint, then why was only Caesar's name struck on them, and not those of the *IIIviri monetales*, as on contemporary coins *RRC* 448-451? It seems that the modern numismatists have better reasons for ascribing this issue to the mint travelling with Caesar,[37] though some part of its staff and equipment might well have come from Rome.

De Salis rightly remarks that all the themes present on the coins with ⊥II occur elsewhere on the coinage of Caesar and his followers in 49–46,[38] but we can hardly assume with certainty that the coins with ⊥II imitated some other series or, on the contrary, were used as their prototypes. For example, Woytek considers that the type with a goddess wearing a diadem and oak-wreath (Venus?) should have appeared for the first time on Caesar's coins with ⊥II, and that only later it should have been adopted by Saserna, moneyer in 48 (*RRC* 448/1).[39] He argues that (1) even in his first imperatorial coin issue (*RRC* 443/1), Caesar had shown great originality in the choice of types; and (2) the oak-wreath on Saserna's coins is not always recognizable, as opposed to that on Caesar's coins. However, some of Saserna's other types are very original: on the obverse of *denarii RRC*

448/2 and *RRC* 448/3 he struck close-up portraits of captive Gauls (man and woman, respectively). As far as I know, the case is unprecedented in Roman Republican coinage.[40] On the contrary, sacrificial tools and the elephant depicted on Caesar's *denarius RRC* 443 all have Republican precedents (*RRC* 406/1 (69 BCE); *RRC* 374/1 (81 BCE), respectively). So, the goddess wearing an oak-wreath might well have been struck for the first time by Saserna, especially since he ought to have been carrying out Caesar's instructions in any case. As for the fact that the oak-wreath is not always recognizable on Saserna's coins, this might well be explained by the engraver's negligence which might have appeared regardless of the originality (or lack thereof) of the coin-type that he was producing. We should abandon attempts to use the coin-type analysis for dating the ⊥II issue more precisely and restrict ourselves to the conclusion that the coins in question were struck in 48. The omission of Caesar's second consulship, moreover, does not exclude their dating to 48, for coins with the simple legend CAESAR and without any indication of his offices or titles were minted even later, when he undoubtedly held the dictatorship and consulship: in 47–46 (*RRC* 458) and 46–45 (*RRC* 468).

Let us pass on to the interpretation of ⊥II. It takes more than just detecting the message Caesar wanted to communicate to his audience. We also need to pose and answer another question: were people able to understand it? This further question is especially important in the case under consideration. A Roman ought to have been able to capture the meaning of ⊥II on the obverse immediately, at a first glance, whether on his own or with the help of some explanation disseminated together with the coins. Otherwise, he would simply have taken ⊥II for a control mark.

Eckel reads the legend as I(mperator) IT(erum).[41] Were the Romans able to decipher it correctly? This is not likely. Until 48, imperatorial acclamations were designated on Roman coins by several letters: IM (*RRC* 367/2-5), IMP (*RRC* 367; 429/2; 437/2-4); IMPE (*RRC* 367/1; 368); IMPER (*RRC* 359/1-2; 374); IMPERAT (*RRC* 365); IMPERATOR (*RRC* 427). Later, Caesar and his subordinates used the abbreviations IM (*RRC* 480/4) and IMP (*RRC* 457, 480/3, 480/5, MP sometimes ligatured). There is only one coin where the word *imperator* is abbreviated simply as I (*RRC* 374/1). The reverse legend consists of the initials of the proconsul responsible for the issue: Q(*uintus*) C(*aecilius*) M(*etellus*) P(*ius*) I(*mperator*). In this case, the meaning of the letter I could be deciphered in one breath, by analogy with other letters (with *Pietas*' head on the obverse as a clue), but in the case of Caesar's issue *RRC* 452, his name is struck on the reverse and ⊥II on the obverse. Such an arrangement of letters makes them more difficult to decipher.

The abbreviation of *iterum* as IT creates even more difficulties. It is unprecedented in Republican coinage: the word *iterum* is either written in full or abbreviated to ITERV (*RRC* 359/1-2). On the coins struck by Caesar and his subordinates, *iterum* is always abbreviated as ITER (*RRC* 456/1, 457/1, 467/1). On parallel Pompeian coins and on coins struck during the civil wars after Caesar's death, *imperator* is almost invariably designated as IMP (except IMPER on *RRC* 480/18-19), and *iterum* as ITER. But the above-mentioned Caesarian coins relate to his second dictatorship (*RRC* 456/1, 467/1) or second consulship (*RRC* 457/1). Did Caesar use the title *imperator iterum* at all, and if he did, was he able to style himself in such a way in 48?

The Meaning of ⊥II on Caesar's Civil War Coinage (RRC 452)

Caesar was proclaimed *imperator* for the first time during his proconsulship in Spain in 61;[42] his Gallic acclamations are not attested, but if we judge by the *supplicationes* which usually followed acclamations, there were three of them: in 57, 55 and 52.[43] So, by the beginning of 48, Caesar already had four acclamations. According to Weinstock, however, Caesar never used the title *imperator* with an ordinal number, and that is why the scholar rejects Eckel's interpretation of ⊥II as I(mperator) IT(erum). The only exception is found in the passages of Flavius Josephus citing Caesar's decrees on the rights of Jews where he is called αὐτοκράτωρ τὸ δεύτερον ('*imperator* for the second time', AJ. 14.10.2(192) and 6(202)), but Weinstock considers this evidence to be Josephus' error as Caesar is called αὐτοκράτωρ καὶ ἀρχιερεὺς δικτάτωρ τὸ δεύτερον ('*imperator* and *pontifex maximus, dictator* for the second time') in the title of one of these decrees.[44] But Zack has recently made a case in favour of the manuscript reading of these passages, as well as αὐτοκράτωρ τὸ τέταρτον ὕπατός τε τὸ πέμπτον δικτάτωρ ἀποδεδειγμένος διὰ βίου ('*imperator* for the fourth time, consul for the fifth time, dictator appointed for life') in the manuscripts of AJ 14.10.7 (211). As a parallel he cites an inscription (*IGR* 4.1715), where Caesar is called αὐτοκράτορος τὸ τρίτον ὑπάτου καὶ ἀρχιερέως μεγίστου. The editors of this inscription usually insert a comma after αὐτοκράτορος and relate τὸ τρίτον to Caesar's consulship,[45] but Zack points out that the numeral was usually placed after the noun and that in this case it should apply to αὐτοκράτορος. According to this reading of the evidence, after the beginning of the civil war Caesar had changed the counting of his imperatorial acclamations, so he styled himself as *imperator I* after his Gallic successes, *imperator II* after the war in Alexandria, *imperator III* after the victory over the king Juba and *imperator IV* after the battle of Munda.[46]

Zack's theory is not free from difficulties. In particular, inscriptions in honour of Pompey indicate that the ordinal number might precede the imperatorial title (*IG* 9.2.1134: τὸ τρίτον αὐτοκράτ[ορα]; *IMT* 324: τὸ τρίτον [αὐτοκράτ]ορα; *IMT* 325: τὸ τρίτον αὐτοκράτορα), so the traditional punctuation of *IGR* 4.1715 can be retained. Furthermore, a question arises as to why, on Zack's theory, Caesar's count of acclamations did not include his victory over Pharnaces, which was honoured with a triumph. It is impossible to examine these questions within the framework of the present paper. However, even if we accept Zack's theory, the title I(*mperator*) IT(*erum*) could have appeared on Caesar's coins only as of March 47 onwards. On the other hand, the heavy *aurei RRC* 452/1 cannot have been issued later than 48. Moreover, it might be added that all the examples of ordinary numbers for Caesar's imperatorial title adduced by Zack are Greek texts where both words are written in full; we know of no Latin examples of this form for Caesar's title. In Roman coinage the only precedent appears on Sulla's coins minted 35 to 36 years earlier (*RRC* 359/1-2), where the word ITERVM is read either in full or with the final 'M' dropped. In Latin inscriptions of Metellus Pius and Pompey, the abbreviation *imp(erator) iter(um)* is used (*ILLRP* 366, 381). So, Caesar's audience could hardly have interpreted the letters on the obverse of *RRC* 452 as I(*mperator*) IT(*erum*).

Now let us consider the theory of Woods, which proposes to interpret the symbol ⊥II as IIT, that is the perfect of the verb *eo* ('to go, walk, move') and to read the obverse and reverse legends as a single sentence CAESAR IIT, which he translates either as a historical perfect 'Caesar advanced' (that is, in Gaul) or as a pure perfect 'Caesar advances' (that is, against Pompey). Woods adduces the famous expression of Caesar *'veni, vidi, vici'* as a parallel and argues that such an issue represented Caesar as a man of action.[47]

A question arises again: was the audience able to understand the message? Woods correctly observes that the legends on Roman coins could begin on one side of the coin and continue on the other side.[48] But I am unable to find a single example of Roman Republican coinage where a finite verb form (rare by itself) and the corresponding subject were placed on opposite sides of the coin. Isolated finite verb forms appear only as a part of common expressions which do not suppose a subject at all: PROVOCO with the scene of *provocatio* (*RRC* 301/1); A(*bsolvo*) C(*ondemno*) on a voting tablet (*RRC* 428/1, 2); L(*ibero*) D(*amno*) on a voting tablet (*RRC* 437/1). In other cases, the whole sentence – regardless of its length – is always placed on the same side of the coin (e.g. *RRC* 420/1, reverse: C(*aius*) (*H*)YPSAE(*us*) CO(*n*)S(*ul*) PRIV(*ernum*) CEPIT; *RRC* 427/2, reverse: MEMMIVS AED(*ilis*) CERIALIA PREIMVS FECIT; *RRC* 485/2, obverse: IIIVIR PRI(*mus*) FL(*avit*)), even at the cost of substantial abbreviations hampering the reading (e.g., *RRC* 419/1, reverse: M(*arcus*) LEPIDUS AN(*norum*) XV PR(*ogressus*) H(*ostem*) O(*ccidit*) C(*ivem*) S(*ervavit*); *RRC* 421/1, reverse: SEX(*tus*) NONI(*us*) PR(*aetor*) L(*udos*) V(*ictoriae*) P(*rimus*) F(*ecit*)).[49] But on the obverse of *RRC* 452, the letters ⊥II are placed to the left of the goddess's head and on the right, there is a free space where the word CAESAR would fit very well. Yet, Caesar's name is placed on the reverse. Therefore, it is rather improbable that ⊥II should be interpreted as the verb IIT.

Nevertheless, let us suppose that the audience was able to read the legend as CAESAR IIT. How could people comprehend its meaning? The main meaning of the verb *eo* is 'to go, walk, move'. In certain contexts, it may mean 'to advance, to attack', for example (to cite Caesar's *commentarii*): *contra hostem* (*BGall.* 7.62.2; *BCiv.* 3.31); *subsidio suis* (*BGall.* 7.62.8), *ea celeritate atque eo impetu* (*BGall.* 5.18.5), *infestis signis ad se* (*BGall.* 6.8.6). In other contexts, *eo* may refer to a retreat (e.g., *BGall.* 1.23.2; 5.31.4). Here the context is missing. If Caesar wanted to strike a legend with the meaning 'Caesar advanced' or 'Caesar advances', it would be more natural for him to use verbs such as *prodeo* (e.g. *BGall.* 1.48.7), *progredior* (e.g. *BGall.* 1.50.1), *advenio* (e.g. *BGall.* 4.14.1), or *promoveo* (e.g. *BGall.* 7.70.6). The verb *eo* is certainly a bad choice, but it was Caesar who considered an accurate choice of words to be the foundation of eloquence.[50]

Let us suppose, however, that Caesar's audience managed to read the legend and understand its meaning correctly. Woods himself admits that CAESAR IIT could be interpreted as an allusion either to Caesar's successes in Gaul, or to his offensive against Pompey. However, if there was the slightest possibility that people would suppose the second meaning (in spite of the Gallic subject of the reverse, such an interpretation would be quite natural as the coins were issued during the war between Caesar and Pompey), such a legend would damage Caesar's reputation rather than strengthen it. It would remind people that Caesar had left his province without authorization by the Senate, in defiance of the *lex Cornelia de maiestate*, that he had invaded Italy and initiated the civil war and now 'advanced' against an army of Roman citizens. The ambiguity of the legend would have been harmful for Caesar's cause, and if he had wanted to glorify his

The Meaning of ⊥II on Caesar's Civil War Coinage (RRC 452)

conquest of Gaul, it would have been safer for him to choose an unambiguous legend, e.g. GALLIA CAPTA, GALLIA DEVICTA, or GALLIA PACATA.[51] Caesar could hardly have wanted his fellow-citizens to read *Caesar iit* on his coins. Therefore, ⊥II cannot be interpreted as a text.

If it is the number LII, what can it mean? Cavedoni relates it to the evidence of Pliny (*NH* 7.92) and Solinus (1.106) that Caesar had won fifty-two battles.[52] In fact, symbols of victory are depicted on the reverse of the coins in question: a Gallic trophy and (on *RRC* 452/4-5) captive Gauls. But Caesar's audience could interpret fifty-two as the number of his victories (without additional clues) only if this number had already been publicly proclaimed. It is absent from Caesar's *commentarii*. Where could Pliny have taken it from? After stating the number of Caesar's victories, Pliny goes on to say that Caesar killed 1,190,000 enemies in his battles, but the number relates only to external wars since Caesar had not wished to give any information on the civil wars (*bellorum civilium stragem non prodendo*). It is natural to suppose that it was Caesar himself who gave the number of enemies slain in his battles, though this information is also absent from his *commentarii*.

There is parallel evidence for Caesar's military successes that can be combined in a single table.

Christopher Pelling argues that the numbers given by Pliny, Plutarch and Appian are derived from the same source, that is from a triumphal inscription of Caesar and/or from the placards presented during his triumph in 46.[53] This is how Pliny and Plutarch use the triumphal tables and inscriptions of Pompey, this time stating their source.[54] As

Table 3.2 Caesar's military successes

Source	Wars	Enemy numbers	Killed	Captured	Battles	Cities seized	Tribes subdued
Nic. Dam. *FGrH*. 130.80	Asia and Europe				302		
Vell. 2.47.1	Gaul		>400,000	>400,000			
Plin. *NH* 7.92	External wars		1,192,000		50 (52?)		
Plut. *Caes*. 15.5	Gaul	3,000,000	1,000,000	1,000,000		>800	300
Plut. *Pomp*. 67.10	Gaul		1,000,000	1,000,000		1,000	>300
App. *Celt*. 1.2.6	Gaul	>4,000,000	1,000,000	1,000,000		>800	400
App. *BCiv*. 2.73	Spain, Gaul, Britain						400
App. *BCiv*. 2.150	Gaul				30		<400
Solin. 1.106			1,192,000		52		

a result, fifty-two battles should be derived by Pliny from the same source. Cavedoni correctly supposes that this number, as well as the number of slain enemies, does not include the statistics of the civil wars – with the possible exception of the African war, which was presented as a victory over king Juba.⁵⁵ Indeed, the tables shown in Caesar's triumph in 46 should have glorified his achievements in Gaul, Egypt, Pontus and Africa, but they should not have mentioned his operations in Spain, Epirus and Thessaly. According to Appian (who evidently used the same source), the share of Gaul is thirty victories out of fifty-two. The other twenty-two victories were won by Caesar later.

There remains the question of how we are to explain Nicolaus' evidence for 302 battles won by Caesar 'in Europe and Asia'. This number is not easily reconciled with the data of Pliny and Appian: even if we suppose that Caesar won fifty-two battles in Gaul alone, it is hard to imagine that this number comprises only a sixth of all his battles in Europe and Asia, not including, notably, his African campaign. Surely, Nicolaus might have used some other source (so too Velleius, whose numbers, on the contrary, are far smaller than those of Pliny, Plutarch and Appian). Or, as Cavedoni suggests, 302 might be the number of all encounters during the military career of Caesar, while fifty-two might relate only to pitched battles (*signis conlatis*, Plin. *NH* 7.92).⁵⁶ But Toher correctly observes that however we interpret the word 'battle', the number 302 is still improbably high, and the number of battles in Caesar's *Bellum Gallicum* approximates just to thirty or thirty-two.⁵⁷ It is possible that τριακοσίαις here should be emended to τριάκοντα, as Jacoby suggests.⁵⁸

Thus, during his triumph in 46, Caesar evidently proclaimed that he had won fifty-two battles (in external wars), including thirty in Gaul. So, the interpretation of ⊥II on his coins as the number of his victories should be abandoned. At the moment of their emission in 48, Caesar could only boast thirty victories.

Let us examine the hypotheses connecting ⊥II as fifty-two on Caesar's coins with the events of the end of the second century BCE. Caspari, who dates the coins *RRC* 452 to April 49, considers ⊥II as fifty-two to be the number of years elapsed between Marius' victories over the Cimbri and Teutons in 102–101 and the release of the issue.⁵⁹ Sumner holds a similar opinion: he dated the issue to 48 but points out that fifty-two years had elapsed between Marius' victories and the termination of Caesar's conquest of Gaul in 50.⁶⁰ That is, Caesar wished to glorify the memory of his uncle and at the same time to emphasize that he himself excelled Marius in war.

Caesar indeed revered Marius' memory and commemorated his victories through the restoration of his trophies;⁶¹ he also compared his own military deeds with those of Marius.⁶² However, what were the chances that a short glance at the coins with ⊥II would evoke Marius and his victories in the minds of the common people? There are no direct references to Marius on these coins: no portrait, no name, no defeated tribes. Gallic trophies (including a *carnyx*, horned helmet and oval shield) depicted on the obverse of *aurei* and *denarii* could in theory allude to the victories over the Cimbri and Teutons,⁶³ but it was far more natural for the audience to relate these with the more recent victories of Caesar, whose name was struck near the trophy. As to the *quinarius RRC* 452/3, the trophy depicted on it is Spanish, not Gallic,⁶⁴ so it could in no way be connected with Marius, but ⊥II is struck on this denomination too.

In short, a Roman soldier who received such coins as his pay would have been required to apply considerable thought in order to recall Marius' victories. First, he had to understand that ⊥II on the obverse signified LII. Next, he had to guess that LII was the number of years. He then had to grasp that the years should have been counted backwards, starting not from the current date (48 BCE), but from the date of the conquest of Gaul (50 BCE).[65] To make this calculation without consular lists to hand would not have been easy. Finally, he had to recall the reason why the consulship of Marius and Catulus had been celebrated. Scarcely anybody would manage to solve this riddle and scarcely anybody would even try to do so. The most obvious solution would be to relate the Gallic trophies with Caesar's conquest and to dismiss ⊥II as a mere control mark.

The same difficulties are produced by Zumpt's hypothesis. This scholar supposes that Caesar's coins with ⊥II were struck in 49 and the letters ⊥II meant that fifty-two years elapsed from the organization of the Transalpine province, which was created in 100 (according to Zumpt), after the defeat of the Cimbri and Teutons (so the year 49 was the fifty-second year after the foundation of the province). Zumpt supposes that Caesar wished to remind his audience of the foundation of Transalpine Gaul to explain on what grounds he was striking the coins, as in 49 he possessed only proconsular powers.[66] Such an explanation could only have confused Caesar's audience. Firstly, ordinary Romans could hardly remember by heart under which consuls Transalpine Gaul had been founded and, still less, how many years had elapsed since then.[67] Secondly, in 49, the allusion to Caesar's province did not legitimize his position; on the contrary, it emphasized that he had left his province and thereby had violated the *lex Cornelia de maiestate*. If Caesar had wanted to remind his audience about his proconsular powers, he would simply have called himself PROCOS on the coins. Lastly, Zumpt's hypothesis cannot be accepted for the simple fact that, as has been demonstrated above, the issue ⊥II should be dated not to 49 but to 48, when Caesar held the consulship; so his Gallic proconsulship became a thing of the past and contributed nothing to legitimizing his position.

Thus, having analysed and excluded all other interpretations, we return to the most widespread theory proposed by Borghesi, according to whom LII signified the age of Caesar. Again, we have to answer the same two questions. Why was the fifty-second year of age of such importance for Caesar? And how could Caesar's audience understand his message?

Let us start with the first question. According to the opinion of most scholars, Caesar wanted to remind his audience that he had achieved his second consulship *suo anno*, observing the statutory ages and intervals between offices.[68] Indeed, Caesar himself stresses in his *commentarii* that he reached the second consulship in accordance with the law (*BCiv.* 1.32.2; 3.1.1). However, if the coins with ⊥II were issued in 48 (as is demonstrated above), this explanation does not work. According to the Sullan law, a man could hold his first consulship in the forty-third year of his age (Cic. *Phil.* 5.48). The second consulship was available to him after an interval of a complete ten years (App. *BCiv.* 2.100), that is, in the fifty-fourth year of his age. If Caesar held the second consulship in 48 BCE at the age of fifty-two, it would mean that at some point he did break the *lex annalis*. Caesar hardly would have wished to suggest such an idea to his fellow citizens;

the more so as the law did not directly state the age requirements for the second consulship, only the interval between the first and second consulships,[69] and it was evident for everyone that between 59 and 48 this interval had indeed elapsed.

According to an alternative hypothesis, ⊥II signified Caesar's age at the time of the battle of Pharsalus which took place on 9 August, less than a month after his birthday.[70] In fact, this suggestion explains nothing. The interval of twenty-eight days between Caesar's birthday and the battle was too long to talk about the coincidence of these events. The age of fifty-two was neither too young nor too old for a victorious general. So why did Caesar choose to attract public attention to it? This is all the stranger when we consider that it was a victory in a civil war, a victory which Caesar, on the contrary, tried to pass over in silence: he did not even send a report about it to the senate (Cass. Dio 42.18.1).

It is equally difficult to answer the second question: how could Caesar's audience understand that ⊥II signified his age? Scholars have drawn a parallel with the *quinarii* of Antony (*RRC* 489/5-6), struck in 43–42 with legends A XL and A XLI, which are also interpreted as indications of Antony's age: on 14 January 42 he turned forty-one.[71] But there is an explicative letter A, that is *anno*, on Antony's *quinarii*. Why did Caesar not use it? If ⊥II really signified his age, such a legend was unprecedented in Roman coinage and Caesar could not expect that people would easily decipher it. And even if they had managed to do so, the conclusion on the legality of Caesar's second consulship would by no means have been self-evident, as the consulship is totally missing from the legend (unlike such issues as *RRC* 457, where Caesar is called COS ITER).

It is possible that both questions have the same answer. It has already been advanced by Hill as an additional suggestion and by Woytek as a means to date the issue more precisely.[72] Both scholars think that the central idea in Caesar's mind was the legality of his second consulship. In my opinion his message was different.

The ⊥II issue, as was the case for all the imperatorial issues of the civil wars, in the first place served as payment to the legionaries. Caesar mentions in his *commentarii* (*BCiv.* 3.78) that after the battle at Dyrrachium, he withdrew to Apollonia with the aim, among other things, of paying his army.[73] Ramsey and Raaflaub date Caesar's setback at Dyrrachium to 9 July 48, and his march to Apollonia and his stay there from 11 to 15 July.[74] As Woytek has pointed out, in this year Caesar's legionaries received their pay on the days close to Caesar's birthday on 13 July.[75] The payment was made in coins with LII. If on that day Caesar turned fifty-two, there would have been no need to explain the meaning of LII to the soldiers.

In the late Republic, the birthday celebration was still a private affair regardless of the public status of the person, but Romans attached great symbolic importance to this holiday.[76] Pompey's decision to celebrate his third triumph in 61 exactly on his birthday confirms that the generals of the Late Republic tried to attract public attention to these dates.[77] Pompey's example was followed by Messala Corvinus in 27 (Tibull. 1.7.1-8; 49-54; 63-64), and by Caligula in 40 CE (Suet. *Cal.* 49.2).[78] Cicero (*Att.* 4.1.4) emphasized that he had timed his return to Italy from exile (on 5 August 57) to coincide with the foundation day of the colony of Brundisium (where he had landed), which in turn coincided with the birthday of his daughter Tullia and the foundation day of the temple of Salus.[79] The news about the battle of Mutina arrived at Rome on the birthday of D. Brutus, and Cicero used this coincidence to support his proposition for the inscribing of Decimus' name in the *fasti* (*Fam.* 11.14.3; *Brut.* 1.15.8). The celebration of a patron's birthday by his clients is well attested already in the early reign of Augustus (Hor. *Carm.* 4.11; Tibull. 1.7),[80] and the whole state celebrated the birthdays of Augustus and his relatives.[81]

The annual public thanksgivings established in 30 in honour of the birthday of the young Caesar (the future Augustus) had as their precedent the celebration of the elder Caesar's birthday. In 45 or 44, public sacrifices were established in honour of Caesar's birthday,[82] and in 42 this day was declared a public holiday.[83] It is possible that Caesar's coins with LII, minted in 48, represent the first stage of the process. Caesar's army endured great hardships at Dyrrachium;[84] a decisive battle with Pompey was in prospect, and at the least Caesar himself strove to force his adversary into action.[85] When Caesar ordered to have his age struck on these coins and to pay his legionaries with them on his birthday, he was creating closer, more personal ties with his army and enhancing the personal loyalty of soldiers to their general, which was crucial in the circumstances of civil war. Such a measure would be far more intelligible to Caesar's soldiers and far more useful to the commander himself than a vague and ambiguous allusion to Caesar's adherence to the *lex annalis* at his election to the second consulship.[86]

Regardless of the letters ⊥II on Caesar's coins *RRC* 452, the issue should be dated to 48 on the basis of the hoard evidence and the analysis of the denominations. As for the letters ⊥II, they in all likelihood indicate the fifty-second birthday of Caesar on 13 July 48, when these coins were distributed among his legionaries. Only in such circumstances would Caesar's message have been clear and fully comprehensible to his audience. The soldiers would have been able to interpret the letters on the obverse without any difficulty or subtle reflection. The coins urged Caesar's legionaries to celebrate their general's birthday in spite of the hardships brought by civil war. So, Caesar was born in 100, and the numismatic data confirm the evidence of Velleius, Suetonius and Appian, and may be reconciled with Plutarch's testimony for Caesar's year of birth.[87] It remains to explain why he held all curule magistracies two years ahead of the legal age, but this problem must be the subject of another enquiry.

Notes

1. On other identifications see: Woytek 2003: 136–7, 142–2; Amela Valverde 2019: 257, with full bibliography.
2. The claim to the trophy's Spanish origin is made by Hollstein, who perceives analogies with the coins of P. Carisius and M. Piso and interprets the trophy as an allusion to Caesar's victory in Spain in 61–60 and his abandoned triumph (Hollstein 2014: 151–7). Tordeur's attempt to identify the round shield as a Macedonian example and to connect the trophy with Caesar's victory at Pharsalus is hardly plausible (Tordeur 2013: 155).

3. See Crawford 1974: 584–9.
4. Borghesi 1862: 495–9; Cesano 1947–9: 109–10; Crawford 1974: 92; Sear 1998: 9–10; Woytek 2003: 143–4; Amela Valverde 2019: 258. On the rendering of 50 as ⊥ see, for example, Cagnat 1914: 31. It also appears as a control-mark on the coins of C. Norbanus (*RRC* 357/1b, 83 BCE), P. Satrienus (*RRC* 388/1b, 77 BCE) and L. Lucretius Trio (*RRC* 390/2, 76 BCE). Cf. also *ILS* 5800 (68 BCE).
5. De Salis 1866: 20–2; Carcopino 1934: 37–42; Crawford 1974: 92; Amela Valverde 2019: 258. For the latter, see Woytek 2003: 147–50.
6. Cavedoni 1854: 93–4 n.76; 1857: 356–7; cf. Solin. 1.106; Plin. *NH* 7.92.
7. For Marius' victory, see Caspari 1911: 103–4; Sumner 1973: 137. For the establishment of the province, see Zumpt 1874: 18–23.
8. For I(mperator) IT(erum), see Eckel 1828: 6; Leone 1986: 76. For the perfect IIT, see Woods 2010: 38–42.
9. Cass. Dio 47.18.5-6. Badian prefers the evidence of Macrobius (1.12.34), according to which Caesar was born on 12 July, as the scholar considers this passage to be a precise citation of the *Lex Antonia* which changed the name of the month Quintilis to Iulius (Badian 2009: 16). But Macrobius does not state here that he is citing the law, in contrast to passage 1.12.35, where a fragment of *senatus consultum* on the renaming of Sextilis in honour of Augustus is introduced by the words *cuius verba subieci*. In this *senatus consultum*, all the events which justified the renaming of Sextilis are enumerated without their precise dates. It is perfectly possible that Antony's law also did not mention Caesar's date of birth and Macrobius stated it by himself using official calendars where it fell on 12 July (cf. Zumpt 1874: 9). As a result, I accept that Caesar was born on 13 July.
10. Suet. *Iul.* 88.1: *sexto et quinquagesimo aetatis anno*; App. *BCiv.* 2.149: ἔτος ἄγων ἕκτον ἐπὶ πεντήκοντα.
11. Plut. *Caes.* 69.1: τὰ μὲν πάντα γεγονὼς ἔτη πεντήκοντα καὶ ἕξ. However, the expression may also be interpreted as 'only fifty-six years'; 'fifty-six years in all'; 'fifty-six years in round numbers', cf. Deutsch 1914: 17–18; Holmes 1923: 1, 436; Hartke 1951: 214 Anm. 1; D'Anto 1957: 128; Leone 1986: 72.
12. See *BHisp.* 31.8 for Munda.
13. Cic. *Phil.* 5.48.
14. Crawford 1974: 92.
15. Battenburg 1980: 45; Woytek 2003: 142–53.
16. Campana 2002a: 17.
17. Amisano 2008: 53–4.
18. Amela Valverde 2019: 258.
19. Amela Valverde 2019: 258.
20. Crawford 1969: 2.
21. Crawford 1974: 90–1. The issue ⊥II closes the Benevento (Italy), Locusteni and Satu Nou (Romania) hoards (a barbarian imitation in the last case), but their composition is unrepresentative and does not allow for a judgement on the date of the coinage (Crawford 1969: 113).
22. *CRR* 1009.
23. *RRC* 452/2. I provide this data on the number of dies only as an illustration: they allow us to estimate approximately the relative volume of different issues. The accuracy of absolute

numbers of dies and (based on them) absolute numbers of issued coins and coins in circulation, as estimated by Crawford, is questionable (Buttrey 1993; Buttrey 1994).

24. Campana 2000: 8–17.
25. Pompey's *aurei* might also have been minted in the 60s (Crawford 1974: 83; Amela Valverde 2010: 205–16). Kopij (2016: 109–27) proposes to date them either to 76–75, or to the first half of 48, but both hypotheses do not explain satisfactorily the mounted figure of a boy attending the *triumphator* on the reverse; according to common opinion the boy is Pompey's son.
26. Campana 2001: 21.
27. Campana 2002a: 19.
28. Campana 2002a: 18.
29. Campana 2002b: 49–52. A half-*aureus* was also minted in 45 (*RRC* 475/2).
30. Campana 2002a: 16.
31. Campana 2002a: 20; Woytek 2003: 149–50.
32. Botrè 2007: 121–34.
33. Whether these *aurei* were minted out of Gallic or Roman gold, in both cases Caesar had to transport ingots across the Adriatic in 48. In 49 Pompey's mint was located in Apollonia (Cic. *Fam.* 13.29.3); when in 48 the city transferred its allegiance to Caesar (Caes. *BCiv.* 3.11), it was natural for him to place his mint there: cf. Caes. *BCiv.* 3.78; more on this passage see *infra*.
34. Though there is a unique coin struck in 85 (*RRC* 352/2), which may be either a *quinarius* or *sestertius*.
35. Woytek 2003: 150–1.
36. De Salis 1866: 21, followed by Grueber 1910: I, 505 n.1; Holmes 1923: 1, 439; Carcopino 1934: 38–9; Cesano 1947–9: 108–10.
37. Crawford 1974: 467; Sear 1998: 9–10; Woytek 2003: 146–7; Amela Valverde 2019: 258–9.
38. A goddess (Venus?) wearing oak-wreath and diadem: *RRC* 448/1 (48 BCE); a veiled goddess (Vesta?): *RRC* 466/1 (46 BCE); sacrificial tools: *RRC* 443/1 (49 BCE), 456/1 (47 BCE), 466/1 and 467/1 (46 BCE); Gallic trophy: *RRC* 448/1 (48 BCE), 468/1–2 (46 BCE), Gallic oval shield, Spanish round shield and carnyx: *RRC* 450/1 (48 BCE); captive Gaul: 448/2 (48 BCE), 468/1–2 (46 BCE).
39. Woytek 2003: 146.
40. Cf. Metcalf 2006: 225.
41. Eckel 1828: 6; followed by Leone 1986: 76. Caesar's coin with the legend IMP ITER, cited by Eckel as an analogy, is missing in all modern catalogues. Evidently it is a forgery or non-existent coin.
42. Plut. *Caes.* 12.4.
43. Caes. *BGall.* 2.35.4; 4.38; 7.90.8. For acclamations and *supplicationes*, see Val. Max. 2.8.7.
44. Joseph. *AJ.* 14.10.2(190); Weinstock 1971, 104–5.
45. Schede 1919: 34, no. 20; *IGR* 4.1715; *IG* 12.6.1.388; Raubitschek 1954: 72, R; *Samos* 273.
46. Zack 2018: 165, Anm. 55; 175–6.
47. Plut. *Caes.* 50.3-4; Suet. *Iul.* 37.2; Woods 2010.
48. Woods 2010: 40–1.
49. Cf. also *BMCRR* II. Africa 10, reverse: EPPIVS LEG(*atus*) F(*landum*) C(*uravit*); Crawford (*RRC* 461/1) proposes to read instead LEG(*atus*) F(*isci*) C(*astrensis*).

50. Cic. *Brut.* 253.
51. See respectively *RRC* 422/1; *RRC* 543/1; cf. Caes. *BGall.* 2.35.1.
52. Cavedoni 1854: 93–4 n.76; Cavedoni 1857: 356–7. It should be observed that MSS of Pliny give *quinquagiens*, but Mayhoff (1875: 23) emends the text with *bis et quinquagiens* citing Solinus, as the source of Solinus' passage (as well as of the two thirds of his text, cf. Brodersen 2011: 70) undoubtedly was Pliny. However, Pelling (2011: 210) considers the text of Solinus, not Pliny, to be erroneous.
53. Pelling 2011: 210–12. In Pelling's opinion, the discrepancy between Plutarch and Appian concerning the numbers of slain enemies and subdued tribes should be explained either by the supposition that Plutarch rounded the exact numbers down and Appian rounded them up, or by the suggestion that Appian's numbers include the achievements not only of Gallic wars but also of the Spanish campaigns of Caesar in 61–60 BCE.
54. Plin. *NH* 3.18; 7.97-98; Plut. *Pomp.* 45.3-4.
55. Cavedoni 1854: 93 n.76; Cavedoni 1857: 357.
56. Cavedoni 1857: 357.
57. Toher 2017: 323.
58. *FGrHist* 407.
59. Caspari 1911: 103–4.
60. Sumner 1973: 137.
61. Suet. *Iul.* 11; Plut. *Caes.* 5.2-3; 6.
62. Caes. *BGall.* 1.40; cf. Plut. *Caes.* 19.4.
63. Cf. *quinarii* of C. Fundanius (*RRC* 326/2, 101 BCE), T. Cloulius (*RRC* 332, 98 BCE), C. Egnatuleius (*RRC* 333, 97 BCE) with similar reverse types: Victory, trophy, *carnyx* and (in the first two cases) kneeling prisoner.
64. Hollstein 2014.
65. Here my reconstruction follows Sumner's hypothesis, as that of Caspari requires us to date the issue ⊥II to 49.
66. Zumpt 1874: 18–23.
67. We have no direct evidence on the date of the foundation of Transalpine Gaul, and Roman administration there was very flexible. Sometimes the eastern part of Transalpine Gaul was combined in one command with Cisalpine Gaul, and its western part was united with Nearer Spain. Transalpine Gaul emerged as a separate province only in 70s and was evidently organized by Pompey. Cf. Badian 1966: 907–10; Ebel 1975: 358–73.
68. De Salis 1866: 20–2; Hill 1909: 103; Grueber 1910: 1, 505–6 n.1; Carcopino 1934: 42; Woytek 2003: 149.
69. Cf. Pompey's case: he was born on 29 September 106 (Vell. 2.53.4; Plin. *NH* 37.13). He had to obtain the senate's permission to hold his first consulship in 70 (Cic. *Leg. Man.* 62), but his second consulship in 55 did not require such permission.
70. Campana 2002a: 17; Amela Valverde 2019: 258.
71. Borghesi 1862: 498–9; Grueber 1910: 1, 505–6 n.1; Woytek 2003: 143; contra: Zumpt 1874: 25–9; Hill 1975: 168.
72. Hill 1909: 103; Woytek 2003: 148–9.

73. Caes. *BCiv.* 3.78. This is the sole passage where Caesar mentions the pay of his legionaries; in other passages only the pay of Pompeians (*BCiv.* 1.23; 87) and auxiliary cavalry (*BCiv.* 3.59) – as well as the doubling of one cohort's pay as a reward (*BCiv.* 3.53) – are mentioned.
74. Ramsey and Raaflaub 2017: 198.
75. Woytek 2003: 148–9. Naturally, Caesar was unable to predict the development of military operations in July 48 with precision, but the approximate date of the next payment was known in advance, so Caesar was able to give orders about the coin legend or even to move the payment closer to his birthday.
76. Feeney 2007: 148–9.
77. Plin. *NH* 37.13.
78. Weinstock 1971: 208–9.
79. To time his return to coincide with his own birthday, Cicero would have waited for five months, which was evidently unacceptable for him.
80. Argetsinger 1992: 180–1 points out that the importance of these celebrations in Roman culture is attested also by 'birthday poems' which had no analogies in Greek literature before Roman times and consequently cannot be regarded as an imitation and can be used as evidence of the longstanding and traditional Roman attitudes on birthdays.
81. Cass. Dio 51.19.2; 54.8.5; for more on this matter see: Weinstock 1971: 209–12.
82. Cass. Dio 54.4, cf. Weinstock 1971: 200, 206, 270 on the date.
83. Cass. Dio 47.18.5-6.
84. Caes. *BCiv.* 3.47-48; Suet. *Iul.* 68. 2; Plut. *Caes.* 39.1-3.
85. Caes. *BCiv.* 3.41, 43-44; 56, 78, 84-85.
86. Why did Caesar not celebrate his birthdays on his military coinage in the following years? Maybe such an opportunity simply did not arise. On his birthday in 47, Caesar was on the march from Tarsus to Mazaca (Ramsey, Raaflaub 2017: 204), but his eastern coinage is quite scarce: only rare *aurei* are known (*RRC* 456), which could not be used as pay for the legionaries. In 46 and 45, Caesar did not wage military operations in the middle of July.
87. See n.11 above.

CHAPTER 4
CREATING ALTERNATIVE LEGITIMACY: OCTAVIAN, SEXTUS POMPEIUS AND DIVINE FILIATION*

Laura Kersten

Although civil war is characterized by armed violence and one can argue that military strength determines the outcome and thus settles the matter through force, Roman civil war leaders were eager to legitimize their power.[1] At first glance, the contest for legitimacy seems to follow Republican models. By Republican legitimacy, I mean power transferred by the Senate and/or the people, and thus deriving from a decree or law, or attributed to an office. In short, power is legitimized institutionally. Such an institutional legitimacy was desirable during civil wars. The Triumvirs Octavian, Marcus Antonius and Lepidus, for example, tried to legitimize their position through the *lex Titia* in 43 BCE, while Cassius and Brutus, who gathered troops in the eastern provinces, were invested with an *imperium* over these from the Senate earlier that year.[2] Both factions thus tried to legitimize their power by using Republican models and were not content to exercise power without an institutional basis, but such legitimacy was unstable. Indeed, as a consequence of the civil war context, it frequently depended on the persons exercising direct control over the city of Rome and on the shifting alliances of the civil war protagonists.[3]

Octavian and Sextus Pompeius can serve as examples for the instability of this sort of legitimacy. Octavian experienced it in connection with the Battle of Mutina in 43. His alliance with Cicero and the Senate before the battle gave him Senate-sanctioned legitimacy and in early January 43 Octavian was able to obtain propraetorian *imperium* as well as the voting privileges of a consul (among other privileges). Yet shortly after the battle in April 43, when alliances and opinion in the Senate had shifted, Octavian's access to the consulate was denied. The consulship to which Octavian aspired was now attainable only with military force, and he therefore marched against Rome in the summer of 43.[4] Sextus Pompeius experienced the instability of institutional legitimacy in connection with his position as *praefectus classis et orae maritimae*, bestowed upon him by the Senate in April 43[5] but then quickly annulled when he was deprived of this position in the summer of 43 in connection with the *lex Pedia*.[6]

In this paper I will argue that during the civil war, both Sextus Pompeius and Octavian created an alternative legitimacy that was not dependent on shifting alliances and developments in Rome and that could, therefore, constitute a more reliable claim to power. In doing so, however, neither took the risk of abandoning traditional, institutional models of legitimacy, though they did take advantage of their roles as the sons and heirs of Pompeius and Caesar, the two protagonists of the preceding civil wars. Florus also seems to emphasize this latter aspect when he describes the role of the civil war protagonists as hereditary:

> The Roman people, after the murders of Caesar and Pompeius, seemed to have returned to their former state of liberty; and they would have done so if either Pompeius had left no children or Caesar no heir, or, what was still more fatal than either of these circumstances, if Antonius, once Caesar's colleague and afterwards his rival in power, had not survived to cause fire and storm in the succeeding age.[7]

In Florus' view, Octavian, Sextus Pompeius, and his brother Gnaeus Pompeius continued the civil war in the footsteps of their fathers, even if Florus does not omit or underestimate Antonius and his contribution to the conflict.

In this paper, however, I want to deal not only with the protagonists' human ancestry, but also their divine filiation. I will show that the two are intertwined. In this regard, it is important to stress that the connection of Roman *gentes* with the divine is nothing new in the resumption of civil wars after Caesar's death in 44. In fact, there are examples of legendary genealogies of Roman *gentes* in late Republican Rome who were said to descend from Greek or Trojan ancestors and/or gods or heroes.[8] Two of the better-known genealogies are those of the Antonii, who were said to descend from Hercules, and the Julii, who claimed a connection to Venus via Aeneas.[9] In particular, (late) Republican leaders were associated with divine descent. Famously, Sulla had already claimed a special connection to Aphrodite/Venus,[10] Caesar advertised his lineage to Venus[11] and the elder Scipio Africanus was said to descend from a god.[12] Although the extent to which such divine ancestry was important for political ambitions has been debated,[13] it clearly was an additional factor in the struggle for prestige and status.

By looking at the narrow context of the renewed civil wars after Caesar's death in 44, I will analyse the use and implications of Sextus Pompeius' and Octavian's divine filiation. I want to show that Sextus Pompeius and Octavian advanced pre-existing connections between Roman *gentes* and the divine to gain an alternative form of legitimacy. Furthermore, I will discuss the way this can be perceived as a breakdown of established models.

In this paper, I will start with Sextus Pompeius and outline his connection to the divine, then analyse the emergence and implications of Octavian's divine filiation before comparing both cases.

1.

Florus writes about Sextus Pompeius' sacrifice to Neptune and describes how he sacrificed a horse, bulls, and gold to the god[14] 'in order to induce the ruler of the sea to allow him to rule in his domain'.[15] The remarkable aspect of this passage is the notion that rule, expressed with the word *regnare*, is supposed to be conferred by a god, not a state institution. The term *regnare* is related to kingship and the divine sphere.[16] It thus brands Sextus' plea as one that exceeds the norms and is unrepublican. Moreover, although not all ancient authors report this sacrifice in the same terms as Florus,[17] it is clear from the other sources that Sextus Pompeius claimed (or perhaps even believed himself) to have power over the sea.

This is particularly visible from two episodes in 42 and 38. Sextus had already lost his position of *praefectus classis et orae maritimae* in summer 43, been proscribed later that same year,[18] and gone on to secure control of Sicily.[19] Following these events, two major naval encounters between Octavian or his generals and Sextus Pompeius occurred off the coast of Sicily. Both encounters, in 42 and in 38, were fought partly in the strait of Messina or close to the promontory of the strait called *Scyllaeum*.

In 42, Octavian sent his general Salvidienus Rufus to prevent Sextus Pompeius' attacks on the Italian coast.[20] After Salvidienus Rufus was successful in his defence of Italy, he attempted to cross the strait of Messina. However, the strong current made the crossing difficult, and he was soundly defeated when he engaged Sextus Pompeius' fleet in combat.[21] While Cassius Dio highlights the superiority of Sextus' ships and naval skills of his crew,[22] Appian emphasizes the natural phenomena that were typical of the strait – the rush of the waves and the current – that Sextus Pompeius and his crew proved able to withstand.[23] Something else is noteworthy in this regard: we read in Cassius Dio that after the battle, Sextus occupied the whole of Sicily, produced triumphal spectacles, and organized a *naumachia*. Additionally, he increased his number of ships, and from that point on dominated the sea and 'assumed a certain additional glory and pride by representing himself to be the son of Neptune, since his father once ruled the whole sea.'[24] So, Cassius Dio informs us not only that Sextus Pompeius represented himself as a descendant of Neptune after a naval victory against Octavian's general, but also that such a representation was connected to his father and his rule over the sea. In writing about Pompeius Magnus' rule over the sea, Cassius Dio certainly means the campaign against the pirates in 67 that was assigned to Pompeius by the *lex Gabinia*[25] and that ancient authors more generally conceptualized as a province extending over the whole (Mediterranean) sea.[26]

In 38, Sextus Pompeius' fleet confronted Octavian, who wanted to join Calvisius Sabinus in the strait for a combined attack on Sicily. This encounter resulted in several naval battles between their respective armadas[27] and the events seemed not to unfold in Octavian's favour (he was obliged to announce that he had survived).[28] The encounters were not decided conclusively in a battle, however, but rather by an unusually fierce storm that led to the destruction of Octavian's fleet. Appian describes in detail the impact of the storm on Octavian's ships, which suffered heavily not only due to the extreme weather, but also due to the decision to lie at anchor in the strait:

> For the narrowness of the place, and the innate difficulty of getting out of it, and the surge of the waves, and the wind whipped into gusts by the surrounding mountains, and the maelstrom in the deep water churning everything up, made it impossible to stay or escape. ... Not even the local inhabitants could remember

there ever being such a terrible storm. In exceeding what was usual and normal, it destroyed most of Octavian's ships and men.[29]

Once again, natural phenomena (and particularly their ferocity in the strait) decided a naval encounter in Sextus Pompeius' favour. Cassius Dio reports that from that time on, Sextus Pompeius not only represented himself as Neptune, but believed himself to be in fact the son of Neptune.[30] Appian mentions such a divine filiation as well, although his first reference to it occurs later, in the aftermath of another naval misfortune in 36.[31] In that context, Appian not only mentions Sextus Pompeius' representation as Neptune's son, but also his faith in the assistance of the gods, since he was twice victorious in summertime naval battles.[32] He further suggests that Sextus' perception of events made him vain, led to his neglect in properly preparing for the final battle for control of Sicily, and prevented him from taking advantage of Octavian's recurring naval misfortunes.[33]

We might think – as research in the last decades has increasingly suggested – that such a connection to Neptune is part of an imperial, non-contemporary, narrative that discredits Sextus Pompeius.[34] Indeed, his representation as Neptune's son received a negative interpretation in both Appian and Cassius Dio.[35] But such a paternal connection to Neptune, who was linked to the destructive force of the sea and the elements, is also detectable in contemporary sources, namely Sextus Pompeius' coinage. I will focus on three coins that make such a connection particularly visible.

The reverse of the first coin issue, which consists of two types, depicts either four ships engaged in a battle (Figure 4.1; *RRC* 483/1) or a sailing galley above which a star is shown (Figure 4.2; *RRC* 483/2) and beneath the galley the inscription Q NASIDIVS naming the person responsible for the minting. The obverse of the coin is particularly illuminating. Both types show the bare head of Pompeius Magnus with a trident and a

Figure 4.1 *Denarius* of Q. Nasidius, *RRC* 483/1; National Museum of Denmark, RP 651.1.

Creating Alternative Legitimacy

Figure 4.2 *Denarius* of Q. Nasidius; *RRC* 483/2; Münzkabinett der Staatlichen Museen zu Berlin, 18213373.

dolphin and the inscription NEPTVNI.[36] Through the attributes of the trident and dolphin, Sextus Pompeius' father is identified as Neptune (or at least syncretized with the sea god)[37] and the inscription spells out whose portrait is depicted on the coin.[38] Although neither Sextus Pompeius' name nor his portrait appears on the coins, which were minted under the authority of Nasidius,[39] it is clear that the coin issue dates to between 44 and 36 (a recent evaluation of hoards points to an early date between 44 and 42)[40] and implies Sextus Pompeius' descent from Pompeius Magnus-Neptune. It is noteworthy that, like the narration in historiographical sources, Sextus Pompeius' connection to Neptune is constructed in reference to his father.

Figure 4.3 *Denarius* of Sextus Pompeius; *RRC* 511/3; Münzkabinett der Staatlichen Museen zu Berlin, 18207996.

Such an identification of Pompeius Magnus with Neptune, with reference to filial or familial *pietas*, is part of another coin issue (Figure 4.3; *RRC* 511/3) minted in Sicily under the name of Sextus Pompeius and with reference to his prefecture. The obverse reads MAG(nus) PIVS and the reverse bears the inscription PRAEF(ectus) CLAS(sis) ET ORAE MARIT(imae) EX S(enatus) C(onsulto).[41] While we can see on the obverse the head of Pompeius Magnus with jug and *lituus*, the reverse shows five figures: on the left and right we can see the Catanaean brothers carrying their parents on their shoulders and in the middle, a person wearing a diadem and a cloak and placing a foot on a ship's prow. This reverse is frequently regarded as representing Pompeius Magnus as Neptune in the middle, flanked by his two sons Gnaeus Pompeius and Sextus Pompeius who (to emphasize filial *pietas*) are depicted as the Catanaean brothers. The mythological brothers were said to have rescued their parents from the eruption of Mount Etna.[42] We can, therefore, not only detect another identification of Sextus' father with Neptune, but we can also see that Sextus Pompeius connected the maritime theme to another topic, namely that of *pietas*. That motif had already played a key role in Sextus Pompeius' coinage on the Iberian Peninsula and continued to do so in his coinage in Sicily.[43] It played a major role in Sextus' (as well as Octavian's) self-representation as the son and heir of the earlier civil war protagonist.[44]

The third coin (Figure 4.4; *RRC* 511/4) is also minted in the name of Sextus Pompeius and bears the same legend as the coin issue described above. On the obverse, a lighthouse surmounted by a statue carrying a trident and rudder and with a foot on a prow is depicted, while in front we see a moving galley with an *aquila* on the prow and a sceptre at the stern. On the reverse one can see the sea-monster Scylla wielding a rudder in both hands. This coin has frequently been connected to one of Sextus Pompeius' victories over Octavian and particularly to his victory in 38. In that battle, he is said to have

Figure 4.4 *Denarius* of Sextus Pompeius (reverse); *RRC* 511/4; Münzkabinett der Staatlichen Museen zu Berlin, 18202271.

reached the safe harbour of Messina (that might be shown on the obverse), while Octavian and his navy suffered greatly in a storm due to anchoring in the Strait of Messina. The force of the sea that threatened Octavian and his fleet in the strait is symbolized on the reverse by Scylla.[45] This is the menacing anthropophagous monster known from the *Odyssey*,[46] who features also in the *Aeneid* of Vergil (Sextus' contemporary), where she is connected to Sicily and a strait.[47] Such an interpretation implies that the terrifying Scylla does not frighten Sextus Pompeius and indeed fights on his side, helping to ensure his victories.[48]

Both coinage and historiography refer to Sextus Pompeius' connection to Neptune and to the origin of this via his natural father Pompeius Magnus. We should not therefore altogether mistrust (as some recent research has suggested) Cassius Dio's and Appian's descriptions and what these tell us about the construction of a link between Sextus Pompeius and Neptune.[49] Rather, imperial historiography and the contemporary sources seem to be in agreement in this case.

In addition, both source types show that the connection is linked to the violence of the sea that seemingly worked in Sextus Pompeius' favour and that he could therefore interpret as assistance from Neptune and the natural elements. The reader may ask why this constructed genealogy was also a claim to power. It implied that Sextus Pompeius alone and no other protagonist of the civil wars could enjoy this kind of connection to Neptune and thus to the sea, because the sea god was, via Sextus' human father, tied to the *gens Pompeia* or (more accurately) to the descendants of Pompeius Magnus, of whom Sextus was the only living son.[50] Furthermore, its function was to claim that the assistance of the sea-god also secured the support of natural elements in combat. Sextus Pompeius thus has power over the sea via Neptune, a conclusion that seems to be reflected in Florus' account, where the historian describes Sextus Pompeius' intention to rule in the sea-god's domain.[51]

Although Sextus seemed to create a divine filiation that, in its internal logic, did not rely on any institutional legitimacy, he was unwilling to abstain from the latter. When the possibility arose and he had access to Rome and its mechanisms of institutional legitimacy, he seized the opportunity. After Caesar's death, a rapprochement with Rome took place and Sextus accepted appointment as *praefectus classis et orae maritimae*, which he struck on his Sicilian coinage,[52] though after he was relieved of the position.[53] He emphasized on his coinage that he received his prefecture EX S(enatus) C(onsulto), thus citing a state institution. In this way, he based his power over the sea not only on divine filiation, but also underpinned it with institutional legitimacy. On his coins, the depiction of Scylla is accompanied by his *praefectus* title. Moreover, when Marcus Antonius and Octavian were willing to negotiate peace with Sextus, he not only became the master of a part of the Roman world[54] (although his power, unlike that of the Triumvirs, was never institutionally acknowledged), but it was also stipulated in the agreement in 39 – the so-called treaty of Misenum – that the Triumvirs would give him access to the state institutions and thus to institutional legitimacy. He was promised the roles of consul and augur.[55] In short, Sextus did not abandon institutional legitimacy, but rather he created an alternative legitimacy that could either complement institutional legitimacy or exist without it. He was to some extent successful because the Roman public connected him to Neptune and responded positively to him.[56]

2.

Parallels between Sextus Pompeius and Octavian have been recognized by others, including Anton Powell, Kathryn Welch, Edward Zarrow, Giovannella Cresci Marrone and Pierre Assenmaker.[57] Indeed, there are striking similarities between the two men when it comes to their position in 44 and their attempt to legitimize their own actions. The similarities highlighted here might also contribute to the debate that has dominated research on Sextus Pompeius since the start of the new millennium.[58] The subsequent rehabilitation of Sextus Pompeius has led to the argument that he was a Republican figure – indeed, the last Republican protagonist – in the late phase of the civil wars.[59] However, this is called into question if we acknowledge that fundamental elements in Octavian's and Sextus Pompeius' bids for legitimacy were both non-institutional and also similar, and that these elements played a role in constructing the legitimacy of the future *Princeps*.

The similarities start with both (Sextus Pompeius and Octavian) intervening as military leaders in the civil wars. As is well known, Octavian had no institutional legitimacy when he decided to recruit soldiers in the wake of Caesar's death.[60] In a similar fashion, Sextus Pompeius had no legal standing when he decided to fight Caesar's governor on the Iberian Peninsula in 45 and 44, after his brother's death.[61] Octavian had been promoted by his great-uncle Caesar. He became *pontifex* in 48, *praefectus urbi feriarum Latinarum causa*, received the *dona militaria* for Caesar's African triumph in 46 (among other honours), and accompanied him to Spain to fight Pompeius' sons.[62] After the Ides of March, Octavian returned from Apollonia to Italy and decided not only to accept Caesar's inheritance and the posthumous adoption, but also to adopt Caesar's name.[63] Furthermore, he took the money Caesar had intended for his Parthian campaign and started to recruit soldiers.[64] Nicolaus of Damascus notes that Octavian's friends told him about his connection to the veterans: 'that [he could induce] those men into an expedition on behalf of Caesar, especially because of his great name. They said the soldiers would readily follow if the son of Caesar was leading them and would do anything he asked'.[65]

Moreover, Octavian did not conceal the basis for his claim to power (although he was eager to hold a position that was institutionally approved),[66] but rather he attempted to legitimize it further through Caesar and his deification, which was officially finalized between 42 and 39.[67] This constitutes one major difference from Sextus Pompeius, whose father was never officially deified. Nevertheless, Sextus also openly advertised his filiation from Neptune, which was connected to his natural father and played a part in his claim to power. Octavian, as is well known, started to call himself *divi filius* on his coinage from 38 at the latest.[68] In addition, coins connected Octavian directly to the deified Caesar. For example, *RRC* 535/1 (Figure 4.5) depicts Octavian on the obverse and Caesar on the reverse, naming Octavian *divi filius* (CAESAR DIVI F) and acclaiming Caesar as

Figure 4.5 Coin (bronze) of Octavian; *RRC* 535/1; ANS 1944.100.6017.

DIVOS IVLIVS. But even before the *divi filius* legend appeared on coins, the divinity of Caesar and his filiation were major topics for Octavian.[69] This is shown by the *ludi Victoriae Caesaris*. During the *ludi* in July 44, the *sidus Iulium*, a comet, is said to have appeared. It was perceived as a sign of Caesar's apotheosis, one that Octavian seemed to enhance by placing a star on the statue of Caesar in the Temple of Venus, which is also depicted on his coinage (also after 27)[70] to demonstrate his father's godlike status.[71] Furthermore, we can see that Caesar played a major role in Octavian's coinage from the outset.[72] An early example dating to 43 is *RRC* 490/2 (Figure 4.6), which depicts Octavian on the obverse and Caesar on the reverse and thus illustrates the succession.[73]

Figure 4.6 *Aureus* of Octavian (obverse); *RRC* 490/2; Münzkabinett der Staatlichen Museen zu Berlin, 18202283.

It is striking that the reference to his divine filiation was not only a stopgap in times when institutional legitimacy was lacking, in 44 as well as probably in 32,[74] but played an important role in Octavian's self-representation throughout the civil war era. This was also the case when he held propraetorian *imperium*, was consul, and governed as triumvir;[75] the nomenclature of *divi filius* also formed part of Augustus' name after 27.[76] So why does Octavian emphasize his filiation and its connection to the divine so prominently if he could have claimed to have institutional legitimacy as consul or triumvir? First, it offered him independence from the institutional legitimacy that Octavian himself had experienced as unreliable in the wake of the Battle of Mutina.[77] Second, it monopolizes a special connection to Caesar and therefore excludes others, namely Octavian's triumviral colleagues Antonius and Lepidus, by virtue of the fact that they were not the sons of Caesar.

Let us consider in more detail the second point. In March 44, Lepidus was *magister equitum* of the deceased dictator and already had a long political and military career.[78] Moreover, he was the person who opposed the conspirators: immediately after the Ides of March, Lepidus gathered the troops on the Campus Martius and is said to have occupied the Forum as well as given a speech that attacked the murderers.[79] In addition, Lepidus was made *pontifex maximus* in the wake of Caesar's death, even though Cassius Dio informs us that the chief priesthood had been made hereditary.[80] Therefore, Lepidus not only held an institutionally legitimized position and had the proper career of a Roman *nobilis* to his credit, but also took a priesthood that, according to Cassius Dio, was earmarked for Caesar's natural or adopted son. However, Caesar's heir Octavian/Augustus did not dare take the priesthood[81] until Lepidus' death in 13 or 12,[82] even though Lepidus was *de facto* already deprived of his political role by 36.[83] Equally, Antonius was in an institutionally legitimized position by the time of the murder. Sole consul after Caesar's death, he had been one of Caesar's close supporters, had accompanied him as a legate to Gaul, and was later augur and tribune, among other positions. In the preceding civil wars, he had not only been propraetor, but also fought with Caesar at Pharsalus and served as *magister equitum*.[84] After the Ides of March, he also rhetorically attacked the murderers and won the goodwill of the populace with his funeral speech by praising Caesar (see cover illustration).[85] On his coinage, Antonius stuck – like Octavian – portraits of himself on the obverse and the deceased Caesar on the reverse.[86]

So, both of Caesar's colleagues (and Octavian's future triumviral colleagues) were by the time of Caesar's death in a better initial position to claim power in Rome and legitimize their actions. They had military and political experience whereas Octavian (although he had fulfilled political duties) was just coming to adulthood. That is why Appian puts the following words into Antonius' mouth:[87]

> My boy, if Caesar had left you the political leadership, along with his estate and name, it would be proper for you to ask me for an explanation of my public decisions, and for me to provide it. But since the Roman people never allowed anyone to succeed to political power, not even the kings, whom they expelled and swore never to put up with any others again – this is the very charge the assassins

make against your father when they say they killed him for acting like a king, no longer as a leader – I am under no obligation to give you an answer on my public decisions.[88]

However, being Caesar's heir was exactly the political capital Octavian possessed and exploited. Part of that was to style himself as *divi filius*, something that neither Lepidus nor Antonius could do. We should also consider the advantage of using his filiation and Caesar's divine aura to appeal to the people who were already responding positively to Caesar's interaction with the divine or his godlike status after death. We learn from the sources about the immense impact that Octavian's filiation and name had on soldiers and clients of Caesar. Already in Greece, but also directly after he arrived in Italy, soldiers welcomed him as Caesar's son. Numerous friends of Caesar and others gathered around him, and the veterans who had served under Caesar were willing to follow him,[89] but the masses in Rome were also inclined to treat Caesar as a god. Already before the *ludi Victoriae Caesaris*, the false Marius mobilized the people to erect an altar for Caesar, an act that was forcibly supressed by Antonius in April 44.[90] Octavian later embraced such tendencies by minting coins that depicted the *sidus Iulium* and named Caesar a god.[91]

So, for Octavian, not only naming himself Julius Caesar, but also referring to his godlike status was a way of gathering Caesar's supporters around himself and distancing them from his triumviral colleagues Antonius and Lepidus.[92] Octavian's filiation emphasized his status as the true heir of the divine Caesar and therefore combined the idea of succession with the god-like status of his ancestor and a seemingly divine aura that allowed Octavian to call himself *divi filius*.

The implications of such legitimacy, which combined divine filiation with being the heir of the dictator Caesar, become apparent when we consider the connection of the *gens Iulia* to the myth of Troy and the goddess Venus (the latter had been already emphasized by Caesar). This connection played an essential role in the visual art and poetry of the Augustan Principate, but before that time Venus and Aeneas (carrying his father Anchises) already featured on Octavian's coinage.[93] Most clearly and most prominently, such implications become visible in the *Aeneid* and the Forum of Augustus,[94] both of which connected the mythological lineage of the Julii to the foundation of Rome as well as to Trojan origins. If we look into Vergil's epic poem, we detect such a connection already in Book One of the *Aeneid* where Jupiter, who is addressing Venus, describes the lineage of Caesar.[95] The lineage begins with Aeneas (who is described as: *sublimemque feres ad sidera caeli magnanimum Aenean*),[96] continues with Ascanius, Rhea Silvia (Ilia) and leads to Romulus and Remus, whose father is Mars, the subsequent foundation of Rome, and finally to Caesar.[97] Furthermore, in Book Six we learn from Anchises in the underworld:

> Here is Caesar and all the seed of Iulus destined to pass under heaven's spacious sphere. And this in truth is he whom you so often hear promised you, Augustus Caesar, son of a god (*divi genus*), who will again establish a golden age in Latium amid fields once ruled by Saturn.[98]

So, not only is Augustus mentioned here by name but he, who is of divine origin (or in other words *divi filius*), is expected to restore the golden age and is the person to whom the whole story of Aeneas' descendants leads.[99] There is a third passage in Vergil of relevance: the shield of Aeneas.[100] On the shield, made by Vulcan, the story of Italy and the triumphs of the Romans are depicted, starting with Ascanius and the twins raised by a wolf. The story does not stop in the mythological past, however. Rather, it also shows various people of the late Republic (e.g. Cato and Catiline) before culminating, at the centre of the shield, with the Battle of Actium and the fight between Octavian and Antonius. Here Augustus is mentioned as 'leading Italians to strife, with Senate and People, the Penates of the state, and all the mighty gods; his auspicious brows shoot forth a double flame, and on his head dawns his father's star'.[101] Roman history thus centres around the event that marks the overcoming of Octavian's last rival and subsequently paved the way for the establishment of his sole rule. Octavian, divinely assisted and protected by his father whose *sidus* appears overhead, is depicted as the fulfilment of Roman history, that is, the person to whom all Roman history leads.

A similar narrative can be constructed from the Forum of Augustus. Of interest here is the fact that the Forum showcased, in the north exedra, Aeneas and the lineage of the Julii, while in the south exedra it displayed Romulus and the *summi viri* of Rome.[102] Augustus' divine father also played an essential role in the Forum. The main building of the Forum was a temple for Mars Ultor, which Octavian had promised after 42 as a consequence of avenging Caesar by defeating his murderers at Philippi.[103] However, not only mythological and deceased persons were shown in the Forum, but also Augustus himself, in the centre of the Forum in a quadriga,[104] thus connecting all these different stories to himself. The Forum tells a strongly suggestive tale, that of the *Princeps'* genealogy which is not only intertwined with the history of Rome and Troy, but is also divine thanks to the deified Caesar, Venus and Mars (via Romulus).[105]

The divine filiation of Octavian/Augustus thus becomes part of a more traditional tale about family origins in Troy, making Augustus' familial genealogy also the genealogy of Roman origins and divine ancestry. Although the gods included in this genealogy are not the only important gods for Octavian/Augustus,[106] the genealogy is a fundamental part of his legitimacy because it declares Augustus (also by including his divine father as the central element and therefore pointing directly to the *divi filius*) to be the one to whom all Roman history leads. Such a genealogical legitimacy, which could be perceived as traditional,[107] also broke with deep-rooted Republican beliefs because it questioned the necessity of institutional legitimacy. However, that did not result in an abandonment of institutional legitimacy. Not only during the civil war, but also after 27 and the establishment of the Principate, Octavian/Augustus used institutional legitimacy and occupied different political offices and priesthoods.[108] Indeed, that lies at the heart of Principate: Octavian/Augustus was particularly concerned with using traditional models for legitimacy or representing them as such. That is not only the case with institutional legitimacy, but also with his divine filiation, which was integrated into a Trojan-Roman genealogy and could therefore appear traditional. However, it exceeded Republican norms by suggesting legitimacy to rule Rome due to filiation and genealogy, implying a divine-dynastic succession. That is why we can perceive the divine filiation as leading to a breakdown – it marks the moment in which alternative models of institutional legitimacy were openly applied and forcefully showcased. Augustus famously pronounced the restoration of the Republic, but he created a political system, the Principate, that is perceived as the end of the Republic. Part of that change is a divine-dynastic legitimacy that irreversibly came to the surface at the end of the Republic and that provided an alternative form of legitimacy.[109]

3.

In summary, both Octavian and Sextus Pompeius highlighted their filiation in the civil wars as a means to acquire more, or a more stable, legitimacy. Both linked their fathers (by adoption or birth) to the divine and thus claimed a divine filiation for themselves. By exploiting such patterns, both men paved a divine-dynastic route to power, if we assume that Sextus Pompeius aspired to a permanent leading position.[110]

There are also discernible differences, however. Whereas Sextus Pompeius' divine filiation connects Neptune and his natural father Pompeius Magnus, and implied a claim to rule the sea, Octavian's divine filiation connected him above all to the god Caesar and, via the mythological lineage of the Julii, to Venus. And if we look at the connection between the Julii and Aeneas as well as Romulus that was emphasized in the Augustan Principate, the whole divine filiation becomes incorporated into a more traditional Roman tale about family origins in Troy and the descent from a god or goddess. Octavian's mythological and historical lineage was thus not restricted to a certain area (or as in the case of Sextus Pompeius, to a certain natural element) nor restricted to a particular god or goddess, since the connection to Caesar, Aeneas and Romulus left space to associate Octavian with more than one god or goddess. The examples I have cited from the Principate show that this led to the claim that Octavian/Augustus represented the fulfilment of Roman history.

The remarkable thing about their divine lineage is not that both rivals asserted it, but rather the way they used it; the link to their fathers made this filiation exclusive to Octavian and Sextus Pompeius. In a way, both enhanced existing models of the connection of Roman *gentes* to the divine, thought to be a part of some noble Republican families, yet at the same time, these examples of divine filiation exceeded Republican norms by claiming a status, and even rule, based on divine-dynastical filiation. That mode of legitimation broke fundamentally with Republican models of institutionally based legitimacy because it did not depend on an office, decree or election.[111] Their divine filiation thus employed seemingly Republican models, but their constructed descent also questioned the Republic itself, as it undermined the political system. Indeed, this is a symptom of the Imperial Age. In the Augustan Principate, Republican models were not abandoned. On the contrary, they were used, but in ways that led to the breakdown of the Republican political system itself.

Notes

*   I am very grateful to the editors of this volume, Richard Westall and Hannah Cornwell, for their suggestions and comments.
1. Bleicken 1990: 108; Rich 2018: 278.
2. For the Triumvirs and the *lex Titia*, see: Kienast 2009: 37–9; Lange 2009: 18 and for Cassius and Brutus and the decree of the senate, see: Welch 2002b: 35–6; Bengtson 1970: 24–40; Kienast 2009: 34; Gowing 1992: 63 n.17; Girardet 1993. While Girardet argues that we should not assume that Brutus and Cassius were totally without legal status (due to being proconsuls in Creta and Cyrenaica) before the decree of the Senate in spring 43, it is difficult to see why they should have been legitimized to recruit troops or command legions in Greece, Macedonia, Illyricum, and the Roman East before the decree of the senate in spring 43. For Cassius' and Brutus' recruitment of troops in the provinces, see: Botermann 1968: 84–108.
3. Access to institutional legitimacy could therefore depend on (military) power and thus could be enforced *per vim*: Börm and Havener 2012: 214.
4. Kienast 2009: 30–7; Alföldi 1976: 112–14; Rich 2018: 280–1; Kienast, Eck and Heil 2017: 53; Lange 2009: 17. Vell. 2.62 is particularly clear about the rift between Octavian and the senate.
5. Woodman 1983: 177–8; Augier 2018: 456.
6. Cass. Dio 47.12.2; 48.17.1; Welch 2002b: 37; Welch 2002a: 17–22; Augier 2018: 457–8.
7. Flor. *Epit.* 2.14.1-3 (tr. Edward S. Forster).
8. Wiseman 1974; Hölkeskamp 1999. For a discussion of how Augustus' promotion of Trojan ancestry shaped the perception of such ancestry in pre-Augustan times, see: Erskine 2001: 15–43.
9. Antonii: Plut. *Ant.* 4.1; 60.3; Julii: Suet. *Iul.* 6.1. For the Triumvirs and other late-Republican dynasts and their divine genealogies, see: Hekster 2006: 24.
10. He was known to be her favourite, but she was not connected to his *gens*. However, as Ramage suggests, we might understand Sulla's special relationship to Venus as pointing also to Venus being the ancestress of the Romans: Ramage 1991: 102. Ramage takes the oracle and dedication Appian mentions as hinting at such an interpretation: App. *BCiv.* 1.97.
11. For Caesar's emphasis of his descent from Venus as well as the connection of the Julii to Venus, see for example: Suet. *Iul.* 6.1; Wiseman 1974: 153; Weinstock 1971: 15–18; 80–90; Erskine 2001: 19–23; Westall 1996.
12. That is due to the rumours that the elder Scipio's conception is connected to an immense serpent: Liv. 29. 19.7; Gell. 6.1.1; Cass. Dio 16.57.39; *De vir. ill.* 49.1; Classen 1963: 319–21; Ogden 2009: 41–4 (with a discussion of when this myth was established).
13. While Wiseman asks: 'With a god in the family tree, who needed consuls?' (Wiseman 1974: 164). Hölkeskamp replies: 'Mit mehr als zwei Dutzend Consuln, diversen Dictatoren und Censoren im Stammbaum, wer brauchte da einen Gott?' (Hölkeskamp 1999: 20).
14. For parallels to horses being cast into the sea, see Albrecht 2020: 277 n.188. Note also Arrian reporting that Alexander the Great sacrificed bulls and different golden items by casting them into the sea: Arr. *Anab.* 6.19.5.
15. Flor. *Epit.* 2.18.3: *ut se maris rector in suo mari regnare pateretur* (tr. Edward S. Forster). Note that in the *Aeneid*, it is Neptune himself who claims an *imperium pelagi*: Verg. *Aen.* 1.138-139.
16. Words formed with the stem *reg-* are not necessarily negatively connoted, but they can relate to the rule of the kings in Rome and Tarquinius Superbus' expulsion. Such a topic was relevant for Sextus' contemporaries due to the rumours that Caesar aspired to be a king or was in fact a king. Therefore, such words could be used in late Republican invectives: Erskine

1991: 106–15; Sigmund 2014: 1–2; 10–13; Murray 1965. The word family can be used to refer to gods: Erskine 1991: 113; Sigmund 2014: 2. For Florus' terminology in this passage, which can be said to be negative, see: Kopp 2020: 274–84.

17. Some sources report a sacrifice but do not mention Sextus' intent to rule in the sea god's domain. Instead, it is reported that he thought he was the son of Neptune and some sources state additionally that he wore a blue cloak to signify his descent from Neptune: App. *BCiv.* 5.100.416-17; Cass. Dio 48.48.5 (both write about the blue cloak); *De vir. ill.* 84.2 (without the blue cloak). See further Massaro 1980.
18. Welch 2002b: 37.
19. For Miltner 1952: 2219–20 Sextus' seizure of Sicily is a direct consequence of his proscription. He therefore dates the seizure to autumn 43. For the chronological uncertainty regarding Sextus' seizure of Sicily, see Welch 2002b: 37–42.
20. Cass. Dio 48.18.1.
21. While Appian does not explicitly state that Salvidienus lost and only mentions that he retreated first, and both lost an equal number of ships (App. *BCiv.* 4.85.360-61), Cassius Dio and the summary of Livy clearly state that Salvidienus was defeated: Cass. Dio 48.18.4; Liv. *Per.* 123.1. See further Hadas 1930: 76.
22. Cass. Dio 48.18.3.
23. App. *BCiv.* 4.85.360.
24. Cass. Dio 48.19.1-2, here 2 (tr. Earnest Cary).
25. For a comparison of Sextus Pompeius' and Pompeius Magnus' commands, see App. *BCiv.* 3.4.11, who informs us that Sextus Pompeius was στρατηγὸν ... τῆς θαλάσσης, καθὼς ἦν καὶ ὁ πατὴρ αὐτοῦ; see further 4.84.353; Augier 2018: 457; Powell 2002b: 108–9. For the *lex Gabinia* and the nature of Pompeius Magnus' command, see Girardet 2007: 22–8 and Loader 1940.
26. While this is not what Velleius Paterculus (2.31.2), who focuses on Pompeius' command being an *imperium aequum* and his power extending fifty miles from the sea, has to tell us about the *lex Gabinia*, other authors emphasize that he received unlimited power over the whole sea: App. *Mithr.* 94.428; held a 'dominion over the sea' as Bernadotte Perrin translates: Plut. *Pomp.* 25.2; and Plin. *HN* 7.27 quotes the *praefatio* of Pompeius' triumph in 61 the following way: CVM ORAM MARITIMAM PRAEDONIBVS LIBERASSET ET IMPERIVM MARIS POPVLO ROMANO RESTITVISSET (...) TRIVMPHAVIT, showing that his command was perceived as an *imperium maris*. Although Appian, Plutarch, and Pliny tell us little about the actual legal dimensions of Pompeius' command, they can demonstrate that the command resulted in the perception that Pompeius had power over the (Mediterranean) Sea. Such a perception is also connected to the *cura annonae* that Pompeius Magnus received in 57, and that Plutarch described as Pompeius being κύριος over land and sea: Plut. *Pomp.* 49.
27. App. *BCiv.* 5.81.342-88.367; Cass. Dio 49.47.
28. App. *BCiv.* 5.87.366.
29. App. *BCiv.* 5.90.377 and 380 (tr. Brian McGing). While Appian describes the storm in greater detail, Cassius Dio also mentions the storm as being the reason why Octavian decided to end his attempts to seize Sicily: 48.48.1-5.
30. Cass. Dio 48.48.5.
31. Octavian's fleet suffered once more from a storm when he tried to approach Sicily to attack Sextus after immense infrastructural and naval preparations in 36: App. *BCiv.* 5.98.408-99.413; Cass. Dio 49.1.

32. App. *BCiv.* 5.100.416-417.
33. App. *BCiv.* 5.100.416 and 418. See further Kersten 2020: 227–9.
34. Gowing 1992: 309–10 discusses the meaning of Sextus' identification with Neptune and whether we should follow Appian's and Cassius Dio's suggestions. See too Welch 2012: 19–20, who deals also with Cassius Dio's and Appian's description and the question of whether later authors depict the way Sextus Pompeius claimed Neptunian ancestry as rightful.
35. Kersten 2020: 224–9; 231; Wendt 2020: 247–9.
36. Each obverse shows the same motif, although Pompeius Magnus' head points on the first type to the left (*RRC* 483/1) and on the second type to the right (*RRC* 483/2).
37. Welch 2012: 154; Trunk 2008: 129; Pollini 1990: 341; Woytek 2003: 504; Hollstein 2020: 162.
38. Hollstein 2020: 162 n.99; Buttrey 2013: 299–300.
39. Therefore, Sextus Pompeius' influence on the coinage leaves room for speculation. While Crawford 1974: I 495 suggested the coins were produced in a mint that was 'moving with Sex. Pompeius' and thus under his direct influence, Estiot 2006: 145; Woytek 2003: 504 and Trunk 2008: 129 suggest the coins were minted in Sicily after Sextus had seized the island. Such an attribution implies the influence of Sextus on the Nasidius-Denarii. Hollstein 2020: 166–7 takes a different approach. He discusses the idea that Nasidius is a Roman moneyer. Such a hypothesis implies a more independent production in Rome.
40. For an overview of the dating, see: Hollstein 2020: 163 n.103. And for his analysis: Hollstein 2020: 165, who argues for a date between 44–42.
41. For a new interpretation of the inscription, see Augier 2018.
42. Zarrow 2003: 132–4; Woytek 1995: 80; Estiot 2006: 142; Hollstein 2020: 142–3; Schäfer 2017: 346. But note La Rocca 1987–8: 267, who interprets the figure in the middle as Pompeius and not Neptune.
43. Not only did Sextus Pompeius slowly transform his name to Magnus Pius (Welch 2012: 108; Syme 1958: 174–5; Trunk 2008: 134; Zarrow 2003: 125–6) but he also minted the personification of *pietas* on his coins: *RRC* 477/1-3. As already shown, his father (and also his late brother) figured in his coinage in Sicily (even once without maritime references on the reverse of *RRC* 511/1).
44. Marrone 1998; Assenmaker 2011; Zarrow 2003. For the meaning of *pietas*, see Marrone 1998: 9; Assenmaker 2011: 97.
45. Liegle 1938; Powell 2002b: 122; 2008: 100–7; Trunk 2008: 134. However, the issue of dating remains. If we attribute the coin to the sea battle in 38, the coins are minted quite late – between 38 and 36. Recent analysis points to an earlier date (between 42 and 39): Hollstein 2020: 154; Estiot 2006: 144–5 and a connection to the battle in 42 against Salvidienus Rufus. But such an early date would not alter the interpretation itself – only attribute it to a different battle.
46. Hom. *Od.* 12.85-100; 118-125; 201-259.
47. Verg. *Aen.* 3.410-428. Intriguingly, in the *Aeneid* Scylla does not eat seamen anymore, but drags them onto the rocks of a strait. That is one way Octavian's crew faced death in the strait of Messina. See further Powell 2008: 100–11.
48. Kersten 2019: 190–3. Note that also *RRC* 511/2 includes on the reverse a reference to Scylla as part of a trophy, connecting Scylla to a victory as well as to the sea-god himself, who is depicted on the obverse and whose trident also forms part of the maritime trophy depicted on the reverse.
49. See n.34 above.

50. As can be seen on the reverse of *RRC* 511/1 and 511/3, that did not prevent Sextus from remembering his late brother and embedding him into his *pietas*-programme; see also *RRC* 477/2-3. Not only was his brother's death in the wake of the Battle of Munda in 45 a reason to include him in a familial *pietas*, but also his brother had already used his father and the notion of *pietas* in his own coinage and political programme: Buttrey 1960; the watchword of the Pompeii's fight against Caesar on the Iberian Peninsula had already been *pietas*: App. *BCiv.* 2.104.430.
51. For more details and the nature of the connection between Sextus Pompeius and Neptune see Kersten 2019.
52. For the coinage see: *RRC* 511/1-4. For the awarding of the prefecture see above n.6.
53. For his loss of the prefecture, see also n. 6. Suggestions for dating *RRC* 511 range from 42–36. Overview: Hollstein 2020: 148–52. A new analysis of coin hoards points to the beginning of that timespan: Estiot 2006: 144–5; Hollstein 2020: 152–5.
54. Cass. Dio 48.36.5; App. *BCiv.* 5.72.30. Achaia, Sicily, Sardinia, and other islands belonged to the domain he received. For an overview of the treaty, see De Souza 1999: 188–9; Berdowski 2011: 38–9.
55. Cass. Dio 48.36.4; App. *BCiv.* 5.72.305. Appian mentions that he was supposed to obtain the consulate *in absentia*.
56. Cass. Dio 48.31.5 informs us that during games in the run-up to the treaty of Misenum, the populace applauded a statue of Neptune during a procession to express their delight in Sextus Pompeius. See further Rosillo-López 2020: 187.
57. Powell 2002b: 107–8; Welch 2002a: 20–1; Zarrow 2003; Marrone 1998; Assenmaker 2011.
58. The new millennium saw a volume edited by Anton Powell and Kathryn Welch in 2002 (Powell and Welch 2002). Robin Seager convincingly entitled his review of the book *Sextus Pompeius: A Rehabilitation* (Seager 2005). In contrast with earlier scholars and especially Ronald Syme, who labelled Sextus Pompeius an adventurer (Syme 1939: 228, see also 166), both editors present a positive image of Sextus Pompeius (Powell 2002a: viii–xv, particularly xv; Powell 2002b: 127, Welch 2002b: 33, 54). For a general overview, see Kersten and Wendt 2020: 5–12.
59. Most clearly Welch 2012: 11.
60. Augustus famously pronounced in his *RGDA* 1.1: *annos undeviginti natus exercitum privato consilio et privata impensa comparavi*. See further: Gotter 1996: 57–8; Alföldi 1976: 73, who writes of a 'Privatarmee'; *privatus*: Lange 2009: 14–15.
61. Welch 2002a: 18.
62. For further honours see: Kienast, Eck, and Heil 2017: 53; Kienast 2009: 3-4; Alföldi 1976: 16–22.
63. Nic. Dam. 18.54-55; App. *BCiv.* 3.11.38.
64. Nic. Dam. 18.55-56; App. *BCiv.* 3.11.38-39; Alföldi 1976: 72; Kienast 2009: 26–7.
65. Nic. Dam. 18.56 (tr. Mark Toher).
66. As mentioned above, Octavian marched against Rome after the Battle of Mutina to obtain the consulship (above n.4) and the Triumvirs institutionally legitimized their position with the *lex Titia*: above n.2.
67. Gesche 1968: 82–91.
68. Gesche 1968: 90; Rowan 2018: 61–2; Sear 1998: 187–90.
69. For further examples and a discussion of when Caesar was perceived as a god, see: Alföldi 1973.

70. In association with *divus Iulius RRC* 540; to Octavian as *divi filius RRC* 535/2; and to Octavian as *divi filius* as well as to the deceased Caesar *RRC* 534/1. For post-27, see *RIC²* Augustus 37a-b; 38a-b; 102; 337; 338; 339; 340.

71. Cass. Dio 45.7.1; Gesche 1968: 68; Kienast 2009: 28; Ramsey and Licht 1997. For an overview of scholarship and discussion of whether the comet actually appeared during the *ludi*, see Matijević 2005: 63–4.

72. Overview: Rowan 2018: 57–65 (in competition with Antonius); Sear 1998: 87–91; see also *RRC* 490/4, 497/2a-d.

73. See further Rowan 2018: 60–1; Sear 1998: 88–9 n.132. On both obverse and reverse we can find the legend C CAESAR. While on the obverse, Octavian is named consul, pontifex, and augur, Caesar is named dictator for life and *pontifex maximus* on the reverse.

74. For Octavian's lack of institutional legitimacy in 44, see above nn.60 and 62. For a discussion of Octavian's institutional legitimation in 32 and the end of the triumvirate, see Bleicken 1990: 69–72; Girardet 2007: 333–62; Börm and Havener 2012: 205–7.

75. *Imperium pro praetore*: 2 January 43; first consulate: 19 August 43; triumvir: 27 November 43 probably until the end of 33 or 28 (for a discussion of this date, see above: n.74): Kienast, Eck and Heil 2017: 53–7.

76. Imperator Caesar Divi filius Augustus; see Syme 1958. For coins and inscriptions also using *divi filius* after 27, see Kienast 2001: 18–24, who argues that there is no turning away from Caesar after the end of civil wars and the beginning of the principate. Note also the entries of 40 and 36 of the Augustan *Fasti Triumphales Capitolini*, which also name Octavian *Divi f.*: *Inscr. Ital.* XIII 1.87, frag. XL. Interestingly, the inscription lists two filiations for Octavian. In addition to *Divi f.* we can read *C. f.* (son of Gaius). In both entries the second reference to Octavian's filiation (son of Gaius) has been carved over an erasure: Cornwell 2013: 19 n.46.

77. As Kienast 2001: 26 puts it: 'Die Abkunft vom Divus Iulius verlieh ihm eine von der Anerkennung durch den Senat unabhängige Legitimation'.

78. Pontifex, master of the mint, aedile, praetor, proconsul, consul, magister equitum: *MRR* 2.228; 275; 288; 293-95; 306; 318-319; Will 1996a.

79. Cass. Dio 44.22.2; Weigel 1992: 98. 44–5. See further Hayne 1971.

80. Cass. Dio 44.5.3; Simpson 2006: 628.

81. There is much speculation about why Octavian/Augustus did not deprive Lepidus of his priesthood: Simpson 2006; Ridley 2005: 297–8. This question seems quite pressing since Bowersock points to the immense importance of the priesthood for Octavian/Augustus and wants to view his accession to the priesthood in direct connection to the Ara Pacis and the themes connected to that monument. Bowersock concludes: 'the altar was also an eternal reminder of an eternal cult, that of Vesta and her priest, the *pontifex maximus*.' Bowersock 1990: 393. We might therefore be inclined to think that one element attached to the chief priesthood is the Romans' descent from Troy through Vesta. Octavian/Augustus represented that Trojan lineage as being directly connected to himself: see pp. 118–20.

82. For the date of death, see Weigel 1992: 98.

83. Kienast 2009: 55; Weigel 1992: 89–93.

84. Will 1996b; Gotter 1996: 41–6; for his offices, see *MRR* 2.236; 238; 254; 258; 260; 272; 286.

85. For the rhetoric, see: App. *BCiv.* 2.124. For Cicero and Antonius' intensified rhetoric of a politics of vengeance in summer 44, see Welch 2019: 67–9. For the funeral speech in particular, see App. *BCiv.* 2.143.599-147.614; Cass. Dio 44.35.4; 44.36-50; Plut. *Ant.* 14.6-8. It is not exactly clear if we should follow the mentioned sources. Welch 2019: 65–6 and

Matijević 2006: 96–110 discuss evidence for attributing a rhetoric of vengeance or at least the condemnation of those who rejoiced in Caesar's murder to another occasion.

86. *RRC* 488/1-2; Newman 1990: 52–5; Rowan 2018: 57–65; Sear 1998: n.118; 123. Note *RRC* 528/1a and 2a depicting a star below the head of Antonius on the obverse. We might be inclined to take the star as pointing to Caesar's apotheosis (or, as Gurval argues, to Antonius' role as *flamen* in the cult of *divus Iulius*): Gurval 1997: 50; see further Pandey 2013: 420. Therefore, we might think Antonius also claimed a special relationship with *divus Iulius*. If we accept that interpretation, we should still acknowledge that there is a fundamental difference between being the son of a god and being the priest of a god. Antonius, probably aware of who would benefit from the divinization, seemingly slowed down the process: Gesche 1968: 70–2; Matijević 2005. There is also a divergent interpretation of what the star signifies: Sear 1998: 165. In addition, we might take into account the fact that Antonius named his son (with Fulvia) Iullus Antonius. Syme interprets this choice of name in the wake of Caesar's death as showing 'loyal attachment to the Julii': Syme 1986: 75, see also 398.

87. Gowing thinks the speech is Appian's own composition: Gowing 1992: 68 n.28. Either way, it underscores the ancient reception of Octavian's position after Caesar's death.

88. App. *BCiv.* 3.18.66-67 (tr. Brian McGing).

89. App. *BCiv.* 3.11.73-40; 3.12.40-41; Nic. Dam. 18.56; Vell. 2.59.5.4–5. See further Botermann 1968: 14–19. However, Cicero and Octavian's stepfather seemingly were not delighted about his change of name and continued to call him Octavius: Cic. *Att.* 14.12.2. For the public reaction to Octavian's new name, see Schmitthenner 1973: 72–6.

90. App. *BCiv.* 3.2.2-4.10; see further Cic. *Att.* 14.6.1; 8.1; *Phil.* 1.5. Kienast 2009: 24. For further attempts at divinization, see Matijević 2005: 57–8.

91. See above n.70.

92. Octavian was apparently quite successful in attracting soldiers, as the desolate end of Lepidus' political and military career after the defeat of Sextus Pompeius in 36 shows: App. *BCiv.* 5.124.512.

93. All coins are minted before 27 BCE: *RRC* 482/1 (44–43 BCE); *RRC* 494/3a-b (42 BCE); *RIC*² Augustus 250/a-b (*c.* 34–29 BCE); *RIC*² Augustus 251 (*c.* 34–29 BCE). For the dates of the coins see: Crawford 1974: I 495; I 502; Sear 1998: 98 no. 150; 87 no. 130; 242 n. 395; no. 397–8; Rowan 2018: 76; 118–19; for an overview on suggestions for dating *RIC*² Augustus 250 and *RIC*² Augustus 251, see Dillon 2007: 35–7.

94. With the Forum Augustus was elaborating a genealogy (and its associated ideology) that was already central to the concept of the Forum Iulium of his adoptive father (see particularly the role of Venus Genetrix within the Forum: Westall 1996).

95. Verg. *Aen.* 1.286: *nascetur pulchra Troianus origine Caesar*. It is not clear if Vergil is referring to Caesar or to Augustus. This ambiguity leaves room for speculation: Horsfall 2013: 539; Holzberg 2015: 680; Austin 1984: 109.

96. Verg. *Aen.* 1.259-260.

97. Verg. *Aen.* 1.257-288.

98. Verg. *Aen.* 6.789-794 (tr. George P. Goold).

99. Cf. Erskine 2001: 17–18.

100. Verg. *Aen.* 8.626-731.

101. Verg. *Aen.* 8.678-681: *hinc Augustus agens Italos in proelia Caesar / cum patribus populoque, penatibus et magnis dis, / stans celsa in puppi, geminas cui tempora flammas / laeta vomunt patriumque aperitur vertice sidus* (tr. George P. Goold).

102. Zanker 2009: 205–6; 213; Ganzert and Kockel 1988: 155; Geiger 2008: 99; see also Ov. *Fast.* 5.545-578; Hist. Aug. *Sev. Alex.* 28.6.
103. Zanker suggests that a statue of the deified Caesar was part of the inner Temple: Zanker 2009: 198; 214. Ganzert argues that the apse of the inner temple could not house the supposed group of statues: Ganzert 2000: 105–6 see also Droge 2011–12: 101–5. There is a discussion of whether a statue of Caesar stood in the *Sala del Colosso*, but this is far from secure and there are also other statues under consideration: Droge 2011–12: 93 n.51; Spannagel 1999: 300–16. For the temple of Mars Ultor that Octavian promised after Philippi, see Suet. *Aug.* 29.1-2.
104. Ganzert/Kockel 1988: 156. The statue in the centre was the binding link between Aeneas and Romulus and thus between Venus and Mars. Therefore, as Droge puts it: 'the line of great men culminated in Augustus': Droge 2011–12: 94.
105. For Venus and Mars, see Zanker 2009: 198–204.
106. There are also tales about a serpent fathering Octavian by Apollo: Suet. *Aug.* 94.4; Cass. Dio 45.1.2-3; Ogden 2009; Kienast 2009: 230–8; Freyburger-Galland 2009: 18–23; for Trojan games at the *ludi Apollinares* of 40, see Cass. Dio 48.20.2; Freyburger-Galland 2009: 22; Lange 2009: 39–46; 166–81. For the connection of the Octavii to Mars, see Suet. *Aug.* 1. We can argue that Mars, as the father of Romulus and Remus, was also integrated into Octavian's Trojan-Roman genealogy. For a general overview of gods that played a central role for Augustus, see Kienast 2009: 227–44.
107. Or at least significant effort was made to suggest such that Trojan ancestry was a Roman tradition, as Erskine discusses: Erskine 2001: 15–43.
108. For an overview of Augustus' offices, honours, and priesthoods, see Kienast, Eck and Heil 2017: 53–8.
109. For the role of dynastical legitimacy and divine filiation in the Principate, see e.g. Gesche 1978.
110. Syme highlights this dynamic from the perspective of names. He compares, inter alia, the naming of Octavian/Augustus and Sextus Pompeius and concludes, for Sextus Pompeius, that the transformation of his name to Magnus Pius 'is revolutionary and foretells the monarchy.' Syme 1958: 175.
111. While I have discussed the connection of divine filiation and Roman tradition, the study could be extended by asking if such a divine-dynastical filiation is an example of a Hellenistic influence on Roman mindsets. For that vast field, see e.g. Chaniotis 2003: 442–3 mentioning similarities regarding the divinity of Hellenistic and Roman rulers, or Ogden 2009, who discusses to what extent the story of Octavian's fathering by a serpent is related to Alexander the Great. See, in addition, the study by Taylor 1931.

CHAPTER 5
NEGOTIATING THE FAILURE OF ROMAN HEGEMONY: THE EXPERIENCE OF ALLIED RULERS DURING THE CIVIL WARS (49–30 BCE)[*]
Bradley Jordan

1. Introduction

Allied rulers have long been recognized as a vital element of the Roman imperial edifice during the late Republic and early Principate. Typically, they provided troops, financial and logistical support for Roman military campaigns, information about regional events and maintained order within their area of influence in exchange for Roman acknowledgement of their position. Such figures are attested across the empire, from Gaul to North Africa, and were especially prevalent in Asia Minor and the Near East. Several – including Deiotarus of Galatia, Juba I of Numidia and Cleopatra VII of Egypt – played critical roles during the civil wars which wracked the Roman state from 49–30, by providing their allegiance and military support to competing *imperatores*. However, the impact of the events of this period on the rulers themselves remains under-researched. To fully understand the development of Roman rule in this period, it is necessary to analyse the experience of allies caught up in civil war: not only the opportunities afforded to them, but also the constraints on their agency and the realities of their junior position *vis-à-vis* Rome. This paper contextualizes allied kingship in the civil war period, the violent and dynamic transition of the central Roman state from a nominally Republican system towards an autocratic empire. Specifically, it addresses the question of how the breakdown of the Roman state between 49–30 affected allied rulers' experience of Roman 'empire'. Following a brief introduction to how allies functioned in the late Republic (here, the first century), this paper, first, assesses the competing demands on allied loyalty in the form of military support; second, it examines how Roman criteria underpinning the recognition of allied rulers changed through the period; and, finally, it investigates allied responses to this shifting landscape. I argue throughout that the events of the civil wars fundamentally altered the experience of Roman allies. On the Roman side, an emphasis on personal loyalty displaced the earlier reliance on dynastic ties or *fait accompli* of locally-held power in deciding whom to set up as rulers. Consequently, allies were forced to pay more attention to the internal politics of the Roman state and develop new strategies for negotiating the relationship. While Augustus later reverted to a dynastic model, this emphasis on personal relationships foreshadowed his broader approach to allies.

2. Allied experience of Roman 'empire' in the late Republic

Before commencing this enquiry, the limits of the available evidence must be acknowledged. The contemporary and near-contemporary written sources for the two decades c. 49–30, including Caesar's account of the civil wars, Cicero's letters, and especially the latter's speech *Pro rege Deiotaro*, are all Roman authored and preserve little of the allied perspective. Later historians, writing under the Principate, with the notable exception of Josephus, concentrate understandably on the movements and actions of major Roman figures.[1] While Strabo's *Geography* preserves a few incidental details, these largely relate to the geographic extent of allied rulers' spheres of influence rather than forming a coherent narrative. Only a handful of relevant coins and inscriptions survive from the period in question and offer a view of the self-presentation of these allied figures. Consequently, this study is necessarily based, on the one hand, on observation of the social dynamics between Roman magistrates and allied rulers, and, on the other, the decisions made by Roman administrators which directly affected allied rulers.

In recent decades, the position of allied rulers *vis-à-vis* the Roman state has been the subject of ongoing reassessment. In his foundational *Foreign Clientelae*, Badian (1958) argued both that the relationships between Rome and extra-Italian states were largely informal and that the *clientelae* of individual aristocrats played an important role in shaping policy. Although scholarship now acknowledges the distinction between Roman *patronatus* and the sociological category of 'patronage', the heuristic value of the latter remains contested. Wendt, for example, has recently argued that, irrespective of the terminology used by contemporaries, allied rulers were indisputably subordinated to the power of the Roman *imperium* and should be considered 'clients' of the Roman state.[2] However, several scholars have argued that the Roman insistence on using the discourse and terminology of *amicitia*, i.e. friendship, should be treated as meaningful. Most convincingly, Burton has highlighted the degree to which *amicitia*, even as a personal relationship, was often unequal and competitive. Pertinently, unlike patronage, which entailed a persistent obligation on the senior participant to protect the interests of the junior, *amicitia* was a looser framework.[3] Cicero, in his philosophical discourse *De amicitia*, has Laelius define *amicitia* as arising from the recognition of *virtus* (in this context, 'moral worth') similar to one's own, consequently strengthened through the exchange of *beneficia* ('favours' or 'gifts'), *studia* ('observing each other's interests'), and growing *consuetudo* ('familiarity').[4] As themes, reciprocity of conduct and loyalty to one another's interests were consistently voiced as major expectations of *amicitia* in Roman contexts.[5]

In practice, personal *amicitia*, as experienced through the letters of Cicero, depended on a stream of reciprocal favours, which created and sustained the relationship. While this suggests a more transactional approach than appears in *De amicitia*, Griffin has shown that the philosophical literature on the subject, from Xenophon through to the imperial period, routinely described 'friendship' as entailing *officia* ('obligations'). In simple terms, the bond of *amicitia* created through granting *beneficia* created an obligation incumbent upon the recipient to reciprocate.[6] While voiced and explored through a vibrant philosophical literature, this system was fundamentally grounded in real social relationships and had political heft. Given Cicero explicitly refers to nearly three quarters of his correspondents, including major antagonists such as M. Antonius, as *amici*, *amicitia*-discourse in a personal sense had a wide semantic range.[7] As an informal and voluntary tie, the invocation of *amicitia* spoke to a series of expectations about two individuals' conduct towards one another without more formal constraints.

The application of *amicitia* to the international sphere entailed some differences, not least an official act of recognition as *amicus et socius populi Romani* ('friend and ally of the Roman People').[8] Crucially, however, the international framework of *amicitia* overlapped in practice with personal *amicitiae* and relationships. While the declaration of a ruler as *amicus et socius populi Romani* formed a political relationship with the Senate and People, such recognition was effected through personal interactions with Roman agents. For example, we learn from Cicero that Ariobarzanes III was recognized as king *ex senatus consulto* on the motion of M. Porcius Cato the Younger in early 51.[9] Cicero reports that the same decree commanded: 'that I [Cicero] protect the king Ariobarzanes Eusebes Philorhomaeus, and that I defend the safety of his person and the integrity of his kingdom, and that I be as a guardian to both king and kingdom' (*Fam.* 15.2.4). However, we also learn that Ariobarzanes owed large sums to both Cn. Pompeius Magnus and M. Iunius Brutus. Both were men of immense influence, and both stood to benefit from his official recognition and continued safety.[10] Moreover, Cicero emphasizes that his counterpart governing Syria, M. Bibulus, refused to address Ariobarzanes as *rex* because, in his words, 'the Senate named him *rex* through my agency and commended him to my care' (*Fam.* 2.17.7).[11]

Importantly, to be successful, petitioners, royal or civic, had to engage personally with senators to secure their support. As early as 167, ambassadors from Teos were honoured for their tireless efforts in soliciting aid from their community's patrons, including at their morning *salutatio*.[12] While monarchs may not have been expected to present themselves in a similar fashion to Roman *clientes*, during the late Republic, several rulers, including Antiochus XIII Asiaticus and Ptolemy XII Auletes, visited Rome personally to petition the Senate. While present in the city, hospitality would often be provided by members of the Roman elite, as was the case with Auletes, hosted by Pompeius.[13] While governor, Cicero had frequent dealings with Antiochus I of Commagene, with whom he was already acquainted from the latter's time in Rome in February 54. The king had petitioned the Senate over a territorial dispute and his right, accorded in 59, to wear the *toga praetexta*. At the time, Cicero, as he exuberantly recounted to his brother, had opposed Antiochus' requests at every turn, partly to make a political point to the consul, Ap. Claudius Pulcher, who himself later preceded Cicero in Cilicia (*QFr.* 2.10.2-3). What is absolutely clear from these examples is the ongoing imbrication of international and personal 'friendships' between Rome, Romans and allied rulers throughout the late Republic.

Our best evidence for the day-to-day relationships between allied kings and Roman state actors during the late Republic comes from Cicero's letters during his governorship in Cilicia in 51/50.[14] During his governorship, both Deiotarus of Galatia and Ariobarzanes of Cappadocia travelled into *provincia Cilicia* to meet with Cicero in person. He also corresponded with Antiochus I of Commagene, Tarcondimotus – a minor ruler recognized by Pompeius in the Amanus range – and Iamblichus, phylarch of the Arabs. In two letters to the Senate, magistrates and People, Cicero recounts for the official record his dealings with the allies, revealing his expectations regarding their conduct.[15] First, in September 51, he writes that ambassadors from Antiochus had informed him of a Parthian army crossing the Euphrates, something later confirmed through letters from Tarcondimotus and Iamblichus.[16] This shows the extent to which allied rulers could provide critical information to Roman commanders. One major problem for pre-modern states was acquiring information regarding potential threats. Where (reliable) allied rulers were employed, Roman officials had a greater network of informants to draw on.[17] For example, Cicero comments on his uncertainties regarding Antiochus' loyalty, noting that 'some' (*nonnulli*) thought *ei regi minorem fidem habendem (esse)* ('that even less faith should be placed in this king') and waited for confirmation from more trustworthy sources. By contrast, he claims Tarcondimotus was regarded as 'the most faithful ally (*fidelissimus socius*) across the Taurus, and the most well-disposed (*amicissimus*) towards the *populus Romanus*' and that Iamblichus was thought 'to think well of and be a friend to our *res publica*' (*Fam.* 15.1.2). Second, Cicero refers to the material support, or rather, the lack of it, he expected to receive from the allies in response to this threat. He reports that he is sure of Deiotarus' loyalty and of support from his army, described elsewhere to Atticus as 'doubling his forces'.[18] However, the other kings, he claims, either cannot or will not provide reliable support: 'Cappadocia is empty, the remaining kings and tyrants reliable neither in resources nor loyalty' (*Fam.* 15.1.6). Though the circumstances did not favour Cicero, his words nevertheless emphasize the fact that Roman magistrates expected material support and loyalty from the allies in times of need.

By contrast, in the same official context, Cicero stresses that provision of support for rulers was even more contingent. He carefully describes the unprecedented nature of the *senatus consultum* enjoining him to protect the person and kingdom of Ariobarzanes, for example, before reporting that he had rejected the ruler's request for Roman troops to support his regime.[19] While Cicero here produces an official account of his actions for the Senate, pre-emptively defending his choices, this observation demonstrates a reluctance on the part of Roman institutions to issue broad instructions for the defence of specific allied rulers. Indeed, as Burton notes, Roman aid to allies in the second century, even where explicitly solicited, more often took the form of embassies and senatorial fact-finding missions than military assistance.[20]

In short, the Roman state expected that allied rulers would furnish local forces and logistical support for their campaigns in the region, suppress unrest in their vicinity and provide information on the events of import.[21] In return, they offered recognition of those rulers' positions and the possibility of support against internal and external threats. The framework of *amicitia* was not legally binding but did provide a firm discursive setting for the relationship between Romans and their allied counterparts.

3. Military support: negotiating a divided *res publica*

One crucial problem facing allied rulers after 49 was deciding which competing faction of Romans (each claiming to represent the *res publica*) to support. While this had been an issue for allies in earlier conflicts, notably the struggle between Sulla and his adversaries (88–81), the increasing connectivity of the Roman world, coupled with the wide-ranging campaigns of participants, contributed a new urgency to this dilemma.[22] For example, the city of Massalia in southern Gaul – a consistent Roman ally since the mid-third century – argued to Caesar that they intended to maintain a principled neutrality. Situated in a strategic location dominating the major land and sea routes from Italy to Spain, the city had consistently benefitted from Roman intervention in the region and had earlier hailed both Pompeius and Caesar as civic *patroni*.[23] After refusing to allow Caesar access to the city, the Massiliotes argued that (Caes. *BCiv.* 1.35):

> They understand that the *populus Romanus* is divided into two parties; it is neither within their judgement, nor their power, to recognize which has the more just cause … Accordingly, they ought to show [the two Roman commanders] equal goodwill, since [the commanders] showed them equal benefactions, and to remain neutral, neither aiding one against the other, nor receiving either into the city or the port.

Notwithstanding this argument, Caesar states that during the negotiations, they admitted the fleet of L. Domitius Ahenobarbus, thereby siding with his opponents.[24] While the truth of this claim cannot be assessed, Westall stresses that the Massiliotes would not have resisted had they been uncertain of success.[25] While Massalia's opposition certainly hindered Caesar's Spanish campaign, stripping him of three legions to invest the city and adding further strain to his supply lines, they were, ultimately reduced to surrender.[26] Without significant aid, the Massiliotes, like most other allied communities were unable to effectively resist either combatant.

Consequently, for most allied rulers, the decision of whom to support was comparatively straightforward. While Caesar was occupied in Italy and Spain in 49, the sources emphasize Pompeius' success in securing troops from several eastern allies.[27] Not only had the latter held the wide-ranging Mithridatic command from 66–61 – affording him a greater level of personal contact with allied rulers in the East than his opponent, whose own commands were in Spain and Gaul respectively – but the governors in the East at the outbreak of civil war overwhelmingly favoured his cause.[28] Deiotarus of Galatia faced a 'choice' similar to that of the Massiliotes. Cicero argues in *Pro rege Deiotaro* that the victorious Caesar should view Deiotarus not as a *hostem* ('enemy') but *amicum officio parum functum* ('a friend deficient in his obligations', *Deiot.* 9) because he preferred his *amicitia* with Pompeius to that with Caesar.[29] This language transferred the offence from the public to the private sphere. Deiotarus' transgression, while serious, was social and personal, not made against the Roman state.[30] Cicero goes on to note that Deiotarus *errore communi lapsus est* ('had fallen into a shared error', *Deiot.* 11) since, being accustomed to following the Senate's commands, he acted to support men who had taken up arms under the Senate's authority and magistrates who had been enjoined to defend the Republic. He further emphasizes the consistency of the information received by Deiotarus. He finally returns to the king's personal relationship with Pompeius, whose victories were well-known, whom he had often supported, and to whom he was bound by ties of *hospitium* and *familiaritas* ('and he came, either asked as a friend, or sent for as an ally, or recalled to service, as one who had learned to obey the Senate', *Deiot.* 12). Similarly, the author of the *bellum Alexandrinum* places in Deiotarus' own words the argument that he was compelled to support Pompeius due to the lack of any means of resisting and the fact that he received no contrary information. He is afforded a similar argument to that of the Massaliotes, viz. it was not his place to judge Roman disputes, simply to obey the Senate's commands (*BAlex.* 67). Finally, this author has Caesar frame his reasons for showing clemency to Deiotarus echo Cicero's emphasis on *amicitia* and *hospitium*, both in a personal capacity and in a broader social framework.[31]

The sources also provide more personal reasons for individual allies to side with a particular commander. Caesar himself recounts the defection of two Gallic brothers, the Allobroges Roucillus and Egus, whom he characterizes as holding *principatus* ('leadership') among their people for many years. He notes the many personal benefactions which he had granted to them, including political support among their own people, as well as land and wealth from defeated opponents. After they were discovered to have colluded at skimming off the pay of Caesar's Gallic cavalry, however, they sought to abscond to Pompeius' camp. Crucially, Caesar adds the detail that, beyond taking money and horses, Roucillus and Egus were accompanied by a 'considerable following' (*magno comitatu*, *BCiv.* 3.59-61).[32] At a minimum, this reveals that the Gallic cavalry included important figures of high status within their home statelets: the Allobroges were allies of Rome in 63 and, despite an uprising in 61, supported Caesar throughout his wars in Gaul.[33] It further demonstrates that Caesar could and did grant individual Gauls spoils and land. Finally, it strongly implies that, despite Caesar's attempts to write his allied contingents out of his account of the civil war, that these men had command over a significant number of their own countrymen.[34]

The discourse of personal *amicitia* and its opposite, *inimicitia*, also surrounds the intervention of allied rulers in North Africa. Caesar explicitly states that the decision of Juba I to assist his adversaries was predicated on an existing relationship of *hospitium* between Pompeius and the Numidian's predecessor, as well as the king's personal hatred for Caesar's *legatus*, C. Scribonius Curio. This latter *inimicitia* sprang from Curio's proposal, while tribune of the *plebs* in 50, to confiscate the kingdom of Numidia and convert it into *ager publicus*.[35] Peer goes so far as to claim that Caesar's own narrative acknowledges Juba's anger as justified.[36] Suetonius also mentions that Caesar himself, defending the interest of a Numidian client against Juba's father, Hiempsal, was personally involved in an altercation with Juba, pulling the latter's beard in frustration (*Div. Iul.* 71). According to Dio, Juba's success prompted the Pompeian senate in Macedonia to honour him as *socius atque amicus populi Romani*. In response, Caesar, honoured his own allies in identical terms, the brothers Bocchus II and Bogud of Mauretania.[37] In later examples, a similar pattern emerges. For example, in June 43, L. Cornelius Balbus, as *quaestor*, absconded to Bogud's kingdom with a significant amount of coin and bullion, possibly hoping to win him to a cause during a particularly complex period of civil strife.[38] Then, in approximately 38, a conflict broke out between the brothers: the victorious Bocchus, aided by Octavian's commanders in Spain, was subsequently recognized as ruler of Bogud's domains, while the latter fled to Antonius.[39] He met his end in 31, defending the port of Methone against an assault led by M. Vipsanius Agrippa.[40]

Allied communities and rulers in the eastern Mediterranean followed this broad trend. Strabo notes that Caecilius Bassus' revolt at Syrian Apameia in 46 had wide support among the minor allies of the region. He explicitly states that the support of one Alchaedamnus, ruler of a nomadic group based near the Euphrates, was predicated on perceived injustices suffered at the hands of Roman governors (16.2.10). Dio frames the success of the rivals P. Cornelius Dolabella and C. Cassius in securing support in terms of individual cities' attitudes towards Caesar, while Appian presents Rhodes, which, like Massalia in 49, sought to equivocate, as refusing to help Cassius out of friendship towards Antonius and Octavian.[41] Matters were further complicated by internal divisions and local rivalries. For example, Oinoanda sided with Brutus to spite their rival Xanthos and Tarsus sought to annex Adana as it supported Cassius.[42] In the absence of easy answers as to which faction of Romans to support, communities and rulers were forced to fall back on alternative strategies, grounded either in their personal experiences of individual Romans or the reactions of their own rivals and friends.[43]

Overall, these examples of military assistance demonstrate two points: first, that allies when faced with the dilemma of choosing a side to identify as the legitimate representatives of the Roman state tended to fall back on existing relationships, both positive and negative, established with major players; second, that in describing these choices, the language of international *amicitia* came increasingly to have a more personal register. As the civil war undermined the institutions of the *res publica*, allied rulers and communities relied on personal bonds of *amicitia* and *inimicitia* to dictate which Romans would receive their military support, with potentially grave consequences.

4. Roman grants of territory, recognition of new rulers

The consequences of choosing which Roman *imperator* to support stretched beyond the immediate risks to the military contingents despatched to the frontlines. Failure to back the right Roman risked reprisals in the inevitable restructuring following each round of victories. Pharsalus, Philippi and Actium were all followed by numerous changes to the constellation of allied rulers. Before Pompeius' wide-ranging reorganization of the East in the mid-60s, the removal and replacement of a reigning, nominally allied, monarch by Rome was unprecedented. Though Polybius reports that some senators sought to induce Attalus II of Pergamum to denounce his brother Eumenes II in return for a kingdom of his own in 167, he ultimately refused.[44] For the most part, Roman recognition of allied rulers reflected the situation on the ground. For example, in 163, the Romans recognized Antiochus V as king in Syria. His rival, Demetrius I Soter, at that time a hostage in Rome, after his escape, return and victory, was recognized in his turn in 160.[45] Similarly, in 158, after Orophernes of Cappadocia deposed his brother Ariarathes V, a Roman ally, the Senate decreed that they should rule together.[46] Throughout the late second and early first centuries, the Roman Senate consistently took a conservative line towards recognizing allied rulers.[47] Only when – as in the case of Jugurtha of Numidia in the late second century – an ally had alienated the Romans to the point of war were they disendorsed.[48] During and after Pompeius' campaigns, however, this pattern was increasingly violated; mostly to Rome's advantage.[49] In 65/64, Pompeius refused to reinstall Antiochus XIII at Antioch, leading to the creation of a Roman *provincia*, Syria. In 65, M. Licinius Crassus began agitating for Egypt to be made tributary to Rome – under the terms of the will of Ptolemy XI Alexander II – and in 63, the *lex agraria* proposed by the tribune Servius Rullus also envisioned the confiscation of Egyptian territory.[50] The ancient sources assert that the primary motive of these proposals was financial and personal.[51] By contrast, Cicero, speaking before the Senate, emphasized the importance of moral standards, as opposed to material considerations, in the treatment of allies: 'I shall not tolerate that this be seen as the policy of our empire, "If you do not give me anything, I will regard you an enemy; if you give me something, I will regard you as an ally and friend"'(*Reg. Alex.* fr. 7).[52] Hekster has highlighted both the complex politics behind the Egyptian throne and the degree to which Ptolemy XII Auletes astutely played off several Roman actors to achieve his desired outcomes in this period.[53] Nevertheless, the promulgation of a *lex* in 58, by P. Clodius Pulcher, appropriating the assets of Auletes' brother, Ptolemy, ruler of Cyprus, presented, as Tiersch stresses, the first occasion on which an allied ruler had been actively deposed by Rome without a previous war.[54] Hitherto, the loose rules of international *amicitia* had been followed. However, the aftermath of repeated civil wars posed two related problems for the Roman victors: how to treat allies who had sided with their opponents in good faith, and how to deal with power vacuums created by the death of allied leaders?

Caesar's decisions in the aftermath of the Alexandrian and Pontic campaigns show a degree of continuity with earlier approaches. Despite Deiotarus' prominent choice of Pompeius' side, Caesar seems to have explicitly recognized his right, granted *ex senatus consulto*, to the title of *rex* over Armenia Minor. By contrast, following complaints from other Galatian leaders, he stripped him of his control of the Trocmi and granted this to Mithridates of Pergamum 'by right of kinship and descent' (*iure gentis cognationis*).[55] This latter individual, already a prominent member of the Pergamene elite community during the late 60s,[56] was the son of Adabogiona, the sister of one Brogitarus, who held the Trocmian tetrarchy during this period and was recognized as *rex* in 58.[57] Mithridates had a close relationship with Caesar, evident from his accompanying the latter to Alexandria after Pharsalus and being despatched to collect reinforcements from Syria and Cilicia when conflict broke out.[58] His support was further rewarded after the defeat of Pharnaces, the son of Mithridates VI Eupator, at Zela in 47. Pharnaces, recognized by the Senate as *socius et amicus rex* in the Crimean Bosporus during the aftermath of Pompeius' eastern campaigns, invaded the province of Pontus-Bithynia in 48.[59] His governor, Asander, immediately revolted and later had him killed, Dio claims in the hopes that the Romans would recognize him as ruler.[60] Instead, Caesar chose to appoint Mithridates. The author of the *Bellum Alexandrinum* calls him 'born from royal stock' (*BAlex*.78) and claims that he served as a companion to the Pontic king for much of his youth. Meanwhile, Strabo, a near-contemporary and well-informed regarding events in Pontus, reports the allegation that Adabogiona acted as a concubine of Mithridates VI and that her son was by him (13.4.3). Whatever the truth, these near-contemporary rumours suggest that Mithridates was either acknowledged as having or was seeking to craft strong links to the former dynasty. Moreover, Asander himself married Dynamis, the daughter of Pharnaces; continued to employ Mithridatic imagery and titulature on his coinage; and was apparently successful in securing Roman recognition.[61] The confirmation of the positions of Hyrcanus, as high-priest in Judaea,[62] and Tarcondimotus, in Cilicia,[63] stand in a similar vein, while the appointment of Lycomedes as priest at Comana was justified through his lineage.[64] Even where Caesar did appoint new rulers, as with Ariarathes in Lesser Armenia or in extending the kingdom of Bocchus II, the beneficiaries were already royals and had clear cultural factors working in their favour. Caesar's record suggests that he preferred to rely on those already wielding power, where possible, or appointing individuals with dynastic links, whether real or asserted.

M. Antonius' decisions in the aftermath of the Parthian invasion of Syria and Asia Minor present a contrast.[65] The fortunes of Herod, known to posterity as 'the Great', offer particular insight into his alternative approach. In 41, Herod's political opponents accused him and his brother Phasael, before Antonius at Antioch, of dominating the government of Judaea, ostensibly that of the Hasmonean Hyrcanus, by force. According to Josephus, Hyrcanus' open support for the pair and the financial inducements the brothers offered led Antonius to appoint them as tetrarchs responsible for the government of Judaea (*AJ* 14.324-329; *BJ*. 1.244). In 40, the Parthians installed the nephew of Hyrcanus, Antigonus Mattathias, as their ruler of Judaea, prompting Herod to flee to Rome. Josephus states that, swayed by his father's loyalty to Caesar, both Antonius and Octavian supported a *senatus consultum* appointing him as king (*AJ* 14.381-385). In the following year, supported by the Roman commander Q. Poppaedius Silo, Herod embarked on a campaign to take back Judaea. Josephus claims that Antigonus argued to Poppaedius that Herod should not be granted the kingship (Joseph. *AJ* 14.403):

> but Antigonus, responding to the things which had been proclaimed by Herod, and before Silo and the Roman army, said that if they gave the kingdom to Herod, a private citizen and Idumaean, that is, a half-Judaean, it would be contrary to <u>their own [sc. the Roman]</u> concept of justice (παρὰ τὴν <u>αὐτῶν</u> δικαιοσύνην), as it was fitting for them to bestow it on one from the [Hasmonean] dynasty, as was their custom. (*Emphasis author's own*)

As Eckhardt demonstrates, Antigonus' argument rested on the claim that it was contrary to justice (δικαιοσύνη) and the custom (ἔθος) of the Romans to appoint as ruler a man who was not a member of the current (Hasmonean) dynasty. Moreover, Herod was not only a private citizen (ἰδιώτης), but an Idumaean, further clarified with the *hapax legomenon*, ἡμιουδαῖος ('half-Judaean').[66] The rhetorical attempt to exclude Herod from the Jewish community, introducing a further barrier to his kingship, relies on a definition of that community by descent, rather than praxis. Josephus preserves other echoes of this critique being levelled against Herod. His mother, Cypros, is explicitly identified as an Arab and not a member of the Jewish or Judaean communities (*BJ* 1.181; *AJ* 14.121). Moreover, Josephus states that Nicolaus of Damascus, a close confidant, invented a genealogy for his father, descending from returnees from Babylon, which demonstrates the importance of this issue to contemporaries.[67] However, the definition of community by descent in this period, was, at minimum, contested. Though Josephus demonstrates that the label 'Idumaean' retained some significance as late as the Flavian period,[68] the region had been integrated within the Hasmonean kingdom and its inhabitants as members of the Jewish faith since the late second century. Herod's grandfather and father had both wielded significant power within the Hasmonean kingdom, the former as *strategos* of Idumaea under Alexander Iannaeus, the latter as a close associate of Hyrcanus.[69] As Josephus emphasizes, the Herodian family's power was rooted in social networks rather than dynastic legitimacy.[70] Finally, most surviving arguments against Herod's legitimacy as ruler concentrate on his lack of orthopraxy.[71] Antigonus' appeal to descent rather than praxis as the marker of Jewishness, though touching on contemporary concerns, was far from a decisive objection.

More substantive, however, was Antigonus' claim that to appoint Herod as king would run contrary to Roman custom. As argued above, during the first century at least, this claim does follow typical Roman practice. Though the text of *1 Maccabees*, dating to the mid-second century, claims that Judas Maccabaeus' desire to seek a Roman alliance was rooted in their propensity to appoint their friends as rulers, and depose their enemies (*1 Macc.* 8:13). The author has a limited grasp of the operation of the Roman state, let alone its policy. As written, this could refer simply to the recognition of rulers without implying an active hand in 'regime change', to use Hekster's term.[72] By 40, however, potential Hasmonean dynasts were thin on the ground: Antigonus' alliance with the Parthians ruled him out; his predecessor as high priest, Hyrcanus, was a Parthian captive in Babylon; while the latter's grandson, Aristobulus (III) remained a youth. Eckhardt has stressed that Herod's marriage to Mariamne may have made him part of the dynasty from a Roman perspective explaining Antigonus' rhetoric of marginalization.[73] Nevertheless, the sources stress throughout the role of Herod's – and his family's – many services for a series of Roman commanders as a factor in his rise to power. The decision of the Roman Senate, advised by Octavian and Antonius, to establish him as *basileus* was not based on dynastic principles but his personal actions and relationships.[74]

However, in 39, Antonius went further: regions which had constituted Roman provinces for generations were bestowed upon local rulers. Lycaonia, mentioned as part of *provincia Asia* in 100, was assigned to Polemo, the son of a rhetorician from Laodicea-on-the-Lycus.[75] Meanwhile, parts of Pisidia, attested as part of *provincia Cilicia* since before 68, were assigned to Amyntas, a Galatian official, who had commanded Deiotarus' forces in the Philippi campaign.[76] Antonius also moved beyond confirming rulers based on the situation on the ground. Several of his appointees had no dynastic link to the region over which they were assigned leadership and some had little cultural connection with their nominal subjects. In plain terms, they were and would remain dependent on Antonius for their exercise of power over their subjects.[77] Though, in his first round of appointments, in 39, Antonius established Darius, son of Pharnaces II and grandson of Mithridates VI, in Pontus, this was an exception.[78] In 36, after the death of Deiotarus, Amyntas was also granted the position of king of Galatia. Though, as already noted, Galatian by birth, a high-ranking official and army commander for Deiotarus, he appears to have had no relation to the Deiotarid dynasty or other tetrarchs.[79] Meanwhile, Polemo's civic upbringing cannot have prepared him well to rule the sparsely inhabited Lycaonian highlands, nor the mountainous, multicultural Pontus, to which he was transferred after the death of Darius.[80] His original tetrarchy was at this point attached to Amyntas' kingdom.[81] For Antonius, as compared to earlier Roman commanders, dynastic legitimacy and cultural familiarity were factors of lesser importance when deciding between potential candidates. This policy may have been designed to ensure that individual appointees remained loyal to the triumvir, since their royal status rested on his continuing power. However, circumstantial evidence implies that, largely, the beneficiaries did not struggle to maintain their authority in the absence of Roman attention. An alternative explanation could be sought in Antonius' apparent attempts to take on the ambitions of Pompeius, who had delighted in his status as the *patronus* of kings and peoples.[82] Antonius' liberality with the title of *rex*, or rather βασιλεύς, is well-attested and an interest in generating a strong cadre of loyal allies able to support him in his rivalry with Octavian in an increasingly polarized empire, may explain his strategy. Crucial, in either case, is the markedly different context shaping Antonius' decisions. In the mid-60s, Pompeius' arrangements – for all his power on the ground in the East – was subject to senatorial oversight, which was in fact exercised.[83] By 41, Antonius, by virtue of the *lex Titia*, could be confident that his arrangements would not be interfered with, while ongoing tensions with Octavian and Lepidus pointed to the likelihood of future conflict.[84] Faced with an unprecedented situation with very few limitations, it is, perhaps, unsurprising that Antonius took an innovative approach.

After Actium, Octavian appears to have implemented a more ruthless policy towards the eastern allies than either Caesar or Antonius. According to Dio, he immediately deposed several minor rulers, including the sons of Tarcondimotus in Cilicia, Alexander of the Emeseni and Lycomedes of Comana (51.2.1-3). Strabo explicitly states that the latter was replaced by Cleon of Gordiucome, who had defected to Augustus before Actium and brought a Mysian contingent with him (12.8.9).[85] That said, these decisions were neither as wholesale nor as permanent as Dio implies. The appointees of Antonius to the major kingdoms, Amyntas in Galatia, Polemo in Pontus, Archelaus in Cappadocia, and Herod in Judaea, all survived. This may in part have been prompted by pragmatism: all seem to have been capable rulers and were well-ensconced in their respective kingdoms. Moreover, in 20, Augustus restored power to the homonymous sons of Tarcondimotus in Cilicia and Iamblichus at Emesa,[86] having already in 25 assigned Mauretania to Juba II, son of Caesar's enemy Juba of Numidia.[87] Cleon's successor at

Comana was Dyteutus, son of the Galatian Adiatorix, whom contemporary accounts claim Octavian initially intended to execute. Strabo, somewhat implausibly, goes so far as to claim that this appointment was motivated by the *Princeps'* remorse (12.3.6, 35).[88] It is worth underlining that upon the death of Amyntas, the majority of the Galatian kingdom became a new *provincia*, with most of Cilicia reverting to Archelaus of Cappadocia.[89] Imperial policy remained fluid – dictated by context and the flow of events – rather than becoming dogmatic. Nevertheless, over the course of his lengthy Principate, the newly minted Augustus chose again and again to prioritize dynastic continuity where possible.[90]

Overall, the civil war period represents a decisive shift in Roman state policy towards the appointment and confirmation of allied rulers, predicated on the outsized power of individual commanders *vis-à-vis* state institutions. While van Wijlick has carefully argued that the scope of bilateral relationships between allied rulers and Rome was unaffected by the outbreak of civil war – an expectation of assistance on request remained and Roman recognition was highly sought – there was, nevertheless, a change in the intensity, an increase in stakes and a new emphasis on personal loyalty as a means of navigating the troubled times.[91] For Caesar, like many of his predecessors, dynastic continuity was a major motivating factor in his decision-making. Even the appointment of Mithridates of Pergamum to rule the Bosporus was linked to near-contemporary rumours of a dynastic connection. However, Antonius' sweeping changes to Roman administrative practice were echoed in his appointment of rulers to kingdoms within which they had little previous legitimacy or, especially in the case of Polemo, connection to. One potential explanation is that, in the absence of meaningful oversight, Antonius' rivalry with his Roman colleagues encouraged him to promote individuals who owed their positions directly to him. Limiting the opportunity for Roman rivals to spring up may also have been a consideration.[92] The precariousness of Roman rule in the East in the aftermath of the Parthian invasion of 40/39 may also have prompted him to depend on the personal loyalty of his appointees in place of enthusiasm of the populace at large. Moreover, by appointing individual rulers, Antonius simplified the process of administration; limiting the amount of resources expended on direct administration of justice and taxation.[93] There is no reason to doubt that contributions of some kind continued to roll in from Antonius' appointees, and we similarly see significant allied military aid attending him both in Parthia, where Polemo was captured, and at Actium.[94] After Antonius' defeat, Octavian moved back in the direction of continuity, albeit with Antonius' appointees as the beneficiaries. Ultimately, however, the victory at Actium underlined the practical point that allied rulers henceforth were to be appointed and confirmed by the new *Princeps*.

5. Allied responses to the breakdown of Roman hegemony

The fragmentation of the Roman state and a concomitant shift in importance away from interstate *amicitiae* towards personal relationships prompted a change in approach by individual allies. While Hekster has shown that this trend was already evident from the

80s, the civil wars after 49 acted as a further violent catalyst.[95] In the aftermath of Pharsalus, having pursued Pompeius to Egypt, Caesar intervened decisively in the ongoing civil war between Ptolemy XIII and his sister Cleopatra VII. Notwithstanding his initial attempts to mediate, stressed throughout his own account,[96] the dictator eventually cemented his most famous lover's power in Alexandria. Moreover, it seems that Caesar may also have returned control over the island of Cyprus to the Egyptian throne. Dio's claim (42.35.4-6) that Caesar designated Arsinoë and Ptolemy XIV as rulers of the island during the initial negotiations is suspect and Strabo (14.6.6) claims that Antonius made this grant without providing a date.[97] However, clear evidence for a Ptolemaic presence exists from 43, when one Serapion, τὸν ἐν Κύπρῳ τῇ Κλεοπάτρᾳ στρατηγοῦντα ('ruling in Cyprus for Kleopatra', App. BCiv. 4.61, 5.9), provided naval assistance to C. Cassius Longinus, while subsequent Ptolemaic governors are attested throughout the 30s.[98] Given Antonius' struggles with political capital during his consulship in 44, the transfer of the island back to Cleopatra likely had already been authorized by Caesar and was perhaps among the *acta* confirmed after the dictator's death.[99]

The sources also accentuate Caesar's personal connection to Mithridates of Pergamum, whom he appointed both as tetrarch of the Trocmi and as *basileus* over the Bosporan kingdom in 47. As noted, Mithridates was a powerful figure in his own right with some connection to both territories. However, the author of the *bellum Alexandrinum* and Strabo both mention his close relationship with Caesar in the context of these decisions. Indeed, the former refers to him as 'a trusted and honoured friend of Caesar'.[100] In the cases of Cleopatra and Mithridates, their personal relationships with Caesar were perceived by contemporaries as the crucial factor behind the benefactions they received.

The ancient sources stress that one driving principle for Antonius' decision-making was his liberality towards his friends and supporters. One major example was his decision in 36 to appoint Archelaus Sisines as ruler of Cappadocia after the summary execution of his predecessor, Ariarathes X, in mysterious circumstances. Sisines' father had held the hereditary priesthood of Ma at Comana, a powerful, semi-independent basis of support within Cappadocia, but had been deposed by Caesar in 47. Intriguingly, Strabo explicitly denies Sisines any relationship to Cappadocia (12.2.11). According to Appian, Antonius appointed him under the influence of his mother Glaphyra, whom he coyly describes as a woman beautiful in appearance (καλὴ φανείση, App. BCiv. 5.7). Octavian's crude invective in the context of the Perusine war, quoted by Martial, strongly implies that they were lovers (Mart. 11.20).[101]

This feeds into Antonius' treatment of his most famous paramour, Cleopatra. In 37, Antonius awarded her control over formerly Ptolemaic territories in Phoenicia, Coele Syria, Cyprus, parts of Cilicia, Judaea and Nabataea.[102] This grant, while extensive, fits easily within the scope of Antonius' broader reorganization of the Roman East. However, in 35/34, he went further, reaffirming Cleopatra's control over these regions, while declaring his children by her rulers in their turn: reportedly, Alexander Helios received Armenia and the East, Cleopatra Selene, Cyrenaïca, and Ptolemy Philadelphus, Syria and Asia Minor.[103] Though most scholars agree that the so-called 'Donations of Alexandria' had minimal impact on the continuing Roman administration of the eastern provinces,[104] numismatic evidence does suggest a change in the status of Cyrenaïca, then governed in conjunction with Crete. First, over thirty specimens of a bronze series, minted in Cyrenaïca, have been found bearing the legend ΑΝΤΩ(νιος) | ΥΠΑ(τος) | Γ (Antonius *cos.* III) on the obverse, and ΒΑΣΙΛ(ισσα) | ΘΕΑ | ΝΕ(ωτέρα) (Queen [Cleopatra] Thea Neotera) on the reverse, associating the two in a position of authority.[105] Second, a bronze series minted at Knossos and Cyrene by one CRAS(sus), most likely P. Canidius Crassus, a close associate and commander for Antonius, began to use crocodile iconography, which Draycott connects to Cleopatra Selene's putative rule.[106] Cleopatra also took care to engage with Antonius' Roman supporters, including Canidius. A celebrated papyrus bears a royal ordinance from 23 February 33 granting the commander and his descendants tax exemptions on his Egyptian estates and set measures of imported wheat and wine.[107] This supplements Plutarch's claim that she persuaded Canidius to intercede with Antonius on her behalf through lavish bribes (Plut. *Ant.* 56.4).[108]

Moreover, the sources highlight the impact that their close relationship had on the fortunes of other allied rulers, for good or for ill. Strabo frames the success of one Aba, who had married into the Teucrid dynasty at Olba, in securing recognition of her power as due to her repeated petitions to both ('but later both Antonius and Cleopatra made that [kingdom, viz. Olba] a gift to her, moved by her petitions', 14.5.10). Similarly, Josephus records that Alexandra, the daughter of Hyrcanus, wrote to Cleopatra asking for her intercession with Antonius to ensure her son, Aristobulus', nomination to the high priesthood of Judaea; again, concerning her confinement by Herod after Aristobulus' appointment; and a third time, seeking justice for Herod's alleged murder of the youth.[109]

Another example of the personalization of allied strategies for engaging with Roman actors can be seen in a well-attested series of bronze coins issued by the Cilician dynast Tarcondimotus after his grant of the title of βασιλεύς in 39.[110] The obverse bears the dynast's portrait in the so-called 'Philorhomaios' style, imitating the veristic portraiture in vogue at Rome during the late Republican period, rather than more idealized Hellenistic models.[111] The reverse iconography shows Zeus Nikephoros, a typical late Hellenistic image, and bears the legend ΒΑΣΙΛΕΩΣ ΤΑΡΚΟΝΔΙΜΟΤΟΥ ('of king Tarcondimotus'), accompanied in the exergue by the epithet ΦΙΛΑΝΤΩΝΙΟΥ ('Philantonios' or 'friend to Antonius'). This adapted the increasingly common first century practice of allied rulers referring to themselves as φιλορώμαιος ('friend to the Romans'), first attested with Ariobarzanes I of Cappadocia in the late 90s or early 80s,[112] and itself drawing on the widespread employment of *philos*-compounds by rulers throughout the Hellenistic period. It is now broadly accepted that use of this title did not indicate a formal status, such as *amicus et socius populi Romani*, but was adopted locally as part of a ruler's self-fashioning for a variety of audiences.[113] In this instance, Tarcondimotus acted an innovator, highlighting his close personal relationship with Antonius in a public fashion and prefiguring the later commonplace φιλόκαισαρ. Suspène suggests plausibly that this strategy negotiated the multi-polarity of the triumviral Roman state, firmly declaring support for one of the major players and recognizing that the city of Rome no longer formed the centre of the imperial edifice.[114]

As the civil wars progressed, personal bonds between Roman actors and individual rulers tended to exert less of a hold. Though Caesar claims in the context of Roucillus and Egus' defection that he received many deserters from Pompeius, especially from Epirus and Aetolia (Caes. *BCiv.* 3.61), there is no evidence that any allied ruler switched sides before Pharsalus. Conversely, during the Philippi campaign, after the first, inconclusive, battle, Amyntas, then commanding a Galatian force on behalf of Deiotarus, switched his support from Brutus to Antonius and Octavian. He may have been accompanied by Rhascyporis, a Thracian leader, who at least abandoned Brutus' cause, while some Germanic troops passed in the opposite direction.[115] Finally, in the prelude to Actium, the sources report several defections by prominent Romans and allied rulers, notably Amyntas, Deiotarus Philadelphus of Paphlagonia, Rhoemetalces of Thrace and Cleon of Gordiucome.[116] The personal characteristics of Roman commanders likely shaped the choices of individual kings. Pompeius, for example, had a record of brutality from his early commands in the Sullan civil war.[117] However, the perception of success seems to have played an important role. Caesar, admittedly with his own agenda, paints a convincing picture of a confident Pompeian camp.[118] By contrast, the situation after the first battle of Philippi was uncertain: while Brutus remained in a strong strategic position, the death of Cassius had a ruinous effect on morale.[119] Similarly, blockaded at Actium, Antonius' forces were suffering from lack of supplies and disease.[120] Even beyond this, the prolonged series of civil wars must have emphasized the risk inherent to backing the wrong Romans.

One final anecdote, relayed by Josephus, illustrates the latitude afforded to allied rulers by the breakdown of Roman authority. In the aftermath of Actium, before rushing to confer with the victorious Octavian, Herod had Hyrcanus, his father-in-law and last surviving male Hasmonean, killed. While the ruler's own autobiography claimed to have uncovered a plot with Malichus of Nabataea to displace him, Josephus argues that this was invented to secure his own position as king (*AJ* 15.161-178; *BJ*. 1.433-434). Importantly, this stands in stark contrast with his later practice. As Czajkowski has demonstrated, Herod repeatedly chose to involve Roman officials in his decision-making over the dynastic machinations of his sons,[121] which should, however, be viewed as a product of the resurgent capacity of the Roman state in the East.

Overall, the evidence shows that the breakdown of the authority and capacity of the Roman state acted as a catalyst for allied leaders to focus their attention on personal relationships with individual Romans instead of institutions. The doubt as to which faction would ultimately be victorious in successive civil conflicts posed a dilemma for most allies and a strong personal relationship with a powerful Roman figure could provide immediate benefactions and a secure starting-point for choosing a side should conflict re-emerge. This is not to say that allied rulers lacked agency, however – several chose to abandon their benefactors when the odds shifted or, like Herod, took advantage of Roman distractions to secure their domestic political situation. The crucial factor in driving allied choices in the chaos of civil war was their interest in their own personal security and protecting their own power base.

6. Conclusions

The breakdown of the Roman state had a major impact on Roman hegemony and the allied 'experience' of empire. Throughout the first century, a considerable overlap had already emerged between the discourses of interstate and personal *amicitia*. As the institutions of the Roman state ceased to function normally and as individual Romans became more powerful the instrumentality of these friendships became more obvious to all participants. The outbreak of civil war further catalyzed this process – as it became impossible to maintain an *amicitia* with a singular Roman state, personal relationships necessarily became more significant in determining which action to take. As Crawford has emphasized, the existence of a Roman citizen diaspora in provincial and allied locales, which supported the rise of alternative state structures, can only have complicated this process for allied agents.[122]

The interests of individual *imperatores* pushed them to grant territory and honours to useful allies, in the hope of retaining their loyalty or demonstrating to others the rewards of choosing the 'correct' side. For their part, the allies themselves were incentivized to prioritize generating strong personal relationships with powerful Roman actors. Individual rulers pursued various strategies to establish these relationships, ranging from the prompt furnishing of military forces and supplies, through the use of iconography, such as Tarcondimotus' use of the title *philantonius*, to the cultivation of personal, even private, relationships. In all cases, the capacity of individual allies to respond to this rapidly changing situation was critical to their maintaining a firm grip on their position.

One reason that Caesar, and later Octavian, did not make large scale changes to the cast of allied rulers, despite many choosing to side with their opponents, may well have been pragmatism. However, Antonius intervened substantially and was apparently successful both in retaining the loyalty of his appointees and choosing capable subordinates. Amyntas and Polemo, the rulers of the two largest allied kingdoms in the East, were retained *in situ* by Octavian, while the ever unpopular Herod, in Judaea, could eventually be spoken of as one of the pre-eminent φίλοι ('friends') of the *Princeps* and his right-hand, Agrippa (Joseph. *BJ* 1.400; *AJ* 15.361). While Josephus certainly exaggerates the closeness of this relationship, Herod was able to demonstrate his loyalty and utility to the regime. In simple terms, he was able to exercise agency in ways which benefitted the man now at the centre of the Roman state. As Josephus had Herod argue to Octavian shortly after Actium: 'I have come to you, having hope of safety in your virtue and anticipating that you consider closely, what kind of friend, not whose friend, I have been' (*BJ* 1.390). As Augustus came to consolidate power within the Roman state, the importance of dynastic principles to the recognition of allied rulers returned. However, his unparalleled influence cemented the primacy of personal relationships in imperial decision-making.

A final example, that of Juba II, son of Juba of Numidia, is revealing. Brought to Rome as a child and exhibited in Caesar's African triumph in 46,[123] he seems to have been educated in Rome, perhaps, as Roller speculates, in the house of Octavia.[124] Dio states that he had accompanied Augustus on campaign, perhaps at Actium or alongside Augustus' own nephew and stepson, Marcellus and Tiberius, in Spain (51.15.6). In 25, he married Cleopatra Selene, the daughter of Antonius and Cleopatra, and was appointed to rule Mauretania, the former kingdoms of Bogud and Bocchus, which appear to have been left without explicitly defined administration since the latter's death in 33 (Str. 17.3.7). Though lacking a specific claim to Mauretania, Juba was indisputably royal, of North African descent, and had enjoyed the benefit of a Roman education and upbringing.[125] However, he was also a member of the imperial household through his marriage to Antonius' daughter Cleopatra Selene. Their son, Ptolemy, was, as Fishwick highlights, 'fatally related to [the *Princeps*] Gaius'.[126] Consequently, in Juba's appointment we see the consequences of two decades of civil war, whereby his personal ties to the *Princeps* fully displaced the concept of state-based *amicitia*.

Notes

[*]   I would like to thank Hannah and Richard for their invitation to contribute and their helpful remarks on draft versions of the paper. I am also grateful to Kimberley Webb for her comments on early versions, as well as Michael Economou, Benedikt Eckhardt and Hugh Elton for valuable conversations and critiques which have improved the final paper. The research was primarily carried out with the welcome support of the Alfried Krupp von Bohlen und Halbach Stiftung during my stay at the Universität zu Köln, graciously facilitated by Prof. Dr Walter Ameling. Naturally, any errors remaining and all views expressed are my own. All dates are BCE, unless otherwise stated. Finally, I am aware of Traina (2023) but have, unfortunately, been unable to take advantage of this recent work; see the discussion in the introduction.

1.   Though occasional moments of clarity exist, note especially Plut. *Ant.* 68.7-8, discussed at Westall 2017: 227–8.
2.   Wendt 2015; cf. Saller 1982: 11–15; Verboven 2002: 50–62; 2003; Winterling 2008: 298–301.
3.   Braund 1984; Eilers 2002: 12–14; Burton 2003: 2011, 28–33; Kaizer/Facella 2010: 15–22; Snowdon 2015. While Suetonius describes rulers as attending on Augustus, togate and *sans* royal insignia, *more clientium* ('in the manner of *clientes*', *Aug.* 60), this use is quite clearly metaphorical (Millar 1996: 162). Similarly, the oft-cited analogy of the second century CE jurist, Proculus, drawn between groups subject to unequal treaties with Rome and personal *clientes* provides a functional comparison in a legal context (Eilers 2002: 12–14; Kaizer and Facella 2010: 16–22). As such, I follow the sources in describing these figures as *reges amici et socii* ('friends and allies') rather than 'client-kings'.
4.   Cic. *Amic.* 29-30.
5.   Brunt 1988: 355–60.
6.   E.g. Cic. *Off.* 1.48; Sen. *Ben.* 3.18.1; Griffin 2003b, esp. 97–9.
7.   Brunt 1988: 361–70; White 2010: 24–6, 122–3; Burton 2011: 63–70.
8.   Braund 1984: 23–6; Burton 2011: 79–81.
9.   Cic. *Fam.* 2.17.7; 15.2.4-8; 15.4.6; Facella 2019.
10. Facella 2019: 196–205.
11. Facella 2019: 194–5, *pace* Shackleton Bailey 1977: 461.

12. *Syll.*³ 656.19-27; Braund 1989: 137–9; Westall 2015a: 28–34.
13. Cic. *Rab. Post.* 6; Siani-Davies 1997: 322.
14. Lintott 2008: 253–67.
15. On the inclusion of these 'official' letters in the corpus and their implications: Martelli 2017. More generally, White 2010: 51–6, 60–1, 167–70.
16. Cic. *Fam.* 15.1.2.
17. For the third and second centuries, Burton 2011: 192–4; see also Cicero's reliance on equestrians such as P. Vedius for information, Cic. *Att.* 6.1.25.
18. Cic. *Fam.* 15.1.6, 15.2.2; *Att.* 5.18.2. It is also to be remarked that two Ciceronian letters from this period emphasize the extent to which information for commanders and the Senate was both crucial and highly contingent. First, in August 51, Cicero wrote to Cato that he had not informed the Senate of a rumoured Armenian raid on Cappadocia, as Antiochus of Commagene (irrespective of his untrustworthiness) had claimed he was doing so and M. Bibulus, possibly arrived in Syria, would be better placed to comment (*Fam.* 15.3.2-3). Then, in September 51, Cicero wrote to Atticus, informing him of a Parthian invasion of Syria, but concerned that his command might be extended, added: *scripsi ad senatum, quas litteras, si Romae es, videbis putesne reddendas* ('I have written to the Senate – if you are in Rome, please look at them and judge whether they should be delivered', *Att.* 5.18.1). In each case, providing information to the Senate was not a foregone conclusion, whereas private letters were naturally expected. Compare Cicero's civil war correspondence, White 2010: 10. Cf. Nicholson 1994.
19. Cic. *Fam.* 15.2.4-8; Facella 2019: 193–4.
20. Burton 2011: 229, 237–43.
21. Braund 1984: 92; Schulz 2015: 38–41.
22. E.g. Hiempsal II of Numidia during the Sullan civil war: Hekster 2012: 188–9.
23. Eilers 2002: 96–7.
24. Caes. *BCiv.* 1.34-36; cf. Cic. *Att.* 10.10.4, 10.12A.3; Vell. 2.50.3; Suet. *Ner.* 2.2.
25. Westall 2017: 141–7.
26. Caes. *BCiv.* 1.35, 2.1-16, 22.
27. In May 48, as Caesar and Pompeius attempted to outmanoeuvre each other outside Dyrrhacium, Cicero's son-in-law, P. Cornelius Dolabella wrote across the lines to persuade him to abandon the Pompeian cause. He argued that despite Pompeius' *gloria* and his *clientela* of kings and peoples, the tide had turned in Caesar's favour. Dolabella dismisses Pompeius' extensive allied support, adding the crucial detail that the latter would boast of his connections (Cic. *Fam.* 9.9.2).
28. Jehne 2015: 303–6.
29. On the *Pro rege Deiotaro* and the unprecedented nature of this 'trial' of an allied ruler: Bringmann 1986; Loutsch 1994: 412–22; Nótári 2012: 101–4.
30. Coşkun 2005:140–2.
31. *BAlex.* 68; see Ritter 1969, persuasively arguing this implies a prior connection between the two men.
32. Caesar's explanatory note at *BGall.* 7.40 that, having been cast out by his tribe, the Aedui, his adversary Litaviccus nevertheless escaped together with his followers (*suis clientibus*), as Gallic custom saw it as sacrilegious to abandon their leaders (*patronos*), indicates both that the deserters may have taken a substantial group with them and that Roman concepts of patronage were more flexible.

33. For the situation in 63, see Cic. *Cat.* 3.4. For that in 61: Caes. *BGall.* 1.6, 7.64; Liv. *Per.* 103.3; Cass. Dio 37.47.1-48.2. For Aeduan support of Caesar in the 50s: Caes. *BGall.* 1.10-11; 3.6; 7.64-65.
34. Kavanagh 2001; Westall 2017: 69–71.
35. Caes. *BCiv.* 2.25.4; Cass. Dio 41.41.3; Luc. 4.688-492; Bertrandy 1990–1: 290; Amela Valverde 2000: 254–7.
36. Peer 2015: 85.
37. Cass. Dio 41.42.7; see Westall 2017: 166–7 on the implications for the free flow of information between the various factions in the civil war.
38. Cic. *Fam.* 10.32.1-2.
39. Cass. Dio 48.45.1-2; cf. Liv. *Per.* 127.6; Roller 2003: 93–4.
40. Str. 8.4.3; Cass. Dio 50.11.3.
41. Cass. Dio 47.30-33; App. *BCiv.* 4.65-68.
42. For Oinoanda and Xanthos, see App. *BCiv.* 4.79. For Tarsus and Adana, see Cass. Dio 47.31.2; Börm 2016; cf. Hispalis and Carteia in Spain, *BHisp.* 35-37.
43. Van Wijlick 2015: 62–3.
44. Polyb. 30.1.1-3.7; Liv. 45.19.1-20.3.
45. Polyb. 31.33.1-4.
46. App. *Syr.* 47; cf. Polyb. 32.10.1-8; Diod. 31.32; Ballesteros Pastor 2008: 46–8.
47. As opposed to interfering in allied state politics, see Hekster 2012: 184 n.2.
48. This conservative approach is seen in their consistent support for deposed or expelled monarchs during the late second and first centuries: e.g. Nicomedes IV of Bithynia and Ariobarzanes I of Cappadocia, against Socrates and Ariarathes, installed by Mithridates VI Eupator (Memnon *FGrH* 434 22.1, 5; App. *Mith.* 10). Contrast with those *reges socii et amici*, who became enemies of Rome, each accused of some violence against Rome or other allies: e.g. Jugurtha (violence against Hiempsal, Adherbal and Roman *negotiatores*: Sall. *BJ.* 12.1-5; 26.3), Mithridates VI (Bithynia and Cappadocia: App. *Mith.* 12); and Ariovistus (Aedui: Caes. *BGall.* 1.35.2, 40.2; App. *Gall.* 22).
49. *pace* Van Wijlick 2020: 232.
50. Plut. *Crass.* 13.1-2; Cic. *Leg. agr.* 2.43-44.
51. Siani-Davies 1997: 312–13; Westall 2017: 286–7.
52. Crawford 2002: 317–18.
53. Hekster 2012: 195–200.
54. Tiersch 2015: 254–60; see Badian 1965: 110–13 with ancient references; Morrell 2017: 116–22.
55. *BAlex.* 67, 78; Str. 12.4.3; Mitchell 1993: 33, 35, with additional references.
56. Cic. *Flacc.* 17, 41.
57. Str. 13.4.3; *I.Didyma* 475.35-41; cf. *OGIS* 348; Cic. *Har. Resp.* 28-29.
58. *BAlex.* 26-28; Joseph. *AJ* 14.127-136.
59. App. *Mith.* 13; *BCiv.* 2.91; Cass. Dio 42.45.1-3.
60. App. *Mith.* 120; Cass. Dio 42.46.4.
61. [Luc.] *Macr.* 17; Cass. Dio 54.24.4; Nawotka 1992: 23, 30–1; Primo 2010: 159–62, cf. *CIRB* 30.

62. Joseph. *BJ* 1.193-200; *AJ* 14.127-138.
63. Wright 2009: 73–4; 2012: 74–5, with earlier literature.
64. *BAlex*. 66; Sullivan 1978: 920.
65. *pace* Van Wijlick 2020, esp. 209–33.
66. Eckhardt 2012: 92–9.
67. See Joseph. *AJ* 16.183-186; Cohen 1999: 17.
68. Appelbaum 2009.
69. Joseph. *AJ* 14.10; Jacobson 2001: 25.
70. Joseph. *AJ* 14.8-12, 43, 120-122; Van Wijlick 2020: 141–2, 154–7.
71. Eckhardt 2012: 94–6.
72. *pace* Hekster 2012; Eckhardt 2012.
73. Eckhardt 2012: 103–4.
74. It should be noted that Antigonus' most efficacious recourse was to simple bribery of individual Roman commanders (Van Wijlick 2015: 57–61).
75. The boundaries of the region initially granted to Polemo evade definition. Strabo, our best-informed source for territorial changes in Asia Minor and chronologically closest, states explicitly that Polemo held Iconium in Lycaonia (12.6.1). Appian suggests that he was assigned 'part of Cilicia' (*BCiv*. 5.75), which, given this region had formed part of *provincia Cilicia* as recently as 50, represents an understandable conflation. More helpfully, Pliny, in a passage likely drawing on Augustan sources, notes the separate existence of a Lycaonian *conventus* district, based around Philomelion, and a Lycaonia tetrarchy, including Iconium (*HN*. 5.95). Syme argued persuasively that this latter territory was that assigned by Antonius to Polemo (Syme 1995: 218–19). Dmitriev's reasons for rejecting this seem to be based on a misunderstanding (2000: 363–6), presuming that Polemo's grant of Lycaonia included the *conventus* district at Philomelion and the 'tetrarchy' based around Iconium. Moreover, while Pliny's evidence may well have post-dated the formation of *provincia Galatia* in 25, we have plentiful evidence for territorial divisions persisting long after their functional obsolescence.
76. Str. 12.5.1, 6.1-6; Mitchell 1994: 102; Coşkun 2008: 135–6.
77. Pilhofer 2020: 81.
78. App. *BCiv*. 5.75.
79. *SEG* 44.1113. Mitchell 1994; Coşkun 2018: 208.
80. Str. 12.6.1, 8.16.
81. Str. 12.6.1.
82. Cic. *Fam*. 9.9.2. Compare Antonius' purchase of Pompeius' house, Cic. *Phil*. 2.71-73; Plut. *Ant*. 10.2; *Caes*. 51.
83. Vell. 2.40.5; Plut. *Luc*. 42.5-6; App. *BCiv*. 2.9; Cass. Dio 37.49.1-50.1.
84. Vervaet 2020: 33–8.
85. cf. Cass. Dio 51.2.2.
86. Cass. Dio 54.9.2.
87. Syme 1995: 163; Roller 2003: 73–4, 98–100; Wright 2012: 77–9.
88. Mitchell 1993: 40–1.
89. Str. 14.5.6; Cass. Dio 54.9.2.

90. Note also, the emergence of complex marriage alliances between these allied dynasts: Jacobson 2001: 24.
91. van Wijlick 2020: 209–33.
92. Cf. his treatment of P. Ventidius, Plut. *Ant*. 34.3-5; Cass. Dio 49.21.1-3.
93. Kaizer and Facella 2010: 36–42; Hekster 2010: 53–5.
94. Plut. *Ant*. 61.1-2; Cass. Dio 50.6.5, 13.5, 8, 14.2; on Polemo: Cass. Dio 49.25.4; Plut. *Ant*. 38.3.
95. Hekster 2012.
96. Caes. *BCiv*. 3.106-112; *BAlex*. 33.
97. Bicknell 1977: 330.
98. For subsequent Ptolemaic governors in the 30s, see *Salamine de Chypre* XIII #97; Mitford 1980: 1292. Compare also coins issued in 44/43 depicting Cleopatra with the infant Ptolemy XV Caesarion and the legend ΚΥΠΡ (e.g. Κύπρος). Svoronos 1904: 1874; Bicknell 1977: 331–4.
99. Bicknell 1977: 331–4.
100. *BAlex*. 26, 78; Str 13.4.3; cf. App. *Mith*. 121.
101. Syme 1995: 144, 148–50.
102. Plut. *Ant*. 36.2; Cass. Dio 49.32.5; cf. Joseph. *AJ* 15.92-95, 1.361.
103. Plut. *Ant*. 54.3-6; Cass. Dio 49.41.1-3.
104. E.g., Welch 2006–7: 189–92; Borgies 2016: 303–7.
105. *RPC* 1.924-925. On the epithet Θεὰ Νε(ωτέρ)α, see Muccioli 2004.
106. *RPC* 1.914, 917; Draycott 2012: 49–52, cf. *RGDA* 27.3.
107. *P. Bingen* 45, with van Minnen 2000: 32–4; Hanson 2001: 304–5.
108. *pace* Pelling 1988: 256.
109. See respectively, Joseph. *AJ* 15.24, 45, and 62-64.
110. *RPC* 1.3871; Plut. *Ant*. 36.2; Str. 14.5.18.
111. Smith 1988: 130–2; Fleischer 1996: 37; Wright 2008: 118.
112. Simonetta 1977: 39–42; with Dmitriev 2006 on the historical debate.
113. Braund 1984: 105–8; Facella 2005: 94–9.
114. Suspène 2009: 47–9.
115. Cass. Dio 47.48.2.
116. Vell. 2.84.2; Plut. *Ant*. 63.3; *Mor*. 207A; Str. 12.8.9; cf. Cass. Dio 50.13.5-8.
117. Val. Max. 6.2.8; though cf. Batstone and Damon 2006: 93–4; Morrell 2017: 4, 65 n.51.
118. Caes. *BCiv*. 3.82-83; cf. Cic. *Att*. 11.4; Plut. *Pomp*. 67.4-68.1.
119. Plut. *Brut*. 46.5; App. *BCiv*. 4.123-124.
120. Vell. 2.84.1-2; Cass. Dio 50.12.8.
121. Czajkowski 2016.
122. Crawford 2008: 634–9.
123. App. *BCiv*. 2.101; Plut. *Caes*. 55.
124. Roller 2003: 61–4.
125. Cf. Suet. *Aug*. 48.
126. Fishwick 1971: 472.

CHAPTER 6
BROTHERS AT THE CROSSROADS: AGRIPPA AND HIS BROTHER IN CIVIL WAR*
Sabina Tariverdieva

In the civil war between Caesar and Pompey, two members of the humble *gens* Vipsania found themselves in the inner circles of the leaders of the opposing parties. Young Marcus Agrippa was the closest childhood friend of Caesar's grand-nephew Octavius and probably took part in Caesar's war against Pompey's sons in 45.[1] We know from Nicolaus of Damascus that, due to his illness, Octavius was unable to go to Spain with Caesar, but instead followed him only after he had recovered. We also know that Octavius took with him only a small number of slaves. Later, however, after his arrival at Caesar's camp, we find Octavius accompanied by three friends whom he wished to take with him on the ship sailing from Tarraco to Carthago Nova.[2] Marcus Agrippa may well have been one of these 'friends'. There are other passages in Nicolaus where he mentions Octavius' friends, and a comparison with other sources shows that Agrippa is usually included in this grouping. Consider, for example, the episode in Apollonia: 'Young Caesar spent three months sojourning here [Apollonia], where he was admired by his *comrades and friends*, marveled at by the whole city and praised by his tutors'.[3] Agrippa is not named here, but, from Suetonius and Velleius, it is clear that he was among these 'comrades and friends' (Vell. 2.59.5; Suet. *Aug.* 94.12). In *FGrHist* 130 F 41, Agrippa is not named either, but we know from Velleius (2.59.5) that it was Agrippa, together with Salvidienus, who advised the young Caesar to accept assistance from the Macedonian legions. Another example is provided by Nicolaus himself: 'And this seemed best to him in his deliberations and to the rest of his *friends* who participated in that campaign and in the actions afterward. These were *Marcus Agrippa*, Lucius Maecenas, Quintus Iuventius, Marcus Modialius and Lucius * *'.[4] Hence, we can assume that, when Nicolaus mentions 'friends' or 'comrades' of Octavius, Agrippa is included among them. That may also be the case in the Spanish episode, and the war in Spain was arguably Agrippa's first military experience.[5] Commenting on this passage, Mark Toher writes that '[i]t is clear from the three comrades ... that Octavius was accompanied to Spain by more than just household servants'.[6] Although this is possible and tempting, it is not necessarily the case. Octavius' friends, including Agrippa, may well have accompanied Caesar to Spain while their ill friend had to stay at home and then they could have simply met again in Caesar's camp, when Octavius arrived following his recovery. In any case, we can be sure that Agrippa was already a close friend of Octavius by 46 (Nic. Dam. *FGrHist* 127 F 16).

As for Agrippa's brother, he supported Cato out of friendship, following him to Africa, where he was taken captive, before Caesar pardoned him at Octavius' request (Nic. Dam.

FGrHist 127 F 16), so he already was close enough to Cato in 49. Here, it is worth noting the Greek wording used by Nicolaus when he describes the relationship between Octavius and Agrippa on the one hand and that between Cato and Agrippa's brother on the other. Of Octavius and Agrippa, he writes: 'there was a particular associate and friend of Octavius, Agrippa, who had been educated at the same place and who was a very special friend of his'; of Agrippa's brother and Cato: 'the brother of Agrippa had supported Cato out of friendship'. Clearly in both cases Nicolaus is talking about friendship (φιλία). In certain contexts, the word φιλία can have the same meaning as the Latin *amicitia*, i.e. personal and political friendship, but the young Octavius could hardly have had a political friendship with his classmate Marcus Agrippa at the age of sixteen. While the case of Agrippa's brother and Cato could well be different and include a political friendship, the relationship between Agrippa and Octavius seems to have been closer and more personal. However, irrespective of these details, the prominence of the two brothers in the opposing parties remain rather curious, since the Vipsanii were neither famous nor noble, and evidently they had not been members of the Roman political elite before the civil war between Caesar and Pompey.[7] D. R. Shackleton Bailey notes that in the civil war between Caesar and Pompey personal sympathies seemed to play much more important a role in choosing sides than social stratum or family loyalty.[8] This seems quite reasonable and possible for the members of the political elite, who had different relationships with one another and the personal component may have well become the decisive one, but the humble origin and obscurity of the Vipsanii makes it worth investigating how and when they got those personal sympathies. In other words, how and why did the two brothers enter the immediate circles of Caesar and Cato, and how were they able to become friends with such figures as Cato and Caesar's grandnephew?

1. What do we know about Agrippa's brother?

We have almost no evidence concerning Agrippa's brother. Indeed, apart from the short episode in Nicolaus discussed above, we have only one, even shorter, mention in Dio Cassius about the moderation of Agrippa, who 'did not accept a triumph, although one was voted at the behest of Augustus, but showed moderation in these matters as was his wont': Dio says that 'once, when asked by the consul for his opinion about his brother, he [Agrippa] would not give it' (Cass. Dio 54.11.6 describing Agrippa's moderation when he declined a Spanish triumph in 19 BCE). It is clear that this episode took place when Agrippa had already acquired power and authority, but its date and exact nature are uncertain. As the name of Marcus Agrippa's father was Lucius (i.e. the inscription on the Pantheon: *CIL* 6.896), and given that Romans usually gave their first son the same *praenomen* as their father, we can assume that Agrippa's brother, who made friends with Cato and took part in the civil war in 47, was the elder brother and bore the name Lucius. As we have almost no information about this man in the sources, it is impossible to say what the difference of age was between him and Marcus. It well may have been two or three years (as it was between Claudii Marcelli brothers (*coss.* 51 and 49) or between the three Antonii who were the sons of M. Antonius Creticus) or more than ten years as may have been the case with the sons of Gnaeus Domitius Ahenobarbus (*cos.* 96).[9]

2. The origin of Marcus Agrippa

As a result, we have to return to the circumstances of Agrippa's early youth and examine the beginning of his friendship with Octavius. This has the potential to shed light on the fate of his brother. As a starting-point, let us examine the origins of the young Caesar and Marcus Agrippa, for the humble origin of the latter is an element often emphasized in the sources. In fact, the origins of Octavius were unpretentious enough. His father, Gaius Octavius, was the first senator in the family (Suet. *Aug.* 2.3).[10] He became praetor in the year 61, after which he was the governor of Macedonia, where soldiers proclaimed him *imperator* (*CIL.* 6.1311). In 59, he died suddenly and therefore did not participate in the consular elections (*MRR* 2.179, 185, 191). It was also said that he practised usury and distributed bribes at the elections (Suet. *Aug.* 3.1; 70).[11] Octavius' grandfather and other paternal ancestors were *equites* from Velitrae, and it is quite likely that one of his great-grandfathers was a freedman (Suet. *Aug.* 1; 2.2–3; 4.2; *ILS* 47=*CIL* 6.1311; Münzer 1937: 1805). Octavius' mother Atia was the daughter of Marcus Atius Balbus, a praetor in the year 60, and Julia, a sister of the dictator Caesar. Balbus' father, that is, Octavius' great-grandfather, came from Aricia. It seems that his family was wealthy and influential in the town, and his ancestors were probably members of the local senate (Suet. *Aug.* 4.1-2).

If we turn now to the family of Marcus Agrippa, our sources often emphasize the humble origin of the great general (Vell. 2.96; Sen. *Controv.* 2.4.12; Tac. *Ann.* 1.3.1; Suet. *Cal.* 23.1), often contrasting Agrippa's achievements with his humble beginnings. It is also interesting to note that Agrippa's grandfather is mentioned neither in the *Fasti Capitolini*, nor in the inscription on the Pantheon.[12] From the text of the *Fasti Capitolini* it is quite obvious that usually the grandfather was mentioned in Agrippa's day. Therefore, this may indicate that he was not a Roman citizen and that the Vipsanii family only received their citizenship after the Social War.[13] Today, there are several theories about the origin of the Vipsanii. Schulze points out that names ending in -*anius* (as well as -*ane*, -*anus*) are usually connected with some geographical place, but he does not give a specific place of this type for the Vipsanii.[14] On the basis of epigraphic evidence, the *gens Vipsania* has been credited with Illyro-Celtic[15] or Illyro-Venetian origins[16], as most of the inscriptions containing this *nomen* appear in Dalmatia and Venetia. However, Jean-Michel Roddaz rightly notes that these inscriptions are difficult to date, so we cannot be sure that any of them predate Agrippa's birth (the opposite is more likely).[17] Wiseman has analysed some of the inscriptions of Agrippa's freedmen and makes the plausible suggestion that the *Marcus Vipsanius Marci libertus* from the *Sergia* tribe mentioned in *CIL* 6.28996 may share the same tribe as his patron. Therefore, Agrippa may have had Marsic or Asisian origins; Sabini and Paeligni also belonged to this tribe, but Wiseman disregards them, as Agrippa's father seems to have been the first Roman citizen in their family.[18] Unfortunately, this remains only a suggestion and cannot be proved decisively.

Overall, I agree with Wiseman's conclusion: 'Agrippa's camouflage of his origins was too efficient [...] the name is found all over Italy thanks to Agrippa and his clients, and may not be accurately localized'.[19]

As such, we have the following picture. Despite his kinship with Caesar, Octavius had rather modest origins, and it can hardly be the case that his childhood was spent only in the company of Roman nobles. His family was more noble and more famous than that of the Vipsanii, but the social divide between the young Octavius (who, at that moment, had not been adopted by Caesar) and Agrippa was not as great as it might appear.

3. Agrippa's acquaintance with young Octavius

Now let us turn to the question of their acquaintance with one another. Today, there exist two main hypotheses. According to the first, Agrippa served in Caesar's army, and it was the dictator who introduced Agrippa to his own grand-nephew Octavius. According to the second, Agrippa and Octavius became acquainted at rhetorical school. Rather more exotic speculation also exists: it has been alleged that Agrippa was Caesar's 'natural son',[20] that he was the 'Prügelknabe' of Octavius,[21] and that his father was the rhetor Atticus Vipsanius, who supposedly taught Octavius.[22] But these last three proposals have not met with serious consideration from scholars. Therefore, I shall concentrate on the first two in what follows.

In the sources, we have Pliny's words about Agrippa's miserable youth (*misera iuventa*, *NH* 7.45) and a rather vague phrase from Manilius – *et Cato fortunae victor, matrisque sub armis miles Agrippa suae* (*Astron.* 1.797-798) – which is sometimes understood to mean that Agrippa started military service early (see below, for detailed analysis of Manilius' text). On the basis of this evidence, Meyer Reinhold makes the following suggestion: at the beginning of the civil war between Caesar and Pompey, Marcus Agrippa, not a member of the elite and the descendant of an obscure family, was enlisted in one of Caesar's legions at the age of only fourteen or fifteen, distinguished himself in the war, and attracted the attention of Caesar, who then introduced the young Agrippa to his grandnephew.[23]

This hypothesis has been challenged by Rudolf Hanslik and Roddaz.[24] First, the age of fourteen or fifteen is too young for a youth to distinguish himself on military service.[25] Second, we know that Agrippa did study with Octavius and was well-educated, as we can see from Pliny's report of Agrippa's 'magnificent oration [...] on the advantage of exhibiting in public all pictures and statues; a practice which would have been far preferable to sending them into banishment at our country-houses' (Plin. *HN* 35.9; tr. by Bostock and Riley). We could hardly expect this from a youth who began his military service at the age of fourteen. Some other considerations can be added to these objections. Pliny mentions Agrippa's *misera iuventa* among his many other misfortunes, which were portended by the unusual manner of his birth (feet first).[26] Some of these misfortunes are obviously exaggerated, for example: the misfortunes brought on Agrippa by his descendants, especially by the two Agrippinae, the younger of whom had not even been born at the time of Agrippa's death; or Augustus' 'grievous tyranny' to which Agrippa was subjected. Thus, the 'miserable youth' may also be a rhetorical exaggeration. But even if not, this passage may well refer to the real misfortunes of Agrippa's youth, namely his participation in the civil wars after the death of Caesar. When Pliny describes the eighteen-year-old young Caesar in 44, he also uses the phrase *in prima iuventa* (*NH* 2.98), So, the word *iuventa* in this passage might also refer to an age above fifteen or sixteen.

As for the text written by Manilius, it is damaged, and the manuscript phrase is incomprehensible if we translate *armis* as 'weapons'.[27] It has been suggested that this word should be interpreted as 'shoulders' and, then, the phrase would mean 'Agrippa, the soldier on his mother's hands'.[28] If we accept this interpretation, the poetic exaggeration is obvious – Agrippa could in no way be a soldier in his infancy. However, this explanation, on which Reinhold bases his hypothesis, is not certain. For example, in the Loeb Classical Library edition another correction is suggested, and this yields another meaning: 'Agrippa, who proved in arms [...] the maker of his destiny'.[29] It has also been suggested that *matris* be read as *patris* or *Martis*, so that the phrase would mean 'the soldier under the arms of the father (meaning father-in-law, Augustus)' or 'the soldier under the arms of Mars'.[30] The version in the Loeb edition seems to me to be the most convincing, but whichever emendation is correct, none of them implies that Agrippa started his military career as early as the age of fourteen or fifteen.

Even if we agree with the hypothesis proposed by Reinhold, however, some further questions arise. First, in order to attract Caesar's attention, the young Agrippa would have had to have earned some kind of distinguished military decoration, but there is not even a hint in the sources of such an event, even though we would expect such an outstanding deed presaging Agrippa's brilliant career to be known to us. Second, let us return to the episode I have already mentioned, which took place after Caesar's return from the African war. Nicolaus reports (*FGrHist* 127 F 16):

> There was a particular associate and friend of Octavius, Agrippa, who had been educated at the same place and who was a very special friend of his. His brother was with Cato and treated with much respect; he had participated in the Libyan War, but was at this time taken captive. Although Octavius had never yet asked anything of Caesar he wanted to beg the prisoner off, but he hesitated because of modesty and at the same time because he saw how Caesar was disposed toward those who had been captured in that war. However, he made bold to ask it, and had his request granted.

It appears from this passage that Octavius studied for some time with Agrippa and that the latter became his closest friend at some time before the year 46, in other words, at the time when Agrippa, according to Reinhold's assumption, ought to have seen military service in one of Caesar's legions. Third, if Caesar thought so well of Agrippa as to introduce him to Octavius, then it is unclear why the young Marcus had to wait for Octavius' help, rather than appealing directly to his protector Caesar. Finally, Reinhold's hypothesis does not explain the friendship of Agrippa's brother with Cato. If Agrippa was introduced to the Roman aristocracy by Caesar, then who did the same thing for his brother (who was equally of humble origin), when did they do it, and how did they do it in such a way that this brother found himself precisely on the opposite side and in the inner circle of Cato?

Challenging Reinhold's hypothesis and drawing on Nicolaus' text, Hanslik assumes that the friendship between Agrippa and Octavius may have begun during their joint study at rhetorical school, as the Vipsanii family was rich enough to give Marcus a good education in Rome.[31] Marx argues, even more specifically, that the two youths became acquainted at Apollodorus' school,[32] and both Toher[33] and Roddaz[34] agree with his assumption. The education of boys was divided into several stages. In the first stage, they studied grammar and arithmetic. Children of members of the upper class were usually educated either in their own homes or in the homes of neighbours or friends who had a specially trained slave teacher, such as Chilo in the house of Cato Major.[35] After that, children were taught by grammarians (at home or at a special school), and only later did their rhetorical education begin. Usually, boys started rhetorical education at twelve to fifteen years of age. So, if we assume that Agrippa and Octavius became acquainted at Apollodorus' school, then it could not have happened any earlier than 51 or 50. However, if Agrippa found himself a student of the same teacher as Octavius and became acquainted with the latter at school, then there is still no answer to the question of when and how his brother (likewise not a member of the Roman *nobilitas*) was introduced to Cato, and by whom? It is my contention that Nicolaus' evidence allows us to propose another hypothesis about the circumstances of Octavius' acquaintance with Agrippa, and this can also provide us with an answer to the question regarding Agrippa's brother.

4. Agrippa and his brother: on opposing sides in the civil wars

At the time of the civil wars, it was possible for members of a single family to fight on different sides, but it is unusual for the Vipsanii brothers, members of the same humble and obscure family, to have found themselves in the inner circles of Caesar and Cato, the leaders of the opposing parties. In my opinion, this could only have happened if the Vipsanii had had a patron among the Roman nobles who was equally well connected with both parties. In fact, it is not difficult to find such a person and, interestingly, it was at his home that the young Octavius spent his childhood and adolescence. Lucius Marcius Philippus, consul in the year 56, gave his daughter from his first wife in marriage to Cato (Plut. *Cat. Min.* 25, 37, 39, 52) and he himself married Atia, Caesar's niece and Octavius' mother, and thus became the stepfather of the future Augustus (Nic. Dam. *FGrHist* 127 F 5; Suet. *Aug.* 8). Nicolaus tells us that, for one thing, Agrippa and Octavius studied together and, for another, that Philippus exerted control over the company kept by his stepson (Nic. Dam. *FGrHist* 127 F 6):

His mother and her husband Philippus watched over him and enquired every day from the teachers and attendants they assigned to accompany the boy what he did, where he went, how he passed the day and with whom he spent his time.

In his article devoted to the role of Philippus in Octavius' life, Michael Gray-Fow accords his stepfather even more importance.[36] According to Gray-Fow, Philippus taught his stepson political strategy and gave him useful advice which Octavius always followed. Many of Gray-Fow's conclusions seem interesting, but they are rather speculative and unsupported by the sources. However, as young Caesar moved to Philippus' house and was at that time around seven years old, when the role of father became more and more noticeable in the life of a Roman boy, there can hardly be any doubt that Philippus played an important role in the young Octavius' life. We can also add that, at some point, Atia Minor, young Caesar's aunt, married the son of Philippus by his first wife, thus adding a new link between the two families (Ovid *Fast.* 6.801; *ex Pont.* 1.2.139).

The case of kinship between Philippus and Cato is more complicated. In the second half of the 60s, Cato married Marcia, Philippus' daughter, divorcing her in the late 50s to allow her to marry the orator Hortensius, with whom she had a child. After the death of Hortensius, Cato again married the daughter of Caesar's relative in the year 49.[37] So Cato took care to ensure close relatives in Caesar's circle, just before the beginning of the civil war. This was remarkable forethought on the part of Cato, the self-styled man of principle.

Let us now consider whether Cato could have formed a friendship with Agrippa's brother in Philippus' house. There is not even a hint of a precise date for Cato's divorce from Marcia in our sources (Plut. *Cat. Min.* 25, 37, 39, 52; Lucan. *Phars.* 2.327ff.; App. *BCiv.* 2.99; Str. 11.9.1; Quint. *Inst. Orat.* 3.5.8, 13; 10.5.13). As Fehrle notes, we can only identify two dates: the *terminus post quem* is Cato's return from Cyprus in May or June 56,[38] as at that time Marcia was still his wife (Plut. *Cat. Min.* 37, 39), and the *terminus ante quem* is Hortensius' death in 50.[39] Citing a passage in Plutarch (*Cat. Min.* 52.3), Means and Dickinson date Cato's second marriage to Marcia to January 49, after the capture of Ariminum by Caesar, but before the abandonment of Rome by Pompey and his associates.[40] Marcia had at least three children by Cato, who was absent from Rome from 58 until the middle of 56 (Luc. *Phars.* 2.331; Plut. *Cat. Min.* 52.3) and may have lost one further child due to lightning.[41] She also had at least one child by Hortensius and may have had more.[42] The date of Cato's first marriage to Marcia is also unknown. Conant argues that it took place sometime in 60, but this dating rests solely on his placing of Marcia's remarriage in '56 or not long after'.[43] However, Plutarch's passage (*Cat. Min.* 25. 4–5) gives no grounds for such an assumption. Marcia's remarriage might have happened in 55–53 or even in 52. The later date seems more likely, as, during the trial of Messala Rufus, Hortensius lamented that, in the case of the condemnation of his nephew, he could find consolation only in the kisses of his grandchildren (Val. Max. 5.9.2). Hence, in 51, when the trial took place (Cic. *Brut.* 328),[44] Hortensius still had no children by Marcia.[45] As evidence that Hortensius' marriage to Marcia was of long duration, one might cite Caesar's reproach that Cato gave Marcia away at a young age (νέαν), in order to get her back rich (Plut. *Cat. Min.* 52). However, Caesar is speaking here about Cato's intentions and motives for divorce, and, at that moment, Cato could hardly have predicted the duration of Hortensius' life. Thus, Caesar was simply saying that Cato was prepared to wait for a long time.[46]

In this way, we can see that, at least in 59–58 and in 56, Cato would have been able to visit the house of Marcius Philippus as his relative and as Marcia's husband. If Cato divorced Marcia at some point in 55–52 (which is perfectly possible), he remained Philippus' relative for several more years, and, during this entire period, both Cato and Philippus remained in Rome. Thus, all the actors had the time and opportunity to meet at the home of Philippus. If Agrippa's father visited the house of Philippus with his sons, the Vipsanii brothers had the opportunity to become acquainted with the relatives of the *paterfamilias*; hence, Agrippa made friends with his coeval Octavius, and his brother fell under the influence of Cato. While Cato was divorced from Marcia, he probably was still able to visit the house of his ex-father-in-law, for Philippus was the grandfather of Cato's children by Marcia. Probably the divorce did not cause a dispute between the families, as Cato convinced Hortensius to obtain Philippus' consent to that marriage, and Philippus, for his part, agreed to Hortensius' request only on the condition that Cato would come to the new betrothal of Marcia and would attest it. So, Cato and Philippus evidently were not in a quarrel, though there are no other details about their relationship in this time in the sources.

The result is of considerable interest. Philippus himself managed to come to no harm in the civil wars, maintaining his neutrality and assuring himself of a relatively secure position. However, the obscure Vipsanii family, connected with him by social ties, suffered an internal breakdown, the brothers having found themselves on different sides in the civil war. As a result, the elder brother remained almost unknown and took hardly any part in political life, whereas the younger brother became one of the greatest generals in history, consul three times, second man in the State and the co-regent of the first Roman emperor, Augustus.

Notes

*   Unless otherwise stated, all dates in this paper are BCE.

1.   Reinhold 1933: 13; Roddaz 1984: 34–5 (including his critique of the Curtius' hypothesis that a cuirassed Agrippa is depicted on an intaglio with the emblems of the *legio VI Ferrata*). Nic. Dam. *FGrHist* 127 F 16: Ἦν εἰς τὰ μάλιστα Καίσαρι τῷ νέῳ συνήθης καὶ φίλος Ἀγρίππας, ἐν ταὐτῷ τε παιδευθείς, καί τινα ἔχων ὑπερβολὴν ἑταιρείας.

2.   Nic. Dam. *FGrHist* 127 F 25.

3.   Unless otherwise stated, all translations of Nicolaus are those of M. Toher and any italics are mine. *FGrHist* 130 F 37: Ὅτι ὁ νέος Καῖσαρ τρίτον ἄγων ἐν τῇ Ῥώμῃ μῆνα ἐνταυθοῖ λοιπὸν παρεπεδήμει, ζηλούμενος μὲν ὑπὸ τῶν ἡλίκων καὶ φίλων, θαυμαζόμενος δὲ ὑπὸ τῶν ἐν τῇ πόλει πάντων, ἐπαινούμενος δ' ὑπὸ τῶν παιδευτῶν.

4.   *FGrHist* 130 F 133: Καὶ ταῦτα αὐτῷ βουλευομένῳ καὶ τοῖς ἄλλοις συνεδόκει φίλοις, οἳ μετεῖχον τῆς στρατείας τῶν τε μετὰ ταῦτα πραγμάτων. Ἦσαν δὲ οὗτοι, Μάρκος Ἀγρίππας, Λεύκιος Μαικήνας, Κόϊντος Ἰουέντιος, Μάρκος Μοδιάλιος καὶ Λεύκιος * *. It seems

probable to me that Toher is right and 'Lucius' should be understood as Lucius Cornificius, close associate of young Caesar and the future prosecutor of Marcus Brutus (interestingly, the prosecutor of Caius Cassius in 43 would be Marcus Agrippa): Toher 2017: 418.

5. Ludwig Curtius even believes that Agrippa is depicted at the time of this war on an intaglio (Curtius 1933: 192–216, esp. S. 210, 214). But Frederik Poulsen rejects this identification (1939: 11–15). This portrait does not seem to me much like the busts which have been securely identified as Marcus Agrippa (for example, Louvre MR 402 or Montemartini MC 2760), so I partially agree with Poulsen's view.
6. Toher 2017: 205.
7. Wiseman 1964: 131–2; Roddaz 1984: 22.
8. Shackleton Bailey 1960b, *passim*, esp. 265–7.
9. Drumann 1906: 13, 18.
10. So he was a *novus homo*, as Wardle notes: Wardle 2014: 87.
11. He may have been an *argentarius* (Shatzman 1975: 387), but the opinion of Wardle that such a profession could not be combined with public political career seems more reasonable: Wardle 2014: 88 with references.
12. Degrassi 1947: 58, 135, 506.
13. Hanslik 1961: 1228; Wiseman 1964: 131–2; Roddaz 1984: 22.
14. Schultze 1904: 531.
15. Marx 1925: 181 Anm. 5.
16. Reinhold 1933: 8.
17. Roddaz 1984: 21–2.
18. Wiseman 1964: 131–2.
19. Wiseman 1964: 132.
20. Wright 1937: 9–10.
21. Gardthausen 1891: 736.
22. Frandsen 1836: 226.
23. Reinhold 1933: 12–14.
24. Hanslik 1961: 1229; Roddaz 1984: 33–4.
25. Pliny states that Agrippa died in his fifty-first year (Plin. *NH* 7.46: *brevitate aevi, quinquagensimo uno raptus anno*) and thanks to Dio we know that this happened in 12 (Dio Cass. 54 28.2-3: Καὶ ὃς τὴν μὲν στρατείαν καίτοι τοῦ χειμῶνος, ἐν ᾧ Μᾶρκος τε Οὐαλέριος καὶ Πούπλιος Σουλπίκιος ὑπάτευον. Therefore, if Agrippa was in the fifty-first year of his life in 12, then he was born in the second half of 64 or the first half of 63.
26. Plin. *NH* 7.45.
27. Housman 1903: 70.
28. Valpy 1828: 180–1.
29. *fictorque sub armis / miles Agrippa suae*.
30. For these and other interpretations, see: Valpy 1828: 180–2; Roddaz 1984: 506 n.43; Feraboli, Flores, Scarcia 1996: 80–1.
31. Hanslik 1961: 1229; Roddaz 1984: 33–4.
32. Marx 1925: 184.

33. Toher 2017: 193.
34. Roddaz 1984.
35. See for example: Bloomer 2015: 233.
36. Gray-Fow 1988, *passim*.
37. The actions of all three seem a little strange: first, Hortensius asks Cato to give him his daughter in marriage (who was married to Bibulus) and, then, his own wife, on the doubtful grounds that he needs more children; Cato gives his pregnant wife to another man; and Marcia agrees to remarry him. Why was Hortensius unable to find an unmarried bride? We have no way to establish the underlying reasons for this 'transaction', but it is possible that Hortensius was aiming to replace Bibulus as Cato's son-in-law. However, Cato did not wish to dissolve his alliance with Bibulus, and it may be that Hortensius asked for Marcia, simply in order to emphasize his desire for an alliance with Cato's family. When Cato agreed, it was perhaps unexpected even for Hortensius. See Drogula (2019: 173–5) for the argument that no such custom ever existed among Romans. Treggiari (2019: 127) also believes that Cato and Hortensius were 'building relationships among themselves, enhancing their own position and that of their descendants'. Kit Morrell suggests the following explanation: Morrell 2017, 101: 'The notorious wife-transfer arrangement between Cato and Q. Hortensius (Plut. Cat. Min. 25) was surely driven by considerations of politics and *amicitia* rather than Stoic doctrine; the philosophical argument recorded by Plutarch was just one of many produced by later writers to justify Cato's actions'. If Morrell is right, then Cato had a very interesting and uncommon understanding of *amicitia* if in his opinion it implied the wife-transfer from one *amicus* to another.
38. Oost 1955: 108.
39. Fehrle 1983: 201–2. With the same view: Conant 1954: 137; Corbier 1991: 656–7.
40. Means and Dickinson 1974: 214 n.27.
41. For a detailed analysis, see Tansey 2013: *passim*, esp. 404. But this also could have happened when Marcia was already Hortensius' wife.
42. Treggiari 2019: 126 n.42. For the suggested descendants of Hortensius and Marcia, see Geiger 1970: *passim*. Corbier argues that either the son of Hortensius and Marcia was adopted by Philippus (*cos.* 56) or by his son (*cos.* 38), or their grandson by Philippus (*cos.* 38): Corbier 1991: *passim*, esp. 695, 701.
43. Conant 1954: 105–6.
44. Alexander 1990: 106 №329 with sources.
45. For more details, see Tansey 2016: 198–9.
46. See Tschiedel (1981: 96–105, esp.: 100–1), who argues that Plutarch's passage cannot be a precise citation of the *Anticato*, as all Caesar's contemporaries knew that only a few years passed between Marcia's marriage to Hortensius and her second marriage to Cato. According to Tschiedel, this interpretation of Caesar's words could have appeared decades after the episode; he cites, as confirmation, Lucan's words that Marcia went to Hortensius young and returned to Cato old (*Phars.* 2.338-341). Maybe that was the error of Lucan himself, or perhaps, as Tschiedel assumes, it was the late erroneous interpretation of Caesar's words.

CHAPTER 7
GHOST WALLS AND VANISHING TOWNS: THE CASE OF CAESAR'S SIEGE OF CORFINIUM BETWEEN HISTORICAL SOURCES AND ARCHAEOLOGICAL-TOPOGRAPHICAL DATA

Vasco La Salvia and Marco Moderato

1. Introduction[1]

Corfinio, today a little village lying within the Peligna valley in the Abruzzi region, Corfinio was an important centrally located site in the late Iron Age, as is documented by the numerous surrounding necropoleis dating to that period. The city was known as *Corfinium* (the name of the Italic and Roman *municipium*) until the early Middle Ages, when the toponym Valva took over. At the end of the eleventh century CE, the city was largely restored by the bishop Trasmund, and its name was changed to Castrum Pentimae or Pentima. Such it remained until 1928, when, in an instance of Fascism's nostalgia for the classical past, Mussolini restored the city's ancient name.[2] Corfinium's unique historical legacy has attracted scholarly attention since the beginning of the nineteenth century. The first professional archaeological research was carried out by Antonio De Nino, who undertook numerous excavations and field surveys in much of the territory in the second half of the nineteenth century.[3] In the 1980s, thanks to van Wonterghem, a volume of the *Forma Italiae* was dedicated to the area of the three Roman municipalities of Sulmo, Corfinium, and Superaequum, providing for the first time a detailed report of all the archaeological finds from these zones and a general historical framework for the development of this territory until the fourth century CE.[4] Almost simultaneously Chris Wickham published his work (1982) on the early medieval history of this area. At the end of that decade a great season of excavations at Corfinium began, within the framework of a project for an archaeological park (unfortunately still unfinished) financed by the Region of Abruzzi in collaboration with the local Superintendency for Cultural Heritage and the Universities of Chieti and Rome Sapienza. Since then, occasional field research on specific monuments and landscape features, linked above all to the pre-Roman and Roman periods, has been carried out in Corfinium and the surrounding area. Moreover, other important excavations at Corfinium have brought to light significant parts of the urban fabric of the Roman city. Between 2013 and 2018 new systematic and extensive archaeological excavations and surveys took place in the area: conducted by a team of archaeologists from the Chieti University, they were under the

Figure 7.1 Corfinium: in Central Italy; 3D rendering of the valley and aerial photo of the present town.

scientific direction of Professors S. Antonelli, V. La Salvia and M. C. Somma, the latter acting as Principal Investigator.[5] Three main sites were investigated:

a. the backyard of the present-day Cathedral of San Pelino
b. a small portion of the Roman Campus
c. an area in the present-day city centre, possibly not far from what was the ancient macellum/forum.

All three yielded evidence of Corfinium's long and variegated history from pre-Roman times to the Middle Ages, providing new data for its topographical reconstruction.

2. Some general topographic remarks on the strategic advantage of the Peligna valley and Corfinium

From a geomorphological point of view, the Peligna valley compels people to use specific natural passes when moving about within its territory. These were well known and readily defended as they coincide with the main river courses. The Aterno river flowing through the gorge of San Venanzio guaranteed access to the Subequano basin and to Superaequum (which, in its turn, allows passage to the Fucino to the southwest). The same area was then connected to the territory of the Vestini Cismontani heading north. Having crossed the valley to the north, the river Aterno receives the waters of Sagittario and Tirino at the height of the valley of Popoli, and then heads northeast to the Adriatic Sea, passing through the ancient territory of the Marrucini towards the port of Ostia Aterni. According to Strabo (5.4.2), Ostia Aterni was used by the Vestini, Peligni and Marrucini long before its conquest by Rome. The Gizio river, instead, which originated in the territory of the present-day municipality of Pettorano and then flowed into Sagittario, was the main link between the area of Corfinium and that of Sulmo. A secondary route that split from this principal itinerary was mainly used as a piedmont road running around the slopes of Mount Morrone. It had a sacred connotation linked to the cult of the waters, highlighted in particular by its direct connection with the present-day sanctuaries of Sant'Ippolito in Corfinium and Ercole Curino near Sulmo.[6] This set of mountain trails, roads, and sheep tracks followed the natural course of crests and valleys running in a northwest–southreast direction. Moreover, they guaranteed numerous outlets to the coast thanks to the course of rivers such as the Aterno and the Fortore. One of the main sections of this road system crossed the Peligna plain. Thus, the control of this network became fundamental for Rome as well, given that it guaranteed easy access both to inner Samnium and to the Adriatic coast. With the conquest and consequent concession of a *foedus* to the Paeligni in 304 BCE, the construction of the Via Valeria became possible. Starting from the Eternal City it reached the Peligna plain intersecting its northwest–southeast axis very near to Corfinium. Under the emperor Claudius, a new road was built connecting this internal part of Abruzzi to via Salaria further north – the Claudia Nova.[7] Subsequently, in 49 CE, the Via Valeria underwent an important restoration and was enlarged particularly in the portion that stretches from Corfinium to the mouth of the Aterno, thus taking the name of Claudia Valeria. This east–west road axis was of paramount importance for Rome both in the phase of expansion and that of the consolidation of its power in the Italian peninsula, as it connected inner Samnium to the Adriatic coast and the main north–south axis of the Roman highways network of the area (viz. the Via Salaria). Thus, the process of Romanization of this territory and that of the 'normalization' of the major road network were deeply interrelated. Furthermore, they determined long-lasting transformations of the landscape, such as centuriation (which recent studies attribute to three different historical moments between the end of the second century BCE and the middle of the first century CE).[8]

Finally, it is necessary to remember that the area under study is highly seismic. Among the numerous historical seismic events that affected and determined the construction techniques of the territory, the earthquake of the second century CE is worth remembering. Documented by the epigraphic evidence, its intensity and repercussions have been evaluated on the basis of the combined archaeological and geological data. Other dramatic earthquakes are attested for 1349, 1456, 1706, 1915 and 1933.[9]

3. The urban development of ancient Corfinium

The choice of Corfinium as a capital in 91 BCE by the Italic League during the Social War,[10] suggests that the city's strategic advantage in wartime was well appreciated. Therefore, it must have been equipped with certain necessary military elements: a fortified city wall and a place to gather the Council of the Italian allies.[11]

The urban surface of the ancient city lay on the high plateau behind a small hill which was occupied by the pre-Roman hillfort. Spreading out from that point, the city covered an area between the Piana San Giacomo terrace on the west to the sacred spot of the so-called Tempio Italico on the east. Urban boundaries are well attested by the presence of several funerary areas which covered the suburban and extra-urban territory, giving us the first clue as to the shape of the settlement itself.

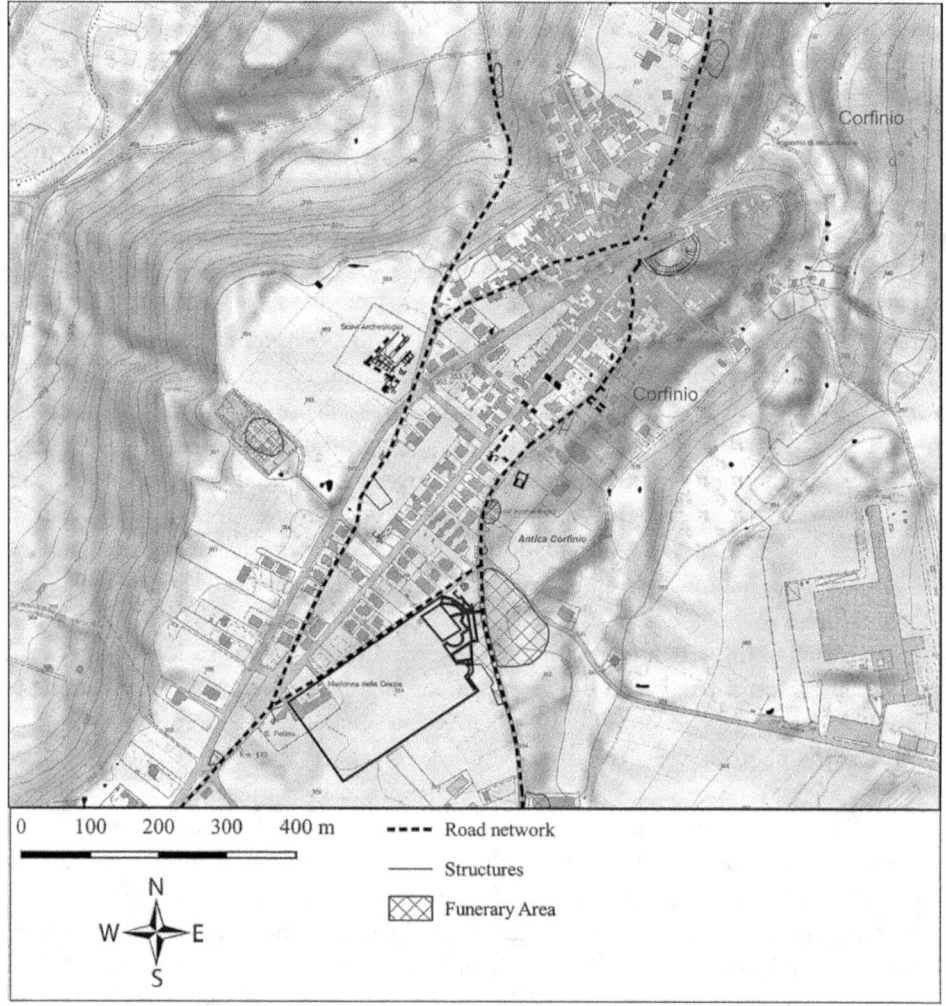

Figure 7.2 Corfinium: plan of the Roman town with known archaeological features.

The city wall would have enclosed the settlement space, securing at least the highest part of the site where the pre-Roman hillfort was located, and probably a large part of the plateau. It is here that archaeological and historical data seem to diverge to a certain degree. Unfortunately, the state of preservation of the ancient walls is rather poor. As late as 1930 the remains of a wall in polygonal ashlar masonry were still visible on the northeastern side of the hill,[12] but they are very hard to locate today. According to van Wonterghem's reconstruction,[13] the urban fortification probably followed the natural shape of the plateau, with gates located where the main regional roads reached the city. The Via Claudia Valeria entered the city from the north, from the valley of the Aterno river, and crossed the city and continued in the direction of the Subequano Valley leading to Rome. From the southeastern side of the city ran Via di Pratola from west to north. In this area De Nino discovered a round-shaped building which he identified as a fortification tower. Today the new road has completely obliterated any relevant archaeological remains.[14] Apart from these remains, there is not any trace of the wall circuit left. However, from the point of view of the reconstruction of the wall circuit, the position of the many different funerary areas surrounding present-day Corfinium and their relationship with the Roman road system allows us to assume at least the existence of some gates. The main gate, as already mentioned, would have been the one through which the Valeria, from the north, entered the town. The large remains of Roman funerary monuments, along the same road axis, might suggest that this was the main entrance. Indeed, the later written sources insist on this area from the early Middle Ages (when the church dedicated to San Pelino was built), identifying it with the significant toponym of Valva, whose *etymon* recalls precisely the opening, the space left by a gate. Moreover, in the Middle Ages, the *Vita* of San Pelino also mentions the presence of an

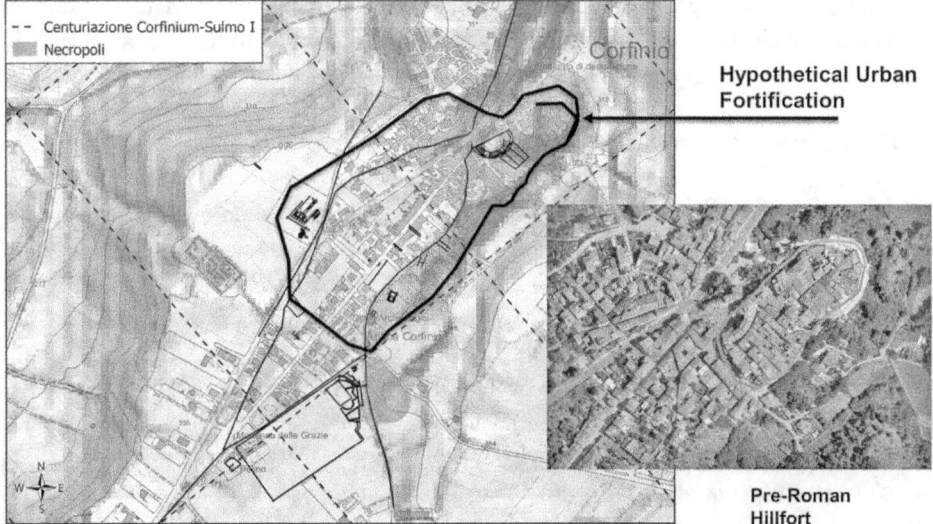

Figure 7.3 Corfinium: urban fortification system.

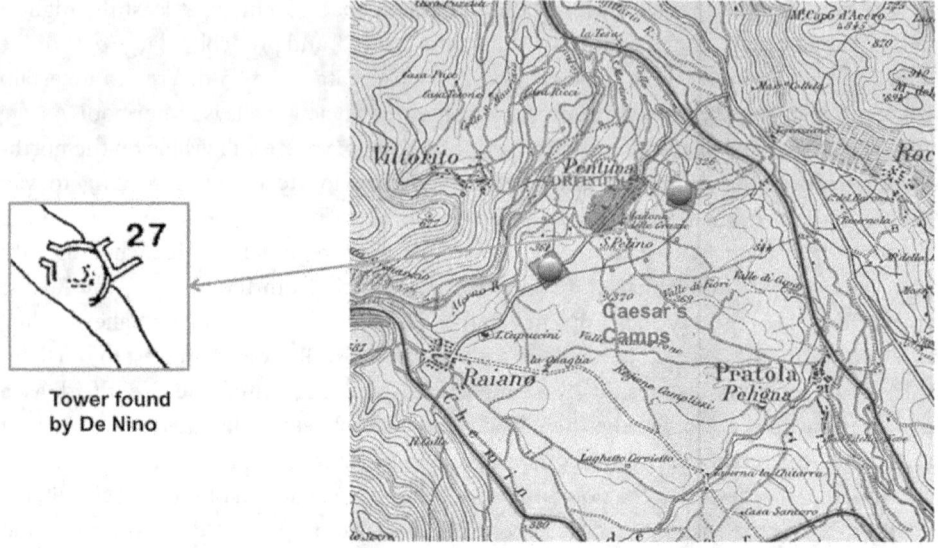

Figure 7.4 Reconstruction of the siege camp adapted from Stoffel 1887's map.

entrance to the city exactly here.[15] Since late antique churches were often built at the edge of the classical city-centre,[16] it is quite likely that at Corfinium, too, the church was built near the walls and a gate. The other gates may have been located near Via di Pratola on the southwestern side of the city,[17] and, possibly near the northeastern side, where the Via Claudia Valeria entered the city. Generally, gates were situated close to ancient thoroughfares entering the urban area, and always near to funerary areas. These latter indicate, quite clearly, the structure of the road network leading to the urban centre.

4. Caesar's siege of Corfinium

On 15 February 49 Caesar faced the troops led by L. Domitius Ahenobarbus near the city of Corfinium. The main written sources for this military engagement are Caesar's *Civil War* and some of Cicero's letters to Atticus.[18] The mention of Corfinium's physical defensive structures in Caesar's account of the siege is another instance where the literary sources stand in marked contrast with the absence of the archaeological evidence. His strategy of the siege was similar to his other military operations, such as those previously employed in Gaul.[19] According to Caesar, after thwarting Domitius' attempt to sabotage the bridge that lay three Roman miles away from the city, Caesar *legionibus traductis ad oppidum constitit iuxtaque murum castra posuit* (Caes. *BCiv.* 1.16.4: 'once his legions were across, halted near the town and made camp up against its wall', tr. Damon 2016). Thus, it appears that he pitched camp not far from the city walls. He was coming from

Firmum and Ausculum and supposedly took the coastal road to Aternum and from there continued on the Via Claudia Valeria. The bridge that Domitius tried to sabotage was probably over the Aterno river in the northern part of the Peligna Valley. The camp might have been located either in the valley north of Corfinium, on a small hill northeast of it or, less likely, in the plateau south-east of the city. This position allowed Caesar to control both the road to Sulmo and the routes toward Apulia, as well as that of the Via Claudia Valeria, thus blocking possible reinforcements from Rome. Yet, he also exposed himself to the danger of being surrounded by his enemies, if Pompey were to come to the aid of Domitius. For his part, Domitius stationed artillery (*tormenta*) along the city walls at several spots of the city (Caes. *BCiv.* 1.17.3). This detail suggests that the walls of Corfinium were equipped with towers able to support war machines and that they overlooked a great part of the area, thus protecting different zones of the city. By that time, Caesar had almost two legions, whereas Domitius commanded more than 33 cohorts. Caesar's strategy was therefore to surround the city with fortifications and to prevent further communication between Domitius and Pompey (Caes. *BCiv.* 1.18.1-2) while gathering resources from the nearby *municipia*. To avoid further danger from the west, another camp was built on the other side of the town. According to Caesar's account (Caes. *BCiv.* 1.18.5), a counter-barrier was installed; in some places the *complexus* was so close to the city that one could describe it as a fence shaped like a *munitio* (Caes. *BCiv.* 1.22.1). The field research of Stoffel, whose results were partially conjectural, calculated that the average distance between the city wall and the Caesarian blockade was 400 metres.[20]

5. Discussion

The archaeological and historical data here presented may be insufficient if taken individually but, if interpreted as a mutual ensemble, may provide new insights into the ancient city and lead us to pose new research questions.

The city walls have today virtually disappeared, both in terms of direct archaeological evidence and as regards indirect sources.[21] Yet, there is no doubt that they existed. Moreover, considering the strategic significance of Corfinium, we can imagine that strong and elaborate fortifications were built, with towers and artillery controlling both the Aterno river valley and the access to the Subequana valley leading towards Rome. This situation is linked to the haphazard preservation of Roman buildings and structures in the ancient city of Corfinium. While the sacred area of the Tempio Italico and the so-called Domus of Piana San Giacomo are well preserved, there are nearly no traces of the city forum, the location of which is still unknown.[22]

Another issue to be considered regarding the ancient townscape of Corfinium is the problem of the management of space and resources. The actual extension of the ancient city is estimated to have been about 20 ha. As Caesar reports, Domitius installed over thirty-three cohorts within the city walls. This means about 13,000 soldiers,[23] without counting the military equipment, civilian followers, animals, food supplies and so on. If

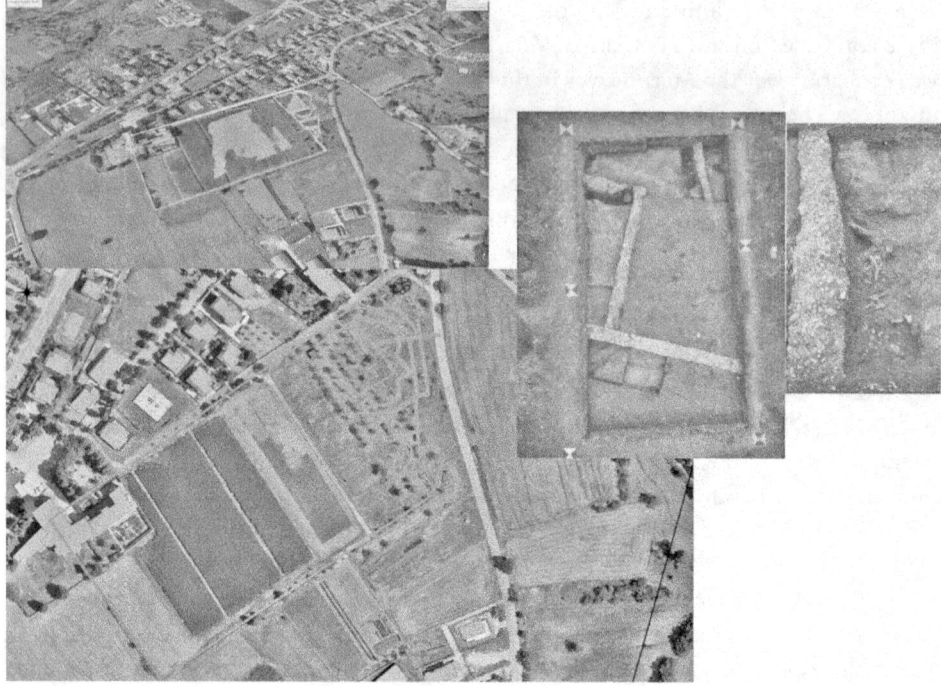

Figure 7.5 Corfinium, *Campus Militaris*: Plan, aerial photo and drone imagery from the excavation.

we calculate 3 m² per person, it would require more than one-fifth of the surface of the city to allocate the soldiers. As mentioned, they were installed inside the city wall, because the proximity of Caesar's blockade would have made it too dangerous for them to camp outside. It remains, thus, to be explained where all these men and materials were placed (Figure 7.5).

The third consideration is directly linked to the previous one. A possible location for this encampment is provided by the so-called Campus. This great architectural complex was located in a suburban area in the southern part of the city. Still partially visible, the buildings were investigated by Antonio De Nino at the end of the nineteenth century, and they are generally dated to the early imperial age.[24] The complex consists of a great rectangular yard (236.85 x 143.1 m) having walls made of carefully executed *opus reticulatum*. On the northeastern side there lay a large pool and three apses. Near the *natatio* and apses are smaller spaces that are more difficult to interpret. This whole portion of the Campus seems to be unattached to the main yard and may be part of a later construction phase. That hypothesis is supported by the modifications of the nearby necropolis of via di Pratola, in which the transition between the Republican and Imperial ages witnessed a general levelling of the area. After this levelling, large, monumental sepulchres were built. Among these, a large monument with a cylindrical body on a square base, probably belonging to an *augur* and *tribunus militum a populo*, was placed in the corner between the road and the campus structure, in a privileged position. The monumentalization is therefore to be linked to a construction boom related to the new imperial municipal elites and their need for self-representation and visibility in the first half of the first century CE.

According to Borlenghi,[25] however, the complex was the result of the monumental reconstruction of an already existing structure dating back to the first century BCE, possibly related to the presence of the capital of the Italic League. That may be the case, as the Campus is aligned with the second centuriation system in place in the Peligna valley, which should be more or less contemporary with the reconstruction of Sulmo after its destruction by Sulla in 81 BCE.[26] The dimensions of the entire structure (about 33,000 m^2 for just the main court) are exaggerated for a *municipium* of Corfinium's size. They represent about one-sixth of the entire city space. Logically, this huge complex ought to have been used by Domitius in his defence strategy. However, the written sources are silent on the matter. Yet, we cannot imagine that Domitius and the defenders of the city left this structure totally unattended. It would have been the perfect spot to settle at least a part of the troops. Unfortunately, this kind of activity rarely leaves archaeological traces. Thus, while for the time being this conjecture remains hypothetical, the current archaeological excavations have confirmed the early date of the complex itself since it overlaps with the last burials of the funerary area of Via di Pratola.[27]

6. The battle for Corfinium: from a minor military skirmish to a major political change

It is now time to consider the siege and capitulation of the city. Although military operations lasted for less than a week and entailed no significant loss of life or employment of effort, they were of paramount significance for the political history of the late Republic. The *Letters* of Cicero complement Caesar's own account of the situation, providing enough evidence for a deeper understanding of the contemporary political turmoil. As has recently been noted by both Marie-José Kardos and Yasmina Benferhat, the siege of Corfinium was the occasion for a change in the political rhetoric of the period.[28] At the same time, it played a major role in shaping a new image of Caesar, which, thereafter, relied on the political language of the *populares*.[29] In this way, Caesar presented himself as a faithful follower of the tradition of the *populus Romanus* in opposition to Pompey, who was now described as a cruel and ruthless leader (also associated with the brutal action of his allied barbarian troops).[30] In Corfinium, Caesar captured five senators, several *equites* and numerous local notables whose safety he guaranteed: exactly starting from these actions conducted in Abruzzi, the political figure of Caesar began to change in an upsurge that would lead him to be considered a champion of moderation. In fact, Cicero himself, until then hostile to the Caesarian political project, seemed to be convinced by Pompey's reluctance to intervene in favour of Domitius in Corfinium, that the ultimate goal of the proconsul was not at all the defence of the Republic but only to serve his personal interests.[31] Indeed, according to Cicero, Pompey was only concerned with maintaining the full number of men in his legions. These feelings culminate in a letter to Atticus (11.6.2) written in November 48, probably as part of the political reflections made after the conclusion of the events in Abruzzo, where cruelty appears to be the main feature of Pompey's character. Clearly, by that time, Caesar had won the psychological war too. The military operations in Corfinium, therefore, apparently 'sealed' the difficult and complicated political history of the previous years (from the Social War 91–88 to the Roman Civil War 83–82).[32] More importantly, the geo-topographical analysis clearly reveals that the city of Corfinium represented a strategic asset in a crucial phase of the Roman civil wars.[33] It was the perfect spot for Domitius and Pompey to surround Caesar's army, as stressed by Domitius himself, in a narrow valley between allied cities (Sulmo and Superaequum), if only Pompey had shown up to rescue Domitius. Instead, it turned out to be a striking victory for Caesar. It allowed him to secure the central part of Italy and, most importantly, Rome was cut off from his enemy army during his march southward. Thus, he did not have to worry about any belligerent action behind him. Moreover, the decision of Pompey to ignore the request for help from Domitius weakened their mutual alliance in favour of Caesar. However, the military-political importance attributed by both sides to the battle of Corfinium may have, to a certain extent, contributed to Caesar's 'rhetorical desire' to accentuate the weight of the defensive structures actually present in the city.[34] This hypothesis could help us to better understand the 'absence' of precise archaeological evidence regarding the city walls or, at the very least, to more effectively understand the difficulties in recognizing these remains on the ground. These questions require further archaeological and field survey work, which has the potential for new insights. For the present discussion, however, we must consider two other elements.

First, from a military and strategic point of view, unless he took Corfinium, Caesar risked being surrounded by Domitius and Pompey's armies. On the contrary, the city's capture opened the way to Rome and made it possible for him to re-enter the *Urbs* without his main adversaries as well as pursuing the Pompeian troops southwards, towards Brindisium, without having to worry about protecting his rear from further enemy attacks.[35]

Moreover, from an ideological (or rather political) perspective, the siege of Corfinium offered Caesar the perfect chance to surprise his contemporaries and offer a public display of his political programme of clemency. In fact, the city of Corfinium was by no means a neutral location. On the contrary, it was still, for a Roman political audience, a highly evocative place, recalling the tragic events of the Social War. For this reason, the way in which Caesar obtained his victory, without unnecessary bloodshed, allowed him to present himself as the only person capable of guaranteeing a peaceful resolution and, at the same time, of definitively completing the process of assimilating the Italic populations,[36] which had really begun only after the census of 70.[37] Hence, it was precisely in Corfinium, to use the words of Grillo, that 'those who have been levied and summoned by Pompeians [as the *Marsi*] defect to Caesar: accordingly at Corfinium Caesar reaps the fruit of his assimilating attitude toward provincials, and the Pompeians reap the fruit of their policies too'.[38] Caesar's policy at Corfinium of liberating defeated political opponents (even the high-ranking ones such as Domitius Ahenobarbus), even at the cost of soon confronting them again, eventually proved successful. Politically effective and useful in military terms, this policy enabled Caesar to achieve the greatest possible consensus. Consensus meant not only winning over public opinion, but also the capacity to absorb into his own ranks the soldiers levied by his opponents. This phenomenon was very important not only from a military point of view, but also on a political level, given the benefits granted to the legions. As soon as hostilities opened, apparently, Caesar was already preparing his 'exit strategy,' or rather, the strategy to politically survive and succeed in civil war. His choice was precisely the opposite of Sulla's: not cruelty and proscriptions, but leniency and amnesty.[39]

7. Conclusion

This paper presents an example of a problem often encountered, viz. a situation where the archaeological evidence and written sources seem to be at variance. Indeed, it is instructive to compare and contrast archaeological and historical data on the siege of Corfinium. Some elements clearly 'visible' in Caesar's account of the event are the walls and the gates of the city (always acknowledged in Latin as an *oppidum*, thus, emphasizing its military connotation) and the acropolis (probably inherited from the late Iron Age hilltop defensive structure), the presence of Caesar's camp, and the deployment of siege equipment. If these were indeed part of the ancient landscape, they have utterly vanished. By contrast, a huge structure such as the Campus, which one would expect to be mentioned in the written accounts, is actually ignored (although it must have existed at the time of the battle). This particular feature of the urban landscape of Corfinium, however, may also simply have been 'named' differently in the ancient sources than expected within the parameters of contemporary historiography. Archaeological and historical data, therefore, need to be contextualized within a multi-disciplinary methodological framework. It should also be considered that the importance attached to these places by the Caesarian narrative (and by his contemporaries as well) may have, to some extent, 'altered' their real material dimension. Therefore, only by bringing together different types of sources and methodologies, such as written accounts, geomorphology, remote sensing, historical, and archaeological investigation, can we hope to achieve plausible historical reconstructions.

Notes

1. This work is the result of joint research. However, authorship of the paragraphs is as follows: Vasco La Salvia (4, 6); Marco Moderato (2, 3, 5); and both (introduction and conclusion).
2. Somma 2015: 282–3.
3. De Nino 1877, 1879, 1880.
4. van Wonterghem 1984.

5. Somma 2015, Somma et al. 2018.
6. van Wonterghem 1984: 73; Moderato and Tornese 2015: 476–7.
7. van Wonterghem 1984: 66; Dionisio 2015: 56.
8. Dionisio 2015: 57, on the centuriation: Chouquer et al. 1987; Soricelli 2011: 488–9.
9. Galadini and Galli 2001: 53–5.
10. Buonocore and Firpo 1991: 155; Isayev 2011; Bourdin 2012: 126.
11. Buonocore and Firpo 1991: 149; Nagle 1973: 373; Bourdin 2012: 336–7, 782.
12. As stated by Colella 1935: 438.
13. van Wonterghem 1984: 132.
14. van Wonterghem 1984: 135–7.
15. Antonelli 2022: 263–78.
16. Chavarria Arnau 2009: 129.
17. Where De Nino reported to find archaeological remains related to a possible city gate, see van Wonterghem 1984: 132–3.
18. On the siege of Corfinium (15–21 February 49) see Caes. *BCiv*. 1,18-23; Liv. *Per.*109; Plut. *Caes*. 34.7-8; Vell. 2.50.1; Suet. *Iul*. 34.1; App. *BCiv*. 2.38; Cass. Dio 41.10.2. See also Cic. *Att*. 8.11A and 8.12B (10–11 February), 8.12.C (16 February), and 8.12.D (17 February) for tensions between Pompey and Domitius Ahenobarbus. *Att*. 8.3.7 (18 February) for information that Caesar was near the walls of Corfinium and Domitius Ahenobarbus was ready for battle; only on 22 February did Cicero learn of Pompey's plans not to fight and to leave Italy (*Att*. 8.4.4); Cic. *Att*. 8.8 for his censure of Pompey for the failure of this plan, see Peaks 1904.
19. Harmand 1961.
20. Stoffel 1887: 13.
21. Specifically, remote sensing, aerial photography, see Moderato et al. 2015: 57–8.
22. As stated by van Wonterghem 1984: 116–18; for an update see Moderato 2022.
23. According to Brunt 1975: 619–20; while Brunt's estimate might be low, it is still a large number of soldiers that had to be housed within the city.
24. Augustan according to Coarelli and La Regina; after 48–49 CE/first half of the second century CE according to van Wonterghem 1984: 159.
25. Borlenghi 2011: 132.
26. The first centuriation system is dated to the Gracchan reforms and the third centuriation system, with a different orientation, is dated to the Augustan period (Soricelli 2011: 490–2). It is highly unlikely that such a building would not respond to the current orientation of the city grid.
27. Burials in this area are broadly dated from early second century BCE to the second century CE (with some sporadic funeral occupation around fourth–fifth centuries CE), cf. van Wonterghem 1984; Romito and Sangiovanni 2008: 195–200. For a deeper stratigraphic reconstruction of the Campus' phases, see Moderato 2022.
28. Benferhat 2005; Kardos 2006.
29. While the rhetorical language of the *populares* might be difficult to identify (see Robb 2010; Arena 2012; van der Blom 2016), Caesar, both in terms of political language and military-strategic behaviour, precisely exemplified his democratic attitude as opposed to that of Pompey and his faction, traditionalist and aristocratic. Caesar followed Roman precedents,

presenting himself as the continuation of recent anti-noble political figures (Marius) and possible ever of third century plebeian general (such as Marcellus): see Brizzi 2010: 98–100 and 102. Certainly, in the reconstruction of the various events of the war, the real protagonists of the military action are almost always the centurions, and not the legates. However, whatever the image that the *commentarii* are intended to project, these 'inferior cadres' of the army seem to have taken on a truly decisive role and autonomy, and to have completely supplanted the officers drawn from the ranks of the *nobilitas* only at the outbreak of the civil war, when many of the legates – such as, for example, Labienus, who had been one of Caesar's best assistants – chose, out of character or convenience, the opposing camp. For the impact of the civil wars on the command structure of the Roman army, see Augier in this volume. Caesar's constant behaviour towards his troops, whose life, expectations and ideals he showed that he shared, should have been dictated not only by functional reasons, but also and above all by political considerations. Attentive to the needs of propaganda, he further exacerbated the Roman tradition of *virtus* and he had to turn more and more decisively towards those models to which he had already been looking. These political devices had the task of establishing an absolute symbiosis between proletarianized soldiers and their commander and to present Caesar as a trustworthy representative of the democratic and popular camp; see, Grillo 2012: 135–6: 'as Caesar explains to Lentulus at Corfinium, he wants to regain his *dignitas*, to defend the rights of the tribunes of the plebs, and to liberate the people oppressed by a faction of few individuals (1.22.5). . . . The *populares* typically exploited the motif of the liberation of the people, and the *Bellum Civile* is filled with catch-words. For instance, Caesar's words to Lentulus at Corfinium (*et se et populum Romanum factione paucorum oppressum in libertatem vindicaret*, 1.22.5) resemble those of Sallust (*vindicare plebem in libertatem at paucorum scelera patefacere*, *Iug*. 42.1), . . ', and 153–4; Canfora 1999: 178–9. Moreover, the fact that Domitius Ahenobarbus' speech to his troops at Corfinium is reported, is not accidental: the promises on the distribution of land, in fact, highlight the enormous inequality in the distribution of wealth, a fact that reinforces Caesar's democratic political perspective that identifies the Pompeians with the 'oligarchs'.

30. Although Pompey was described as cruel in other contexts, as Steel 2013 has articulated, such descriptions remain mere rhetoric. The influence of the political struggle on this characterization of Pompey is, in fact, clearly demonstrated in Cicero's concerns surrounding the siege of Corfinium, wherein Pompey's cruelty is clearly associated with political misbehaviour, see Dowling 2000: 309–10. Moreover, it should be noted that although cavalry units (300 men) from Noricum arrived at Corfinium to his aid, Caesar (Caes. *BCiv*. 1.18.5) seems to have prevented their nocturnal movements (precisely in order to impede their possible excesses) and also that the raids attributed to his auxiliary barbarian troops (in Gomphi and Metropolis in the following year) are reported by the sources precisely in open contrast to what happened at Corfinium, underlining the difference in the political and military context; for the portrayal of Caesar as a Republican hero see, Grillo 2012: 37 with selected bibliography in n.2. As for the Barbarians troops, see Grillo 2012: 117–18.

31. For the divergence of views between Pompey and Ahenobarbus, see Vervaet 2006: 936 and 946–8, cf. Grillo 2020: 122.

32. See Grillo 2020: 131–2. The effects of Caesar's political and military moves at Corfinium 'transformed' him into the perfect anti-Sulla, while it was Pompey who took on the features of the dangerous dictator. It was precisely from the events of Corfinium that Caesar built the cornerstone of his political trajectory, distancing himself from the Sullan model, which did not foresee the persecution of his own political enemies but the construction of a wide democratic consensus: see, Canfora 1999: 166–9; Grillo 2012: 156. For a recent evaluation of Caesar's clemency as a political strategy and as an anti-aristocratic political model, see Brizzi 2017: 150–1. See also Cornwell and Zucchetti in this volume.

33. See Grillo 2012: 37; Grillo 2020: 133.
34. The fact that the outcome of the battle was considered by contemporaries to be crucial for the destiny of the Republic is well outlined in Grillo 2020: 123–4 who, not by chance, quotes Cicero (*Att.* 8.5.2) explicitly recalling how the future of the Republic was at stake in Corfinium and, on the other hand, how Caesar presented himself as the only one able to resolve a serious and dangerous impasse without further and useless bloodshed.
35. Canfora 1999: 188, according to what can be deduced from the analysis of the sources, Domitius Ahenobarbus himself had pointed out to Pompey the senselessness of his strategic choice. Caesar himself, in fact, in the *Commentarii*, on the basis of the information gained during and after the war campaign, reports about the attempts of Domitius – besieged by Caesar at Corfinium – trying to make Pompey reconsider his plan, even when Pompey had already retreated to Apulia, sending him envoys familiar with the geomorphological characteristics of the territory (the central Apennines) who had to convince Pompey to come to their aid. The importance that Domitius attached to this mission was such that Domitius himself promised his messengers a substantial reward in case of success. The strategic proposal of Domitius foresaw the use of the two armies (supposing that Pompey had returned immediately to the north, joining Domitius in the defence of Corfinium), which, taking advantage of the difficulties of the terrain, could easily block Caesar and cut off his supplies. Otherwise – Domitius argued – he, with more than thirty cohorts and a large number of senators and officers, would be in serious difficulty.
36. Grillo 2020: 129–33.
37. Brizzi 2017: 209.
38. Grillo 2020: 132.
39. Canfora 1999: 169.

CHAPTER 8
THE CHANGING FACE OF THE COMMAND STRUCTURE DURING THE CIVIL WARS (49–30 BCE)

Bertrand Augier

In Roman armies one of the key elements of military discipline[1] was the *sacramentum* (oath), which included a clause of general obedience to the orders of the magistrate *cum imperio* (with the power of command), who obtained compliance from the common soldiers through his coercive power,[2] or via his officers.[3] Every soldier took this oath, either when beginning his service, during the *dilectus* (levy),[4] or when receiving a new general.[5] With the *sacramentum*, a soldier not only swore allegiance to the commander but was also transformed from a *quiris* (citizen) into a *miles* (soldier), no longer subject to *ius* (civil law), but to *fas* (divine law).[6] The *fas disciplinae* (military law) was everything the gods imposed through the orders of the *imperatores*, i.e. military rule and discipline.[7] The *sacramentum* invested the magistrate *cum imperio* as having principal jurisdiction over the army. He was assisted by the rather elaborate and formal chain of command which played a large role in the discovery and punishment of the soldiers' offences and in preventing indiscipline.[8]

Even though the *sacramentum* continued to be taken by soldiers,[9] the period of civil wars which ended the Roman Republican period was characterized by an apparent weakness of discipline caused by the multiplication of offences such as mutiny, desertion and fraternization, but also by the *levitas* (bonhomie) that *imperatores* (generals) had to display towards their troops.[10] The question of soldiers' consent was crucial,[11] as they never lost their citizen status and their freedom of speech.[12] The late Republican soldier was primarily a citizen vested with certain important rights, strengthened by the *leges de provocatione* (appellate legislation), in the second century BCE.[13] In addition, despite the oaths and various military regulations, soldiers were always able to express their opinions freely, especially when the legitimacy of their commanders was at stake. The *imperatores* were not warlords,[14] and soldiers still possessed a very strong civic spirit.[15]

Since the gulf between senatorial commanders and the common soldiery could be considerable, the *imperatores*, particularly during the civil wars, had to legitimate themselves to the soldiers,[16] especially through political propaganda.[17] Nevertheless, during the civil wars, the armies may not have been as uncontrollable as has been argued.[18] In a context of political crisis, what military sociologists call 'command' – i.e. the legal frame of authority, or what we might call in Weberian terms rational-legal authority – could indeed be contested. As scholarship has long demonstrated, it gave more room to charismatic and informal authority, based on what is often called 'leadership' (i.e. social influence).[19]

In such a context, an important element of the troops' consent to an *imperator*'s cause was the hierarchical structure of the *exercitus* (army), i.e. the officers. The *tribuni militum* (tribunes of the soldiers), *praefecti* (vice-commanders) or *legati* (lieutenants), all of senatorial or equestrian rank, composed a chain of command which enabled the downward flow of directives[20] to aim at the execution of orders and the enforcement of discipline.[21] In a letter addressed to M. Cato in January 50, Cicero attributes to the absence of officers (*legati* and *tribuni militum*) and centurions the indiscipline of the cohorts he found upon arrival in Cilicia in 51.[22] The anonymous author of the *Bellum Alexandrinum* underlined the responsibility of the Caesarian officers during the mutiny of 47: 'and the flattering indulgence shown to their troops by the military tribunes and legionary commanders was giving rise to many practices opposed to military custom and usage which tended to undermine strict discipline.'[23]

The rebellion was a direct consequence of the weakening of discipline, as the military tribunes, and probably the legates 'who were in charge of the legions', failed to enforce it. Exemplary behaviour was traditionally expected from the middle military cadres, who had to inspire the troops with the necessary confidence to obtain obedience. It was particularly the case of *tribuni militum*: 'This was the province of the tribune, who was outstanding in his knowledge of weapons, his strength of body, and the rectitude of his lifestyle.'[24]

Physical courage, skilled handling of weapons and irreproachable morality were all aristocratic virtues that inspired confidence among their subordinates, and consequently served to maintain social control over the legions. Soldiers obeyed their officers because they knew them on a day-to-day basis and saw them on the battlefield. These ethical requirements were exacerbated during the civil wars, as the officers played a large role in the troops' mobilization in favour of the *imperatores*, and they were extended to superior officers such as the *legati*, who exerted a significant influence on their soldiers at the end of the Republican period. Indeed, when Labienus, one of Caesar's most important legates, rallied to Pompey in January 49, Cicero interpreted this as a significant reversal for Caesar: 'He has had a body blow in the defection of T. Labienus, the most distinguished of his officers, who has refused to be party to his criminal enterprise.'[25]

The term *auctoritas* (authority) underlines Labienus' particular status and abilities, which made him worthy of voluntary allegiance and trust.[26] One key element of his *auctoritas* was certainly his rank of *praetorius* (former praetor), but also and primarily the fact that he had displayed the qualities of a commander during the Gallic campaigns of Caesar. His military value was recognized by his commander as well as his subordinates. Indeed, *auctoritas* existed only insofar as the superior military abilities of the officer were acknowledged by his subordinates.[27] So, this quality can be viewed as military leadership (i.e. an ability to influence the action of the army in an informal way), or rather as charismatic authority,[28] which augmented or decreased according to the officer's *virtus* (i.e. 'valour' or 'courage'), which was the traditional measure of manliness,[29] and was often associated with *fortitudo* (physical courage),³⁰ in the Roman conception of *auctoritas*.³¹ The close association between *virtus* and *auctoritas* is illustrated, for a lower level of military hierarchy, by the fact that Caesar himself called the centurion T. Balventius *vir fortis et magnae auctoritatis* ('a brave man having considerable authority').³² The link between fighting excellence and authority over the troops rarely occurs in the evidence for late Republican armies,³³ but Nathan Rosenstein has shown that commanders' authority was traditionally legitimated by moral qualities such as *virtus*, rather than through technical competence.³⁴ This was the case with Labienus, who again displayed outstanding bravery when fighting against Caesar's troops in Africa in 46.³⁵

Virtus, moreover, was a key element in officers' legitimacy. It was fundamental for bridging the social and economic gap which existed between aristocratic officers and their subordinates.³⁶ The speech Antonius delivered before Caesarian veterans at Brundisium in December 44, evoking his service under the murdered dictator, is particularly revealing: 'What friendship and what zeal I had for Caesar while he lived, what dangers I braved in his service, you, who have been my fellow-soldiers and sharers in these events, know full well.'³⁷

Not only *virtus*, of course, but also an ability to withstand the fatigues of war and triumph over difficulties and hardships are the key elements of Antonius' exemplarity as an officer, helping him to bridge the social distance with his men and establish a charismatic authority.³⁸ This maintained his prestige and provided a common standard of behaviour.³⁹ The system of interiorized social rules, values and representations in which the members of the *exercitus* recognize each other regulated collective behaviour and created consensus around Antonius.⁴⁰ The military competence of the officers can therefore be considered as a social construct: from a sociological point of view, it can be conceived as a skillset which enabled an individual to deal with a situation in a way the community considered suitable.⁴¹

In the officers' case, emphasis on *virtus* did not mean they had to display boldness on the battlefield. On the contrary, they often curbed the soldiers' enthusiasm, and channelled the soldiers' *impetus* and *animus* (i.e. onslaught and enthusiasm). They could appear as the guarantors of a defensive conception of courage,⁴² inherited from the manipular organization of the legions, in which the fundamental duty of a *miles* was to never abandon his position.⁴³ They played then a leading role in a form of 'routinization' of *virtus*, through *disciplina militaris* (however, never complete, since an aggressive courage was, at the same time, expected from soldiers by *imperatores* such as Marius or Caesar). However, the officers' attitude during military operations seems to have evolved during the civil wars, as officers often encouraged the commander-in-chief during the *consilia* (staff meetings) to go on the offensive,⁴⁴ sometimes directly challenging his decisions.⁴⁵ Lendon has pointed out that disagreements did not arise over strategic considerations, but rather the *imperator*'s alleged lack of aggressiveness, opening the way for accusations of cowardice and weakening the authority of the *imperator* over the troops.⁴⁶ Since a military commander's political legitimacy and authority was especially open to question by his opponents in time of civil war, this kind of attitude was a way for officers, who were also political partisans, to drive the *imperator* to reassert his authority. Accounts of officers exposing themselves to danger are in fact very rare, and this behaviour seems to have been tolerated only in the case of defeat,[47] or when coming from younger elite officers, who traditionally fought on the front lines.[48] Ancient authors utterly disapproved of excessive displays of courage: the indiscipline of Flavius Gallus, probably a *tribunus militum* under Antony during the retreat following his Parthian campaign, who ignored the orders of his superiors and exposed himself and his subordinates to danger is highly criticized by Plutarch,[49] and the τόλμα (*audacia*, i.e. daring) Octavian's *legatus* L. Cornificius displayed in 38 in attacking the ship of Sex. Pompeius' admiral Demochares was παράβολος (*temerarius* or rash) according to Appian.[50]

Within this general framework, the officer's authority over the troops therefore largely depended on his attitude on the battlefield, that is to say his ability to integrate his words and gestures within the behavioural framework of civic values. This was part of an aristocratic *ethos* within which *virtus* was central. This conformity with the aristocratic *ethos* was also the basis for officers' military reputation, as is clear in the *Corpus Caesarianum*. For instance, the *praefectus equitum* C. Volusenus Quadratus, who served under Caesar in Gaul, was renowned for his bravery: 'Volusenus possessed 'outstanding courage' (*eam virtutem quae singularis erat in eo*).[51] His *virtus* was recognized by his superiors, for Caesar's legate M. Antonius entrusted him with the difficult task of hunting down the Gallic chief Commius in 51, but it was also recognized by his subordinates, for during the campaign of Pharsalus in 48, Roucillus and Egus, the two Allobroges who deserted to Pompey, wanted to assassinate him as a token of their new allegiance.[52] This kind of exemplarity was an important factor for the morale or attitude of the soldiers.[53] It was, for example, at the exhortation of the military tribune C. Vulteius Capito that some Caesarian soldiers, when they were surrounded by Pompeian troops on the island of Curicta in 49, committed a collective suicide so as not to fall into the enemy's hand.[54] By their leadership officers not only initiated, but also maintained vertical group cohesion between soldiers and their officers. Apart from this 'rank cohesion', a horizontal 'peer cohesion' among soldiers also depended on the quality of the officer's leadership.[55] Military leadership can be considered a symbolic relationship between officers and soldiers that resulted in the establishment of a *Weltanschauung* (in the Freudian meaning of the term) specific to this particular group.[56]

We can assume that officers who exercised leadership over the soldiers could serve as intermediaries between the soldiers and their *imperatores*. This applies particularly to middle cadres such as the *tribuni militum*, who were, together with the centurions, in contact with their subordinates on a daily basis. They were in a position to intercede on the soldiers' behalf with the *imperator*. For instance, when Caesar threatened to inflict decimation on the *legio IX*, which had mutinied at Placentia in 49, the officers mediated, as Appian's account makes clear: 'The officers threw themselves at Caesar's feet in supplication.'[57] A similar pattern can be observed during another mutiny in Campania in 47. Caesar gathered his soldiers in a *contio*, and notified them of their dismissal, provoking their despair. According to Cassius Dio: 'When they had reached this stage and one of their leaders also, either on his own impulse or as a favour to Caesar (the younger), had said a few words and presented a few petitions on their behalf.'[58]

Here, too, some officers, whose rank is unknown, argued the case of their soldiers. So, the armies of the civil wars were characterized by bidirectional and intense modes of communication between the commanders and the rank and file of the *exercitus*. As De Blois has shown in several seminal works, the military middle cadres were able to influence the rank and file of the armies: the *imperatores* who were entering upon a course of doubtful legality and therefore needed to maintain control over their troops perforce relied on these officers.[59]

Of great importance in producing soldiers' consent to their commander's action were the *contiones militares* (gatherings of soldiers) that the magistrate *cum imperio* assembled, for example, before battle in order to give a speech to galvanize soldiers.[60] These *contiones* also had an informative role, and functioned as political assemblies during these years, allowing the *imperator* to win over his troops to his cause and obtain their agreement. For instance, it was during such a *contio* that Caesar related to his soldiers the reasons why he had crossed the Rubicon in 49.[61] It was also in front of their gathered troops that Antony, Octavian and Lepidus announced the agreement they had reached near the Lavino river.[62] Just as in Roman political life, the *contiones* might be an arena where soldiers demonstrated their disagreement or pressed their commander for a choice in line with their expectations: Lepidus' soldiers manifested great enthusiasm in May 43, when he announced his intention to join Antony.[63] These *contiones*, just like those which took place in Rome, were political gatherings where public opinion was formed and consensus might crystallize about the *imperator*'s action. As brokers between the two poles of soldiery and *imperator*, the officers were fundamental in creating consensus and controlling the flow of information, e.g. relaying the speech of an *imperator* during a *contio*. This is precisely what happened before the first battle of Philippi in 42:

> When they had taken their stand facing each other, exhortations were addressed to each side, partly to the armies collectively and partly to the separate bodies of troops, according as the speakers were the generals or the lieutenants or the lesser officers; and much that was said consisted of the necessary advice called for by the immediate danger and also of sentiments that bore upon the consequences of the battle – words such as men would speak who were to encounter danger at the moment and were looking forward with anxiety to the future.[64]

Information was transmitted according to what we might term a subsidiarity principle. The expression 'partly to the armies collectively and partly to the separate bodies of troops' suggests an alternation between commanders addressing the whole army and smaller meetings between officers and the units under their direct orders. Complementary methods, these compensated for the communication difficulties raised by the armies' enormous size. However, use of the military chain of command as a communication channel between troops and their *imperatores* shows that after Caesar's death the armies in general and Caesarian veterans in particular had become autonomous political entities needing to be handled with care.[65] Indeed, according to the expression attributed by Cassius Dio to Fulvia and Lucius Antonius, the soldiers became *senatores caligati*,[66] making political choices and mediating between the *duces*.

Similarly, in the late spring of 44, a delegation of Caesarian veterans went to the consul Antony's house to ask him to treat Octavian less harshly: 'The tribunes of Antony's guard, who had served under the elder Caesar, and who were then in the highest favour with Antony, urged him to refrain from insult, both on their own account and on his own, as he had served under Caesar and had obtained his present good fortune at Caesar's hands.'[67] The meeting occurred in the *atrium* of Antony's house, and the delegation's interaction with the consul recalls the rituals of a patron-client relationship,[68] as these *tribuni militum* were ex-centurions promoted by Antony. Nevertheless, their origins and also their function as intermediaries between soldiers and *imperator* designated them as spokesmen of the troops: that is why Antony treated them with consideration.

There are other examples of this specific political role of the *tribuni militum*, especially after the Ides of March.[69] One significant episode occurred at the end of 44, when Antony punished his mutinous soldiers in Brundisium: 'Antony, however, being still angry at the outbreak, or from some other suspicion, changed their tribunes'.[70] The ταξιάρχοι here are probably the *tribuni militum*: to better control his troops, Antony chose to replace these restless intermediaries, who contributed to the questioning of his prominence, with devoted partisans. However, we know that this replacement had absolutely no effect on the soldiers' loyalty, since a few days after this episode, the *legio IV* and the *legio Martia* defected to join Octavian: 'So for the time being the soldiers were quiet, but when they arrived near the capital on the way to Gaul they mutinied, and many of them, despising the lieutenants who had been set over them, changed to Caesar's side; in fact, the Martian legion, as it was called, and the Fourth went over to him in a body.'[71] The ὑποστρατήγοι in Cassius Dio's account are probably the *tribuni militum*. Newly nominated officers, their leadership was questioned by the soldiers because they did not have a shared history of service, and therefore were unable to counteract the centrifugal forces inside the legions.

The officers sometimes outgrew their role as intermediaries and took the lead in challenging the *imperator*'s authority. This happened during the mutiny Octavian faced in September 36 after his victory at Naulochus. His soldiers behaved like those who asked Caesar for immediate discharge during the great mutiny of 47,[72] acting like a pressure group conscious that their *imperator* still needed them for the Illyrian campaign being planned. The young Caesar tried to stamp out the revolt by delivering a speech and awarding honours to his soldiers and middle cadres, but one of them, the *tribunus militum* Ofilius, publicly rejected his proposals:

> and (young Caesar) now gave to the legions additional crowns, and to the centurions and tribunes purple-bordered garments and the dignity of chief councillors in their native towns. While he was distributing other awards of this kind, the tribune Ofellius exclaimed that crowns and purple garments were playthings for boys, that the rewards for soldiers were lands and money. The

multitude cried out 'Well said', whereupon Caesar descended from the platform in anger. The soldiers gathered round the tribune, praising him and railing at those who did not join with them, and the tribune said that he alone would suffice to defend so just a cause. After saying this he disappeared the following day, and it was never known what became of him.[73]

The soldiers demanded the same privileges as the veterans discharged after the campaign of Philippi in 42, and Ofilius, as leader and mouthpiece of the protest, was carrying a slogan which had become usual from Caesar's time, i.e. land and money (χωρία καὶ χρήματα).[74] He was a middle cadre, and probably a son of the municipal elite of Italy: military service for this type of officer was an opportunity for enrichment and reinforced his local prominence by promotion into the *ordo equester*.[75] But, as L. De Blois has stated, this does not mean that their loyalty lay primarily and exclusively with their commander.[76] These officers needed land to ensure their belonging to the eighteen equestrian centuries: profit was a central motivating factor for their enlistment,[77] as was the case with the *milites*.[78] Their leadership during mutinies can therefore be explained by common interest.

So, during the civil wars, the *imperatores* had to deal with undisciplined officers, who might threaten their political interests and the cohesion of the *exercitus*. We know that Ofilius mysteriously disappeared the day after his speech, probably executed by order of Octavian. But commanders usually privileged a different strategy of punishment, viz. shaming and disgracing cowards or offenders. It appears that a double standard of discipline existed in the Roman armies, since corporal punishment was rarely used against the officers.[79] One of the most spectacular of shaming punishments was demotion or dishonourable discharge (*missio ignominiosa*),[80] which became an increasingly formalized means of punishment in these decades.[81] For instance, after a naval disaster near Thapsus in 46, Caesar gathered his troops in a *contio* and publicly laid the blame on certain military tribunes as well as centurions:

> Inasmuch as you, Gaius Avienus, in Italy have stirred up soldiers of the Roman people against the state and have committed acts of plunder in various municipal towns; inasmuch as you have proved useless to me and to the state (...); for these reasons I hereby discharge you with ignominy from my army and direct that you leave as soon as possible and be quit of Africa this day. You also, Aulus Fonteius, I dismiss from my army, for having proved a mutinous military tribune and a disloyal citizen.[82]

Two *tribuni militum*, C. Avienus and A. Fonteius, were called *seditiosi*, since they probably led the mutiny Caesar had to face the year before, and then acted *contra morem militarem*. They were both dismissed *cum ignominia*. The importance of such shaming ceremonies can be explained by the fact that it seemed inappropriate to subject senatorial and equestrian officers to corporal punishment.[83] Officers who underwent *ignominiosa missio* became *infames*:[84] they were still Roman citizens, but were stigmatized and excluded from civic life.⁸⁵ Such a shaming punishment, in an anthropological sense, had a considerable impact on aristocrats, questioning their very prominence in the city,⁸⁶ as it induced a downgrading in the civic hierarchy. For instance, among the list of grounds for disqualifying persons from eligibility from local magistracies, the *tabula Heracleensis* mentions '(anyone) whom a general because of disgraceul conduct has ordered or shall have ordered to leave the army'.⁸⁷ The social death implied by the *ignominiosa missio* might appear a more suitable punishment for members of the civic elite. Indeed, the symbolic violence and loss of status involved partly compensated for and made physical violence more acceptable to the soldier-citizens. But another explanation is in my opinion more important. During the civil wars most of the officers (if not all) were *privati* appointed by a magistrate *cum imperio*, as the elections of *tribuni militum* did not exist anymore.⁸⁸ They probably were not enlisted according to the traditional manner of the *dilectus*, probably were not *milites* from a legal perspective, and probably did not swear the regular *sacramentum*.⁸⁹ Consequently, if we accept this premise, they were legally not subject to the *fas disciplinae* and were legally immune from corporal punishments.⁹⁰

However, we must note that references to shaming punishments are particularly scarce for the period of the civil wars. Maybe the influence some officers might exert over the troops dissuaded the *imperatores* from dismissing them too quickly. More important is the fact that they were at the same time political allies and members of powerful equestrian or senatorial lineages; the *imperatores* could not risk alienating these powerful supporters by punishing one of their prestigious subordinates too harshly. The officers Caesar dishonourably discharged in 46 BCE were indeed all members of the Italian municipal elite, whose lower social capital exposed them to such a punishment and did not have to be given the benefit of the *imperator*'s *levitas*. Moreover, a commander could not treat his officers too harshly. Because of their particular status, they could also shift allegiance more easily, without breaking the *sacramentum*: this last element may also explain the tortuous political path taken by many of these aristocrats during the civil wars. What was at stake more than ever in this particularly troubled period was political survival. These officers, as aristocrats, were no exception.

Notes

1. About *disciplina militaris* as embedded in Roman political and cultural ideologies: Phang 2011: 127. For an important and challenging analysis of this traditional thesis: Machado 2021 (who however exaggerates the transformation of the late Republican armies into tools that could be used to gain political power).
2. Etzioni 1971 drew a classification of complex organizations, based on their ability to obtain consent from its members, influenced by three types of power (coercive, remunerative, normative), each one characterized by a specific modality of integration (alienation, discipline and participation).
3. Polyb. 6.21.2 (cf. Dion. Hal. 11.43.2; Hinard 1993: 254).
4. Nicolet 1976: 141.

The Changing Face of the Command Structure During the Civil Wars (49–30 BCE)

5. Cic. *Off.* 1.36-37; Livy 3.53.
6. Tondo 1963: 25; Harmand 1967: 300; Le Bonniec 1969: 105; Nicolet 1976: 141; Linderski 1984: 75–6; Rüpke 1990: 86–8.
7. Tac. *Ann.* 1.19.3; cf. Vendrand-Voyer 1983: 56.
8. Chrissanthos 2013: 322.
9. See for instance Caes. *BCiv.* 2.28.2 and 32.7-9; App. *BCiv.* 2.47.
10. Harmand 1967: 272–9.
11. Skocpol 1979: 279 sheds light on the importance of the armies' discipline during a *coup d'état* (cf. Caplow and Vennesson 2000: 110–11).
12. Chrissanthos 2004.
13. Lovisi 1999: 166–70; Cadiou 2018: 207–9. For example, the officers who molested soldiers could be publicly tried (Val. Max. 6.1.10-11).
14. *Contra* Keaveney 2007: 4–7, 35, 41 and 97 (cf. Holland 2003: 88–9, 305, 341–2, 368, 393; Sheppard 2006: 7, 29; Fields 2008; Mackay 2009: 337; Capogrossi Colognesi 2014: 214; Zarecki 2014: 162). Rich 2018: 277–88 for a nuanced discussion on warlordism in late Republican Rome; another seminal paper is Rosenstein 2018.
15. Cadiou 2018: 265–6 and n.672, *contra* Bloch and Carcopino 1952 [1932]: 122; Harmand 1967: 65; Nicolet 1976: 510; Nicolet 1979: 330; Gabba 1973: 67; De Blois 1987: 12 and 58; Patterson 1993: 107; Erdkamp 2006: 294; De Blois 2007:169; Alston 2007: 182–3.
16. Phang 2008: 76.
17. Laignoux 2010.
18. Cadiou 2018: 319–39.
19. Sheffield and Till 2003.
20. Lang 1965; Isaac 1995: 23.
21. Soeters et al. 2006: 240.
22. Cic., *Fam.* 15.4.2.
23. *BAlex.* 65.1.
24. Veget. 2.12.2.
25. Cic., *Fam.* 16.12.4.
26. Hellegouarc'h 1963: 296–7.
27. About *auctoritas*, 'elle [était] fondée sur la conviction que celui qui en est pourvu possède des «capacités» qui le rendent digne de leur soumission et de leur confiance: elle [supposait] l'approbation et l'adhésion volontaire de ceux sur lesquels elle s'exerce' (Hellegouarc'h 1963: 302; cf. Cic., *Top.* 78 and *Leg. Man.* 43, 45 and Schulz 2010).
28. Augier (2023) on charisma in the late Republican armies.
29. Harris 1979: 39–40; Rosenstein 1990: 117–21; Lendon 2005: 176–7, 188–9.
30. Combès 1966: 215 and 271.
31. Cicero often links *auctoritas* to *virtus*: Cic., *Inv.* 1.5; *Balb.*, 4.10. Cf. Hellegouarc'h 1963: 298–9.
32. Caes. *BGall.* 5.35.6.
33. The only other occurrence for the Republican period is M. Petreius, *legatus* of C. Antonius Hybrida (*cos.* 63 BCE) at the battle of Pistoria in 62 (Cic., *Sest.* 12), precisely considered as *homo militaris* by Sallust (Sall. *Cat.* 59).

34. Rosenstein 1990: 130.
35. *BAfr.* 16.
36. Phang 2008: 95–6; Augier 2016a.
37. App. *BCiv.* 3.33.128.
38. Phang 2008: 240.
39. Phang 2008: 95–6.
40. Ouellet 2005: 83–4.
41. The notion of collective representations, defined in particular by M. Mauss and E. Durkheim, and used by historians like R. Chartier, can be defined as the way in which a community gives form and meaning to its experiences, stages a coherent system representation of the world.
42. Augier 2016b.
43. Pol. 6.37.10-11.
44. Caes. *BCiv.* 1.71-72, 3.74.2 (cf. App. *BCiv.* 2.64); *BAfr.* 82; Plut. *Caes.* 40.1, *Pomp.* 67-68.1 (cf. Caes. *BCiv.* 3.82); App. *BCiv.* 4.516. The advice could however be sometimes more contrasted (Caes. *BCiv.* 1.67, 2.30-31; cf. *BGall.* 3.5, 5.28-30).
45. However, this is not a particularity of the late Republican period: this was also the case before the battle of Pydna in 168 BCE (Liv. 44.37.10-40.1; Plut. *Aem.* 17.6; cf. Hammond 1984: 33 and Lendon 2005: 199).
46. Lendon 2005: 200.
47. It is well illustrated by M. Porcius Cato's death during the battle of Philippi (Plut. *Cat. Min.* 73.5, *Brut.* 49.9; App. *BCiv.* 4.135).
48. Wiedemann 1996: 98. Cf. Cic. *Off.* 2.45.
49. Plut. *Ant.* 42.
50. App. *BCiv.* 5.86.
51. Caes. *BGall.* 8.48.
52. Caes. *BCiv.* 3.60 (if we accept the identification between this C. Volusenus and C. Volusenus Quadratus).
53. For instance, Cicero's son displayed great valour during the campaign of Pharsalus and gained the affection and confidence of the soldiers as well as of Pompey (Cic. *Off.* 2.45). On morale: MacMullen 1984: 448; cf. Kellet 1982: 319–22 and English 1996: 90.
54. Luc. 4.539-581; Flor. 2.13.33.
55. Nuciari 2006: 64. We have according to Harris 2006: 304 and Phang 2011: 107–8 no explicit evidence for the existence of membership in one small 'primary group' or unit, creating powerful loyalties between the soldiers.
56. Ouellet 2005: 80–1.
57. App. *BCiv.* 2.47.195.
58. Cass. Dio 42.53.5.
59. De Blois 2000: 23 (cf. *ibid.* 1992 and 1994).
60. On military *contiones*: Pina Polo 1989: 199–217.
61. Caes. *BCiv.* 1.7-9.
62. Cass. Dio 46.56.2.
63. Cic. *Fam.* 10.21.4.

The Changing Face of the Command Structure During the Civil Wars (49–30 BCE)

64. Cass. Dio 47.42.2.
65. De Blois 2000: 23-24.
66. Cass. Dio 48.12.3 (cf. Ferriès 2007: 196). The expression βουλὴ καλιγᾶτα used by Cassius Dio is a translation from *senatus caligatus*.
67. App. *BCiv.* 3.29.112.
68. Mangiameli 2012: 48–9.
69. For example, App. *BCiv.* 3.32.125-126 and 5.20.79.
70. App. *BCiv.* 3.44.183.
71. Cass. Dio 45.13.3.
72. Chrissanthos 2001.
73. App. *BCiv.* 5.128.531-533.
74. Keppie 1983: 105.
75. Demougin 1983: 289; Augier 2016b.
76. De Blois 2000: 29.
77. Augier 2016b.
78. Cadiou 2018: 339–55 who shows that it should not be considered as a sign of the proletarization of the Roman armies at the end of the Republican period.
79. Phang 2008: 288 (cf. Watson 1969: 125).
80. *D.*3.2.2.2 (Ulp. 6 *ad ed.*) and 49.16.13.3 (Macer 2 *De Re Mil.*).
81. Giuffrè 1974: 242–63. For a similar procedure: Caes. *BCiv.* 3.74.1 (cf. Liv. 3.29.1-2; 27.13.9; Tac. *Ann.* 1.44.5).
82. *BAfr.* 54.4.
83. *Contra* Phang 2008: 141.
84. *D.*49.16.13.3 (Macer 2 *De Re Mil.*), 3.2.1.pr (Iul. 1 *ad ed.*), 3.2.2.pr. (Ulp. 6 *ad ed.*).
85. Thomas 2007: 300; Bur 2018.
86. Phang 2008: 112 and 141.
87. *RS* 1: 357-391, n.24 (l.120-121: *quemve imperator ignominiae caussa ab exercitu decedere iusit iuserit*).
88. *StR3* 1, 119–20, 221 and 228–9=*DP* 1, 136–7, 252 and 260; Smith 1958: 60–1; Gruen 1974: 112–13; Goldsworthy 1996: 14.
89. They could, however, be part of the exceptional *sacramenta* (e. g. App. *BCiv.* 1.66; Caes. *BCiv.* 1.76, 3.13.3–4, 3.87).
90. Phang 2008: 112 (cf. Lendon 1997: 248–9).

CHAPTER 9
THE CIVIL WAR OF 43–42 BCE AND ARMY FINANCES
François Gauthier

In his famous description of the Roman Republic's political system, Polybius argues that consuls could not obtain supplies, pay, and clothing for their armies without the approval of the Senate.[1] There is disagreement among modern scholars as to what extent Roman generals in the middle and late Republic were really dependent on the Senate for supplies and pay. Some defend the view that the Romans quickly implemented regular provincial taxation to fund armies operating far from Rome, notably in Spain.[2] Others, however, believe that the Romans instead made *ad hoc* requisitions of money, food, and auxiliaries from populations located near war zones, a phenomenon that has been labelled a 'war economy'.[3]

Regardless of the side one chooses to defend in this debate, it seems clear that Roman generals were not entirely dependent on the *aerarium* (treasury) for the maintenance of their armies. For example, in the early years of the Second Punic War, the Roman commanders operating in Spain wrote to the Senate that they needed a great many things for the army but that they would obtain these *in situ* if no funds were available in Rome. The supplies ended up being provided by three companies of private entrepreneurs, and the soldiers' pay was supplied by local resources.[4]

The coming of civil war as well as several episodes of political instability earlier in the first century BCE caused a certain decentralization in the financing of Roman armies as well as the use of improvised measures. Indeed, the faction that did not control Italy, and thus lacked access to the *aerarium*, had to find other means of funding its troops. For example, during his campaign against Mithridates, Sulla, cut off from a Rome controlled by his enemies, billeted his soldiers in private houses, and demanded that the owners provide them with food and money.[5] He commandeered the treasures of the sanctuaries of Epidaurus and Olympia as well as the wealth of the Delphic Amphictyony.[6] He also inflicted an enormous fine of 20,000 talents on the province of Asia and required 2,000 talents from Mithridates.[7] He surely intended to use this money to finance the war against his enemies in Italy. Indeed, he was so hard-pressed for funds that his soldiers even offered him money out of their own pocket to fight his opponents, something that he refused.[8] In addition to this, some of the money later raised from proscriptions in 82–81 was certainly used to reward his army.[9] Subsequently, during the Spanish campaign against Sertorius, Pompey bitterly complained in 74 about the lack of funds from Rome, claiming that for three years he had mostly paid for the upkeep of his army himself and had received less than a year's worth of what was needed. He asserted that he had spent all his personal credit and would not be able to continue fighting without funds from Rome.[10]

Although Pompey's resources may indeed have been exhausted by his expenditure in Spain, he eventually gained the means to potentially finance another campaign himself, if necessary. Indeed, during his eastern campaigns in the 60s, he supported an eastern king in his bid to regain the throne. Cicero mentions a later heir of that king, Ariobarzanes III, still repaying the debt several years later: the thirty-three talents (about 200,000 *denarii*) handed over per month did not even cover the interest Pompey was demanding. He also supported Tigranes of Armenia in exchange for a sum of 6,000 talents (36 million *denarii*), and the final sum agreed upon was supposedly even greater than that.[11] At the end of his eastern campaigns, Pompey was able to give 25 million *denarii* to each of his staff officers.[12] Clearly, the amounts of wealth available to generals like Pompey were reaching levels unimaginable just a few decades earlier.

Caesar likewise used his own funds to pay for some of his troops in Gaul. According to Suetonius, he raised extra legions out of his own pocket for his campaigns, and defrayed the cost of their *stipendium* until 56.[13] He did eventually receive public money to pay for all his legions but was nevertheless able to finance some of them for quite some time, much like Pompey in Spain. A final example is that of Lucullus. According to Plutarch, when the Roman general captured the Armenian capital Tigranocerta in 69, the royal treasure it contained allowed him to finance the war without funds from Rome, something about which he boasted.[14] This was, of course, done for political reasons, but the fact remains that the money allowed Lucullus a certain degree of financial independence in the field.

This contribution will examine the civil war of 43–42 that culminated in the battle(s) of Philippi, and it will argue that this conflict continued the trend towards the decentralization of army financing and exemplifies to the extreme the main features of Roman war financing in the Republic: improvisation, *ad hoc* requisitions, and the exploitation of fiscal regimes already in place. Indeed, the armies gathered for the campaign leading to the battle of Philippi were of an enormous size. None of the battles fought during the previous rounds of civil war could match the numbers of combatants involved at Philippi.[15] The cost of fielding such troops was immense and forced commanders on both sides to use expedients that were unsustainable in the long run.

1. Strength of the armies

1.1 Cassius and Brutus

Cassius and Brutus originally left Italy without any forces.[16] However, some of Pompey's soldiers who had survived the battle of Pharsalus joined Brutus' ranks in Thessaly, presumably enticed by the money he received from Asia; volunteers from Italy came to him as well.[17] Once he arrived in Illyria, Brutus took over from the province's former governor the three legions stationed there. To these three legions, he added five more, including two legions entirely made up of Macedonians and trained to fight in the Roman fashion.[18] There were presumably large numbers of non-Romans recruited in other legions as well to bolster their strength as Pompey had done before confronting

Caesar at Dyrrachium and Pharsalus. In addition to this, he also recruited large numbers of cavalry, light-armed troops, and archers.[19] Cassius took command of twelve or thirteen legions in Syria and Palestine, two of which were perhaps composed of provincial natives.[20] However, Cassius did not bring all of these legions to Philippi, as some were sent elsewhere.[21] Thus, Cassius and Brutus commanded some twenty-one legions, of which about seventeen were engaged at Philippi.[22] These seventeen legions cost 20.4 million *denarii* in *stipendium* (25.2 million for all twenty-one legions). Cassius and Brutus also had 17,000 cavalrymen from many regions of the Mediterranean; these included Gauls, Lusitanians, Thracians, Illyrians, Parthians, Thessalians, Spaniards, Arabs, and Medes.[23] Finally, in addition to their land forces, both Cassius and Brutus had assembled a navy of about 200 ships.[24]

1.2 Mark Antony and Octavian

Following the war of Mutina and the establishment of the Triumvirate, Mark Antony and Octavian had twenty legions each, although only nineteen of these were present at Philippi. The legionary strength of the triumviral army was probably around 100,000 men since Appian indicates that their legions were at full strength.[25] In terms of cavalry, Octavian and Antony had 13,000 horsemen at their disposal, including Thracians, 'barbarians', and 2,000 Lacedaemonians.[26] The Triumvirs had also built a fleet of their own to transport their army into Greece. Since a force of seventy ships was enough to destroy most of Octavian's fleet at Brundisium,[27] it has been proposed that the strength of the triumviral fleet was likely no more than sixty ships.[28]

2. Expenditure

2.1 Cassius and Brutus

As highlighted above, according to the strength of their army, Cassius and Brutus needed some 20.4 million *denarii* for the *stipendium* of their seventeen legions.[29] The 17,000 cavalry were mostly provided by allies. In the Republic, it was customary for allied communities to pay the contingents they were sending to the Roman army. However, this practice started to change during the civil wars, and auxiliary units financed by Roman generals begin to appear.[30] Still, in this case it seems reasonable to argue that most auxiliary units were probably financed by their own communities because of the already very important sums of money required to pay such a huge army. The upkeep of

Table 9.1 Opposing forces at Philippi in 42 BCE

	Cassius and Brutus	Antony and Octavian
Legions	17	19
Cavalry	17,000	13,000

the fleet also necessitated large amounts of money. Roman sailors in the Republic were paid by the state, but there is unfortunately no information about the value of this pay.[31] There are two categories of people to consider here. Marines were legionaries temporarily serving on ships, probably receiving the same *stipendium* as their comrades serving on land. Rowers, however, were most often drawn from the poorest elements of society who did not meet the property qualification for service in the land army. Writing about the imperial period, some scholars have proposed that sailors received as much as imperial auxiliary infantrymen, who were paid less than legionaries.[32] More recently, Michael Taylor has suggested that Republican sailors and legionaries received the same pay.[33] I find this suggestion attractive even though there is no hard evidence to prove it. For the sake of simplicity, I will follow Taylor and assume that sailors (marines and rowers) received the same pay. According to Polybius, Roman quinqueremes in the First Punic War had a crew of 420, that is 120 marines and 300 rowers.[34] However, the number of marines could vary greatly as more would be added from the land army in preparation for a naval battle. I will therefore only calculate the rowers' *stipendium*. Thus, the 200 ships attested required at least some 13.5 million *denarii* in *stipendium* or perhaps lower if some of the ships were crewed by Greek allies. Furthermore, Brutus and Cassius felt they had to be extremely generous with their men because many had served under Caesar, and they feared that their loyalty might waver in the presence of his heir.[35] To put things in perspective, to honour their promise of 4,500 *denarii* to their seventeen legions, Cassius and Brutus needed some 230–267 million *denarii* (see Table 9.2 below).

2.2 Mark Antony and Octavian

On the side of the Triumvirs, Octavian and Antony had to pay some 20.5 million *denarii* in *stipendium* for the 100,000 legionaries they mobilized against their enemies. Since their 13,000 cavalry are described as non-Roman, I will assume that the majority were paid by the polities providing them.[36] The sixty ships required about 4 million *denarii* in *stipendium* for rowers.

This is only a fraction of the money that the Triumvirs had to find. Indeed, like their enemies, they also offered lavish donatives to their men, so much so that it made the *stipendium* look like a triviality. For example, after the first battle of Philippi, Antony and Octavian promised 5,000 *denarii* to their surviving soldiers, some 84,000 men.[37] This meant a total amount of 420 million *denarii*(!). Octavian's gift of 2,500 *denarii* to his ten legions in 43 adds another 100 to 125 million *denarii* to the total. All in all, the cost of *stipendium* and donatives (if they were all really paid) for the Triumvirs reaches 520 to 545 million *denarii* (more than 100,000 talents, see Table 9.2 below). In addition to money, the Triumvirs promised settlement in eighteen Italian towns to their troops to strengthen their will to fight.[38] Finally, Lawrence Keppie has suggested that after the campaign one or often two legions were settled on the territory of each town selected. He identified the following cities used to settle veterans: Ancona, Aquinum, Ariminum, Asculum, Beneventum, Bononia, Capua, Concordia, Cremona, Firmum, Hadria, Hispellum, Luca, Nuceria, Pisaurum, Teanum, Tergeste, and Venusia.[39]

The Civil War of 43–42 BCE and Army Finances

Table 9.2 Gifts to soldiers 43–42 BCE[40]

Date	Sum of Money	Source	Beneficiaries, Total Sum
43: Octavian to 10 legions	2,500 (plus 2,500 promised)	App. *BCiv.* 3.94.387; Cass. Dio 46.46.6	*c.* 40,000–50,000 men, 100–125 m. *denarii*
42: Antony and Octavian after first battle of Philippi	5,000 (promised)	App. *BCiv.* 4.120.507; Plut. *Ant.* 23.1	*c.* 84,000 men, 420 m. *denarii*
42: Brutus and Cassius on the eve of Philippi	1,500	App. *BCiv.* 4.100.422	*c.* 70,000–85,000 men, 105–127 m. *denarii*
42: Brutus, after first battle of Philippi	1,000 (Appian) 2,000 (Plutarch)	App. *BCiv.* 4.118.498; 5.30; Plut. *Brut.* 44.4; 46.1	*c.* 62,000–77,000 men, 62–77 m. *denarii* (Appian) *c.* 62,000–77,000 men, 124–140 m. *denarii* (Plutarch)

3. Sources of income

As mentioned at the beginning of this chapter, Roman war financing in the Republic was characterized by the use of *ad hoc* measures complementing regular ones. The campaign of 43–42 was no exception. This included cash requisitions (also known as extortion), extraordinary taxes, regular taxation, and (in the case of the Triumvirs) proscriptions. These measures have sometimes been labelled a 'war economy', as opposed to a model in which armies were strictly funded by regular provincial taxation. In fact, the armies fielded in this campaign were so large and the donatives promised so high, that generals needed to extract as much money as possible from the areas they controlled in order to be able to pay their troops.

According to Plutarch, state income before Pompey's expedition in the East in the early 60s was on the order of 50 million *denarii*, at a time when Rome did not experience civil war and was in control of most of its provinces. Pompey's campaign increased the state revenues to 85 million *denarii*.[41] However, as Nathan Rosenstein and Michael Taylor have recently demonstrated, the revenues of the Roman state were actually very volatile as they relied to a large extent on plunder and war indemnities.[42] If Plutarch's figure is accepted as roughly accurate, it nevertheless seems small compared to the cost for the armies I have proposed earlier. It is thus not surprising to hear a lot in our sources about generals desperately trying to raise money as immense sums were needed to pay for tens of thousands of soldiers.[43]

3.1 Cassius and Brutus

In the spring of 44, Brutus and Cassius had sent envoys to collect money in Asia and Bithynia.[44] Later, after Brutus reached Asia, he gathered some 16,000 talents (*c.* 100

million *denarii*) from the taxes collected there.[45] In addition to this, the quaestor in Syria gave him a further 500,000 *denarii*.[46] Writing to Cicero in April 43, Brutus mentioned that money was among the things he needed the most.[47] Therefore, in 42, Brutus kept going and took 150 talents (900,000 *denarii*) from the Lycians.[48]

Meanwhile, Cassius also obtained money in Asia after his arrival in 44.[49] In 43, he sent his cavalry to kill the king of Cappadocia on charges of plotting against him and seized his royal treasury.[50] He then demanded 1,500 talents (9 million *denarii*) from Tarsus. Lacking the money, the townspeople were compelled to sell all public property to gather the necessary funds, including temple offerings. When they realized that this was not enough, they had to sell citizens into slavery to acquire more money.[51]

Cassius punished Rhodes because of its resistance to him by demanding all its gold and silver: 800 talents in total (4.8 million *denarii*). He also fined the city for 1,500 additional talents (9 million *denarii*).[52] Finally, in addition to this, Cassius and Brutus demanded ten years' worth of tribute from Asia. This amounted to an unknown, yet surely tremendous amount of money.[53] In total, it has been calculated that Cassius and Brutus collected between 25,000 and 30,000 talents in Asia and Lycia (150 to 180 million *denarii*, see Table 9.3 below).[54]

Table 9.3 Attested sources of income for Cassius and Brutus

Location/ Community	Date and Source	Sum/Goods	Type of Transaction
Bithynia	44, App. *BCiv.* 3.6	Money and ships	Taxes
Greece	44, App. *BCiv.* 3, 63; 4.75; Plut. *Brut.* 24–25; Cass. Dio 47.21.3	16,000 talents (=96 million *denarii*) +500,000 *denarii*	Tribute and fundraising
Asia	44, Cass. Dio 47.26.1	–	Tribute
Tarsus	43, App. *BCiv.* 4.64	1,500 talents	Confiscation of public money and selling of the population
King of Cappadocia	43, App. *BCiv.* 4.63	Personal wealth of the king	Confiscation
Asia	43/42, App. *BCiv.* 4.82; 5.2; 5.5	Unknown, likely considerable	Extraordinary tribute imposed (worth ten years)
Rhodes	42, Plut. *Brut.* 32; Cass. Dio 47.33.4	Plut.: 800 talents +500 in fine	Extraordinary contribution/fine
Lycia	42, Plut. *Brut.* 32; App. *BCiv.* 4.81; 4.82	150 talents, plus precious metal and ships	Extraordinary contribution/fine

3.2 Octavian and Mark Antony

Octavian had inherited the wealth of his adoptive father, Caesar. He could also count on the property of his biological father, his mother, and stepfather.[55] Furthermore, after he learned of Caesar's death in early 44, Octavian sent for the money prepared for Caesar's planned campaign against the Parthians, some of which was in Brundisium.[56] As a result, he acquired a sum that was probably considerable. However, the resources of Italy were severely depleted by the Mutina campaign that took place in early 43.[57] Yet, as more money was needed to finance the campaign against Cassius and Brutus, new expedients had to be devised.

In August of 43, Octavian marched on Rome and demanded to be reimbursed with public money for what he had spent on his army.[58] Following the alliance of Octavian, Lepidus and Mark Antony, the Triumvirs embarked on a large-scale programme to finance their army. They issued proscription lists, putting to death and confiscating the property of some 300 senators and 2,000 equestrians. Since this was not sufficient for the needs of their enormous forces, they were reduced to reintroduce the *tributum* (suspended in 167) and to burden the population with additional harsh demands for money and duties on houses, sales, leases, and personal wealth.[59] Money was also taken from temples and contributions were even demanded from rich women, something that created an outcry among them.[60] Despite all these measures, the Triumvirs were short of some 200 million *denarii* for the coming war.[61] Therefore, the proscriptions were extended the following year, although this time it did not entail the death of those listed.[62] After they had landed in Greece, Mark Antony and Octavian relied primarily on the resources of Macedon and Thessaly, for their enemies' naval superiority prevented their bringing in money and supplies from other provinces.[63]

The tremendous clash at Philippi eliminated both Brutus and Cassius, but it did not put an end to the financial misery of Asia Minor. Indeed, despite their victory, the Triumvirs were still in need of money to honour the promises they had made to their soldiers. For instance, Mark Antony is said to have asked for land in Asia Minor for his men, notably around Ephesus. Plutarch reports that Mark Antony asked for more money even after Asia gave him the fantastic sum of 200,000 talents (1.2 billion *denarii*!) though this is surely an exaggeration to emphasize Mark Antony's lack of self-control. Nevertheless, it eloquently illustrates the financial burden of the civil war armies.[64] Unsurprisingly, modern research has usually argued that the cities of Asia Minor went bankrupt as a result of the hardships they endured.[65] However, more recently, François Kirbihler has pointed out that there do not seem to be interruptions in the lists of magistrates tasked with the organization of certain festivals in Miletus and Ephesus for the years 44 to 41.[66] Such magistrates had to pay with their own money for the duties associated with the position. In times of financial difficulties, the lack of candidates for such magistracies could lead to a god being 'appointed' in lieu of a citizen. In such cases, temple treasuries would take care of the required expenditure.[67] That being said, even if Ephesus and Miletus may have fared better than other communities, there can be no doubt that the cities of Asia Minor suffered from a tremendous financial burden. When

Table 9.4 Attested sources of income for Octavian and Antony

Location/Community	Date and Source	Sum/Goods	Type of Transaction
Rome	44, Cic. *Phil.* 2.93	175 million *denarii*	Money left by Caesar seized by Antony in the temple of Ops (likely spent in the Mutina campaign)
Italy	44, Plut. *Ant.* 15	24 million *denarii*	Taken from Caesar's property and given by Calpurnia
East	44, Nic. Dam. *Vita* 18	Considerable	Money for Caesar's campaign against the Parthians demanded by Octavian
Italy	43, App. *BCiv.* 4.5-7	Property of 300 senators and 2,000 equestrians confiscated	Proscriptions
Mostly Italy	43, Cic. *Fam.* 12.30	Likely considerable	Reintroduction of the *Tributum* (war-tax)
Italy	43, Cass. Dio 46.31.3; 47.14.2; App. *BCiv.* 4.34	Likely considerable	Extraordinary taxes
Italy	43, App. *BCiv.* 4.3; 4.5; 4.32-34; 5.13; 5.22; 5.24; 5.27; Cass. Dio 48.12.4	Likely considerable	Money taken from temples
Italy	42, Cass. Dio 47.16	Likely considerable	Extension of proscriptions

Sulla imposed a fine of 20,000 talents on Asia Minor after the First Mithridatic War, the cities were so hard pressed that they had to borrow money at very high rates of interest so that the total sum amounted to 120,000 talents.[68] We can therefore assume a similar level of distress in 44–42 since we are talking about a more or less equal order of magnitude.

4. A juggernaut funded by a 'war economy'?

What kind of model is implied by the financial measures of Roman civil war? It used to be thought that the end of *tributum* in 167 meant that the provinces were now all taxed to fund their Roman masters' treasury.[69] However, the gradual implementation of provincial taxation did not follow a systematic and uniform plan applied to all provinces.

Rather, the Roman state used a variety of ways to extract resources from the provinces. Sometimes pre-existing fiscal regimes were used, such as in Sicily, while in other cases, informal requisitions of money, supplies, and auxiliaries were preferred.[70] So, whereas provincial resources were used by Rome for its army in various ways, it cannot be stated that they quickly replaced the revenues brought by the *tributum* paid by Roman citizens as the implementation of provincial taxation was a long and gradual process.[71] In fact, the suspension of *tributum* in 167 shows a certain lack of long-term planning in terms of military financing. It is worth remembering that the *tributum* had been the steadiest source of income to finance soldiers' *stipendium* since its introduction in the early Republic and what allowed Rome to field armies in the first place.[72] Despite the increase in military expenditure in the first century as a result of the enfranchisement of the Italians and Caesar's increase in pay, no provisions were ever made to create a reserve of emergency funds comparable to what Athens did before the Peloponnesian War. On that occasion, the Athenians had accumulated 6,000 talents on the Acropolis, mostly provided by the payments made by the subject-allies.[73]

According to Philip Kay, the cost of the army between 99 and 50 BCE was about 1.1 billion *denarii*, while state income amounted to roughly 1.7 billion *denarii* for the same period.[74] However, neither the Triumvirs nor Caesar's assassins had access to the resources of the entire empire, yet they raised enormous armies whose total cost was certainly higher than what a 'normal state budget' of *c*. 85 million *denarii* could afford, notably because of the donatives repeatedly promised.[75] Therefore, generals had to focus on solutions that allowed them to extract as much money as possible from the areas they controlled. By doing so, they were continuing a trend that started with civil war itself in the time of Sulla. Moreover, the unprecedented decentralization of coin production attests the efforts of minting enough money to pay the huge mass of soldiers mobilized for the war.[76] Even if one disagrees with the concept of a 'war economy' for earlier periods of the Republic, it can surely be applied to the civil war of 43–42.[77]

After the final defeat of Mark Antony at the battle of Actium in 31, Octavian found himself in command of some 500,000 soldiers, a formidable force whose members desired rewards for their toil during years of civil strife.[78] This enormous mass of soldiers was not to be trifled with if another civil war was to be avoided. Paying and rewarding such a large army required immense quantities of cash as Octavian knew from his experience of the Philippi campaign as well as earlier ones in Italy. Maintaining armies of this size and giving them lavish handouts was bankrupting the state, forcing generals to levy special taxes and confiscate property and money everywhere they brought their armies. Such measures were hardly conducive to the pacific and lasting establishment of a new regime. Something had to be done on both the strategic and institutional levels to put an end to such improvisation. A system mixing plunder, war indemnities, taxation and *ad hoc* measures had worked for most of the Republican period, but the sheer size of the civil wars broke down this model of financing. Augustus changed this by introducing new taxes to finance the standing army he created.[79] These reforms ensured that from the reign of Augustus onward, the army would be funded by a new military treasury rather than by extortion and improvisation.[80]

Notes

1. Pol. 6.15.2-5: 'The consul, when he leaves with his army invested with the powers I mentioned, appears indeed to have absolute authority in all matters necessary for carrying out his purpose; but, in fact, he requires the support of the people and the Senate, and is not able to bring his operations to a conclusion without them. For it is obvious that the legions require constant supplies, and without the consent of the Senate, neither corn nor clothing, nor pay can be provided; so that the commander's plans come to nothing, if the Senate chooses to be deliberately negligent and obstructive'.
2. France 2006: 1–17; 2007a: 171–6; 2007b: 333–68; 2021; Cadiou 2008: 498.
3. Ñaco del Hoyo 2010: 169–82.
4. Liv. 23.48.4-49.4; also 23.21.1-4; Badian 1972: 16–20.
5. Plut. *Sull.* 25.2.
6. Plut. *Sull.* 12.5-9.
7. Plut. *Sull.* 22-33; 25.2; *Luc.* 4.1; 20; App. *Mithr.* 63.261. On the Mithridatic war, see Ñaco del Hoyo et al. 2011: 291–304; Ñaco del Hoyo and Arrayás-Morales 2016: 3–19.
8. Plut. *Sull.* 27.3.
9. App. *BCiv.* 1.95.442-444.
10. Sallust *Hist.* 2.98.M; Plut. *Luc.* 5.3; *Pomp.* 20.1.
11. Cic. *Att.* 6.1.3; 6.3.5. See also Westall 2017: 301–2.
12. Plin. *NH* 37.17; Tan 2017: 9–10; Shatzman 1975: 389–92.
13. Suet. *Iul.* 24.2: 'he added to the legions which he had received from the state others at his own cost'.
14. Plut. *Luc.* 29.7-10. The phrase is similar to that of Cato found in Livy 34.9.12: *bellum se ipse alet*. It is perhaps relevant to also mention here the famous quotation from Crassus found in Plutarch concerning the importance of an aristocrat's ability to finance an army, cf. Plut. *Crass.* 2.7.
15. App. *BCiv.* 3.46.190; 3.47.191; 3.66.270-271; 3.78.320; 3.79.324; 3.83.342; 3.91.373; 3.97.399-403. The forces involved at Pharsalus, Thapsus, and Munda were large (cf. Caes. *BCiv.* 3.4; *BAfr.* 59; 62; *Bhisp.* 30; Plut. *Pomp.* 64.1), but those at Philippi were even bigger, cf. Plut. *Brut.* 38.5. See also Brunt 1971: 485–7; von Domaszewski 1894: 157–88.
16. Plut. *Brut.* 28.7. See also Rawson 1986: 101–19.
17. Plut. *Brut.* 25-26; Cass. Dio 47.21; Cic. *Ad Brut.* 2.4.4. Many of these men were non-Romans, cf. Caes. *BCiv.* 3.4; Plut. *Pomp.* 64.2.
18. App. *BCiv.* 4.75.317; 3.79.324: 'and since he approved the valour of the Macedonians he raised two legions amongst them, whom, too, he drilled in the Italian discipline.'; Cic. *Phil.* 10.13-14.
19. App. *BCiv.* 4.75.318; *Ill.* 13.37.
20. App. *BCiv.* 78.318; Cass. 47.28.1. I follow here the suggestion of Brunt 1971: 476–7 and 486, arguing that two of his twelve legions might have been one of the legions recruited by King Deiotarus in Pontus, cf. *BAlex.* 34. The other one may have been composed of a nucleus of Roman troops left in Alexandria and reinforced by natives.
21. App. *BCiv.* 4.63.272; 74.315; 86.367.
22. Brunt 1971: 473, 487; Keppie 1997: 90.

23. Auxiliaries are again attested from nearly everywhere in the Roman world: Gauls, Lusitanians, Thracians, Illyrians, Thessalians, Iberians, Arabians, Medians, and Parthians, cf. Appian *BCiv.* 4.88.373. Appian later (4.108.454) gives the figure of 20,000 horsemen. Brunt 1971: 484, '[…] one may suspect that in all the new provincial units non-citizens were readily accepted or conscripted, especially if they had a veneer of Roman culture'. Brunt's point about Roman culture seems dubious as it is doubtful whether a Roman general would have enquired about the cultural background of his recruits.
24. App. *BCiv.* 3.63.259; 4.72.306: eighty ships; 74.315: sixty ships; 82.345; 86.367: fifty ships; 115.480: 130 ships; Cass. Dio 47.33.4: taking over Rhodian ships; Plut. *Brut.* 24.5; 28.3; 30.1; Kromayer 1897: 439–42.
25. App. *BCiv.* 4.3.9; 108.454; Brunt 1971: 480–8.
26. App. *BCiv.* 4.108.454; Plut. *Brut.* 41; 50. See also Moles 2017: 373.
27. App. *BCiv.* 5.26.104.
28. App. *BCiv.* 5.26.104; Plut. *Brut.* 47.3-4; App. *BCiv.* 4.115-116; Kromayer 1897: 445; Brunt 1971: 507.
29. Pay alone must have required huge amounts of cash: Frank 1933: 334, 'When the armies of the various generals rose to 70 and more legions, the expense involved would have used every penny of income even if the stipend had been the normal one of 120 denarii.' Also, 340–2 with sources. Taylor (2017: 152–3) has suggested an 'operative' cost of one million *denarii* for a legion in the mid-first century. This was before Caesar's increase in *stipendium* and must thus be increased substantially. Cf. Suet. *Iul.* 26.3: 'He doubled the pay of the legions for all time.' (*Caesar legionibus stipendium in perpetuum duplicavit*). Note that a common rate of pay for Hellenistic mercenaries was six obols (= 1 *denarius*), cf. Griffith 1935, 302; Thomsen 1973: 194–208; Rathbone 2007: 158–75. It is not impossible that credit was used in these operations: Harris 2019: 158–89. Most scholars agree that Caesar's pay increase resulted in a *stipendium* of 225 *denarii*. On this topic, see: Boren 1983: 446–50; Speidel 1992: 87–106; Alston 1994: 113–23; Pedroni 2001: 115–30. I argue that the increase in *stipendium* was matched by Caesar's enemies to limit desertions. This brought the cost of a legion in *stipendium* to about 1.2 million *denarii*.
30. Caes. *BCiv.* 3.59-60; *BAfr.* 6.1; 8.5; Speidel 2016: 93–4; Gauthier 2019: 251–68. I do not take for granted that legions no longer included a limited contingent of Roman cavalry but include them in the cost of a legion.
31. Liv. 24.11.7-9.
32. Starr 1960: 81; Watson 1969: 101–2; Reddé 1986: 557–8.
33. Taylor 2017: 153, quoting Pol. 10.35.5.
34. Pol. 1.26.7; 10.35.5; Liv. 24.11.7-9. Taylor 2017: 153, thinks that Roman quinqueremes would normally carry fewer marines than the figure of 120 provided by Polybius.
35. App. *BCiv.* 4.89.374. On donatives during the civil wars, see Laignoux 2014a: 223–4.
36. It is important to note that Roman citizen cavalry is still attested in the period, and it is now clear that there are no grounds to believe that Gaius Marius disbanded it. On this topic, see Cadiou 2016: 53–78.
37. App. *BCiv.* 4.120.507; Plut. *Ant.* 23.1.
38. Cass. Dio 47.14.2; App. *BCiv.* 4.3.12. On veteran settlement, see Keppie 1983: 58–69; Gabba 1953: 101–10. On donatives, see also Laignoux 2017: 71–94.
39. Keppie 1983: 63–4.
40. See Scheidel 2007: 330–1 for a table of cash handouts covering a longer timeframe.

41. Plut. *Pomp.* 45.4.3. The exact meaning of the passage in which Plutarch describes by how much money Pompey increased Rome's revenues has been debated. The Greek text says that there were already 50 million *denarii* from the taxes (ἐκ τῶν τελῶν), and that, through the places Pompey gained (προσεκτήσατο), they (i.e. the Romans) were taking (λαμβάνουσιν) 85 million *denarii*.
42. Taylor 2017: 169–70; Rosenstein 2016: 114–30.
43. On similar measures during the Caesarian civil war, see Westall 2017: 63; 90; 130.
44. App. *BCiv.* 3.6.18.
45. App. *BCiv.* 3.63.259; 4.75.316; Cass. Dio 47.21.3. The validity of the figure is questioned by Kirbihler 2013: 358, 'Quand on sait que sous Auguste les revenus de l'Empire entier devaient osciller autour de 400–450 ou plus probablement 500 millions de sesterces, il est impossible d'accepter ce nombre en année courante.' On taxation during that period, see Günther 2015: 213–27.
46. Plut. *Brut.* 25.1; Cass. Dio 47.21.3.
47. Cic. *Brut.* 2.3.5.
48. Plut. *Brut.* 32.4; App. *BCiv.* 4.82.345.
49. Cass. Dio 47.26.1.
50. App. *BCiv.* 4.63.272.
51. App. *BCiv.* 4.64.275.
52. Plut. *Brut.* 32.4; Cass. Dio 47.33.4. On this episode, see Westall 2015b: 125–67.
53. App. *BCiv.* 5.2.3-6; 5.24.
54. Kirbihler 2013: 359; Migeotte 2014: 412–13.
55. Suet. *Iul.* 83; Nic. Dam. *Vita* 13; Liv. *Per.* 116; App. *BCiv.* 3.23.89; Shatzman 1975: 357–62; Ridley 1980–1: 29.
56. Nic. Dam. *Vita* 18; Cass. Dio 45.3.2.
57. App. *BCiv.* 4.5.18; Cic. *Ep. ad Caes. iun.* frag. 5; Cass. Dio 46.31.3-4. The treasury was so depleted that certain games could not take place.
58. Cic. *Phil.* 5.53; Cass. Dio 46.29.3.
59. Cic. *Fam.*12.30; Cass. Dio 46.31.3; 47.14.2; proscriptions: App. *BCiv.* 4.5-7. Also: Cic. *Brut.* 1.18.5. On proscriptions, see Laignoux 2013: 367–85.
60. Money taken from temples: App. *BCiv.* 4.32-34; 5.13.53; 5.22.87; 5.24.97; 5.27.106; Cass. Dio 48.12.4; *RGDA* 1.24. See also Hopwood 2015: 305–22.
61. App. *BCiv.* 4.31.134. Also, Scuderi 1979: 341–68.
62. Cass. Dio 47.16.2-5.
63. App. *BCiv.* 4.117.494.
64. App. *BCiv.* 5.3.11; 5; 6; 13; 15.60; 22.86-87; Plut. *Ant.* 24.4-5: Asia would have given Antony 200,000 talents. See also Woytek 2003: 365–412. On the sources tendency to rhetorical exaggeration for large monetary figures, see Duncan-Jones 1994: 16–19; Scheidel 1996: 222–38.
65. Frank 1933: 341, 'Asia was bankrupt for a generation.' See also Ñaco del Hoyo et al. 2015: 35–55.
66. Kirbihler 2013: 361–2. On the other hand, there were interruptions in similar lists after the Mithridatic wars.

67. Migeotte 2014: 353–4.
68. Plut. *Sull.* 25.4; *Luc.* 20.4; App. *Mithr.* 63.261; Santangelo 2007: 111–33; Migeotte 2014: 330–1.
69. Arnold 1914: 194.
70. On Spain, see Richardson 1986; on Sicily, see Prag 2007: 68–100; also, Ñaco del Hoyo 2007: 226–30. See also the comprehensive study of France, 2021.
71. Lintott 1993: 70–96; Ñaco del Hoyo 2007: 218–31.
72. Rosenstein 2016: 114–30; Taylor 2020: 126–8.
73. Thuc. 2.13.3-4. On the enfranchisement of the Italians, see Nicolet 1978: 1–11. On Caesar's increase in pay, see n.29 above.
74. Kay 2014: 298; 300.
75. See n.41 for state income in the early 60s.
76. Hollstein 2000: 130, 'Die Jahre des Bürgerkrieges nach der Ermordung Caesars erlebten eine nie dagewesene Streuung von Prägeorten für römische Aurei und Denare über den Mittelmeerraum'. See also Crawford 1974 (I): 94–102; Woytek 2003: 467–528; Laignoux 2014b: 147–69.
77. On the concept of war economy, see Ñaco del Hoyo 2010: 169–82.
78. *RGDA* 3.3.
79. *RGDA* 17.2; Cass. Dio 55.25.3-6; Suet. *Aug.* 49.2; Tac. *Ann.* 1.78.
80. For the cost of the early imperial army, see the calculations of Duncan-Jones 1994: 33–7. For the cost of the late imperial army, see also Duncan-Jones 1990: 105–18.

CHAPTER 10
SALLUST'S MITHRIDATES AND THE CULTURAL TRAUMA OF CIVIL WAR
Jennifer Gerrish

1. Introduction*

All war creates damage both physical and psychic, but civil war inflicts an additional wound: destabilization of collective national identity as citizen is pitted against citizen. This ambiguity made the triumviral civil war not just an atrocity, but also, according to modern theorists, a collective or cultural trauma. Some scholars have suggested that an integral part of the healing process is normative inversion, the process of reconstituting community identity against the counter example of the trauma's perpetrators; recalling the atrocity of a foreign culture's violation of the community's values reinforces the perceived barbarity of the outsiders and, by contrast, the validity of the community's own values.

However, in the case of civil war, both perpetrators and victims are members of the same community with presumably – or at least formerly – shared values. This contribution argues that Sallust's Mithridates demonstrates the failure of normative inversion in the context of the triumviral civil war and the futility of trying to process Rome's ongoing trauma. As a foreign king and the only non-Roman in the *Histories* with extended *oratio recta*, Mithridates could have provided a barbarian 'Other' against which the audience might reconstitute a sense of shared Roman identity. However, Sallust's Mithridates fails to adhere to barbarian archetypes and is even assimilated to the figures of the triumvirs and the historian himself. By using Mithridates to destabilize the distinction between 'Roman' and 'barbarian', Sallust suggests that the healing function of normative inversion fails in the context of the traumatic triumviral conflicts and raises the grim possibility that a collective sense of Roman identity cannot be recovered.[1]

2. Sallust's *Histories*

2.1 The text

Sallust's *Histories*, composed around 39–35 BCE, survive to us in approximately 500 fragments, the majority of which are brief quotations passed down by the grammarians. Thanks in part to the grammarians' diligence in preserving context and book numbers, the overall architecture of the *Histories* is generally well-established, and the fragments have been allocated to five books.[2] The main narrative seems to begin with the death of

Sulla in 78 and appears to break off during the debate over the *lex Gabinia* in 67; the intended terminus of the work is unknown, and it is thought to have been left unfinished at the author's death around 35. In addition to the 500 or so individual fragments (mostly citations by grammarians), we also possess four speeches and two letters from the *Histories* that have been preserved in a separate manuscript tradition. The two letters, one from Pompey to the Senate and the other from Mithridates to King Arsaces, belong to separate years and books, but much like the speeches also seem to function as a pair (as I shall discuss below).

2.2. The historiographical programme of the Histories

At the narrative level, the *Histories* are an account of the turbulent years following Sulla's death. However, I have argued elsewhere that this densely allusive work is also a trenchant, but implicit critique of the triumviral regime.[3] The historical parallels between narrative time (the 70s and 60s) and compositional time (the early 30s) offered Sallust abundant material for comparison, and he artfully amplified or exaggerated those pre-existing parallels.[4] So much was the same: civil turmoil as the *res publica* struggled to reconstitute itself in the wake of a dictator's death was accompanied by competing claims to *libertas*, *pietas*, *res publica restituta*, and so forth, as the cowed Senate deferred to the strongman whose fortune appeared brightest or whose army appeared strongest at any given moment. There was generational continuity, as well. Most obvious were the Lepidi; the rebellion of Marcus Aemilius Lepidus, consul of 78, was featured in Book One, and his son Marcus Aemilius Lepidus was a member of the ruling Triumvirate under whose regime Sallust wrote. Add to this: Pompey Magnus and Sextus Pompey, Marcus Antonius Creticus (pr. 74 BCE) and Marcus Antonius the Triumvir, and Lucius Marcius Philippus, step-grandfather of the Triumvir Octavian.

Using these natural parallels and continuities as a foundation, Sallust layered his account of the post-Sullan era with allusions to contemporary events and figures. For example, the aforementioned revolt of Lepidus was depicted in such a way as to recall the recent siege of Perusia. Both uprisings were located in Etruria, and in both cases, suffering Italians followed demagogues who professed to be taking up the cause of the dispossessed in the wake of civil war. These structural echoes were underscored with literary ones, particularly in the speech of Philippus against Lepidus, in which numerous linguistic, stylistic and thematic echoes of Cicero's *Philippics* have been identified.[5] In another passage to which we will return shortly, Pompey's letter to the Senate, we find an additional example that demonstrates how the *Histories*' slippage of time works in both directions. Under-provisioned and overmatched by Sertorius, Pompey writes to the Senate from Spain asking for reinforcements and supplies. Should the Senate refuse his requests, he says, he will be forced to march into Italy with his army, 'bringing the whole Spanish War' with him.[6] Pompey's threat to bring a war from Spain into Italy obviously evokes Hannibal, but the idea of armed Romans moving towards the city probably also evoked the memory of the marches by Sulla and Caesar; and, most recently for Sallust's audience, Octavian.

The method of 'analogical historiography' through which Sallust presents his critique of contemporary politics and society via his portrayal of the past achieves multiple aims. First, historical allusion encourages readers to approach the narrative with a critical eye and peel back its layers like an onion. Not merely an academic exercise, this type of interrogation was necessary for the preservation of history and truth under a regime that engaged in multiple media to promote its own versions of 'history' and 'truth'.[7] Second, allusion is a form of literary repetition and, as such, underscores the reiterative nature of civil war (one of Sallust's themes).[8]

This repetition may also have a therapeutic effect. In *Remembering, Repeating, and Working-Through* and *Beyond the Pleasure Principle* Sigmund Freud observed that trauma victims often seem compelled to return to and even re-enact their trauma in real life or in dreams.[9] These indirect repetitions, Freud theorized, allow the trauma sufferer to retroactively attempt to master the original trauma. Cathy Caruth, whose work has examined the intersection of literature, collective memory, and psychoanalytic theories of trauma, has 'scaled-up' this theory to the level of cultural trauma.[10] Focusing on 'insistently recurring' words, images, and motifs in literature and film, she has argued that these repeated textual returns function like recurring nightmares as the narrator attempts belatedly to understand and repair the original wound.[11] The historical allusions in Sallust's *Histories* may perform a similar function, if, as I shall argue, the triumviral civil wars may be said to constitute a cultural trauma.

3. Theories of cultural trauma

3.1 Trauma theory and ancient historiography

In recent years, scholars of the Greco-Roman world have shown an increasing interest in the role of trauma in classical texts. As is often the case with 'new' applications of theory, trauma theory was first explored in poetry, specifically Homer and Greek tragedy, and has largely focused on combat trauma and post-traumatic stress disorder in ancient narratives.[12] Scholars of historiography have been slower to embrace trauma theory, but recent work in this vein shows promise of future inquiry.[13]

3.2 Cultural trauma and normative inversion

Since the label 'trauma' is used variously by laypeople, mental health professionals and academics of various stripes, it will be useful to briefly outline the terms under which I argue the civil wars constituted a 'cultural trauma'. In attempting to create a working definition of 'cultural trauma', Jeffrey Alexander argued that the difference between *a terrible thing that happens to a community* and a *collective or cultural trauma* is that '[c]ultural trauma occurs when members of a collectivity feel they have been subjected to a horrendous event that leaves indelible marks upon their group consciousness, marking their memories forever and changing their future identity in fundamental and irrevocable ways'.[14] We might also consider the evocative description by Kai Erickson, distinguishing between individual and collective trauma in his account of the aftermath of a devastating flood in the coal mining region of West Virginia:

> By individual trauma I mean a blow to the psyche that breaks through one's defenses so suddenly and with such brutal force that one cannot react to it effectively [...] By collective trauma, on the other hand, I mean a blow to the basic tissues of social life that damages the bonds attaching people together and impairs the prevailing sense of communality. The collective trauma works its way slowly and even insidiously into the awareness of those who suffer from it, so it does not have the quality of suddenness normally associated with 'trauma'. But it is a form of shock all the same, a gradual realization that the community no longer exists as an effective source of support and that an important part of the self has disappeared.[15]

In the context of these definitions, I would suggest that the Roman civil wars of the first century BCE may defensibly be described as a cultural trauma. The various contributions of this volume demonstrate the widespread breakdown of models during the civil wars, as traditional systems of morality, politics, economics, patronage, and so forth failed under the pressures of internecine strife. The concomitant breakdown of shared identity can be witnessed in the anguished literary sources of the period (including and beyond Sallust).[16] As has been noted, one of the characteristics of a cultural trauma according to Alexander's criteria is that it fundamentally changes the community's self-definition and spurs the creation of new boundaries and markers of identity. One means by which this occurs is the process of what Jan Assmann termed 'normative inversion'.[17] The fracturing of community identity is one of those elements that constitute trauma rather than just an awful event; in particular, cultural trauma brings with it the sense that the values that unite a group have been compromised. Normative inversion is the process of what Assmann also describes as 'contra-distinctive self-definition'[18] – in short, we reconstitute our sense of shared identity by uniting against the outside group (often, but not always foreign) that perpetrated our trauma. For example, we might consider the concomitant rise of 'patriotism' and virulent anti-Muslim sentiment in the United States as a response to the 9/11 attacks (although that is a complicated example, as is discussed in the conclusions below).

The problem presented by the triumviral civil wars, of course, is that the atrocities – land confiscations, proscriptions and so forth – were committed by members of the same community as their victims. Alexandra Eckert has used Valerius Maximus' treatment of the Sullan proscriptions as one example of how to negotiate this. Valerius explicitly compares Sulla's atrocities with Hannibal's cruelty:

> L. Sulla, quem neque laudare neque vituperare quisquam satis digne potest, quia, dum quaerit victorias, Scipionem se populo Romano, dum exercet, Hannibalem repraesentavit.
>
> Val. Max. 9.2.1

> Lucius Sulla, whom no one is able to either praise or reproach sufficiently, because when he was seeking victories, he showed himself to be a Scipio to the Roman people, but when he achieved them, he recreated Hannibal.

As Eckert summarizes, '[c]omparing the cruelty of the Roman Sulla with the non-Roman Hannibal underlines the extreme transgression of Roman values by Sulla.'[19] In other words, a *real* Roman did not do this to us; *our* identity and values are intact.

The example of Valerius Maximus and Sulla is thus relatively straightforward. For Sallust, it cannot be this simple, for at least two reasons. First, Sallust tends to eschew simplicity and the obvious. As was discussed above, the *Histories* are intricately and densely allusive and there are almost invariably multiple interpretive layers at work. Second, Valerius Maximus wrote under Tiberius, at a great remove from the civil wars (both in basic chronology and political climate). Sallust, on the other hand, was writing the *Histories* in the early 30s, when the civil wars were far from over (even Sextus Pompey and Lepidus had not yet been 'eliminated') and it is arguably impossible to assess fully the impact of a trauma that is still being inflicted.[20] Furthermore, while Sallust was no longer active in politics, no one was out of the Triumvirs' reach, and it may be doubted whether Sallust's former association with Caesar afforded him any particular protection. In sum, calling Octavian a 'second Hannibal' would not do. An allusive exploration of normative inversion, however, would be consistent with Sallust's historiographical programme.

4. Mithridates and the failure of normative inversion

4.1 The letter of Mithridates

The letter of Mithridates (4.60 R) purports to be a message from the Pontic king to Arsaces, king of Parthia, requesting aid against the Roman forces led by L. Lucullus. Much of the scholarship on the letter of Mithridates has focused on the question of its authenticity. The prevailing view (with which I concur) is that the letter may well reflect familiarity with the rhetoric and views of the historical Pontic king, but it was probably composed with a free hand by Sallust.[21] Accordingly, we might reasonably ask what sort of historiographical role this letter may have played.

For the ancient historians, the direct speech attributed to their characters (in our case, in the form of a letter) provided the author with opportunities to exercise creativity and emphasize themes or arguments of the larger narrative.[22] One potential function of Mithridates' letter would be to position him as a foreign Other against which Sallust's audience could try to reclaim a Roman identity; in other words, Sallust could have made Mithridates a *locus* for therapeutic normative inversion. Models were available. In historiography we might think of Caesar's Critognatus, who advocated for cannibalism to survive the siege of Alesia in Book 7 of the *Bellum Gallicum*. The use of the Other for self-definition was a common motif in tragedy as well (e.g. the cruel and violent Thracians, Taurians, and Egyptians of Euripides),[23] and Sallust's awareness and use of tragic material is apparent.[24]

Thus, Sallust easily *could* have barbarized Mithridates, but he avoids doing so. Numerous scholars have noted the ways in which ancient historians also do the *opposite* of 'Othering', using 'barbarian' figures to actually destabilize the differences between Greeks and Romans and barbarians, often as part of a critique of some aspect of Greek or Roman society. Again, Sallust would have had historiographical models for this.[25] Furthermore, his own Jugurtha is a liminal figure upon whom 'Roman' characteristics are projected; Jugurtha then turns a perverted version of his 'Roman' virtues back against Rome.[26] I suggest that Sallust's Mithridates is operating in this tradition as well. Previous scholarship has identified multiple ways in which Mithridates seems to be assimilated to Roman intellectual and rhetorical traditions. Bikermann and Alheid have demonstrated Mithridates' use of traditional oratorical structures,[27] while Adler has described how Mithridates voices an eloquent and informed critique of Roman foreign policy.[28] I would like to suggest another way in which Sallust 'de-barbarizes' Mithridates: the Pontic king seems to act as a cipher for the historian himself.

I have argued elsewhere that many major characters in the *Histories* have a metahistorical function and that Sallust uses them to reflect on the changing role and utility of history under the Triumvirs, who were aggressive propagandists and who tried to 'write' the narrative of their own history by simply declaring their own version of the 'truth' to be fact.[29] Mithridates seems to perform a similar historiographical task as figures like Sertorius, Spartacus and Pompey, simultaneously enacting the roles of the 'sincere' historian (like Sallust) and the 'false' historian (like the Triumvirs).

4.2 Mithridates as 'sincere' historian

First, to note the obvious: the words of Mithridates are presented not in a speech, but in a *letter*, a written medium. Rather than dismissing this as a case of *variatio*, I would suggest that this choice is actually indicative of the letter's programmatic purpose as part of Sallust's larger reflection on historiography. This reading is supported by the role played by the other extant letter, the letter of Pompey, in Sallust's historiographical exploration. As a historical actor, Pompey was keen to control the representation of his deeds himself rather than leaving it up to future historians (except the one he famously hired).[30] As was mentioned above, Pompey wrote to the Senate from Spain in the winter of 75/4 requesting aid for his campaign against Sertorius. In this letter, Pompey explicitly expresses doubts about the value of narrating the past:

> *quid deinde proelia aut expeditiones hibernas, oppida excisa aut recepta enumerem, quando res plus valet quam verba? castra hostium apud Sucronem capta et proelium apud flumen Durium [. . .] satis clara vobis sunt*
>
> 2.86.6 R[31]

> Why should I enumerate, then, the battles or winter expeditions, the towns razed or captured, since actions are stronger than words? The enemy camp captured at the Sucro and the battle at the Durius River . . . these things are famous enough to you.

Pompey follows this bit of *praeteritio* with a more effective tactic: the threat of violence. As was mentioned earlier in the discussion of triumviral resonances, Pompey says that he will be compelled to bring the army 'and the whole Spanish War' with it back into Italy should the Senate fail to send aid (2.86.10). Mere words can achieve less than action; or, rather, specifically words that record and review the past can achieve less than violence (or the threat thereof). Rome had always preferred men of action to men of words (*Cat.* 8), and Sallust's Pompey seems to suggest that, in the fog of civil discord that hung over both the narrative time and the time of composition, the work of recording history had lost its value. What need was there to record the past when the victorious party would establish their own version of it anyhow?

Mithridates, on the other hand, *does* rely on *verba*, and specifically words that record the past, as he tries to use the narrative of history to persuade Arsaces to action. The main body of the letter (sections 5–15) is a brief historical overview that describes Roman interactions and hostilities in the East since the Third Macedonian War (171–168 BCE). That is, Mithridates does exactly the opposite of what Pompey recommends, and in doing so aligns himself with the role of the traditional historian. The two letters thus function as a pair through which Sallust demonstrates both hope and doubt about the utility and value of the historian's craft.[32]

There are further linguistic clues in the letter suggesting its programmatic historiographical function. In the first sentence after the salutation a connection is drawn between Mithridates and Sallust the historian with a close echo of the preface of the *Catiline*.

omnes qui secundis rebus suis ad belli societatem orantur considerare debent

4.60.1 R

All those who are asked during times of prosperity to make an alliance for waging war should consider …

omnis homines, qui sese student praestare ceteris animalibus, summa ope niti decet

Cat. 1.1

All men who seek to surpass the other animals should strive with the greatest effort.[33]

This seeming allusion to the *Catiline*'s preface connects Mithridates with an important programmatic passage in which Sallust explicitly discussed the value of historiography (*Cat.* 3, 8).[34] Unlike the *Catiline* and *Jugurtha*, the *Histories* appear not to have contained a defence of history-writing in the proem,[35] but rather the work as a whole seems to function as an extended and allusive meditation on historiography.[36] In light of this reading, the connection with the *Catiline*'s preface is an implicit nod to Sallust's earlier defence of the historian's role and signals to the reader that Mithridates' letter may be read programmatically as part of Sallust's historiographical reflection.

Mithridates' repeated use of the language of vindication also suggests his role in Sallust's historiographical exploration. Twice in his letter Mithridates uses vocabulary associated with the idea of vindication:

atque ego ultus iniurias Nicomedem Bithynia expuli Asiamque spolium regis Antiochi recepi et Graeciae dempsi grave servitium

4.60.11

But I avenged my injuries: I drove Nicomedes out of Bithynia, I recovered Asia and the spoils taken from King Antiochus, and I freed Greece from bitter servitude.

namque pauci libertatem, pars magna iustos dominos volunt, nos suspecti sumus aemuli et in tempore vindices adfuturi

4.60.18

Indeed, few men want freedom, but a good number want fair masters. We are under suspicion as rivals and as potential avengers.

Both examples here might sensibly be understood to mean 'vindication' in the literal sense; Mithridates is certainly bent on revenge. However, there are other contemporary examples of writers using the language of vindication to allude to writers' ability to 'rescue' historical actors from obscurity.

non ego nobilium scriptorum auditor et <u>ultor</u>
grammaticas ambire tribus et pulpita dignor

Horace, Epist. *1.19.39-40*

I, the audience and avenger of great writers,
do not deign to canvass the tribes of grammarians and their desks.

vel me hercule etiam ut laudem eorum iam prope senescentem, quantum ego possem, ab oblivione hominum atque a silentio <u>vindicarem</u>

Cicero, De orat. *2.7*

and, moreover, [my purpose was] that, to the extent that I am able, I rescue the glory of these men, already near decline, from the forgetfulness of men and from silence.

Horace and Cicero each use language from the semantic field of vindication to emphasize the writer's ability to preserve *memoria* and prevent the works and deeds of men from being lost to history. In the case of the *Histories*, reading the language of vindication from a meta-literary position might bring new meaning to Sallust's description of Spartacus' death in 71:

haud impigre neque <u>inultus</u> occiditur

4.31 R

he [Spartacus] died, most boldly and not unavenged

It is easy to understand from this fragment that Spartacus fought bravely until the end; this echoes Sallust's depiction of Catiline's death (*Cat.* 60-61) and is how later readers like Plutarch seem to have interpreted it (*Crass.* 11.6-7). However, we might also understand this remark as an acknowledgment of Sallust's power as a historian. The *Histories* are our earliest source for the Spartacus War and there was no particular reason for Sallust to highlight Spartacus as an individual. His accomplishments against Rome were impressive but previous slave revolt leaders had been depicted almost interchangeably as archetypal barbarians.[37] Sallust's Spartacus, however, seems to have been a complex and 'Romanized' figure (much like Sallust's Mithridates).[38] Spartacus' elevation to a level of narrative prominence shared by figures like Pompey and Sertorius demonstrates the historian's enduring ability to shape the past; by using the language of vindication, Sallust's Mithridates may be making a similar claim for the value of writing history.

4.3 Mithridates as 'false' historian

Mithridates thus acts as a counterbalance to Pompey insofar as he embodies the positive value of historiography: he preserves and 'vindicates' the past rather than manipulating it. However, it is worth noting that Mithridates' version of Roman history is not precisely Roman history as we know it. As Raditsa and Adler have detailed, this is a fairly tendentious and exaggerated account of Roman activities in the East.[39] While the core tenets of Mithridates' argument may be defensible (e.g. the charge of Roman rapacity), he uses omissions, simplification and exaggeration to amplify his claims. For example, Mithridates asserts that the Romans accepted the surrender of Perseus, son of Philip, at Samothrace, but then tortured and killed him with sleep deprivation (4.60.7); while the point (Roman treachery) is sound enough, in order to make it Mithridates has compressed two different events that occurred eight years apart (Perseus' flight to Samothrace after Pydna and his death in 162).[40] In another example, Mithridates asserts that, upon the death of Nicomedes, the Romans 'stole away (*diripuere*) Bithynia' from Nicomedes' rightful heir, although a variety of other sources attest that Nicomedes had disowned his children and willed Bithynia to Rome.[41]

Considering these distortions, Mithridates appears less like a 'sincere' historian and more like the 'false historians' of whom Sallust was so deeply critical. His 'history' is selective and curated, shaped in the interest of personal and political gain rather than according to the principle of 'truthful' representation.[42] Likewise, the Triumvirs co-opted various media to spread their own tendentious version of history, one in which they had restored the Republic and put an end to civil wars; in their hands history became a weapon against the feeble Senate and a tool with which to manipulate the Roman people.[43] Furthermore, as Adler notes, the exaggerations in Mithridates' letter are not necessarily obvious, even to the experienced student of history, and there are enough defensible claims and 'facts' in the letter to camouflage.[44] The best propaganda, of course, is insidiously plausible, since outlandish fabrication is unlikely to persuade anyone except the most fervent and zealous partisans who did not need convincing in the first place. The Triumvirs seemed to recognize this principle, as evidenced by their scrupulous yet superficial adherence to Republican customs and language while ignoring or even dismantling the cultural and political *mores* and structures of the Republic. Mithridates mirrors the Triumvirs by striking a similarly calculated balance between something like 'truth' and rhetorical manipulations.

Mithridates thus plays the role of both the 'sincere' and 'false' historian, demonstrating, on the one hand, the enduring power of *verba*, while at the same time undercutting this message by demonstrating how easily words can be manipulated to serve the purpose of the speaker or writer. Still, in either case, Mithridates is assimilated to Roman figures representing Roman values (at least in theory). Does this Romanize Mithridates? Does it barbarize the Romans? I would suggest that it does both, and that this is precisely the point. Rather than representing an outsider with foreign values against whom Romans can unite, Sallust's Mithridates contributes to the overall sense of category confusion so typical of ancient historiography in general and civil war narratives in particular.[45]

5. Conclusions: Sallust as witness to trauma

In civil war it is difficult to differentiate *socii* from *hostes*, and Sallust underscores this confusion by destabilizing the distinction between foreign characters and Romans. By enacting this confusion in Mithridates, who is the only foreigner with direct speech in the *Histories*, Sallust suggests that the traumas inflicted by the triumviral civil wars cannot be mitigated through the process of normative inversion and raises the possibility that it will not, in fact, be possible to recover a shared sense of Roman identity.

Sallust also calls attention to how easily the natural human drive toward normative inversion could be exploited by those with an interest in redirecting the triumviral narrative. I have already mentioned the simultaneous flourishing of patriotism and bigotry in the post-9/11 United States. Perhaps some of those sentiments arose organically, but it has become, I think, quite clear that the administration of President George W. Bush and the American military were instrumental in cultivating those attitudes to provide pretexts for invading Iraq and Afghanistan. Sallust may have recognized a similar effort by the Triumvirs, who had many reasons to divert attention from their own civil conflicts to foreign ones, whether or not they actually existed. As excellent students of history, the Triumvirs were well aware of the Roman public's unease with celebrating civil war victories. Antony and Lepidus would have recalled (and

Octavian had surely heard about) Caesar's quadruple triumph in 46, at which he paraded the images of several of his defeated Roman foes to the great disapproval of his audience (App. *BCiv.* 2.101). The Triumvirs' tricks are familiar to us: Sextus Pompey becomes a pirate, and Cleopatra, not Mark Antony, the target of war. In this reading, the warning of the *Histories* becomes even more dire. Not only does Sallust believe it is not possible to repair the social fabric, but the unravelling of the *res publica* might even be hastened by the cynical exploitation of those who are still hopeful for unity, as the Triumvirs use the spectre of barbarians at the gates to draw attention away from their own violent discord.

Notes

* Due to Covid-related delays, a substantial interval elapsed between the writing of this paper and its publication. I would like to note two excellent monographs on Sallust that have been published since this paper was written, which, had they been available, would no doubt have enriched this discussion: Andrew Feldherr's *After the Past: Sallust on History and Writing History* (2021) and Edwin Shaw's *Sallust and the Fall of the Republic* (2021). In addition, Alexandra Eckert also has a more recent chapter on trauma and cultural identity which readers may find useful to consult ('Coping with Crisis: Sulla's Civil War and Cultural Identity', in Kloosters and Kuin (eds), *After the Crisis: Remembrance, Re-anchoring and Recovery in Ancient Greece and Rome* (2020). Many thanks to Hannah Cornwell and Richard Westall for their patience and persistence in bringing this volume to fruition despite the disruptions posed by the Covid pandemic.
1. This chapter builds upon arguments in my 2019 monograph, *Sallust's* Histories *and Triumviral Historiography*, particularly the discussions of trauma theory (pp. 47–60) and characters as ciphers for the historian (pp. 73–105). The case study here advances those arguments by using the character of Mithridates (not discussed at length in the book) to tie together these two lines of inquiry and demonstrate the close relationship between the traumatic experience of the Roman civil wars and the practice of writing history, particularly (near) contemporary history.
2. Maurenbrecher 1891–3 has been the standard edition for over a century but may be eclipsed by Ramsey's excellent 2015 Loeb edition, which I have used here.
3. Gerrish 2019, especially 35–72.
4. On these historical parallels and Sallust's awareness of them, see, e.g., Syme 1964: 219–24 and Gerrish 2019: 35–43.
5. Morawski 1911. The originality of Sallust's speeches and letters has been discussed at length in scholarship. At the extremes, some suggest that they are more or less faithful reproductions of historical speeches and letters (e.g. Tannenbaum 2005), while others argue that they are pure Sallustian inventions expressing contemporary concerns (e.g. Perl 1965 and 1967; Mellor 1999). A reasonable (and, in my opinion, persuasive) middle ground has been carved out by scholars like Büchner 1960 and Syme 1964, who make the case that Sallust's speeches are composed freely in the author's own natural style and that they preserve the concerns of the narrative time as accurately as possible while also leaving room for the interpolation of the author's other interests; while they require some chronological disentangling, the speeches can thus reveal to us some combination of the time they depict, the time in which they were written, and the author's perspective on both. Steed 2017 provides an excellent recent overview of the question and defence of this 'middle ground' position.

On the authenticity of the speech of Philippus specifically see Sapere 2014: 226 (with additional bibliography).

6. 'You are all that's left: unless you come to my aid, although I do not wish it but as I predicted my army will march from here into Italy, bringing with it the entire Spanish War' (2.86.10 R).

7. For good overviews of triumviral propaganda and messaging, see Osgood 2006; Wallmann 1989; Zanker 1988: 33–78.

8. See Gerrish 2019: 47–61 for this theme in Sallust; for the idea of civil war's repetitive nature in other authors, see also Quint 1993 on Vergil and Joseph 2012 on Tacitus.

9. While Freudian theory has generally been replaced by other approaches in the mental health fields, psychoanalytic theory continues to be a dynamic field of literary study. For Freudian and other psychoanalytic approaches to classical texts, in addition to Caruth (discussed above) see, e.g., Bowlby 2009; Oliensis 2009; Zajko and O'Gorman 2013.

10. See, e.g., Caruth 1996 and 2013.

11. Caruth 1996: 5: 'My main endeavor is, rather, to trace in each of these texts a different story, the story or the textual itinerary of insistently recurring words or figures. The key figures my analysis uncovers and highlights [...] in their insistence, here engender stories that in fact emerge out of the rhetorical potential and the literary resonance of these figures, a literary dimension that cannot be reduced to the thematic content of the text or to what the theory encodes, and that, beyond what we can know or theorize about it, stubbornly persists in bearing witness to some forgotten wound.'

12. Shay 1994 and 2002 were pioneering texts in this field. More recently, see Meineck and Konstan 2014.

13. E.g. Jarratt 2019; Mehl 2014; Eckert 2014.

14. Alexander 2004: 1.

15. Erickson 1976: 153–4. Cf. also Smelser 2004: 44: 'We may now advance a formal definition of cultural trauma: a memory accepted and publicly given credence by a relevant membership group and evoking an event or situation which is a) laden with negative affect, b) represented as indelible, and c) regarded as threatening a society's existence or violating one or more of its fundamental cultural presuppositions.'

16. For example, Vergil's *Eclogues* 1 and 9 depict the vast differences in fortune among Italian landowners and highlight the widening gaps between civilians and veterans and between Italy and the city of Rome; on the gulf between 'Roman' and 'Italian' identities around this time see also Propertius 1.22. Horace's *Epodes* suggest that civil war is, in fact, an inevitable component of the Roman identity (*Epod.* 7) and that some part of the population might be better served by escaping Rome entirely (*Epod.* 16).

17. Assmann 1997, especially 55–74 and 216–18.

18. Assmann 1997: 216.

19. Eckert 2014: 270. Cicero used the same rhetorical trick against Caesar, as Westall 2017: 70 points out (*Att.* 7.11.1-3).

20. Cf. Caruth 1996: 18: 'For history to be history of trauma means that it is referential precisely to the extent that it is not fully perceived as it occurs; or to put it somewhat differently, that a history can be grasped only in the very inaccessibility of its occurrence'.

21. See n.5 above on the authenticity of Sallust's speeches and letters. On the letter of Mithridates in particular, see Bikerman 1946: 131–2; Büchner 1982: 229; Raditsa 1969: 6; Ahlheid 1988: 67–8; McGushin 1994: 174. At the other pole, Stier 1969: 447 argues that Sallust's version is copied from a specific archival document, see Stier 1969: 447. McGing

1986: 154–61 seeks a middle ground and suggests (unpersuasively, in my view) that Sallust meticulously imitated authentic Pontic propaganda. It is perhaps worth noting that Fronto specifically cites the letter of Mithridates (along with Sallust's letter of Pompey and the letter of Nicias in Thucydides) as an example of the literary license assumed by the historians (*Ad Verum* 2.1.15).

22. E.g. Pausch 2010.
23. See Hall 1989.
24. E.g. Skard 1956: 57–74 and Dué 2000.
25. For example, see Pelling 1997 on Herodotus and Baragwanath 2016 on Xenophon.
26. See, e.g., Levene 1992: 59–60.
27. Bikermann 1946 and Alheid 1988.
28. Adler 2011: 15–35. Adler particularly emphasizes the issue of national identity in Sallust's use of Mithridates to critique foreign policy, and notes Sallust's subversion of expectations: 'Sallust was capable of criticizing Rome and even valorizing barbarians' complaints against it [...] It is thus incorrect to assume that Roman historians inevitably discussed barbarians with the implicit motive of justifying Roman conquest. On the contrary: at times Roman historians present deep-seated criticisms of their own society' (16).
29. Gerrish 2019: 73–6.
30. For example, in order to downplay the distasteful appearance of civil war (and, perhaps more to the point, ensure his eligibility for a triumph), Pompey celebrated his victory in Spain not as the defeat of Sertorius, but of the Spanish tribes: 'he set up the trophies on the ridges of the Pyrenees for his conquests of the Spanish' (3.63 R). Cf. Pliny, *NH* 7.96 and Flor. 2.10.1.
31. Text and numbering of the *Histories* is that of Ramsey (2015).
32. Paired speeches were a regular feature of ancient historiography, often employed to show both sides of a situation, theme, or conflict; the tradition stretches back as far as Homer.
33. This word pairing appears three additional times in Sallust's extant works in programmatically significant passages. It occurs twice in speeches (at *Cat.* 51.1, the opening of Caesar's speech regarding the Catilinarian conspirators and *Jug.* 14.17, the speech of Adherbal) and once in Sallust's comments about his fellow historian Sisenna at *Jug.* 95.2. It also appears in a description of Roman soldiers in battle (*Jug.* 97.5) and in a fragment of the *Histories*' geographical excursus on the land of the Isauri (2.70 R); without context, it is difficult to say whether this passage had programmatic import, but I have argued elsewhere that geographical digressions are often tied closely with major themes of the text; see Gerrish 2019: 106–45.
34. Cf. *Jug.* 4.
35. Scanlon 1998, esp. 223–4.
36. Gerrish 2019, esp. 73–105.
37. Cf. Diodorus Siculus' depictions of Eunus and Damophilus, leaders in the First Sicilian Slave War of 135–132 (34/5.2.1-48).
38. Gerrish 2019: 88–94.
39. See Stier 1969; Raditsa 1969 and Adler 2011 for a full accounting of the distortions and factual errors in the letter of Mithridates.
40. Adler 2011: 22 and Raditsa 1969: 123.
41. Adler 2011: 23 and Stier 1969: 445. Among Sallust's near-contemporaries cf. Cic. *Agr.* 2.40 and Liv. *Per.* 93.

42. While there should be no doubt that every historian manipulated, invented or passed over items as they saw fit, Sallust's claims about the absence of partisanship from his work (*quod mihi a spe, metu, partibus rei publicae animus liber erat*, *Cat.* 4 and *neque me divorsa pars in civilibus armis movit a vero*, 1.6 R) suggest his hostility toward the use (or abuse) of history for political gain in particular.

43. Cf. the play produced by the quaestor L. Cornelius Balbus at Gades in 43, in which Balbus celebrated and no doubt amplified his own role in the siege of Dyrrachium during the war between Caesar and Pompey; see Westall 2019: 54–5 and in this volume.

44. Adler 2011: 20: 'In order for the ancient reader to recognize the exaggerations in Mithridates' letter, he would have to possess an encyclopedic knowledge of Roman foreign policy in the East. It is hard to believe that many ancient Romans could have immediately discovered the distortions Sallust's Mithridates offers – distortions that modern scholars were able to detect only after extended careful research.'

45. While ancient audiences were comfortable with some types of category confusion (for example, literary genres were less rigidly defined than in modern critical studies), unease about the inversions of civil war seems to have been a common preoccupation of historians in particular. The trope originated with Thucydides' famous excursus on the *stasis* in Corcyra (3.82) and has echoes in later writers like Sallust (cf. *Hist.* 1.12 M) and Tacitus (on which see, e.g. Gerrish 2021: 486–90.

CHAPTER 11
TOWARDS A NEW ARCHAEOLOGY OF THE LOST *HISTORIES* OF C. ASINIUS POLLIO*
Richard Westall

Arguably the most influential work of the twentieth century to deal with Roman history, *The Roman Revolution* (1939) of Sir Ronald Syme changed the way that ancient historians viewed their subject. The traditional themes of politics and war were reinstated, in place of the nineteenth-century emphasis on laws and constitutional structure, albeit now analysed through the prism of prosopography. There were precedents for this prosopographical approach, both in the English-speaking world and in the German academy. Lewis Namier had published his prosopographical analysis of early modern Britain at the start of that same decade (1930), and amongst the German practitioners of note figured not only Friedrich Münzer of the previous generation (whose contributions to the Pauly-Wissowa encyclopaedia remain fundamental points of departure for serious scholarship), but also Wilhelm Drumann (whose multi-volume history of the Roman Republic had the signal feature of being organized as a prosopographical encyclopaedia). Münzer's monograph on the Roman nobility appeared in 1920, whereas the latter's work, originally published 1834–44, was revised and published anew by Paul Groebe 1919–29. Nonetheless, neither of these works had the galvanizing effect to be seen from the reception eventually accorded to Syme's monograph, which came to be viewed as a historiographical classic in the years after the Second World War. The constitutional approach epitomized by Theodor Mommsen (who received the Nobel Prize for literature in 1902), which depended on a long-term view of Roman jurisprudence from Romulus to Justinian, was superseded by a prosopographical approach, which favoured the study of the late Republic and early Principate and encouraged a focus on the transformation of society and government's external forms brought about by the Roman civil wars. While it is now rare to find reference to the work of Theodor Mommsen or T. Rice Holmes, both of whom were once universally cited, the work of Syme continues to be commonly cited as an authoritative basis for Roman history.

Indeed, it is not uncommon to find contemporary scholars citing Syme's work as though it were on a par with the testimony of the ancients. Obviously, that is problematic. For modern interpretations can never be viewed as being on a par with ancient sources.[1] However, the error is itself due in part to the very style of the *Roman Revolution* and the spirit in which Syme composed that work. Allowing himself the freedom of the essayist, Syme wrote a historical work that was anything but neutral or impartial. While eschewing open partisanship for the losing side in the Roman civil wars of the late Republic, he struck a pose that unequivocally evoked that of the senator C. Asinius Pollio (76/5 BCE– 4/5 CE), a Caesarian partisan and *quondam* political ally of the triumvir M. Antonius. In fact, it might be said that Syme not only channelled the spirit of the *novus homo* to write a history of the Republic that privileged the oligarchy and its traditions, but also undertook to write a more perfect version of what Pollio ought to have written. While Pollio, like his fellow Caesarian C. Sallustius Crispus (likewise intimately associated with Caesar's victories in north Africa in the 40s), composed *Historiae* that dealt with a rather limited span of time, Syme made the revolutionary decision to compose a history written in the spirit of those historians, but dealing with the entire timespan of the life of Augustus. In short, Syme undertook to write the history of the transition from the Republic to the Principate as it ought to have been written, whether by Sallust, Pollio or Tacitus.[2]

Scholarship, of course, never remains fixed, and new findings frequently reveal that the old certitudes were mistaken. Working on the basis of an erroneous premise, Christopher Columbus accidentally discovered a new world. In like fashion, working on the basis of nineteenth-century philologists' reconstruction of the *Historiae* of Pollio,[3] Syme created a new historiographical masterpiece that has proved as influential as that of his ancient predecessor. For a long time, in part thanks to the authority of Syme and the persuasive nature of his re-interpretation of the history of the late Republic and early Principate, that reconstruction of the *Historiae* of Pollio has gone generally unchallenged. However, as has been anticipated by other scholars in recent decades (viz. John Henderson and A. J. Woodman), a close reading of the evidence calls into question the basis for the commonly accepted reconstruction of Pollio's lost work. The present contribution offers a re-reading of the evidence that argues that Pollio's *Historiae* had a rather different shape than that which has usually been thought. Of more limited temporal scope (49–40), Pollio's work was in many ways similar to the *commentarii* of Caesar dedicated to the civil war of 49–48, but marked by a flair for the dramatic and a penchant for self-referentiality to be expected of literature produced after the last round of Rome's civil wars.

1. Historian and dramatist

Of no little significance is the well attested fact that Pollio was a dramatist.[4] Indeed, Horace pointedly refers to his dramatic production when discussing the Caesarian officer's account of the civil wars in the opening piece of Book 2 of the *Odes* (Hor. *Carm.* 2.1.9-12):

> Let dire tragedy's Muse be absent
> from the theatres only briefly: presently,
>   once you have set public affairs in order,
>   you will again seek lofty duty with Cecropian boot.

While expressing admiration for the senior statesman's public service in composing an account of recent history, the lyric poet (and veteran who had formerly fought on the other, losing side) expresses the hope that engagement in historiography is merely a brief respite from Pollio's true literary calling.[5] The way in which Horace looks forward to Pollio's resumption of the writing of Greek-style tragedies (*Cecropio ... cothurno*) is suggestive, calling to mind the *otium* that awaited the magistrate once he had finished with his duty to the Roman community at large.[6] Horace implies that it is Pollio's activity as a *littérateur* and not as a statesman that is more congenial: past tragedies are less distressing. In a poem that exalts Pollio's account of the civil wars, the vision of the historian as a tragedian must be seen as implying a dramatic vividness (*enargeia*) of historical narrative.

That Pollio wrote tragedies on Greek themes in Latin is abundantly attested. Horace also in the *Satires*, Vergil in the *Eclogues* and Tacitus in the *Dialogue on Orators* refer to this production.[7] However, neither the number of tragedies that he wrote, nor their precise titles and content are known. Horace, Vergil and Tacitus all speak vaguely of tragedies in the plural, and they do not specify their contents beyond indicating that they were appropriate for the Athenian stage. That Horace in the *Satires* cites Pollio as *the* example of a Roman author writing tragedies on Greek themes in Latin is suggestive of their stylistic finesse, but that is all.

It is to be observed that Pollio's predilection for tragedy is one that he appears to have shared with a fair number of his peers between the late Republic and the early Principate. Best known, because of the simple fact that they survive intact, are the tragic productions of Seneca the Younger.[8] Of this corpus of nine works, six appear indebted to Euripides (*Hercules furens, Troades, Medea, Phaedra, Phoenissae, Thyestes*), four to Sophocles (*Oedipus, Hercules Oetaeus, Troades, Thyestes*) and two to Aeschylus (*Agamemnon, Phoenissae*).[9] However, Pollio's older contemporaries are also attested as having indulged in writing Greek-style tragedies in Latin. So, for instance, Q. Tullius Cicero 'translated' multiple tragedies from Greek into Latin during his time as an officer serving under Caesar in Gaul in the 50s.[10] In like fashion, Caesar produced an *Oedipus* at some point, arguably during one of his provincial appointments in the 60s or 50s.[11] So, too, Augustus is known to have attempted to produce an *Ajax*.[12] The fact that Pollio, like Q. Cicero, produced a number of tragedies bespeaks a certain affinity for the genre and a sensibility for dramatic themes and their representation.

2. The significance of a preposition

With very rare exceptions,[13] modern scholars have held that the narrative of the *Historiae* of Pollio commenced with the year 60 and proceeded in annalistic fashion down to some point in the 40s or 30s. While there has been intense debate over the precise year of their conclusion (favourite candidates: 42, 35 or 30), the scholarly consensus is that they began with the consulate of Q. Metellus and L. Afranius.[14] Horace speaks of civil war (*motum ... civicum*) originating *ex Metello consule* (Hor. *Carm.* 2.1.1), and his language is normally taken to mean that the *Historiae* began with the establishment of the 'First Triumvirate'. A re-reading of Horace's opening description of the *Historiae* is in order (Hor. *Carm.* 2.1.1-8):

> Civic unrest going back to Metellus' consulate,
> war's causes and excesses and means,
> >   Fortune's inconstancy and leaders'
> >   portentous alliances, weapons
> bespattered with blood yet unavenged:
> it is a work loaded with the die's danger
> >   you undertake, and you make your way
> >   through fires overlaid with treacherous ash.

Horace's language is far more ambiguous than the traditional interpretation admits. Indeed, there are a number of reasons why the traditional interpretation of the first line's *ex Metello consule* as indicating a commencement of the *Historiae* in 60 cannot stand.

First, there are no signs of the use of Pollio's narrative in the surviving historiography for the 50s. Plutarch and Appian, to be precise, signally fail to offer a coherent, detailed and trustworthy narrative for these years. This curious state of affairs has one of two explanations: either they preferred another source to Pollio or Pollio's work did not cover this period. Since they do make use of evidence deriving from Pollio for the events of the 40s, it must be concluded that Pollio's narrative was unavailable to them for the previous decade. In short, no such narrative existed because the *Historiae* of Pollio commenced later than is commonly inferred from the testimony of Horace.

Secondly, the traditional interpretation makes nonsense of the semantic thrust of the opening lines of the ode *Motum ex Metello consule civicum*. The poet is not interested in providing a pedestrian, straightforward description of the work for some future librarian.[15] Rather, he is concerned to offer an impressionistic sense of the content and themes of the *Historiae*. Civic unrest, causes, fortune, leaders' fatal concord and weapons bespattered with sacrilegious blood – these are the topics that Pollio boldly proposes to relate in his account of contemporary history. Horace is manifestly not interested in offering a precise, aseptic taxonomy of Pollio's latest literary work. To take the poet as giving readers the equivalent of the publication data to be found on the back of a modern book's title page is to engage in the error of anachronistic application of modern categories and models.[16]

Third and last, but most significant, linguistic considerations show the traditional interpretation cannot be allowed to stand. The poet has utilized the wrong preposition, if modern interpreters are right in their rendering of the Latin. Had Horace wished to express the idea that Pollio began the *Historiae* with, or rather 'from', the consulate of Metellus and Afranius, then he ought to have written *ab* instead of *ex*. That is clear enough from the titles of historical works dealing with the late Republic and Principate: Livy's *Ab urbe condita*,[17] Pliny the Elder's *A fine Aufidi Bassi*,[18] or Tacitus' *Ab excessu divi Augusti*.[19] Moreover, the lexica reveal a distinction in the use of the prepositions *ex* and *ab*. Whereas *ab* is normally used to signify 'from' a particular time or moment,[20] *ex* as a rule means 'out of' or 'originating from'.[21] Indeed, this difference in use, commonly enunciated in Latin grammars, has a distinct parallel in Greek that is likewise illustrated in textbooks (Figure 11.1); for bilingual authors such as Horace and Pollio this parallel is

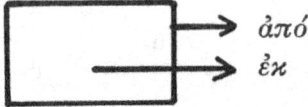

Figure 11.1 Diagram illustrating the use of the prepositions ἀπό and ἐκ, from Hansen and Quinn 1992: 54.

not insignificant.[22] Hence, it seems preferable to render the first line thus: 'Civic unrest originating in the consulate of Metellus'. Finally, it is worth observing that Horace could have deployed *ab*, but instead chose *ex* even though the metre would allow for either preposition. In short, the Latin preposition *ex* in this instance arguably possesses a causal rather than a temporal force.

In view of these considerations, the traditional use of Horace's words to reconstruct the *Historiae* as a work commencing in 60 ought to be abandoned. Poets are quite punctilious in their choice of words, and the use of the preposition *ex* instead of *ab* renders null and void *a priori* the interpretation that puts the phrase on a par with the titles of other historical works of the late Republic and early Principate.

3. The chronological parameters of the *Historiae*

Once the red herring of the traditional interpretation of the opening line of Horace's testimony has been laid to rest, it is possible to appreciate the second to fourth lines of the second stanza for what they have to offer. Having indicated the subject of Pollio's historical work, Horace goes on to provide general chronological parameters before venturing into a more detailed, lyrical survey of what is covered. Horace offers what appear to be allusions to two specific historical moments in the period covered by Pollio. Neither particular names nor the details of these events are furnished, but the singular aspect of each episode is such as to render the allusion transparent for those acquainted with the period covered. Indeed, there was little cause for the poet to name explicitly what the historian had treated explicitly in his work, for it would be well known to the wider audience as well as the addressee (viz. Pollio), and words of possible ill omen were arguably to be avoided by the *vates*. Consequently, the modern consensus offers a very imperfect appreciation of Horace's introductory description of the *Historiae* of Pollio.

Standing in apposition to the direct objects of the verb 'you undertake' (line 7: *tractas*) that have just been listed in lines 1–5, the phrase of line 6 deftly employs an allusion to the opening episode of civil war in 49 to characterize the nature of the *Historiae* of Pollio as a whole (Hor. *Carm.* 2.1.6): 'a work loaded with the die's danger' (*periculosae plenum opus aleae*). Pollio the historian is likened to the protagonist of his narrative in its opening phase, C. Caesar, whom Pollio is known to have reported as having uttered the memorable phrase 'May the die roll high'.[23] For Pollio the *Caesarianus*, this was no small meed of praise.[24] Of greater interest to the modern student, on the other hand, is the fact that Horace has chosen to single out for use this opening episode of civil war. From the testimony of Plutarch, it emerges clearly that Pollio figured amongst those who accompanied Caesar in his initial invasion of Italy. Pollio is named in the account furnished by Plutarch, and that fact not only establishes that the episode figured memorably in Pollio's *Historiae*, but also corroborates the interpretation advanced here. In a work of historiography marked by its author's protagonism as an ancient witness to history,[25] it was altogether inevitable and appropriate that Pollio should have commenced with an episode in which he had participated. This, indeed, is the first demonstrable instance of Pollio's influence upon the later historiography of the Roman civil wars of 49–30.[26]

In a striking instance of chiasmus, Horace goes on to make another allusion that complements what has just been stated. Deploying an image that has puzzled the most acute of commentators,[27] Horace emphasizes yet again the danger inherent in the undertaking of writing an account of contemporary history (Hor. *Carm*. 2.1.7-8): 'you make your way / through fires overlaid with treacherous ash' (*et incedis per ignis / suppositos cineri doloso*). Once more the conceit of the author's assimilation to the protagonists of his narrative is crucial to a proper appreciation of Pollio's lost account. Bringing their own experiences to bear upon the text, modern readers have been tempted to follow Macaulay in seeing a reference to a volcanic eruption[28], understood an earthquake metaphor,[29] or sought an even more exotic explanation.[30] Nonetheless, none of these explanations is congruent with the situation depicted by Horace, who explicitly draws attention to the deceptive nature of the ashes in question. As has been remarked by one perceptive pair of commentators, who end their discussion inconclusively and without any attempt at identification, Horace's language seems to represent 'the smouldering remains of a conflagration'.[31] It just so happens that there is one conflagration of note on record for this epoch, that which devastated the ancient Etruscan city of Perusia and brought that community's siege by the younger Caesar to a terrible conclusion in 40.[32] Pollio's role in the affair was lacklustre, as he failed to bring relief to the city precisely on account of the treacherous political circumstances of the siege. Although once again no 'fragment' has been identified,[33] it is virtually certain that Velleius Paterculus' reference to the episode was conditioned by his reading of the *Historiae*.[34] If that be accepted, then we have confirmation that here Horace is referring to an episode occurring towards the very close of Pollio's historical work.

The *tableaux* of Caesar at the Rubicon and the devastated ruins of Perusia – if these interpretations of the allusions be accepted – form a diptych in which Horace deftly synthesizes the whole of the period treated by Pollio in the *Historiae*. Overall, they point to Pollio's writing a historical narrative that dealt only with the decade of the 40s, nothing more nor less.[35]

4. The implications of Gades

Renowned for its cult of Hercules, the former Phoenician foundation and Roman municipality of Gades lay situated at the westernmost margin of the Mediterranean world of the Greeks and Romans. Important as a hub for commerce, this flourishing port city regularly saw the passage of the governors of Hispania Ulterior and their administrative assistants. According to the testimony of Strabo, Gades counted some 500 *equites* as belonging to its civic community.[36] Amongst these figured the elder Cornelius Balbus, famed as a collaborator of the elder Caesar, and that man's notorious nephew. The elder Balbus' relationship with Caesar will have been strengthened, if not in fact established, by the fact of Caesar's sojourns in the city. The first occurred while Caesar was serving as quaestor to the governor Antistius in 69,[37] and the second took place when Caesar returned as a governor of Hispania Ulterior in his own right in 61.[38] Eventually to achieve the honour of a suffect consulate in 40, the elder Balbus owed his political rise to the economic resources that he was able to make available to Caesar in the latter's pursuit of further political aims.[39] No less suggestive of the city's economic importance is the fact that the Roman *eques* C. Gallonius was active there as an agent securing an inheritance that had been left to the fantastically wealthy L. Domitius Ahenobarbus (*cos.* 54).[40]

It is therefore not surprising to find that Pollio had occasion to refer to Gades in the course of the *Historiae* when dealing with contemporary history. The problem for a modern audience arises from the fact that Pollio's treatment has been shorn of its historical context,[41] much like a miniature cut out of a medieval manuscript because of its value as a beautiful artefact in its own right. From an anecdote reported by Valerius Maximus, it is known that Pollio wrote of the Gaditane ruler Arganthonius in Book 3 of the *Historiae* (Val. Max. 8.13 ext. 4): 'In fact, Asinius Pollio, not the least part of Roman literature, records in the third book of his histories that (Arganthonius) lived for one hundred and thirty years.' Reports going back to the Archaic period stressed the longevity of the legendary ruler of Tartessus in furthest Spain.[42] The item is of interest because Valerius Maximus clearly indicates that Pollio dealt with the subject of Spain in Book 3 of the *Historiae*. What was the occasion for adducing this item?

Application of Occam's razor points to this report as evidence for Pollio's dealing with the campaign of Caesar against the lieutenants of Pompeius Magnus in Spain in mid-49.[43] To be precise Pollio must have been describing Caesar's lightning-swift campaign against Varro, which involved the capitulation of Gades as well as the transferral of the whole of the province's allegiance to Caesar. No other episode in Spain can be satisfactorily adduced to explain Pollio's interest in the region so early in the *Historiae*. Economy of evidence and hypotheses is preferable. To postulate a reference to Caesar's governorship in 61/60[44] or a civic quarrel in 56/55[45] is to grasp at straws in an attempt to avoid the most straightforward solution.[46]

It bears emphasizing that there is no evidentiary basis for believing that Pollio provided his readers with a detailed account of the events of the 50s, much less that he provided a multi-book *archaeologia* covering the period 130–60. No fragments are explicitly linked to anything before the crossing of the Rubicon in 49.[47] Conversely, the jejune nature of Appian of Alexandria's account of events in the 50s and the uneven quality of Plutarch's treatment of those same years together point to two fundamental conclusions that are contrary to what was the scholarly consensus of the nineteenth and twentieth centuries: Pollio was not their source for this material and Pollio did not cover this period in the *Historiae*.[48]

5. *Libertas* and Caesar

Assuredly, a *Leitmotif* that loomed large in the *Historiae* was the *libertas* for which Caesar and his partisans claimed they were waging civil war. In the interview with Lentulus Spinther (*cos*. 57) on the eve of the fall of Corfinium, Caesar had enunciated even more forcefully than at Ariminum the fundamental idea informing his decision to wage war: 'to free himself and the Roman people from oppression by a faction of the few'.[49] This was a slogan that gained traction, as can be seen by the way in which Caesar returns to it at the opening of the battle of Pharsalus.[50] After a brief summary of his own speech in indirect speech, Caesar cedes the stage to the re-enlisted centurion Crastinus, 'a man of exceptional bravery' (Caes. *BCiv*. 3.91.2):

> You who once were under my command, follow me, and give your general the help that you have promised. This one battle remains. After it is done, he will have again his honour and we our freedom.

Such was the call to arms launched before the mêlée, or at least such is the version that Caesar saw fit to transmit to posterity. Whether these are Crastinus' *ipsissima verba* or a version improved by Caesar, the important thing is that they seemed not only plausible, but also appropriate. From the mass of corroborative evidence, e.g. the reprisal of the phrase *in libertatem vindicare* by Caesar Augustus and the attempt to associate the end of the free Republic with the deaths of C. Cassius and M. Brutus, there can be little doubt that Caesar is more or less accurately reporting what was said and believed amongst his partisans. Therefore, as a *Caesarianus* writing an account of these years of civil war, Pollio will naturally have given new life to the questionable trope that Caesar's individual honour was intimately linked to the freedom of the Republic.[51]

Indeed, Pollio's use of this trope can be seen already in one of the three surviving letters of his correspondence with Cicero in early 43. As governor of Hispania Ulterior in 44–43, Pollio found himself courted by Cicero as the latter sought to garner all possible support for a campaign against M. Antonius.[52] In his desire to form a grand coalition against Antonius, Cicero left no commander of troops untested, regardless of that individual's ties to the former dictator. Soldiers were desperately needed if Antonius were to be suppressed. Hence, the elderly *consularis* devoted attention to such marginal figures as the young Caesar and Pollio. Neither callow youth nor geographical remoteness represented a bar to being pressed into service in Cicero's campaign to destroy Antonius. Pollio, a friend and colleague of Antonius, responded tardily and in veiled language that might be welcomed by Caesar's former collaborators as well as by Cicero himself (Cic. *Fam*. 10.31.3, tr. Shackleton Bailey):

> If, therefore, we have an attempt to place supreme power once again in the hands of one man, I profess myself his enemy, whoever he is. There is no danger on behalf of freedom from which I shrink or seek to be excused.

Pollio professed a warm regard for the welfare of the Roman commonwealth, but he went on to make a statement that could just as readily have been uttered by Caesar in 49–48 while prosecuting the war against Pompeius (Cic. *Fam.* 10.31.5, tr. Shackleton Bailey):

> So you must think of me as one who is, first, most eager for peace (I am unashamedly anxious that none of our fellow-countrymen should perish) and, second, ready to defend my country's freedom and my own.

Caesar, too, had professed an overriding concern for peace, just as he had prosecuted war on the pretext that his individual freedom was to be identified with that of his country. No less sibylline in his expressions of commitment than had been the young Caesar, Pollio deployed language characteristic of the epoch, language which should have troubled Cicero. For the modern historian of ideas, the important thing to observe is that this language illustrates a direct continuity, in the person of Pollio, from the civil wars of the 40s through to the historiography of the 20s.[53]

Yet another instance of Pollio's interest in the theme of *libertas* and the government of the Republic may be discerned in his use of the spoils (*manubiae*) acquired through the campaign that he conducted against the Parthini while governor of Macedonia in 40–39.[54] One of the numerous building projects to change the appearance of Rome between the late Republic and early Principate,[55] this monument needs to be understood as Pollio's attempt to leave a lasting impression upon the landscape of the imperial capital. A newcomer (*novus homo*) to the Senate,[56] he wished to create a building of public utility that would not only guarantee his own memory in the years to come, but also ensure the future political success of his descendants. A compromise between ideals and reality, the building thus realized expressed the patron's ambitions and plans for the future. The choice that Pollio made is most eloquent. Redefining the space adjacent to the Forum of Caesar, he created a monumental public building destined for the maintenance of the censors' records and installed Rome's first public libraries (Greek and Latin) in this structure.[57] The name of this structure was *Atrium Libertatis*, or the Courtyard of Freedom.[58] For a *novus homo* of Italic stock who derived from one of the families that had initially been ranged against the Republic in the Social War of 91–88, this choice of monument was on a par with the creation of the Basilica Porcia by Cato the Elder during his time as censor.[59] It embodied in grandiose and lasting form the senator's adherence to the aristocratic ideals of the Republic and identified him with the proper functioning of Roman government. Both monuments, not surprisingly, had analogues in their patrons' historiographical work,[60] which sought to achieve the same end in another medium. The choice of name, which was new to this monument, is emblematic of how Pollio viewed his political choices as a devoted *Caesarianus* and consonant with his other attested activities.⁶¹ Fittingly, the inclusion of the image of the *Pompeianus* M. Terentius Varro (who figured among those the Triumvirs had initially proscribed and was the only living author to be represented in this building⁶²) represented freedom of thought as regards the liberal arts and literature.⁶³

6. Fighting against Cato

What stood at the centre of the *Historiae*? If the transmitted information of 17 books be taken as correct and the chronological *termini* of 49 and 40/39 be accepted, then it would appear that the campaign in north Africa against the forces led by Cato the Younger and Scipio was the subject of the centrally situated Book 9 of Pollio's *Historiae*. That especial emphasis was placed upon this campaign seems independently evident from the testimony of Horace, who singles out Cato and Africa for unmistakeable reference in the poem that he dedicated to Pollio and that author's new masterpiece. Of the numerous protagonists and places to figure in the annals of those tumultuous years, only Cato and Africa are singled out for explicit mention and actually named by Horace, aside from the poet's apostrophe of Pollio himself.⁶⁴ Casting aside the allusion that characterizes his sensitive handling of the contested theme of civil war, Horace in two successive quatrains names the Roman leader and the province that was the scene of fatal engagements (Hor. *Carm*. 2.1.21-28):

> Already I seem to hear mighty leaders
> covered with not inglorious dust
>   and all the world subdued
>   save the truculent spirit of Cato.
> Juno (and whoever of the gods better disposed
> to the Africans) had impotently abandoned
>   the unavenged land, but now has offered the victors'
>   descendants in sacrifice to the shade of Jugurtha.

The defeat of Cato by Caesar offers occasion for dilation upon civil war's tragedy and a temporary abandonment of the Pindaric style that is a regular feature of Horatian description. Apparently, contemporaries were struck by Pollio's account of the campaign of 47–46, wherein the earlier defeat of Caesar's lieutenant Scribonius Curio was avenged and Africa once again secured as a source of grain and olive oil for the imperial metropolis.⁶⁵

It might be suggested that Africa stood at the centre of Pollio's oeuvre not merely by chronological chance, but also on account of its fundamental significance as the site where the contest for power was ultimately decided. Despite the fact that the sons of Pompeius Magnus were to attempt to continue the struggle in Spain, the defeat of the forces opposed to Caesar in Africa marked the effective conclusion of the first cycle of civil war in the 40s.⁶⁶ With the defeat of Cato and Scipio in Africa, no one of equal authority – *pace* Labienus and his aspirations – survived from the generation of Caesar and Pompeius Magnus to lead the anti-Caesarian forces. The torch had passed to the next generation and, as is evident from the trajectory of Sextus Pompeius, it would take them some time to re-group and re-assert themselves as a viable military opposition.[67]

Cato the Younger was a problematic figure on numerous counts, from a Caesarian perspective. Memorably immortalized by Sallust in his account of the Catilinarian conspiracy penned at the close of the 40s, Cato's rivalry with Caesar went back decades.[68] Caesar composed an invective against the dead Cato that was so vile as to provoke a written response from Cicero, notwithstanding the latter's tendency to avoid crossing Caesar in public after enjoying Caesar's clemency. Only Horace offers clear testimony as to how Pollio dealt with the figure of Cato, and this testimony strongly suggests that he was anything but favourable. Horace writes of Cato as 'gloomy' or 'truculent' (*atrox*), deploying an adjective that admits of no positive interpretation.[69] In view of the fact that Cato re-opened his abdominal wound to carry out his intention of suicide in defeat, the epithet of 'truculent' seems a fitting description of his resolute behaviour as leader of the defeated party. Whether Pollio applied this adjective to Cato or not, it may therefore be inferred that he did not pass over in silence – or without judgement – the decision taken by Cato to prefer death over Caesar's clemency. The act of suicide was yet another instance of the unreasoning obstinacy of Caesar's enemies that had rendered civil war necessary. Unwilling to negotiate, they had preferred death and destruction over life and liberty. Pollio manifestly did not belong to that obdurate group of senators who cultivated the memory of Cato as a leader who had sacrificed his life in the attempt to defend liberty and the Republic.[70]

7. Judgement on Cicero

By good fortune, as it were, Seneca the Elder not only preserved Pollio's obituary for Cicero, but also remarked upon the nature of Pollio's account of the statesman's death (*FRHist* 56 F7). Whereas the obituary reveals grudging respect for his predecessor, the narrative account (now lost) is reported to have been unambiguously malevolent (*mortem . . . maligne narrat*). Moreover, Pollio was alone (*solus ex omnibus*) in offering an unfavourable account of Cicero's death. This independence of judgement is noteworthy, not only because it reveals Pollio taking a stance none of his peers and contemporaries considered tenable, but also because it was taken at a time (mid-20s) when the rehabilitation of Cicero was already well under way.[71] Notwithstanding his proclaimed concern for *libertas*, Pollio did not consider Cicero to be a role model to be held up for emulation. On the contrary, he reckoned him pitiable by virtue of the manner of his death. In Pollio's judgement, Cicero had composed numerous works of enviable craftsmanship and manifest significance, but the manner of his death had defined his life as wretched.[72]

Pollio's judgement on the death of Cicero cannot be viewed in isolation from the two men's position on the figure of M. Antonius and his role in Roman politics in the 40s.

Cicero's depiction of Antonius as a latter-day Helen of Troy who was responsible for the outbreak of civil war in 49 is infamous.[73] So, too, are the attacks of 44–43 that were committed to posterity in the form of the *Philippicae*.[74] Cicero sought to have Antonius declared a public enemy (*hostis publicus*) and proved successful, to his undoing. With the death of the two *consules ordinarii* of 43, the realignment of the younger Caesar with Antonius was merely a matter of time, and proscriptions followed naturally from that reformation of the Caesarian party. Antonius paid Cicero back in kind, having him eliminated as a public enemy.[75] Pollio, whose actions in 44–43 had contributed to the survival of Antonius and the re-affirmation of his primacy amongst the heirs of Caesar acting as the leaders of the Caesarian party, had remained loyal to Antonius' memory even when the rest of Italy prepared to follow the younger Caesar into war against Antonius at the close of the 30s. Therefore, it comes as no surprise that Pollio should have assumed a position that defended the inherent justice of Antonius' decision to proscribe Cicero and other presumed enemies of the Republic. The injustice of the Proscriptions is so obvious to modern students of the period that no one seems to have considered the possibility that an ancient contemporary might have written a historical account that justified the choice.[76] Yet, it would appear that that was precisely what Pollio did. At the very least, it must be conceded, Pollio considered the most distinguished victim of the Proscriptions not to have been deserving of commiseration, and that is tantamount to reckoning the death of Cicero as justified and the Proscriptions as a necessary evil. Pollio's position on the Proscriptions, in other words, must have been close to that which he attributed to Caesar as the victorious leader looked upon the masses of dead scattered over the battlefield of Pharsalus.[77]

It is worth recalling that Pollio's collaboration with Antonius goes back to 47, if not earlier. During the tenure of Antonius as *magister equitum*, there were disturbances in Rome. The cause was P. Cornelius Dolabella's attempt, as tribune of the *plebs*, to pass a law that would cancel debts.[78] Antonius opposed this, reinforced in his stance by the belief that Dolabella had also been engaged in adulterous relations with his wife Antonia.[79] When Dolabella occupied the Forum Romanum in an attempt to force the issue, street-fighting and bloodshed ensued.[80] During this whole episode, Pollio, present in Rome as a tribune of the *plebs*, was active as an advisor and partisan of Antonius.[81] Whether or not the two men had served together in Gaul under Caesar at the end of the 50s, their service for the Caesarian cause in 49–48 did result in their being amongst those of the victorious party to return first to Rome from the East. That collaboration seems to have been mutually beneficial, for Pollio needed little urging to decide in 44–43 that the cause of the Republic was identical with the cause of Antonius, and he would persevere in that opinion over the next decade. In short, Pollio appears to have been that rarest of political animals: a politician consistent in his views and allegiances even in the midst of civil war.

8. Loyalty to Antonius

In his account of the campaign undertaken against Antonius at the close of the 30s, the elderly Augustus looked back proudly upon how he had united the whole of Italy under his leadership.[82] The reality was more prosaic. As is remarked by Suetonius, there was a significant exception in the form of the city of Bononia (Bologna), which was bound by ties of patronage to the figure of Antonius.[83] Moreover, politicians in Rome at the very summit were themselves divided, notwithstanding the attempt to create an appearance of unanimity. This is revealed by the anecdote that Velleius reports regarding the figure of Pollio in the comments introducing his treatment of that conflict (Vell. 2.86.3):

> Let us not pass over in silence a memorable deed and saying of Asinius Pollio. Although he had stayed in Italy after the peace of Brundisium and had never looked upon the queen nor mingled with Antonius' partisans after the latter had been unmanned by passion, when Caesar asked him to join him for the Actian campaign, he responded, 'My actions on behalf of Antonius are greater, but his on my behalf are better known. So, I shall withdraw myself from your contest, and I shall be the prize of the winner.'

This *recusatio* indeed exhibits no explicit criticism of the war,[84] but the example offered by the *consularis* is striking, and in all likelihood it was within the context of the senatorial debate on whether or not to declare war against Antonius that Pollio memorably refused to participate in the destruction of his former leader.[85] The invitation is unlikely to have been made behind closed doors,[86] but rather to have occurred during the very public preparations for the war that the younger Caesar had decided was necessary.

In view of his long-standing allegiance to Antonius, the notion that Pollio could have concluded the *Historiae* with an account of the defeat and destruction of Antonius and Cleopatra VII ought never to have been entertained.[87] What historian ever sets out to write an account that will make himself look bad? As any speaker or writer worth their salt knows, omission is a potent weapon, and Pollio surely left out of his account of contemporary history an affair that can hardly have redounded to his credit. To have included it would have laid him open to charges of being either an ingrate at the moment of crisis or stupid in a more felicitous age, and even a compromised enemy such as Plancus would have felt emboldened to give him grief. Silence is far more difficult to attack.

By closing with some felicitous memory such as his consulate in 40 or his triumph a year later,[88] Pollio could set up for readers a nice antithesis between the golden promise of the early 30s and the recurrence of civil war and fraternal bloodshed yet again at the end of the 30s. Pollio had done his part as a statesman, and for a moment it had appeared that peace might follow. By implication, the onus for the renewal of conflict fell squarely upon the shoulders of the younger Caesar and those of Antonius' partisans who abandoned either their leader (e.g. Plancus) or their magistracy (e.g. Sosius). Whereas the name of Plancus was indissolubly linked in Roman annals to the national disaster of Philippi in 42,[89] that of Pollio was no less strongly attached to the Pact of Brundisium and that agreement's promise of peace two years later.[90] Moreover, despite the hostile actions of the younger Caesar, Pollio had stood his ground in 40, unlike C. Sosius in 32, and he had even taken steps to secure a peaceful settlement between the younger Caesar and Antonius. For someone for whom being a *Caesarianus* had meant being a loyal partisan of Antonius in the latter half of the 40s and during the 30s, Pollio had every reason to focus upon a date that would enable him to highlight the honourable role that he himself had played in past events. Hence, arguably the triumph that he had celebrated for victories obtained in Macedonia in 39, or more plausibly the Pact of Brundisium and the triumphal reception accorded to the younger Caesar and Antonius when they entered Rome late in 40.[91] Even though Pollio and his colleague Cn. Domitius Calvinus (*cos. iter.*) were replaced by suffect consuls, the accomplishment was theirs and theirs were the names that were attached to the year. Closing with this triumphal entry would, indeed, have allowed Pollio to contrast implicitly the promise of the year in which he stood at the helm of the ship of state with those (42, 32) of the time-servers who by their actions had signally failed Antonius and the Republic.

Perhaps the most decisive argument for the conclusion of the *Historiae* in 40, however, is the absence or extremely modest attention given in the historical narratives to the triumph celebrated by Pollio over the Parthini in 39. Indeed, those who believe that most of the narrative of the *Emphylia* of Appian of Alexandria was taken from the *Historiae* of Pollio must resort to some extravagant hypothesis to explain the omission, alleging for instance 'something discreditable about the triumph'.[92] The omission is all the more striking in view of Appian's use of Augustus' *De vita sua* to create the last portion of the *Illyrikê*. Are we to believe that Pollio, an author noted for emphasizing personal autopsy as a historian and his own role in the civil wars of the 40s,[93] described the events of the 30s and yet downplayed or omitted his own role in them? Far better and more consistent is the thesis that he omitted the 30s from the narrative of the *Historiae* altogether.[94] In accordance with Occam's razor, the unknowns postulated ought to be kept to a minimum. Since the annalistic nature of the *Historiae* is not in doubt, the simplest and most economical solution is to posit that Pollio brought them to a close on a note of promise with the triumphal return of the triumvirs to Rome after having concluded the Peace of Brundisium. At the time of writing (viz. mid-20s), Pollio can hardly have expected to be overtaken by the historical work of Livy, much less have anticipated being mined by Seneca the Elder and thereby condemned to oblivion. Moreover, for contemporaries, the new Atrium Libertatis will, with its monumental dedicatory inscription,[95] have seemed sufficient guarantee for the eternal memory of Pollio's martial victory over a Balkan people during his time as governor of Macedonia.

9. The audience of the *Historiae*

Who constituted the audience of the *Historiae*? What reader(s) did Pollio imagine as initially making use of his work of contemporary history? Whom did he wish to persuade of his version of events? These questions merit further reflection, even though it is self-evident that historians (not to be confused with apologists) essentially write their works for the sake of informing future generations. By writing *historiae* rather than *commentarii*, Pollio was laying claim to a concern with the intellectual formation of future generations.

This manifestly puts him within the tradition of Herodotus and Thucydides. However, further reflection points to the possibility of refining this analysis. Specifically, Pollio appears to have been interested in having a voice in the formation of the ruling class of tomorrow, viz. senators and *equites*. It is surely an intriguing coincidence that Pollio is known from the testimony of Horace to have been composing the *Historiae* in the late 20s, which was the very period when his son C. Asinius Gallus (*cos*. 8) came of age. Born in the course of 40, during his father's consulate, Gallus was reportedly the child whose birth was celebrated by Vergil as marking the opening of a new age.[96] Whatever one might think of that claim, apparently made by none other than Gallus himself, it is hard not to be struck by the fact that Pollio dedicated himself to writing an account of the experiences of the civil wars of the 40s in the very years in which his teenage son came of age. Fathers, as is well known, trained their sons for participation in public life, and the composition of the *Historiae* was arguably merely another facet of this training for future engagement on the public stage of imperial Rome. For those who might be sceptical, it is worth observing that Pollio was keenly aware of the significance of the nexus between politics and the education of the younger generations. Exemplary of that fact is his virulent reaction to the injury incurred by his grandson M. Claudius Marcellus Aeserninus (*pr*. CE 19) during the celebration of the *lusus Troiae* in or shortly after 2, the year in which the Senate declared Caesar Augustus 'the father of the fatherland'.[97] Pollio used the incident as a pretext for discontinuing a rite that he viewed as inherently contrary to the proud tradition of liberty associated with the Republic. Anything that valorized the Trojan origins of the *princeps* – contemporaries would by now have thought of the ritual's description in the poetic work of Vergil – was to be contested, as it implicitly subordinated the Senate to the emperor. In his perception of the nexus between education and politics, Pollio, it is worth remarking, was not particularly innovative. Indeed, it might be argued that this *novus homo* was merely taking yet another page from the playbook of Cato the Elder, who had written various works for the instruction of his son as a future member of the Senate. Amongst Cato the Elder's works there had figured a history of Rome. Therefore, in view of the Roman tendency to view literature as having a practical finality, it is not far-fetched to imagine Pollio as having written the *Historiae* for his son as a manual of introduction to the practice of contemporary politics in imperial Rome.[98] Fathers educated their sons in the ways of politics, and history was a supremely political form of literature at Rome.

* * *

The *Historiae* of C. Asinius Pollio have disappeared. They failed to make the leap across the chasm of transmission from papyrus roll to codex. Indeed, there is doubt whether they were still being read by the time that Plutarch, Suetonius, and Appian came to compose their historical works in the late first and second centuries CE.[99] Nevertheless, even though the route of direct transmission was broken, traces of Pollio's influence on other authors of civil war can be discerned or inferred. So, for instance, one significant borrowing by Livy is well documented: the account of the death of Pompeius Magnus. Thanks to source analysis (*Quellenforschung*), Livy's debt to Pollio is certain in spite of the fact that both Livy's and Pollio's accounts have perished.[100] From what has been proposed in the preceding pages, it might be argued that Livy's very way of structuring his narrative for the years 49–40 was heavily indebted to the work of Pollio. After all, Livy used nineteen books (109–27, according to the *Periochae*) for the same period covered by Pollio in seventeen books. Moving on in time, we find another secure instance of knowledge and use of Pollio in the account of the civil wars that was composed by Seneca the Elder. It is to Seneca that we owe our knowledge of Pollio's obituary for Cicero, which happens to be the longest of the surviving fragments of the *Historiae*. Arguably influenced by Pollio's penchant for the picturesque and dramatic, Seneca the Elder wrote an account that appears to have been intensively mined by such authors of the Second Sophistic as Plutarch and Appian. Still further on in time, when he came to write an account of civil war and the Flavian emperors under whom he had flourished, Tacitus seems to have turned to Pollio for inspiration. Aside from the breadth and depth of treatment that he accorded to contemporary history in his own *Historiae*, Tacitus, as a *novus homo*, appears to have been influenced by Pollio's choice of topics (e.g. the theme of civil war and a focus upon events comparable to the siege and firing of Perusia) and arguably shared his pessimism regarding deity and disaster or the iniquity of human behaviour.

Notes

*   I am deeply grateful to Hannah Cornwell, Jennifer Gerrish and Susan M. Treggiari for their helpful comments and salutary criticism, which have substantively improved this paper. Collegial assistance, of course, does not imply agreement, and I am alone responsible for all remaining errors.

1. For this phenomenon, see Powell 2002a: x; Welch 2012: 34 n.6.
2. Syme 1939: 4–7.
3. See esp. Kornemann 1896: 557–692.
4. Néraudau 1983: 1732–50. For Pollio's political career, by contrast, readers are referred to Ferriès 2007: 335–41; Wiseman 1971: 215 (no. 50); PIR^2 A1241. Overall, see *FRHist* 1.430-445 and Bruhns 1978.
5. With the jussive subjunctive of *desit*, Horace projects his own desires onto Pollio. For Horace's past allegiance in civil war, see Osgood 2006: 212–14. For Pollio's possible involvement in Horace's return to peacetime life, see Williams 1995: 303–4.
6. Cf. Brunt 1986; Balsdon 1960, on Cicero and this conceit. Of course, there is Horatian paradox in the application of *munus* to Pollio's pastime.
7. Hor. *Serm.* 1.10.42–43; Verg. *Ecl.* 8.9-10; Tac. *Dial.* 21.7.
8. Perhaps to be dated to the latter half of the 40s CE: von Albrecht 1997: 1170 n.1.
9. von Albrecht 1997: 1178.
10. Cic. *QFr.* 2.15.3; 3.1.13; 3.6.7; 3.9.6.
11. Suet. *Iul.* 56.
12. Suet. *Aug.* 85.

13. Havas 1980; Henderson 1996: 59–136 (= Henderson 1998: 108–62); Woodman 2003: 191–216 (= Woodman 2012: 127–44).
14. So, for example, Pelling 1988: 27; Mazzarino 1966: 2.397; Syme 1939: 8; cf. Haller 1967: 113; Woodman 2003: 203. For the most recent statement of this consensus, see Harrison 2017: 45, 47–8.
15. *Pace* Harrison 2017: 47–8; Nisbet and Hubbard 1978: 11, 'may even be echoing a sub-title'.
16. Cf. Turner 2019: 38–9, who goes so far as to suggest that Horace is proposing ideas to Pollio.
17. For the ancient tradition for Livy's work, see Klotz 1926: 818.
18. Plin. *NH* praef. 20; Plin. *Epist.* 3.5.6. For this work and its influence on the historiographical tradition, see the remarks of Barbara Levick (*FRHist* 1.532-534) in her superlative introduction.
19. For the ancient tradition for Tacitus' work, see Schwabe 1900: 1576; cf. Goodyear 1972: 85–7.
20. *TLL* 1.36-39; *OLD* 1-3 s.v. 'ab, abs, a', here B.11.
21. *TLL* 5.1104, 1106. *OLD* 628-629 s.v. 'ex, e', *pace* the citation of this passage under §9. It is worth adding, as Hannah Cornwell reminds me, that, in the *fasti triumphales*, triumphs are *de* + ethnic group but *ex* + geographical area.
22. Allen and Greenough 1903: 131 §220b (overview of prepositions); 131 §221 no. 1.b (*a, ab*); 133 §221 no. 11.b (*e, ex*); Hansen and Quinn 1992: 54 fig. (primary semantic difference between ἀπό and ἐκ).
23. Plut. *Caes.* 32.6; *Pomp.* 60.2; cf. Suet. *Iul.* 32; App. *BCiv.* 2.35.140.
24. Cf. Nisbet and Hubbard 1978: 15. Indeed, one is reminded of the fact that Cornelius Balbus the Younger claimed Caesar as the model for his own actions.
25. Morgan 2000.
26. This is unfortunately obscured by the presentation of the fragments of Pollio in *FRHist*, for the text of Plutarch does not constitute a 'fragment' in the classical sense of the word and is therefore omitted from those assembled there. The methodological issues involved in identifying and publishing fragments are complicated and require extended treatment elsewhere.
27. Nisbet and Hubbard 1978: 15–16.
28. In this instance, given the omens that attended the assassination of C. Caesar, we ought to think of Mt Etna rather than Mt Vesuvius. To my knowledge, no one has made this obvious suggestion.
29. Woodman 2003: 211.
30. See Nisbet and Hubbard 1978: 16, for the ritual of firewalking.
31. Nisbet and Hubbard 1978: 16.
32. Prop. 2.1.29; Vell. 2.74.4; App. *BCiv.* 5.49; Cass. Dio 48.14.5. See Westall 2016: 61, for discussion of Cassius Dio's account.
33. Cf. *FRHist* no. 56.
34. Vell. 2.74.3, draws attention to the signal failure of L. Munatius Plancus (*Plancus, Antonianarum adiutor partium, spem magis ostenderat auxilii, quam opem ferebat Antonio*). This is typical of Pollio's tendency to engage in invective against his former brother-in-arms.
35. Aside from the fact that this (firing of Perusia) finds a parallel in Tacitus' inclusion of the destruction of Pompeii and other cities of Campania, there is the key fact that this war atrocity occurred during the year marked by the consulate of Pollio in 40.

36. Str. 3.2.3 C169.
37. Gelzer 1968: 32.
38. Gelzer 1968: 63, assigning the initial acquaintance to 69.
39. For the suffect consulate, see Syme 1939: 131, 220. Overall for his career, see *FRHist* 1.383-384. It bears emphasizing that he was adopted by Theophanes as a part of the pact of 60: Cic. *Balb.* 57; *Att.* 7.7.6; cf. SHA, *Max. Balb.* 7.3 (= *FRHist* 41 T1).
40. Caes. *BCiv.* 2.18.2; Westall 2017.
41. Cf. Drummond, at *FRHist* 3.521: 'in either case the context would be beyond recovery'.
42. For the identification with Gades, see *FRHist* 3.521.
43. Cf. Caes. *BCiv.* 2.17-21. According to the chronological table at Kraner, Hofmann and Meusel 1906: 372, this took place in the early autumn of 49.
44. Cic. *Balb.* 43; Plut. *Caes.* 12; Cass. Dio 37.52.3.
45. Cic. *Fam.* 10.32.2.
46. Drummond, at *FRHist* 3.521. Indeed, it is curious that none of those who do so suggest a reference to 69-68, when Caesar was quaestor in Further Spain: *MRR* 2.136 n.7 (for the date).
47. The latter point was well made by Zecchini 1982: 1285, 'Indizi sicuri di un'ulteriore prosecuzione (*sc.* after Philippi) non ce ne sono'.
48. Cf. Bellemore 2005: 225-57, esp. 227 (for Plutarch's reliance on a variety of sources for 59).
49. Caes. *BCiv.* 1.22.5: *ut se et populum Romanum factione paucorum oppressum in libertatem vindicaret.*
50. Cf. *RGDA* 1.1, Hurlet 2020: 176-7 (discussing Augustus' reprisal of this Caesarian theme).
51. Cf. Caes. *BCiv.* 1.7; Bosworth 1972: 456; Wirszubski 1950: 103-4. See also Westall 2017: 49-57; Zucchetti (in the present volume).
52. See Gelzer 1972.
53. Cf. Morgan 2000: 65-8, regarding *libertas* and Pollio's authorial stance in the *Historiae*.
54. The matter is not altogether certain and has been much debated. For the identification of Macedonia as Pollio's province, see Syme 1937: 39-48 (= Syme 1979: 1.18-30); Osgood 2006: 255 n.18. Arguing for Illyricum instead: Bosworth 1972: 463-8. Yet others have proposed instead a roving commission combining Macedonia and Illyricum: André 1949: 22-3; Woodman 1983: 192-6. In the most detailed of recent discussions (Drummond 2013: 433), the solution of Macedonia is preferred, but the possibility of Illyricum not excluded.
55. Suet. *Aug.* 29.5.
56. Wiseman 1971: 215 (no. 50).
57. Plin. *NH* 7.115; 35.10; Isid. *Orig.* 6.5.2; cf. Ovid. *Trist.* 3.1.71-72. For discussion of these libraries, see Casson 2001: 80-108; Osgood 2006: 296. For overall cultural context, see Rawson 1985: 39-45; Fedeli 1988: 31-64. The idea that Pollio gave one or more readings of the *Historiae* within this setting is attractive (e.g. Dalzell 1955: 27; Fantham 1996: 71; Roller 2019: 196 n.23). For the testimony of Seneca the Elder regarding the readings instituted by Pollio, see Dalzell 1955: 20-8.
58. Coarelli 1993: 133-5; Amici 1999: 229; cf. Purcell 1993, for an alternative identification.
59. Steinby 1993: 187.
60. For Cato the Elder, see the brief but incisive comments of Leigh 2000: 44-5.

61. The list of fourteen Hellenic works of art known to have adorned the structure (reproduced by Osgood 2006: 296) suggests a possible ideological link to the Theatre of Dionysus at Athens, just as the choice of location points to a linking of *libertas* to the person of C. Caesar in polemical contrast with the 'tyrant slayers', who had occupied the Capitoline after assassinating the Dictator.
62. Plin. *NH* 7.115, explicitly drawing a parallel between the action of Pollio and that of Pompeius Magnus when he awarded Varro a 'naval crown' for his activities in the campaign against piracy.
63. Cf. Morgan 2000: 66; Fantham 2003: 116–17; Bloomer 2015: 52, 243 n.4, highlighting the 'symbolic value' of Varro, but unfortunately confusing the two Caesars.
64. It should be remarked, however, there may be two allusions to Pompeius Magnus: the phrase *magnos . . . duces* at line 21 (Nisbet and Hubbard 1978: 23) and the rhetorical question *quae caret ora cruore nostro?* at line 36 (Lyne 1995: 94). Whereas the form of the first may be explained as an instance of a rhetorical plural, the point of the latter is that Pompeius' truncated corpse was left lying unceremoniously abandoned on the beach of Pelusium, where he had hoped to find safety with the young Ptolemy XIII. Pollio's description of that episode of civil war made a strong impression upon contemporaries, even providing the inspiration for Vergil's description of the dead Priam: Moles 1983: 287–8 (= Moles 2023: 2.131–3).
65. Naturally, Pollio's own role in the failed expedition of Curio in 49 made him even more eager to stress his having taken part in the successful expedition led by Caesar a couple years later. Pollio, readers will remember, had managed to escape from the *débacle* with a limited portion of the troops that had been brought to Africa from Italy and Sicily.
66. Even though the fourth and last triumph was ostensibly over the African allies of Scipio and not the Roman commanders themselves (Lange 2016: 109–10), Caesar's month of four triumphs in 46 BCE indicates Caesar's belief and hope at the time that civil war was effectively at an end.
67. Welch 2012.
68. La Penna 2013: 266.
69. Hor. *Carm.* 2.1.24; cf. *OLD* 199 s.v. 'atrox, ocis'; Nisbet and Hubbard 1978: 24 ('complimentary only by way of paradox'). It can hardly be a coincidence that Caesar represented the dying Cato in the triumph that he celebrated in Rome for this civil war victory: App. *BCiv.* 2.101.419.
70. For reception of the figure of Cato under the Principate, see Griffin 1986: 64–77, 192–202; Goar 1987: 23–76; Afzelius 1941: 190–203. See also, for a useful re-evaluation of Cicero's own testimony regarding Cato as a Stoic and an orator, Stem 2005: 37–49.
71. This rehabilitation was a corollary of the destruction of M. Antonius. One of the consuls at the time of receipt of the news of Antonius' death was none other than Cicero's own son (Cass. Dio 51.19.4). That Agrippa was married to Atticus' daughter Caecilia Attica will likely have facilitated the *volte-face*. The political career of the Princeps had completed a full revolution, from defender of the Republic to despotic dynast and back to defender of the Republic.
72. It is to be remarked that Pollio refuses to instantiate his polite appraisal of Cicero's literary accomplishments. For a detailed discussion of evidence overall, see now Roller 2019: 109–30.
73. Cic. *Phil.* 2.55; cf. Plut. *Cic.* 6.1.
74. Cf. App. *BCiv.* 4.20.77.
75. Cf. App. *BCiv*, 4.8.32; 4.19.73-20.82.
76. It is perhaps worth adding that Appian, too, found them intrinsically unjustified.

77. Suet. *Iul.* 30.4; Plut. *Caes.* 46.1-2 (= *FRHist* 56 F3).
78. Plut. *Ant.* 9.1.
79. Plut. *Ant.* 9.2.
80. Plut. *Ant.* 9.3-4.
81. Plut. *Ant.* 1-4; Sumner 1971: 260–1; cf. Pelling 1988: 136.
82. *RGDA* 25.2.
83. Suet. *Aug.* 17.2; Cass. Dio 50.6.3.
84. As observed, for instance, by Drummond at *FRHist* 1.434.
85. For the order followed in debate, see Talbert 1984: 240–1; of especial note the testimonies of Gell. 14.7.9; 4.10.1; Cass. Dio 54.15.5-6. In view of his seniority and his recent change of allegiance, one suspects that Munatius Plancus was the first of the *consulares* to be asked for his opinion on the matter.
86. Cf. Syme 1939: 291.
87. For an example of the scholarship arguing for a conclusion in 30, see Pelling 1988: 27 (citing earlier work).
88. See Westall 2016: 64–5.
89. Cf. Hor. *Carm.* 3.14.27-28.
90. Cf. Syme 1939: 217.
91. Cass. Dio 48.31.
92. Bosworth 1972: 468.
93. Morgan 2000: 55, 'Assertions of autopsy were ... an important and recurrent feature of Pollio's *Histories*'.
94. Cf. *FRHist* 1.438-439, noting that the certain evidence of fragments goes no further than 43.
95. Cf. Suet. *Aug.* 29; Isid. *Orig.* 6.5.2: *de manubiis*.
96. Serv. ad. Verg. *Ecl.* 4.11. For evolving historical context and the identification of the child, see Clausen 1994: 125–6.
97. Suet. *Aug.* 43.2.
98. As Hannah Cornwell reminds me, although a philosophical work, Cicero's *De officiis* utilizes *exempla*, including the perceived tyranny of Caesar, as a lesson in politics for his son. For this work as an element in the education of young M. Cicero, see Treggiari 2015: 246, 250. As readers will remember, Cicero was a *novus homo*, like Cato the Elder and Pollio.
99. E.g. Drummond, at *FRHist* no. 56.
100. Moles 1983: 287–8 (= Moles 2023: 2.131–3). For the vexed (and related question) of Appian's relationship to Livy, see most recently Stevenson 2015: 272 (limited to App. *BCiv.* 2.48-91); Westall 2015: 157, 159; Westall 2013.

BIBLIOGRAPHY

Abbreviations according to L'Année Philologique.

Adler, E. (2011), *Valorizing the Barbarians: Enemy Speeches in Roman Historiography*, Austin.
Afzelius, A. (1941), 'Die politische Bedeutung des jüngeren Cato', *C&M* 4: 100–203.
Ahlheid, F. (1988), 'Oratorical strategy in Sallust's letter of Mithridates reconsidered', *Mnemosyne* 41: 67–92.
Albrecht, J. (2020), *Die Religion der Feldherren: Vermittlung und Inszenierung des Krieges in der späten römischen Republik*, Heidelberg.
Alexander, J. C. (2004), 'Toward a theory of cultural trauma', in J. C. Alexander, R. Eyerman, B. Giesen, N. J. Smelser and P. Sztompka (eds), *Cultural Trauma and Collective Identity*, 1–30, Berkeley.
Alexander, M. C. (1990), *Trials in the Late Roman Republic, 149 BC to 50 BC*, Toronto.
Alföldi, A. (1973), 'La divinisation de César dans la politique d'Antoine et d'Octavien entre 44 et 40 avant J.-C.', *RN* 15: 99–128.
Alföldi, A. (1976), *Oktavians Aufstieg zur Macht*, Bonn.
Allély, A. (2012), *La déclaration d'hostis sous la République romaine*, Bordeaux.
Allen and Greenough 1903 = Ayer, M. (2014), *Allen and Greenough's New Latin Grammar for Schools and Colleges*, (Dickinson College Commentaries), Carlisle, PA: https://dcc.dickinson.edu/grammar/latin/credits-and-reuse
Alston, R. (1994), 'Roman military pay from Caesar to Diocletian', *JRS* 84: 113–23.
Alston, R. (2007), 'Warfare and the state: B. The military and politics', in P. Sabin, H. Van Wees and M. Whitby (eds), *The Cambridge History of Greek and Roman Warfare*, vol. 2: *Rome from the Late Republic to the Late Empire*, 176–97, Cambridge.
Althusser, L. (1965), 'Contradiction et surdétermination', in L. Althusser, *Pour Marx*, 87–108, Paris.
Althusser, L. (1969), 'Contradiction and overdetermination', in L. Althusser, *For Marx*, 15–35, London.
Amela Valverde, L. (2000), 'Numidia y la "clientela" pompeyana: La acción de los políticos de la República romana en el extranjero', *Iberia* 3: 253–64.
Amela Valverde, L. (2010), 'El áureo de Cn. Pompeyo Magno (RRC 402/1)', *ETF(hist)* 23: 205–16.
Amela Valverde, L. (2019), 'La serie *RRC* 452 de César', *Revista numismática: OMNI* 13: 252–64.
Amici, C. M. (1999), 'Atrium Libertatis', in E. M. Steinby (ed.), *Lexicon topographicum urbis Romae*, vol. 5, 229, Roma.
Amisano, G. (2008), *L'oro di Roma: Dalle origini al 27 a.C.*, Cassino.
André, J. (1949), *La vie et l'oeuvre d'Asinius Pollion*, Paris.
Antonelli S. (2022), 'Connessioni adriatiche: la complessa vicenda del culto di San Pelino tra Corfinium e Dyrrachium', in S. Antonelli, V. La Salvia, M. C. Mancini, O. Menozzi, M. Moderato and M. C. Somma (eds), *Archaeologiae. Una storia al plurale: Studi in Memoria di Sara Santoro*, 263–78, Oxford.
Appelbaum, A. (2009), '"The Idumaeans" in Josephus' *The Jewish War*', *JSJ* 40: 1–22.
Arena, V. (2012), *Libertas and the Practice of Politics in the Late Roman Republic*, Cambridge.
Arena, V. (2020), 'The notion of *Bellum Civile* in the last century of the Republic', in F. Pina Polo (ed.), *The Triumviral Period: Civil War, Political Crisis and Socioeconomic Transformations*, 101–26, Zaragoza, Sevilla.

Bibliography

Argetsinger, K. (1992), 'Birthday rituals: Friends and patrons in Roman poetry and cult', *ClAnt* 11.2: 175–93.

Armitage, D. (2017), *Civil Wars: A History in Ideas*, New York.

Arnold, W. T. (1914), *The Roman System of Provincial Administration to the Accession of Constantine the Great*, 3rd edn, rev. by E. S. Bouchier, Oxford.

Assenmaker, P. (2011), 'Les défunts Pompée et César dans les propagandes de leurs héritiers: l'exploitation politique des conceptions philosophiques et religieuses liées à la mort à la fin de la République', in J. Andreu, D. Espinosa and S. Pastor (eds), *Mors omnibus instat: Aspectos arqueológicos, epigráficos y rituales de la muerte en el occidente romano*, 95–111, Madrid.

Assmann, J. (1997), *Moses the Egyptian*, Cambridge, MA.

Augier, B. (2016a), 'L'autorité ne va pas sans prestige, et le prestige sans éloignement? Le cas des officiers dans les légions tardo-républicaines', in R. Baudry and F. Hurlet (eds), *Le prestige à Rome à la fin de la République et au début du Principat*, 91–103, Paris.

Augier, B. (2016b), Homines militares: *Les officiers dans les armées romaines au temps des guerres civiles (49–31 av. J.-C.)*, PhD thesis, Université Paris Nanterre.

Augier, B. (2018), 'Sextus Pompée, un imperator (il)légitime à plus d'un titre: nouvelles interprétations autour de la titulature praef. clas. et orae marit. ex s. c.', *MEFRA* 130(2): 451–66.

Augier, B. (2023), 'Le charme discret de la hiérarchie: pratiques charismatiques et commandement des troupes à la fin de la République', in J.-P. Guilhembet, R. Laignoux and P. Montlahuc (eds), *Le charisme en politique – Max Weber face à l'Antiquité grecque et romaine*, 85–118, Rome.

Austin, R. G. (ed.) (1984), *P. Vergili Maronis, Aeneidos: Liber Primus*, Oxford.

Badian, E. (1958), *Foreign Clientelae (264–70 B.C.)*, Oxford.

Badian, E. (1962), 'Waiting for Sulla', *JRS* 52: 47–61.

Badian, E. (1965), 'M. Porcius Cato and the annexation and early administration of Cyprus', *JRS* 55: 110–21.

Badian, E. (1966), 'Notes on Provincia Gallia in the late Republic', in R. Chevallier (ed.), *Mélanges d'archéologie et d'histoire offerts à André Piganiol*, 2.901–18, Paris.

Badian, E. (1972), *Publicans and Sinners: Private Enterprise in the Service of the Roman Republic*, Ithaca, NY.

Badian E. (2009), 'From the Julii to Caesar', in M. Griffin (ed.), *A Companion to Julius Caesar*, 11–22, Malden, MA.

Ballesteros Pastor, L. (2008), 'Cappadocia and Pontus, Client kingdoms of the Roman Republic from the Peace of Apamea to the beginning of the Mithridatic Wars (188–89 B.C.)', in Altay Coşkun (ed.), *Freundschaft und Gefolgschaft in den Auswärtigen Beziehungen der Römer (2 Jh. v. Chr.-1 Jh. n. Chr.)*, 45–63, Frankfurt.

Balsdon, J. P. V. D. (1960), 'Auctoritas, dignitas, otium', *CQ* 10: 43–50.

Baragwanath, E. (2016), 'The character and function of speeches in Xenophon', in M. A. Flower (ed.), *The Cambridge Companion to Xenophon*, 279–98, Cambridge.

Batstone, W. W. (2010), 'Catiline's speeches in Sallust's *Bellum Catilinae*', in Dominic H. Berry and A. Erskine (eds), *Form and Function in Roman Oratory*, 227–46, Cambridge.

Batstone, W. W. and C. Damon (2006), *Caesar's Civil War*, Oxford.

Battenberg, C. (1980), *Pompeius und Caesar: Persönlichkeit und Programm in ihrer Münzpropaganda*. Diss. Marburg.

Beck, H. and U. Walter (eds) (2001–4) *Die frühen römischen Historiker*, Wissenschaftliche Buchgesellschaft Darmstadt.

Bellemore, J. (2005), 'Cato's opposition to Caesar in 59 BC', in K. Welch and T. W. Hillard (eds), *Roman Crossings: Theory and Practice in the Roman Republic*, 225–57, Swansea.

Beloch, J. (1886), *Die Bevölkerung der griechisch-römischen Welt*, Leipzig.

Benferhat, Y. (2005), 'D'*iniuria* à *lenitas* dans le *Bellum ciuile* de César', *VL* 173: 11–25.

Bengtson, H. (1970), *Zur Geschichte des Brutus*, München.

Bibliography

Berdowski, P. (2011), 'The Treaty of Misenum (39 BC) and the "Fourth Tyrant"', in S.Ruciński, K. Balbuza and K. Królczyk (eds), *Studia Lesco Mrozewicz ab amicis et discipulis dedicata*, 31–46, Poznań.

Bertrandy, F. (1990–1), 'L'aide militaire de Juba Ier aux Pompéiens pendant la guerre civile en Afrique du Nord (50–46 avant J.-C.)', in *Histoire et archéologie de l'Afrique du Nord: actes du IVe colloque international réuni dans le cadre du 113e Congrès national des sociétes savantes, Strasbourg, 5–9 avril 1988*, 289–97, Paris.

Bicknell, P. J. (1977), 'Caesar, Antony, Cleopatra and Cyprus', *Latomus* 36(2): 325–42.

Bikerman, E. (1947), 'La lettre de Mithridate dans les "Histoires" de Salluste', *REL* 24: 131–51.

Bleicken, J. (1990), *Zwischen Republik und Prinzipat: Zum Charakter des Zweiten Triumvirats*, Göttingen.

Bloch, G. and J. Carcopino (1952), *Histoire romaine, t. II: La République romaine de 133 à 44 avant J.-C.*, vol. 1 *Des Gracques à Sylla*, 3rd edn, Paris.

Blom, H. van der (2016), *Oratory and Political Career in the Late Roman Republic*, Cambridge.

Blomart, A. (2021), 'The prayers of *evocatio* and *devotio*: Between religious ritual and Roman law', *AAntHung* 60(3–4): 399–416.

Bloomer, W. M. (ed.) (2015), *A Companion to Ancient Education*, Chichester.

Boren, H. (1983), 'Studies related to the *stipendium militum*', *Historia* 32(4): 427–60.

Borghesi, B. (1862), *Oeuvres complètes*. T. 1, Paris.

Borgies, L. (2016), *Le conflit propagandiste entre Octavien et Marc Antoine. De l'usage propagandiste de la* vituperatio *entre 44 et 30 a.C.n.*, Bruxelles.

Borlenghi, A. (2011), *Il campus: organizzazione e funzione di uno spazio pubblico in età romana; le testimonianze in Italia e nelle province occidentali*, Thiasos [Monografie] 1, Roma.

Börm, H. (2016), 'Hellenistische Poleis und römischer Bürgerkrieg: Stasis im griechischen Osten nach den Iden des März (44 bis 39 v. Chr.)', in H. Börm, M. Mattheis and J. Wienand (eds), *Civil War in Ancient Greece and Rome: Contexts of Disintegration and Reintegration* (Heidelberger althistorische Beiträge und epigraphische Studien, 58), 99–125, Stuttgart.

Börm, H. and W. Havener (2012), 'Octavians Rechtsstellung im Januar 27 v. Chr. und das Problem der "Übertragung" der *res publica*', *Historia* 61(2): 202–20.

Börm, H., M. Mattheis and J. Wienand (eds) (2016), *Civil War in Ancient Greece and Rome: Contexts of Disintegration and Deintegration* (Heidelberger althistorische Beiträge und epigraphische Studien, 58), Stuttgart.

Börm, H, U. Gotter and W. Havener (eds) (2023), *A Culture Civil War? Bellum civile and Political Communication in Late Republican Rome* (Heidelberger althistorische Beiträge und epigraphische Studien, 65), Stuttgart.

Botermann, H. (1968), *Die Soldaten und die römische Republik in der Zeit von Caesars Tod bis zur Begründung des Zweiten Triumvirats*, München.

Botrè, C. (2007), 'Alcune considerazioni sulla prima coniazione aurea di Cesare', *RIN* 108: 121–33.

Bourdin, S. (2012), *Les peuples de l'Italie préromaine: identités, territoires et relations interethniques en Italie centrale et septentrionale (VIIIe–Ier s. av. J.-C.)*, (BEFAR, 350), Roma.

Bowersock, G. W. (1990), 'The pontificate of Augustus', in K. A. Raaflaub and M. Toher (eds), *Between Republic and Empire: Interpretations of Augustus and His Principate*, 380–94, Berkeley.

Bowlby, R. (2009), *Freudian Mythologies: Greek Tragedy and Modern Identities*, Oxford.

Braund, D. C. (1984), *Rome and the Friendly King: The Character of the Client Kingship*, London.

Braund, D. C. (1989), 'Function and dysfunction: Personal patronage in Roman imperialism', in A. Wallace-Hadrill (ed.), *Patronage in Ancient Society*, 137–52, London.

Breed, B., C. Damon and A. Rossi (eds) (2010), *Citizens of Discord: Rome and Its Civil Wars*, Oxford.

Briguglio, S. (2017), *Fraternas acies: saggio di commento a Stazio, Tebaide, 1, 1–389*, Alessandria.

Bringmann, K. (1986), 'Der Diktator Caesar als Richter? Zu Ciceros Reden "Pro Ligario" und "Pro rege Deiotaro"', *Hermes* 114(1): 72–88.

Bibliography

Brizzi, G. (2010), 'Eloquentia militarique re aut aequavit praestantissimorum gloriam aut excessit (Suet. Caes.55). Cesare soldato: strategia e immagine', in G. Urso (ed.), *Cesare: precursore o visionario?* 85–103, Pisa.

Brizzi, G. (2017), *Ribelli contro Roma: Gli schiavi, Spartaco, l'altra Italia*, Bologna.

Brodersen, K. (2011), 'Mapping Pliny's world: The achievement of Solinus', *BICS* 54(1): 63–88.

Brown, R. D. (1999), 'Two Caesarian battle-descriptions: A study in contrast', *CJ* 94(4): 329–57.

Bruhns, H. (1978), *Caesar und die römische Oberschicht in den Jahren 49–44 v.Chr. Untersuchungen zur Herrschaftsetablierung im Bürgerkrieg*, Göttingen.

Brunt, P. A. (1965), 'Amicitia in the late Roman Republic', *Proceedings of the Cambridge Philological Society* n.s. 11: 1–20.

Brunt, P. A. (1971), *Italian manpower, 225 BC–AD 14*, Oxford.

Brunt, P. A. (1975), 'Two great Roman landowners', *Latomus* 34: 619–35.

Brunt, P. A. (1986), 'Cicero's *officium* in the civil war', *JRS* 76: 12–32.

Brunt, P. A. (1988), *The Fall of the Roman Republic and Related Essays*, Oxford.

Brunt, P. A. (1990), *Roman Imperial Themes*, Oxford.

Bucher, G. S. (2000), 'The origins, program, and composition of Appian's *Roman history*', *TAPhA* 130: 411–58.

Büchner, K. (1960), *Sallust* (1st edn), Heidelberg.

Büchner, K. (1982), *Sallust* (2nd edn), Heidelberg.

Buongiorno, P. (ed.) (2020), *Senatus consultum ultimum e stato di eccezione: Fenomeni in prospettiva*, Stuttgart.

Buonocore, M. and G. Firpo (1991), *Fonti latine e greche per la storia dell'Abruzzo antico*, Padova.

Bur, C. (2018), *La citoyenneté dégradée: Une histoire de l'infamie à Rome (312 av. J.-C.-96 apr. J.-C.)*, Roma.

Burton, P. J. (2003), '*Clientela* or *amicitia*?: modelling Roman international behaviour in the middle republic (264–146 B.C.)', *Klio* 85(2): 333–69.

Burton, P. J. (2011), *Friendship and Empire: Roman Diplomacy and Imperialism in the Middle Republic (353–146 BC)*, Cambridge.

Burton, P. J. (2016), 'Deditio (Surrender)', in S. E. Phang, I. Spence, D. Kelly and P. Londey (eds) *Conflict in Ancient Greece and Rome: The Definitive Political, Social, and Military Encyclopedia*, 857–8, Santa Barbara, CA.

Buttrey, T. V. (1960), 'The "Pietas" denarii of Sextus Pompey', *NC* 20(6): 83–101.

Buttrey, T. V. (1993), 'Calculating ancient coin production: Facts and fantasies', *NC* 153: 335–51.

Buttrey, T. V. (1994), 'Calculating ancient coin production II: Why it cannot be done', *NC* 154: 341–52.

Buttrey, T. V. (2013), 'Grammar and history: Thoughts on some late Roman Republican coins', in P. G. van Alfen and R. B. Witschonke (eds), *Essays in Honour of Robert Russo.* 295–304, Zürich.

Cadiou, F. (2008), *Hibera in terra miles: Les armées romaines et la conquête de l'Hispanie sous la République (218–45 av. J.-C.)*, Madrid.

Cadiou, F. (2016), 'Cavalerie auxiliaire et cavalerie légionnaire dans l'armée romaine au Ier s. a.C.', in C. Wolff and P. Faure (eds), *Les auxiliaires de l'armée romaine: Des alliés aux fédérés*, 53–78, Paris.

Cadiou, F. (2018), *L'armée imaginaire: Les soldats prolétaires dans les légions romaines au dernier siècle de la République*, Paris.

Cagnat, R. (1914), *Cours d'épigraphie latine*, 4th edn, Paris.

Campana, A. (2000), 'Monete d'oro della Repubblica romana (IV–VII): Emissioni di Lucio Cornelio Silla (84–80 a. C.)', *Panorama Numismatico* 144: 5–11 and 145: 12–17.

Campana, A. (2001), 'Monete d'oro della Repubblica romana (VIII): Emissione di Gneo Pompeo Magno (71 a. C.)', *Panorama Numismatico* 148: 20–4.

Campana, A. (2002a), 'Monete d'oro della Repubblica romana (X–XII): Emissioni al tempo della guerra civile tra le battaglie di Farsalo e di Tapso (48–46 a.C.)', *Panorama Numismatico* 164: 10–20.

Bibliography

Campana, A. (2002b), 'Monete d'oro della Repubblica romana (XIII–XV): Emissioni tra la battaglia di Tapso e la morte di Caio Giulio Cesare (46–44 a.C.)', *Panorama Numismatico* 162: 45–52.
Canfora, L. (1999), *Giulio Cesare: Il Dittatore Democratico*, Roma.
Caplow, T. (1992), 'Coalitions', in E. F. Borgatta and M. L. Borgatta (eds), *Encyclopaedia of Sociology*. Vol. 1, 208–12, Basingstoke.
Caplow, T. and P. Vennesson (2000), *Sociologie militaire: Armée, guerre et paix*, Paris.
Capogrossi Colognesi, L. (2014), *Law and Power in the Making of the Roman Commonwealth*, tr. L. Kopp, Cambridge.
Casson, L. (2001), *Libraries in the Ancient World*, New Haven.
Carcopino, J. (1934), 'La naissance de Jules César', *Mélanges Bidez* (Annuaire de l'Institut de philologie e d'histoire orientals), 2: 35–69, Bruxelles.
Carter, J. M. (ed.) (1991), *Julius Caesar: The Civil War: Books I & II: Edited with an introduction, translation & commentary*, Warminster.
Carter, J. M. (ed.) (1993), *Julius Caesar: The Civil War: Book III: Edited with introduction translation and commentary*, Warminster.
Caruth, C. (1996), *Unclaimed Experience: Trauma, Narrative, and History*, Baltimore.
Caruth, C. (2013), *Literature in the Ashes of History*, Baltimore.
Caspari, M. (1911), 'On the dated coins of Julius Caesar and Mark Antony', *NC* 11: 101–8.
Cavedoni, C. (1829), *Saggio di osservazioni sulle medaglie di famiglie Romane ritrovate in tre antichi ripostigli dell'agro Modenese negli anni MDCCCXII, MDCCCXV e MDCCCXXVIII*, Modena.
Cavedoni, C. (1854), *Ragguaglio storico archeologico de' precipui ripostigli antichi di medaglie consolari e di famiglie romane d'argento*, Modena.
Cavedoni, C. (1857), 'Compte rendu du *Description générale des monnaies de la République romaine, communément appelées médailles consulaires*, par H. Cohen', *RN* 2: 346–62.
Cesano, S. L. (1947–9), 'Le monete di Cesare', *RPAA* 23/24: 103–51.
Chandlar, D. and R. Munday (2011), *A Dictionary of Media and Communication*, Oxford.
Chaniotis, A. (2003), 'The divinity of Hellenistic rulers', in A. Erskine (ed.), *A Companion to the Hellenistic World*, 431–45, Oxford.
Chavarría Arnau, A. (2009), *Archeologia delle Chiese: Dalle origini all'anno Mille*, Roma.
Chouquer, G., M. Clavel Leveque, F. Favory and J.-P. Vallat (eds) (1987), *Structures agraires en Italie centro-méridionale: cadastres et paysages ruraux*, (CEFR, 100), Roma.
Chrissanthos, S. G. (2001), 'Caesar and the mutiny of 47 BC', *JRS* 91: 63–75.
Chrissanthos, S. G. (2004), 'Freedom of speech and the Roman republican army', in I. Sluiter and R. M. Rosen (eds), *Free Speech in Classical Antiquity* (Mnemosyne suppl. 254), 341–67, Leiden.
Chrissanthos, S. G. (2013), 'Keeping military discipline', in B. Campbell and L. A. Tritle (eds), *The Oxford Handbook of Warfare in the Classical World*, 312–29, Oxford.
Clark, A. J. (2007), *Divine Qualities: Cult and Community in Republican Rome*, Oxford.
Classen, C. J. (1963), 'Gottmenschentum in der römischen Republik', *Gymnasium* 70: 312–38.
Clausen, W. V. (1994), *A Commentary on Virgil, Eclogues*, Oxford.
Cloud, D. (1994), 'The constitution and public criminal law', in J. A. Crook, A. Lintott, E. Rawson (eds), *Cambridge Ancient History IX: The Last Age of the Roman Republic, 146–43 B.C.*, 491–530, Cambridge.
Coarelli, F. and A. La Regina (1984), *Abruzzo, Molise*, Roma.
Coarelli, F. (1993), 'Atrium Libertatis', in E. M. Steinby (ed.), *Lexicon topographicum urbis Romae*, vol. 1, 133–5, Roma.
Cohen, S. J. D. (1999), *The Beginnings of Jewishness: Boundaries, Varieties, Uncertainties*, Berkeley.
Colella, N. (1935), 'Corfinium – Ricerche di topografia', *Atti e Memorie del Convegno Storico Abruzzese-Molisano* 2: 435–45.

Bibliography

Collins, J. H. (1959), 'On the date and interpretation of the *Bellum Civile*', *AJPh* 80: 113–32.
Collins, J. H. (1972), 'Caesar as political propagandist', *ANRW* 1.3: 922–66.
Combès, R. (1966), *Imperator: Recherches sur l'emploi et la signification du titre d'imperator dans la Rome républicaine*, Paris.
Conant, J. M. (1954), *The Younger Cato: A Critical Life with Special Reference to Plutarch's Biography*. PhD thesis: Columbia University.
Constantinou, C. (1996), *On the Way to Diplomacy*, Minneapolis, MN.
Corbier, M. (1991), 'La descendance d'Hortensius et de Marcia', *MEFR* 103(2): 655–701.
Cornago, N. (2016), '(Para)diplomatic cultures: old and new', in J. Dittmer and F. McConnell (eds), *Diplomatic Cultures and International Politics: Translations, Spaces and Alternatives*, 17–94, London.
Cornell, T. J. (eds) (2013), *The Fragments of the Roman Historians*, 3 vols, Oxford.
Cornwell, H. (2013), *PAX·TERRA·MARIQVE: Rhetorics of Roman victory 50 BC–AD 14*, DPhil thesis: University of Oxford.
Cornwell, H. (2014), 'The Construction of One's Enemies in Civil War', in R. Westall (ed.), *The Roman Civil Wars: A House Divided*, *Hermathena* 196–7: 41–67.
Cornwell, H. (2017), *Pax and the Politics of Peace: Republic to Principate*, Oxford.
Cornwell, H. (2020), 'A framework of negotiation and reconciliation in the Triumviral Period', in F. Pina Polo (ed.), *The Triumviral Period: Civil War, Political Crisis and Socioeconomic Transformations*, 149–70, Zaragoza, Servilla.
Coşkun, A. (2005), '*Amicitiae* und politische Ambitionen im Kontext der *causa Deiotariana* (45 v. Chr.)', in A. Coşkun (ed.), *Roms auswärtige Freunde in der späten Republik und im frühen Prinzipat*, 127–54, Göttingen.
Coşkun, A. (2008), 'Das Ende der ‚romfreundlichen' Herrschaft in Galatien und das Beispiel einer ‚sanften' Provinzialisierung in Zentralanatolien', in A. Coşkun (ed.), *Freundschaft und Gefolgschaft in den auswärtigen Beziehungen der Römer (2. Jh. v.Chr. – 1. Jh. n.Chr.)*, 133–64, Frankfurt am Main.
Coşkun, A. (2018), 'Prolegomena to the study of "warlordism in later Hellenistic Anatolia"', in T. Ñaco del Hoyo and F. López Sánchez (eds), *War, Warlords, and Interstate Relations in the Ancient Mediterranean*, 204–31, Leiden.
Crawford, M. H. (1976), 'Hamlet without the Prince?' *JRS* 66: 214–17.
Crawford, J. W. (2002), 'The lost and fragmentary orations', in J. M. May (ed.), *Brill's Companion to Cicero: Oratory and Rhetoric*, 305–30, Leiden.
Crawford, M. H. (1969), *Roman Republican Coin Hoards*, London.
Crawford, M. H. (1974), *Roman Republican Coinage*, 2 vols, London.
Crawford, M. H. (2008), 'States waiting in the wings: Population distribution and the end of the Roman Republic', in S. Northwood and L. de Ligt (eds), *People, Land, and Politics: Demographic Developments and the Transformation of Roman Italy, 300 BC–AD 14* (Mnem. suppl., HACA 303), 631–43, Leiden.
Curtius, L. (1933), 'Ikonographische Beiträge zum Porträt der Römischen Republik und der Julisch-Claudischen Familie', *MDAI(R)* 43: 182–243.
Czajkowski, K. (2016), 'Justice in client kingdoms: The many trials of Herod's sons', *Historia* 65(4): 473–96.
D'Anto, V. (1957), 'Sviste ed errori nei dati cronologici di Svetonio e di altri biografi minori', *AFLN* 7: 117–43.
Dalzell, A. (1955), 'C. Asinius Pollio and the early history of public recitation at Rome', *Hermathena* 86: 20–8.
Damon, C. (2015), *C. Iuli Caesaris commentariorum, libri III De bello civili*, Oxford.
Damon, C. (2016), *Caesar: Civil War* (Loeb Classical Library 39), Cambridge, MA.
De Blois, L. (1987), *The Roman Army and Politics in the First Century B.C.*, Amsterdam.
De Blois, L. (1992), 'Roman officers and politics: The manipulation of the military cadre in the period 44–36 BC', *Laverna* 3: 104–26.

Bibliography

De Blois, L. (1994), 'Sueton, *Aug.* 46 und die Manipulation des mittleren Militärkaders als politisches Instrument', *Historia* 43(3): 324–45.

De Blois, L. (2000), 'Army and society in the late Roman Republic: Professionalism and the role of the military middle cadre', in G. Alföldy, B. Dobson and W. Eck (eds), *Kaiser, Heer und Gesellschaft in der römischen Kaiserzeit: Gedenkschrift Eric Birley*, 11–31, Stuttgart.

De Blois, L. (2007), 'Army and general in the late Roman Republic', in P. Erdkamp (ed.), *A Companion to the Roman Army* (Blackwell Companions to the Ancient World. Ancient History), 164–79, Malden, MA.

De Ligt, L. (2012), *Peasants, Citizens, and Soldiers: Studies in the Demographic History of Roman Italy 225 BC–AD 100*, Cambridge.

De Nino, A. (1877), 'Pentima', *NSA* (1877): 211–17.

De Nino, A. (1879), 'Corfinio', *NSA* (1879): 315–20.

De Nino, A. (1880), 'Pentima', *NSA* (1880): 143–6

De Salis (1866), 'Date de la naissance de Jules César', *RA* 14: 17–22.

De Souza, P. (1999), *Piracy in the Graeco-Roman World*, Cambridge.

Degrassi, A. (ed.) (1947), *Inscriptiones Italiae: 13. Fasti et Elogia. Fasciculus I. Fasti Consulares et Triumphales*, Roma.

Demougin, S. (1983), 'Notables municipaux et ordre équestre à l'époque des dernières guerres civiles', in M. Cébeillac-Gervasoni (ed.), *Les bourgeoisies municipales italiennes aux IIe et Ier siècles av. J.-C.*, 279–98, Paris.

Der Derian, J. (1993), 'Diplomacy', in J. Krieger (ed.), The Oxford Companion to Politics of the World, 244–66, Oxford.

Deutsch, M. E. (1914), 'The year of Caesar's birth', *TAPhA* 45: 17–28.

Dillon, J. N. (2007), 'Octavian's finances after Actium, before Egypt: The CAESAR DIVI F / IMP CAESAR coinage and Antony's legionary issue', *Chiron* 37: 35–48.

Dionisio, A. (2015), *La valle del Sagittario e la conca Peligna: Abruzzo, tra il IV e il I secolo a.C: dinamiche e sviluppi della romanizzazione* (BAR international series 2735), Oxford.

Dmitriev, S. (2000), 'Observations on the historical geography of Roman Lycaonia', *GRBS* 41(4): 349–75.

Dmitriev, S. (2006), 'Cappadocian dynastic rearrangements on the eve of the first Mithridatic War', *Historia* 55(3): 285–97.

Dowling, M. B. (2000), 'The clemency of Sulla', *Historia* 49(3): 303–40.

Dowling, M. B. (2006), *Clemency and Cruelty in the Roman World*, Ann Arbor.

Draycott, J. (2012), 'The symbol of Cleopatra Selene: Reading crocodiles on coins in the late Republic and early Principate', *AClass* 55: 43–56.

Droge, A. J. (2011–12), 'Finding his niche: On the "autoapotheosis" of Augustus', *MAAR* 56-7: 85–112.

Drogula, F. K. (2019), *Cato the Younger: Life and Death at the End of the Roman Republic*, Oxford.

Drumann, W. (1906), *Geschichte Roms in seinem Übergange von der republikanischen zur monarchischen Verfassung: oder, Pompeius, Caesar, Cicero und ihre Zeitgenossen nach Geschlechtern und mit genealogischen Tabellen*, Bd. 3: Domitii-Julii, Leipzig.

Drummond, A. (2013), 'Asinius Pollio', *FRHist* no. 56 = *FRHist* 1.430-445; 2.854-867; 3.521-530.

Dué, C. (2000), 'Tragic history and barbarian speech in Sallust's *Jugurtha*', *HSPh* 100: 311–25.

Duncan-Jones, R. P. (1990), *Structure and Scale in the Roman Economy*, Cambridge.

Duncan-Jones, R. P. (1994), *Money and Government in the Roman Empire*, Cambridge.

Ebel, C. (1975), 'Pompey's organization of Transalpina', *Phoenix* 29: 358–73.

Eckel, I. (1828), *Doctrina numorum veterum*, Vol. 6, Wien.

Eckert, A. (2014), 'Remembering cultural trauma: Sulla's proscriptions, Roman responses, and Christian perspectives', in E.-M. Becker, J. Dochhorn, E. Kragelund Holt (eds), *Trauma and Traumatization in Individual and Collective Dimensions: Insights from Biblical Studies and Beyond*, 262–74, Göttingen.

Bibliography

Eckert, A. (2020), 'Coping with crisis: Sulla's civil war and cultural identity', in J. Kloosters and I. N. I. Kuinn (eds), *After the Crisis: Remembrance, Re-anchoring and Recovery in Ancient Greece and Rome*, London.

Eckhardt, B. (2012), '"An Idumean, that is, a half-Jew": Hasmoneans and Herodians between ancestry and merit', in B. Eckhardt (ed.), *Jewish Identity and Politics Between the Maccabees and Bar Kokhba: Groups, Normativity, and Rituals*, 91–115, Leiden.

Eilers, C. (2002), *Roman Patrons of Greek Cities*, Oxford.

English, A. D. (1996), *The Cream of the Crop: Canadian Aircrew, 1939–1945*, Montreal.

Erdkamp, P. (2006), 'Army and society', in N. Rosenstein and R. Morstein-Marx (eds), *A Companion to the Roman Republic*, 278–96, Malden, MA.

Erickson, K. (1976), *Everything in Its Path: Destruction of Community in the Buffalo Creek Flood*, New York.

Erskine, A. (1991), 'Hellenistic monarchy and Roman political invective', *CQ* 41(1): 106–20.

Erskine, A. (2001), *Troy Between Greece and Rome: Local Tradition and Imperial Power*, Oxford.

Estiot, S. (2006), 'Sex. Pompée, la Sicile et la monnaie: Problèmes de datation', in Jacqueline Champeaux and Martine Chassignet (eds), *Aere perennius: En hommage à Hubert Zehnacker*, 125–53, Paris.

Etzioni, A. (1971), *Les organisations modernes*, Gembloux.

Evans, R. J (1991), 'Candidates and competition in consular elections at Rome between 218 and 49 BC', *AClass*, 34(1): 111–36.

Facella, M. (2005), 'Φιλορώμαιος καὶ Φιλέλλην: Roman perception of Commagenian royalty', in O. Hekster and R. Fowler (eds), *Imaginary Kings: Royal Images in the Ancient Near East, Greece and Rome*, 87–104, Stuttgart.

Facella, M. (2019), 'Cicerone e il *senatus consultum* su Ariobarzane III di Cappadocia', in P. Buongiorno, S. Lohsse and F. Verrico (eds), *Miscellanea senatoria*, 191–213, Stuttgart.

Fantham, E. (1972), *Comparative Studies in Republican Latin Imagery*, Toronto.

Fantham, E. (1996), *Roman Literary Culture: From Cicero to Apuleius*, Baltimore.

Fantham, E. (2003), 'Three wise men and the end of the Roman Republic', in E. Fantham (ed.), *Caesar Against Liberty? Perspectives on his Autocracy*, 96–117, Cambridge.

Fedeli, P. (1988), 'Biblioteche private e pubbliche a Roma e nel mondo romano', in G. Cavallo (ed.), *Le biblioteche del mondo antico e medievale*, 29–64, Bari.

Feeney, D. (2007), *Caesar's Calendar: Ancient Time and the Beginning of History*, Berkeley.

Fehrle, R. (1983), *Cato Uticensis*, Darmstadt.

Feldherr, A. (2021), *After the Past: Sallust on History and Writing History*, Chichester.

Feraboli, S., E. Flores and R. Scarcia (eds) (1996), *Manilio: Il poema degli astri (Astronomica)*, Milano.

Ferri, G. (2017), 'La *devotio*: per un'analisi storico-religiosa della (auto)consacrazione agli dèi inferi nella religione romana', *MEFRA* 129(2): 349–71.

Ferriès, M.-C. (2007), *Les partisans d'Antoine: des orphelins de César aux complices de Cléopâtre*, Pessac.

Fields, N. (2008), *Warlords of Republican Rome: Caesar versus Pompey*, Barnsley.

Fishwick, D. (1971), 'The annexation of Mauretania', *Historia* 20(4): 467–87.

Flamerie de Lachapelle, G. (2011), '*Clementia*: Étude de vocabulaire (à propos de Sen., *Clem.*, II, 3,1)', *REA* 113(1): 147–65.

Fleischer, R. (1996), 'Hellenistic royal iconography on coins', in P. Bilde, T. Engberg-Pedersen, L. Hannestad and J Zahle (eds), *Aspects of Hellenistic Kingship*, 28–40, Aarhus.

Flower, H. I. (2018), 'Servilia's *consilium*: Rhetoric and politics in a family setting', in H. van der Blom, C. Gray and C. Steel (eds), *Institutions and Ideology in Republican Rome: Speech, Audience and Decision*, 252–64, Cambridge.

France, J. (2006), '*Tributum* et *stipendium*: La politique fiscale de l'empereur romain', *RD* 84(1): 1–17.

France, J. (2007a), 'Deux questions sur la fiscalité provinciale d'après Cicéron, *Ver.* 3.12', in J. Dubouloz and S. Pittia (eds), *La Sicile de Cicéron: Lectures des Verrines*, 169–82, Besançon.

France, J. (2007b), 'Les catégories du vocabulaire de la fiscalité dans le monde romain', in J. Andreau and V. Chankowski (eds), *Vocabulaire et expression de l'économie dans le monde antique*, 333–68, Bordeaux.

France, J. (2021), *Tribut: Une histoire fiscale de la conquête romaine*, Paris.

Franchet d'Espèrey, S. (1999), *Conflit, violence et non-violence dans la «Thébaïde» de Stace*, Paris.

Frandsen, P. S. (1836), *M. Vipsanius Agrippa: Eine historische Untersuchung über dessen Leben und Wirken*, Altona.

Frank, T. (1933), *An Economic Survey of Ancient Rome*, vol. 1, Baltimore.

Freyburger-Galland, M.-L. (2009), 'Political and religious propaganda between 44 and 27 BC', *Vergilius* 55: 17–30.

Fucecchi, M. (2011), 'Partisans in civil war', in P. Asso (ed.), *Brill's Companion to Lucan*, 237–56, Leiden.

Gabba, E. (1953), 'Sulle colonie Triumivirali di Antonio in Italia', *PP* 8: 101–10.

Gabba, E. (1973), *Esercito e società nella tarda Repubblica romana*, Firenze.

Gaertner, J. F. and Hausburg, B. (2013), *Caesar and the Bellum Alexandrinum: An Analysis of Style, Narrative Technique, and the Reception of Greek Historiography*, Göttingen.

Galadini, F. and P. Galli (2001), 'Archaeoseismology in Italy: Case studies and implications on long-term seismicity', *Journal of Earthquake Engineering* 5(1): 35–68.

Ganzert, J. (2000), *Im Allerheiligsten des Augustusforums*, Mainz.

Ganzert, J. and V. Kockel (1988), 'Augustusforum und Mars-Ultor-Tempel', in M. Hofter (ed.), *Kaiser Augustus und die verlorene Republik: Eine Ausstellung im Martin-Gropius-Bau, Berlin, 7 Juni–14 August 1988*, 149–99, Mainz.

García Riaza, E. (2020), 'Information exchange and political communication in the Triumviral period: Some remarks on means and methods', in F. Pina Polo (ed.), *The Triumviral Period: Civil War, Political Crisis and Socioeconomic Transformations*, 281–300, Zaragoza, Servilla.

Gardthausen, V. E. (1891-1904), *Augustus und seine Zeit*, 2 vols, Leipzig.

Gauthier, F. (2019), 'Auxiliaries and war financing in the Republic', *JAH* 7: 251–68.

Geiger, J. (1970), 'M. Hortensius M. f. Q. n. Hortalus', *CR* 20(2): 132–4.

Geiger, J. (2008), *The First Hall of Fame: A Study of the Statues in the Forum Augustum*, Leiden.

Gelzer, M. (1968), *Caesar: Politician and Statesman*, tr. P. Needham, Oxford.

Gelzer, M. (1972), 'Die drei Briefe des C. Asinius Pollio', *Chiron* 2: 297–312.

Gerratana, V. (ed.) (1975), Antonio Gramsci. *Quaderni del Carcere*, 4 vols, Torino.

Gerrish, J. (2019), *Sallust's Histories and Triumviral Historiography: Confronting the End of History*, London.

Gerrish, J. (2021), 'Sertorius, Civilis, Rome and exile in Tacitus' Histories', *CW* 116(4): 473–98.

Gesche, H. (1968), *Die Vergottung Caesars*, Kallmünz.

Gesche, H. (1978), 'Die Divinisierung der römischen Kaiser in ihrer Funktion als Herrschaftslegitimation', *Chiron* 8: 377–90.

Gill, S. (2003), *Power and Resistance in the New World Order*, Basingstoke.

Girardet, K. M. (1993), 'Die Rechtsstellung der Caesarattentäter Brutus und Cassius in den Jahren 44-42 v. Chr.', *Chiron* 23: 207–32.

Girardet, K. M. (2007), *Rom auf dem Weg von der Republik zum Prinzipat*, Bonn.

Giuffrè, V. (1974), *La letteratura 'de re militari'. Appunti per una storia degli ordinamenti militari*, Napoli.

Goar, R. J. (1987), *The Legend of Cato Uticensis from the First Century B.C. to the Fifth Century A.D. With an Appendix on Dante and Cato* (Collection Latomus, 197), Brussels.

Golden, G. K. (2013), *Crisis Management During the Roman Republic: The Role of Political Institutions in Emergencies*, Cambridge.

Goldsworthy, A. K. (1996), *The Roman Army at War (100 BC–AD 200)*, Oxford.

Bibliography

Goodyear, F. R. D. (ed.) (1972), *The Annals of Tacitus: Books 1–3*, Cambridge.
Gotter, U. (1996), *Der Diktator ist tot! Politik in Rom zwischen den Iden des März und der Begründung des Zweiten Triumvirats*, Stuttgart.
Gowing, A. M. (1992), *The Triumviral Narratives of Appian and Cassius Dio*, Ann Arbor.
Gray-Fow M. J. G. (1988), 'A stepfather's gift: L. Marcius Philippus and Octavian', *G&R* 35(2): 184–99.
Griffin, M. (1986), 'Philosophy, Cato, and Roman suicide', *G&R* 33(1): 64–77 and *G&R* 33(2): 192–202.
Griffin, M. (2003a), '*Clementia* after Caesar: from politics to philosophy', in F. Cairns and E. Fantham (eds), *Caesar Against Liberty? Perspectives on his Autocracy*, 157–82, Cambridge.
Griffin, M. (2003b), '*De Beneficiis* and Roman society', *JRS* 93: 92–113.
Griffith, G. T. (1935), *The Mercenaries of the Hellenistic World*, Cambridge.
Grillo, L. (2012), *The Art of Caesar's Bellum Civile: Literature, Ideology, and Community*, Cambridge.
Grillo, L. (2018), 'Speeches in the *Commentarii*', in L. Grillo and C. B. Krebs (eds), *The Cambridge Companion to the Writings of Julius Caesar*, 131–43, Cambridge.
Grillo, L. (2020), 'Caesar and the crisis of Corfinium', in J. Klooster and I. N. Kuin (eds), *After the Crisis: Remembrance, Re-anchoring and Recovery in Ancient Greece and Rome*, 121–34, London.
Grueber, H. A. (1910), *Coins of the Roman Republic in the British Museum*, London.
Gruen, E. S. (1969), 'The consular elections for 53 B.C.', in J. Bibauw (ed.), *Hommages à Marcel Renard* 2.311–21, Bruxelles.
Gruen, E. S. (1974), *The Last Generation of the Roman Republic*, Berkley.
Günther, S. (2015), 'Financing the civil wars – the case of duties and taxes', *MBAHWS* 33: 213–27.
Gurval, R. A. (1997), 'Caesar's comet: The politics and poetics of an Augustan myth', *MAAR* 42: 39–71.
Hadas, M. (1930), *Sextus Pompey*, New York.
Hall, E. (1989), *Inventing the Barbarian: Greek Self-Definition through Tragedy*, Oxford.
Haller, B. C. (1967), *Asinius Pollio als Politiker und zeitkritischer Historiker*, Münster.
Hammond, N. G. L. (1984), 'The battle of Pydna', *JHS* 104: 31–47.
Hansen, H. and Quinn, G. M. (1992), *Greek: An Intensive Course*, 2nd rev. edn, New York.
Hanslik, R. (1961), 'Vipsanius [2]', *RE* IXA: 1226–75.
Hanson, A. E. (2001), 'Papyrology: Minding other people's business', *TAPhA* 131: 297–313.
Harmand, J. (1961), 'Un témoignage archéologique sur les bulletins césariens', *REA* 63: 31–44.
Harmand, J. (1967), *L'armée et le soldat à Rome de 107 à 50 avant notre ère*, Paris.
Harris, W. V. (1979), *War and Imperialism in Republican Rome, 327–70 B.C.*, Oxford.
Harris, W. V. (2006), 'Readings in the narrative literature of Roman courage', in S. Dillon and K. E. Welch (eds), *Representations of War in Ancient Rome*, 300–20, Cambridge.
Harris, W. V. (2019), 'Credit-money in the Roman economy', *Klio* 101(1): 158–89.
Harrison, S. (ed.) (2017), *Horace: Odes, Book II. Cambridge Greek and Latin Classics*, Cambridge.
Hartke, W. (1951), *Römische Kinderkaiser: Eine Strukturanalyse römischen Denkens und Daseins*, Berlin.
Havas, L. (1980), 'Asinius Pollio and the fall of the Roman Republic', *ACD* 16: 25–36.
Hayne, L. (1971), 'Lepidus' role after the Ides of March', *AClass* 14: 10917.
Hekster, O. (2006), 'Descendants of gods: Legendary genealogies in the Roman Empire', in L. De Blois, P. Funke and J. Hahn (eds), *The Impact of Imperial Rome on Religions, Ritual and Religious Life in the Roman Empire*, 24–35, Leiden.
Hekster, O. (2010), 'Trophy kings and Roman power: a Roman perspective on client kingdoms', in T. Kaizer and M. Facella (eds), *Kingdoms and Principalities in the Roman Near East*, 45–55, Stuttgart.
Hekster, O. (2012), 'Kings and regime change in the Roman Republic', in C. Smith and L. M. Yarrow (eds), *Imperialism, Cultural Politics, and Polybius*, 184–202, Oxford.

Hellegouarc'h, J. (1963), *Le vocabulaire latin des relations et des partis politiques sous la République*, Paris.
Henderson, J. (1996), 'Finishing off the Politics: Horace's Ode to Pollio, 2,1,' *Materiali e discussioni per l'analisi dei testi classici* 36: 59-136
Henderson, J. (1998), *Fighting for Rome: Poets and Caesars, History and Civil War*, Cambridge.
Hill, G. F. (1909), *Historical Roman Coins from the Earliest Times to the Reign of Augustus*, London.
Hill, P. V. (1975), 'Coin symbolism and propaganda during the wars of vengeance (44-36 B.C.)', *NAC* 4: 157-207.
Hinard, F. (1993), '*Sacramentum*', *Athenaeum* 81: 251-63.
Hoare Q. and G. Nowell-Smith (eds) (1971), *Antonio Gramsci: Selections from the Prison Notebooks*, New York.
Hölkeskamp, K.-J. (1999), 'Römische *gentes* und griechische Genealogien', in G. Vogt-Spira and B. Rommel (eds), *Rezeption und Identität: Die kulturelle Auseinandersetzung Roms mit Griechenland als europäisches Paradigma*, 3-21, Stuttgart.
Hölkeskamp K.-J. (2000), '*Fides – deditio in fidem – dextra data et accepta*: Recht, Religion und Ritual in Rom', in C. Bruun (ed.), *The Roman Middle Republic: Politics, Religion, and Historiography, c. 400-133 B.C.*, 223-50, Rome.
Hölkeskamp, K.-J. (2013), 'Friends, Romans, countrymen: addressing the Roman people and the rhetoric of inclusion' in C. Steel and H. van der Blom (eds), *Community and Communication: Oratory and Politics in Republican Rome*, 11-28, Oxford.
Hölkeskamp, K.-J. (2020), *Roman Republican Reflections: Studies in Politics, Power, and Pageantry*, Stuttgart.
Hölkeskamp, K.-J. (2022), 'Political culture: Career of a concept', in V. Arena and J. R. W. Prag (eds), *A Companion to the Political Culture of the Roman Republic*, 4-19, Chichester.
Holland, T. (2003), *Rubicon: The Triumph and Tragedy of the Roman Republic*, London.
Hollstein, W. (ed.) (2000), *Metallanalytische Untersuchungen an Münzen der Römischen Republik*, Berlin.
Hollstein, W. (2014), 'Caesars spanische Statthalterschaft im Münzbild', in R. Lehmann, B. Hamborg, A. V. Siebert, S. Vogt and C. E. Loeben (eds), *Nub Nefer – Gutes Gold: Gedenkschrift für Manfred Gutgesel*, 151-7, Rahden.
Hollstein, W. (2020), 'Die Münzprägung des Sextus Pompeius in Sizilien', in L. Kersten and C. Wendt (eds), *Rector maris: Sextus Pompeius und das Meer*, 141-85, Bonn.
Holmes, T. R. (1923), *The Roman Republic and the founder of the Empire*, Oxford.
Holzberg, N. (ed.) (2015), *Publius Vergilius Maro, Aeneis*, Berlin.
Hopwood, B. (2015), 'Hortensia speaks: an authentic voice of resistance?' in K. Welch (ed.), *Appian's Roman History: Empire and Civil War*, 305-22, Swansea.
Horsfall, N. (ed.) (2013), *Virgil, Aeneid 6: A Commentary*, Berlin.
Housman, A. E. (ed.) (1903), *M. Manilii astronomicon: Liber primus*, London.
Hurlet, F. (2020), 'The *Auctoritas* and *Libertas* of Augustus: Metamorphosis of the Roman *Res Publica*', in C. Balmaceda (ed.), *Libertas and Res Publica in the Roman Republic*, 170-88, Leiden.
Isaac, B. (1995), 'Hierarchy and command-structure in the Roman army', in Y. Le Bohec (ed.), *La hiérarchie de l'armée romaine sous le Haut-Empire*, 23-31, Paris.
Isayev, E. (2011), 'Corfinium and Rome: Changing place in the Social War', in M. Gleba and H. W. Horsnæs (eds), *Communicating Identity in Italic Iron Age Communities*, 210-22, Oxford.
Jacobson, D. M. (2001), 'Three Roman client kings: Herod of Judaea, Archelaus of Cappadocia and Juba of Mauretania', *PalEQ* 133: 22-38.
Jarratt, S. (2019), 'Historiographical trauma: The case of Polybius', in A. Karanika and V. Panoussi (eds), *Emotional trauma in Greece and Rome: Representations and reactions*, 111-22, New York.

Bibliography

Jehne, M. (2010), 'Erfahrungsraum und Erwartungshorizont bei Julius Caesar', in G. Urso (ed.), *Cesare: precursore o visionario? Atti del convegno internazionale, Cividale del Friuli, 17–19 settembre 2009*, 311–32, Pisa.

Jehne, M. (2015), 'From *patronus* to *pater*: The changing role of patronage in the period of transition from Pompey to Augustus', in M. Jehne and F. Pina Polo (eds), *Foreign Clientelae in the Roman Empire: A Reconsideration*, 297–319, Stuttgart.

Jehne, M. (2017), 'Why the Anti-Caesarians failed: Political communication on the eve of the civil war (51 to 49 BC)', in C. Rosillo-López (ed.), *Political Communication in the Roman World*, 201–30, Leiden.

Johnston, A. C. (2018), '*Nostri* and the "other(s)"', in L. Grillo and C. B. Krebs (eds), *The Cambridge Companion to the Writings of Julius Caesar*, 81–94, Cambridge.

Jones, C. P. (1971), *Plutarch and Rome*, Oxford (repr. 1972 with corrections).

Jönsson, C. and M. Hall (2003), 'Communication: An essential aspect of diplomacy', *International Studies Perspectives* 4: 195–210.

Joseph, T. (2012), *Tacitus the Epic Successor*, Leiden.

Kahn, A. D. (1973), 'The Crastinus incident', *CO* 50(5): 52–5.

Kaizer, T. and M. Facella (2010), 'Introduction', in T. Kaizer and M. Facella (eds), *Kingdoms and Principalities in the Roman Near East*, 15–42, Stuttgart.

Kalinka, E. (1912), 'Die Herausgabe des *Bellum Civile*', *WS* 34: 203–7.

Kalyvas, S. N. (2006), *The Logic of Violence in Civil War*, Cambridge.

Kardos M.-J. (2006), 'La «déformation historique» dans le livre I du *Bellum civile*: le témoignage de Cicéron et de la Correspondance', *VL* 175: 19–35.

Kavanagh, B. (2001), 'The citizenship and *nomen* of Roucillus and Egus', *AHB* 15: 163–71.

Kay, P. (2014), *Rome's Economic Revolution*, Oxford.

Keaveney, A. (2007), *The Army in the Roman Revolution*, London.

Kellett, A. (1982), *Combat Motivation: The Behavior of Soldiers in Battle*, Boston.

Keppie, L. J. F. (1983), *Colonisation and Veteran Settlement in Italy, 47–14 B.C.*, London.

Keppie, L. J. F. (1997), 'The changing face of the Roman legions: (49 BC–AD 69)', *PBSR* 65: 89–102.

Kersten, L. (2019), 'NEPTVNI: Sextus Pompeius' göttliche Genealogie und das Meer', in O. Schelske and Ch. Wendt (eds), *Mare nostrum – mare meum: Wasserräume und Herrschaftsrepräsentation*, 175–201, Hildesheim.

Kersten, L. (2020), 'Der vierte Tyrann: Sextus Pompeius im Narrativ des Appian', in L. Kersten and Ch. Wendt (eds), *Rector maris: Sextus Pompeius und das Meer*, 211–33, Bonn.

Kersten, L. and C. Wendt (2020), 'Einleitung' in L. Kersten and C. Wendt (eds), *Rector maris: Sextus Pompeius und das Meer*, 1–22, Bonn.

Kienast, D. (2001), 'Augustus und Caesar', *Chiron* 31: 1–26.

Kienast, D. (2009), *Augustus: Prinzeps und Monarch*, 4th edn, Darmstadt.

Kienast, D., W. Eck and M. Heil (2017), *Römische Kaisertabelle: Grundzüge einer römischen Kaiserchronologie*, 6th edn, Darmstadt.

Kirbihler, F. (2013), 'Brutus et Cassius et les impositions, spoliations et confiscations en Asie mineure durant les guerres civiles (44–42 a.C.)', in M.-C. Ferriès and F. Delrieux (eds), *Spolier et confisquer dans les mondes grec et romain*, 345–66, Chambéry.

Klooster, J., and I. N. I. Kuin (eds) (2020), *After the Crisis: Remembrance, Re-anchoring and Recovery in Ancient Greece and Rome*, London.

Klotz, A. (1911), 'Zu Caesars *Bellum Civile*', *RhM* 66: 80–93.

Klotz, A. (1926), 'Livius 9', *RE* XIII,1: 816–52.

Konstan, D. (2005), 'Clemency as a virtue', *CPh* 100: 337–46.

Kopij, K. (2016), 'The context and dating of the Pompey's aureus (*RRC* 402)', *NAC* 45: 109–27.

Kopp, H. (2020), 'Thalassokratōr, Seekönig – oder doch (nur) Flottenpräfekt? Zur Terminologie der "Seeherrschaft" des Sextus Pompeius bei Appian und Florus', in L. Kersten and Ch. Wendt (eds), *Rector maris: Sextus Pompeius und das Meer*, 259–90, Bonn.

Kornemann, E. (1896), 'Die historische Schriftstellerei des C. Asinius Pollio: Zugleich ein Beitrag zur Quellenforschung über Appian und Plutarch', *Jahrb. f. cl. Phil.*, Suppl. 22: 557–692.

Kraner, F., F. Hofmann and H. Meusel (eds) (1906), *C. Iulii Caesaris Commentarii de Bello Civili*, 11th edn, Berlin.

Krebs, C. B. (2018), 'More than words: The *commentarii* in their propagandistic Context', in L. Grillo and C. B. Krebs (eds), *The Cambridge Companion to the Writings of Julius Caesar*, 29–42, Cambridge.

Kromayer, J. (1987), 'Die Entwicklung der römischen Flotte vom Seeräuberkriege des Pompeius bis zur Schlacht von Actium', *Philologus*, 56: 426–91.

La Penna, A. (1952), 'Tendenze e Arte del *Bellum civile* di Cesare', *Maia* 5: 191–233.

La Penna, A. (2013), *La letteratura latina del primo periodo augusteo (42–15 a.C.)*, Bari.

La Rocca, E. (19878), 'Pompeo Magno "novus Neptunus"', *BCAR* 92: 265–92.

Laclau, E. (2005), *On Populist Reason*, London.

Laclau, E. and C. Mouffe (2001), *Hegemony and Socialist Strategy: Towards a Radical Democratic Politics*, 2nd edn, London.

Laignoux, R. (2010), 'La construction du pouvoir personnel durant les années 44–29: processus de légitimation', thèse dactylographiée, Université de Paris I – Panthéon Sorbonne.

Laignoux, R. (2013), 'Justifier ou contester les confiscations des guerres civiles : l'économie discursive des sanctions patrimoniales à Rome dans les années 44–31 a.C.', in M.-C. Ferriès and F. Delrieux (eds), *Spolier et confisquer dans les mondes grec et romain*, 367–85, Chambéry.

Laignoux, R. (2014a), 'Des guerres à prix d'or: multiplication et cérémonialisation des distributions exceptionnelles à la fin de la République', in M. Reddé (ed.), *De l'or pour les braves! Soldes, armées et circulation monétaire dans le monde romain*, 199–227, Bordeaux.

Laignoux, R. (2014b), 'Frapper monnaie entre 49 et 31 av. J.-C.: les guerres civiles romaines comme laboratoire d'unification monétaire', in J. Dubouloz, S. Pittia (eds), *L'imperium Romanum en perspective: Les savoirs d'empire dans la République romaine et leur héritage dans l'Europe médiévale et moderne*, 147–69, Besançon.

Laignoux, R. (2017), 'Les chefs et leurs troupes: s'assurer la fidélité des soldats pendant les guerres civiles des années 44-30', *HiMA* 4: 71–94.

Lang, K. (1965), 'Military organizations', in J. G. March (ed.), *Handbook of Organizations*, 838–78, Chicago.

Lange, C. H. (2009), *Res publica constituta: Actium, Apollo and the accomplishment of the Triumviral assignment*, Leiden.

Lange, C. H. (2014), 'The logic of violence in Roman civil war', in R. Westall (ed.), *The Roman Civil Wars: A House Divided*, *Hermathena* 196-7: 69–98.

Lange, C. H. (2016), *Triumphs in the Age of Civil War: The Late Republic and the Adaptability of Triumphal Tradition*, London.

Lange, C. H. (2017), '*Stasis* and *bellum civile*: A difference in scale?', *Critical Analysis of Law* 4(2): 129–40.

Lange, C. H. (2021), 'The Pursuit of Consensus in Roman Civil War (Writing): Thoughts on Hindsight', in G. Urso (ed.), *Popularitas: Ricerca del consenso e 'populismo' in Roma Antica*, 213–40, Roma.

Lange, C. H., and Vervaet, F. J. (eds) (2019), *The Historiography of Late Republican Civil War* (Historiography of Rome and Its Empire, 5), Leiden.

Le Bonniec, H. (1969), 'Aspects religieux de la guerre à Rome', in J.-P. Brisson (ed.), *Problèmes de la guerre à Rome*, 101–15, Paris.

Lees, C. (2001), 'Coalition', in J. Michie (ed.), *Reader's Guide to the Social Sciences*, vol. 1, 224–6, London.

Bibliography

Leigh, M. (2000), 'Primitivism and power: the beginnings of Latin literature', in O. Taplin (ed.), *Literature in the Roman World*, 4–26, Oxford.
Lendon, J. E. (1997), *Empire of Honour: The Art of Government in the Roman World*, Oxford.
Lendon, J. E. (2005), *Soldiers and Ghosts: A History of Battle in Classical Antiquity*, New Haven.
Leone, M. (1986), 'L'anno di nascità di Cesare', *Seia* 3: 65–76.
Levene, D. (1992), 'Sallust's *Jugurtha*: An historical fragment', *JRS* 82: 53–70.
Liegle, J. (1938), 'Ein Münzbild des Sextus Pompeius', in J. Allan, H. Mattingly and E. S. G. Robinson (eds), *Transactions of the International Numismatic Congress organised and held in London by the Royal Numismatic Society, June 30–July 3 1936*, 211–13, London.
Liguori, G. (2006), *Sentieri gramsciani*, Roma.
Liguori, G. (2015), *Gramsci's pathways*, Leiden.
Linderski, J. (1984), 'Rome, Aphrodisias and the *Res Gestae*: The *genera militiae* and the status of Octavian', *JRS* 74: 74–80 (= idem (1995), *Roman questions: Selected papers*, 147–53, Stuttgart).
Lintott A. W. (1993), *Imperium Romanum: Politics and Administration*, London.
Lintott, A. W. (1999), *The Constitution of the Roman Republic*, Oxford.
Lintott, A. W. (2008), *Cicero as Evidence: A Historian's Companion*, Oxford.
Lo Cascio, E. (1997), 'Le procedure di *recensus* dalla tarda repubblica al tardo antico e il calcolo della popolazione di Roma', in *La Rome impériale: Démographie et logistique. Actes de la table ronde, Rome, 25 mars 1994*, (CEFR, 230), 3–76, Roma.
Lo Cascio, E. (2001), 'Recruitment and the size of the Roman population from the third to the first century BCE', in W. Scheidel (ed.), *Debating Roman Demography* (Mnemosyne Suppl. 211), 111–37, Leiden.
Loader, W. R. (1940), 'Pompey's command under the *Lex Gabinia*', *CR* 54(3): 134–6.
Lobur, J. A. (2019), 'Civil war and the biographical project of Cornelius Nepos', in C. H. Lange and F. J. Vervaet (eds), *The Historiography of Late Republican Civil War* (Historiography of Rome and Its Empire, 5), Leiden.
Lockyear, K. (2013), *Coin Hoards of the Roman Republic Online, Version X*, New York, available at http://numismatics.org/chrr/ (accessed on 3 November 2019).
López Barja de Quiroga, P. (2019), 'The *Bellum Civile Pompeianum*: The war of words', *CQ* 69(2): 700–14.
Lounsbury, R. C. (1975), 'The death of Domitius in the *Pharsalia*', *TAPhA* 105: 209–12.
Loutsch, C. (1994), *L'exorde dans les discours de Cicéron* (Coll. Lat., 224), Brussels.
Lovano, M. (2002), *The Age of Cinna: Crucible of Late Republican Rome*, Stuttgart.
Lovisi, C. (1999), *Contribution à l'étude de la peine de mort sous la République romaine, 509–149 av. J.-C.*, Paris.
Low, S. (2017), *Spatializing Culture: The Ethnography of Space and Place*, Abingdon.
Lyne, R. O. A. M. (1995), *Horace: Behind the Public Poetry*, New Haven.
Macfarlane, R. T. (1996), '*Ab inimicis incitatus*: On dating the composition of Caesar's *Bellum Civile*', *SyllClass* 7: 107–32.
Machado, D. (2021), 'Deconstructing *Disciplina*: Disentangling Ancient and Modern Ideologies of Military Displine in the Middel Republic', *AJPh* 142(3): 387–424.
Mackay, C. S. (2009), *The Breakdown of the Roman Republic: From Oligarchy to Empire*, Cambridge.
MacMullen, R. (1984), 'The legion as a society', *Historia* 33(4): 440–56.
Mangiameli, R. (2012), *Tra «duces» e «milites»: Forme di comunicazione politica al tramonto della Repubblica*, Trieste.
Marincola, J. (1997), *Authority and Tradition in Ancient Historiography*, Cambridge.
Marrone, G. C. (1998), '*Pietas* di Ottaviano e *pietas* di Sesto Pompeo', in G. C. Marrone (ed.), *Temi Augustei: Atti dell'incontro di studio Venezia*, 7–20, Amsterdam.
Martelli, F. (2017), 'The triumph of letters: Rewriting Cicero in *ad Fam.* 15', *JRS* 107: 90–115.
Marx, F. (1925), 'M. Agrippa und die zeitgenössische römische Dichtkunst', *RhM* 74: 174–94.

Bibliography

Maschek, D. (2018). *Die römische Bürgerkriege: Archäologie und Geschichte einer Krisenzeit*, Darmstadt.
Massaro, M. (1980), 'Il mantello azzurro di Sesto Pompeo e un frammento trascurato di Livio', *RFIC* 108: 403–21.
Mastrocinque, A. (2021), '*Sacratio capitis*, *devotio*, and blood in the Roman law and religion', *AAntHung* 60(3–4): 241–7.
Matijević, K. (2005), 'Marcus Antonius und die Vergottung Caesars', in K. Matijević and H. H. Steenken (eds), *Rom, Germanien und das Reich: Festschrift zu Ehren von Rainer Wiegels anlässlich seines 65. Geburtstages*, 46–79, St. Katharinen.
Matijević, K. (2006), *Marcus Antonius: Consul, Proconsul, Staatsfeind. Die die Politik der Jahre 44 und 43 v.Chr.*, Rahden.
Maurenbrecher, B. (ed.) (1891–1983), *C. Sallusti Crispi Historiarum Reliquae*, Leipzig.
Mayhoff, C. (ed.) (1875), *Plini Secundi C. Naturalis historiae libri XXXVII*, Vol. 2, Libri 7–15, Leipzig.
Mazzarino, S. (1966), *Il pensiero storico classico*, 3 vols, Bari.
McGing, B. (2020), *Appian. Roman History, Volume IV: Civil Wars, Books 1–2*, Loeb Classical Library 5, Cambridge (MA).
McGing, B. C. (1986), *The Foreign Policy of Mithridates VI Eupator, King of Pontus*, Leiden.
McGushin, P. (1987), *Sallust: Bellum Catilinae: Text with Introduction and Notes*, Bristol.
McGushin, P. (1994), *Sallust: The Histories*, Vol. 2, Oxford.
Means, T. and S. Dickinson (1973–4), 'Plutarch and the family of Cato Minor', *CJ* 69: 210–15.
Mehl, A. (2014), 'Individual and collective psychiatric traumas in ancient historiographical literature', in E.-M. Becker, J. Dochhorn and E. Kragelund Holt (eds), *Trauma and Traumatization in Individual and Collective Dimensions: Insights from Biblical Studies and Beyond*, 244–61, Göttingen.
Meineck, P. and D. Konstan (eds) (2014), *Combat Trauma and the Ancient Greeks*, New York.
Mellor, R. (1999), *The Roman Historians*, London.
Metcalf, W. E. (2006), 'Review of Bernhard Woytek: *Arma et Nummi. Forschungen zur römischen Finanzgeschichte und Münzprägung der Jahre 49 bis 42 v. Chr.*', *SNR* 85: 222–30.
Migeotte, L. (2014), *Les finances des cités grecques aux périodes classique et hellénistique*, Paris.
Millar, F. (1996), 'Emperors, kings and subjects: The politics of two-level sovereignty', *SCI* 15: 159–73.
Miltner, F. (1952), 'Pompeius [33]', *RE* XXI, 2: 2213–50, Stuttgart.
Mitchell, S. (1993), *Anatolia: Land, Men, and Gods in Asia Minor. Volume I: The Celts in Anatolia and the Impact of Roman Rule*, Oxford.
Mitchell, S. (1994), 'Termessos, King Amyntas, and the war with the Sandaliôtai: A new inscription from Pisidia', in D. H. French (ed.), *Studies in the History and Topography of Lycia and Pisidia: In Memoriam A. S. Hall*, 93–105, Ankara.
Mitchell, T. N. (1971), 'Cicero and the *senatus consultum ultimum*', *Historia* 20(1): 47–61.
Mitford, T. B. (1980), 'Roman Cyprus', *ANRW* 2.7.2: 1285–384.
Moderato, M. (2022), 'Il Campus Militaris di Corfinio (AQ): interpretazioni topografiche e dati stratigrafici a confronto', in S. Antonelli, V. La Salvia, M. C. Mancini, O. Menozzi, M. Moderato and M. C. Somma (eds), *Archaeologiae: Una storia al plurale. Studi e ricerche in memoria di Sara Santoro*, 341–7, Oxford.
Moderato, M. and Tornese, M. (2015), 'Il paesaggio storico di Corfinio (AQ) tra Tardantichità e alto Medioevo', in P. Arthur and M. L. Imperiale (eds), *VII Congresso nazionale di archeologia medievale: Palazzo Turrisi, Lecce, 9–12 settembre 2015*, 476–80, Firenze.
Moderato, M., V. La Salvia and L. Pompilio (2015), 'Applicazione Diagnostica Archeologica a Corfinio (AQ)', in P. Arthur and M. L. Imperiale (eds), *VII Congresso Nazionale di archeologia medievale: Palazzo Turrisi, Lecce, 9–12 Settembre 2015*, 57–60, Firenze.
Moles, J. H. (1983), 'Virgil, Pompey, and the Histories of Asinius Pollio', *CW* 75(5): 287–8.

Bibliography

Moles, J. L. (2017), *A Commentary on Plutarch's* Brutus. With updated bibliographical notes by Christopher Pelling (Histos suppl. 7): https://histos.org/documents/SV07.MolesBrutus.pdf

Moles, J. L. (2023), *The Collected Papers*, 2 vols, Leiden.

Morawski, C. (1911), 'De oratione Philippi apud Sallustium', *Eos* 17: 135–40.

Morello, R. (2018), 'Innovation and cliché: The letters of Caesar', in L. Grillo and C. B. Krebs (eds), *The Cambridge Companion to the Writings of Julius Caesar*, 223–34, Cambridge.

Morgan, L. (2000), 'The autopsy of C. Asinius Pollio', *JRS* 90: 51–69.

Morrell, K. (2017), *Pompey, Cato, and the Governance of the Roman Empire*, Oxford.

Morstein-Marx, R. (2004), *Mass Oratory and Political Power in the Late Roman Republic*, Cambridge.

Morstein-Marx, R. (2009), '*Dignitas* and *res publica*: Caesar and Republican legitimacy', in K.-J. Hölkeskamp and E. Müller-Luckner (eds), *Eine politische Kultur (in) der Krise? Die 'letzte Generation' der römischen Republik*, 115–40, München.

Morstein-Marx, R. (2013), 'Cultural Hegemony' and the Communicative Power of the Roman Élite' in C. Steel and H. van der Blom (eds), *Community and Communication: Oratory and Politics in Republican Rome*, 29–47, Oxford

Morstein-Marx, R. (2021), *Julius Caesar and the Roman People*, Cambridge.

Mouffe, C. (1977), 'Hegemony and Ideology in Gramsci', in C. Mouffe (ed.), *Gramsci and Marxist Theory*, 168–204, London.

Muccioli, F. (2004), 'La titolatura di Cleopatra VII in una nuova iscrizione cipriota e la genesi dell'epiteto Thea Neotera', *ZPE* 146: 105–14.

Münzer, F. (1937), 'Octavius [13]', *RE* XVII: 1805.

Murray, R. J. (1965), 'The attitude of the Augustan poets toward *rex* and related words', *CJ* 60(6): 241–6.

Ñaco del Hoyo, T. (2007), 'The late Republican West: Imperial taxation in the making?', in O. Hekster, G. de Kleijn and D. Slootjes (eds), *Crises and the Roman Empire: Proceedings of the Seventh Workshop of the International Network Impact of Empire, Nijmegen, June 20–24, 2006*, 218–31, Leiden.

Ñaco del Hoyo, T. (2010), 'The Republican war economy strikes back: A "minimalist" approach', in F. Kirbihler and N. Barrandon (eds), *Administrer les provinces de la République romaine*, 171–80, Rennes.

Ñaco del Hoyo, T. and I. Arrayás-Morales (2016), 'Rome, Pontus, Thrace and the military disintegration of the world beyond the Hellenistic East', in D. Slootjes and M. Peachin (eds), *Rome and the World Beyond Its Frontiers*, 3–19, Leiden.

Ñaco del Hoyo, T. and F. López Sánchez (eds) (2018), *War, Warlords, and Interstate Relations in the Ancient Mediterranean*, Leiden.

Ñaco del Hoyo, T., B. Antela-Bernárdez, I. Arrayás Morales and S. Busquets-Artigas (2011), 'The ultimate frontier between Rome and Mithridates: War, terror and the Greek poleis (88–63 BC)', in O. Hekster and T. Kaizer (eds), *The Frontiers of the Roman World*, 291–304, Leiden.

Ñaco del Hoyo, T., B. Antela-Bernárdez, I. Arrayás Morales and S. Busquets-Artigas (2015), 'Roma o Mitrídates. Las póleis griegas en su última encrucijada (89–63 a.C.): cuatro casos de estudio', *Faventia* 37: 35–55.

Nagle, D. B. (1973), 'An allied view of the Social War', *AJA* 77(4): 367–78.

Nawotka, K. (1992), 'Asander of the Bosporus: His coinage and chronology', *AJN* 3–4: 21–48.

Néraudau, J.-P. (1983), 'Asinius Pollion et la poésie', *ANRW* 2.30.3: 1732–50.

Newman, R. (1990), 'A Dialogue of power in the coinage of Antony and Octavian (44–30 B.C.)', *AJN* 2: 37–63.

Nicholson, J. (1994), 'The delivery and confidentiality of Cicero's letters', *CJ* 90(1): 33–63.

Nicolet, C. (1976), *Le Métier de citoyen dans la Rome républicaine*, Paris.

Nicolet, C. (1978), 'Le *stipendium* des alliés italiens avant la guerre sociale', *PBSR* 46: 1–11.

Nicolet, C. (1979), *Rome et la conquête du monde méditerranéen*, T. 1: *Les Structures de l'Italie romaine*, Paris.

Nisbet, R. G. M. and M. Hubbard (1978), *A Commentary on Horace: Odes: Book II*, Oxford.
Nótári, T. (2012), 'Handling of facts and strategy in Cicero's speech in defence of King Deiotarus', *Nova Tellus* 30(2): 99–116.
Nuciari, M. (2006), 'Models and explanations for military organization: An updated reconsideration', in G. Caforio (ed.), *Handbook of the Sociology of the Military*, 61–85, New York.
Ogden, D. (2009), 'Alexander, Scipio and Octavian: Serpent-siring in Macedon and Rome', *SyllClass* 20(1): 31–52.
Oliensis, E. (2009), '*Freud's Rome: Psychoanalysi and Latin Poetry. Roman Literature and Its Contexts*, Cambridge.
Oost S. I. (1955), 'Cato Uticensis and the annexation of Cyprus', *CPh* 50: 98–112.
Osgood, J. (2006), *Caesar's Legacy: Civil War and the Emergence of the Roman Empire*, Cambridge.
Osgood, J. (2014), *Turia: A Roman Woman's Civil War*, Oxford.
Osgood, J. (2019), 'Caesar, civil war and *Civil War*', in C. H. Lange and F. J. Vervaet (eds), *The Historiography of Late Republican Civil War* (Historiography of Rome and Its Empire, 5), 137–59, Leiden.
Ouellet, E. (2005), 'Le leadership militaire et les forces armées canadiennes: apports à la théorie sociologique', in F. Gresle (ed.), *Sociologie du milieu militaire: les conséquences de la professionnalisation sur les armées et l'identité militaire*, 73–86, Paris.
Pandey, N. B. (2013), 'Caesar's comet, the Julian star, and the invention of Augustus', *TAPhA* 143(2): 405–49.
Patterson, J. (1993), 'Military organization and social change in the later Roman Republic', in J. Rich and G. Shipley (eds), *War and Society in the Roman World*, 92–112, London.
Pausch, D. (ed.) (2010), *Stimmen der Geschichte: Funktionen von Reden in der antiken Historiographie*, Berlin.
Peaks, M. B. (1904), 'Caesar's movements, January 21 to February 14, 49 b.c.', *CR* 18: 346–9.
Pedroni, L. (2001), 'Illusionismo antico e illusioni moderne sul soldo legionario da Polibio a Domiziano', *Historia*, 50(1): 115–30.
Peer, A. (2015), *Julius Caesar's* Bellum Civile *and the Composition of a New Reality*, Farnham.
Pelling, C. B. R. (ed.) (1988), *Plutarch: Life of Antony*, Cambridge.
Pelling, C. B. R. (1997), 'East is East and West is West – or are they? National stereotypes in Herodotus', *Histos* 1: 51–66.
Pelling, C. B. R. (ed.) (2011), *Plutarch: Life of Caesar. Translated with an Introduction and Commentary*, Oxford.
Perl, G. (1965), 'Die Rede Cottas in Sallusts Historien', *Philologus* 109: 75–82.
Perl, G. (1967), 'Die Rede Cottas in Sallusts Historien', *Philologus* 111: 137–41.
Perrin, B. (1884), 'The Crastinus episode at Palaepharsalus', *TAPhA* 15: 46–57.
Phang, S. E. (2008), *Roman Military Service: Ideologies of Discipline in the Late Republic and Early Principate*, Cambridge.
Phang, S. E. (2011), 'New approaches to the Roman army', in L. L. Brice and J. T. Roberts (eds), *Recent Directions in the Military History of the Ancient World*, 105–44, Claremont.
Picone, G. (ed.) (2008), *Clementia Caesaris: Modelli etici, parenesi e retorica dell'esilio*, Palermo.
Pilhofer, P. (2020), 'Die Geschichte des ‚Rauhen Kilikien' unter den Römern', *Klio* 102(1): 71–120.
Pina Polo, F. (1989), *Las contiones civiles y militares en Roma*, Zaragoza.
Pina Polo, F. (ed.) (2020), *The Triumviral Period: Civil War, Political Crisis and Socioeconomic Transformations*, Zaragoza, Servilla.
Pollini, J. (1990), 'Man or god: Divine assimilation and imitation in the late Republic and early Principate', in K. A. Raaflaub and M. Toher (eds), *Between Republic and Empire: Interpretations of Augustus and His Principate*, 334–63, Berkeley.
Poulsen, F. (1939), *Römische privatporträts und prinzenbildnisse*, København.
Powell, A. (2002a), 'Introduction', in A. Powell and K. Welch (eds), *Sextus Pompeius*, vii–xvi, Swansea.

Bibliography

Powell, A. (2002b), '"An island amid the flame": The strategy and imagery of Sextus Pompeius, 43–36 BC', in A. Powell and K. Welch (eds), *Sextus Pompeius*, 103–33, Swansea.
Powell, A. (2008), *Virgil the Partisan: A Study in the Re-integration of Classics*, Swansea.
Powell, A. and A. Burnett (eds) (2020), *Coins of the Roman Revolution 49 BC–AD 14: Evidence without Hindsight*, Swansea.
Powell, A. and K. Welch (eds) (2002), *Sextus Pompeius*, Swansea.
Prag, J. R. W. (2007), '*Auxilia* and *gymnasia*: a Sicilian model of Roman imperialism', *JRS* 97: 68–100.
Primo, A. (2010), 'The client kingdom of Pontus between Mithridatism and philoromanism', in T. Kaizer and M. Facella (eds), *Kingdoms and Principalities in the Roman Near East*, 159–79, Stuttgart.
Purcell, N. (1993), 'Atrium Libertatis', *PBSR* 61: 125–55.
Purcell, N. (2012), 'Rivers and the geography of power', *Pallas* 90: 373–87.
Quagliati, Q. (1904), 'Regione II (Apulia). V. Carbonara – Ripostiglio di monete repubblicane d'argento', *NSA* Ser. 5 (1): 53–65.
Quint, D. (1993), *Empire and Empire*, Princeton, NJ.
Raaflaub, K. A. (1974), *Dignitatis contentio: Studien zur Motivation und politischen Taktik im Bürgerkrieg zwischen Caesar und Pompeius*, München.
Raaflaub, K. A. (2003), 'Caesar the liberator? Factional politics, civil war, and ideology', in F. Cairns and E. Fantham (eds), *Caesar Against Liberty? Perspectives on his Autocracy*, 35–67, Cambridge.
Raaflaub, K. A. (2007), 'Caesar and Augustus as Liberators?', in E. Baltrusch (ed.), *Caesar*, 229–61, Darmstadt.
Raaflaub, K. A. (2009), '*Bellum Civile*', in M. Griffin (ed.), *A Companion to Julius Caesar*, 175–91, Malden, MA.
Raaflaub, K. A. (2010a), 'Creating a grand coalition of true Roman citizens: On Caesar's political strategy in the civil war', in B. Breed, C. Damon and A. Rossi (eds), *Citizens of Discord: Rome and Its Civil Wars*, 159–70, Oxford.
Raaflaub, K. A. (2010b), 'Between tradition and innovation: Shifts in Caesar's political propaganda and self-presentation', in G. Urso (ed.), *Cesare: precursore o visionario? Atti del convegno internazionale, Cividale del Friuli, 17–19 settembre 2009*, 141–57, Pisa.
Raaflaub, K. A. (ed.) (2017a), *The Landmark Julius Caesar*, New York.
Raaflaub, K. A. (2017b), 'The Roman *commentarius* and Caesar's commentaries', in K. A. Raaflaub (ed.), *The Landmark Julius Caesar*, 203–9, New York.
Raaflaub, K. A. (2017c), 'The *Civil War* as a work of propaganda', in K. A. Raaflaub (ed.), *The Landmark Julius Caesar*, 246–54, New York.
Raaflaub, K. A. (2018), 'Caesar, literature, and politics at the end of the Republic', in L. Grillo and C. B. Krebs (eds), *The Cambridge Companion to the Writings of Julius Caesar*, 13–28, Cambridge.
Raditsa, L. (1969), *A Historical Commentary to Sallust's Letter of Mithridates*, PhD diss., Columbia University.
Ramage, E. S. (1991), 'Sulla's propaganda', *Klio* 73(1): 93–121.
Ramsey, J. T. (2015), *Sallust: Fragments of the Histories; Letters to Caesar*, Loeb Classical Library 522, Cambridge, MA.
Ramsey, J. T. (2016), 'How and why was Pompey made sole consul in 52 BC?' *Historia* 65(3): 298–324.
Ramsey, J. T. and L. A. Licht (1997), *The Comet of 44 B.C. and Caesar's Funeral Games*, Atlanta, GA.
Ramsey J. T. and K. A. Raaflaub (2017), 'Chronological tables for Caesar's wars (58–45 BCE)', *Histos* 11: 162–217.
Rathbone, D. (2007), 'Warfare and the state: A. Military finance and supply', in P. Sabin, H. Van Wees and M. Whitby (eds), *The Cambridge History of Greek and Roman Warfare*, vol. 2: *Rome from the Late Republic to the Late Empire*, 158–76, Cambridge.

Raubitschek, A. E. (1954), 'Epigraphical notes on Julius Caesar', *JRS* 44: 65–75.
Rawson, E. (1985), *Intellectual Life in the Late Roman Republic*, London.
Rawson, E. (1986), 'Cassius and Brutus: the memory of the Liberators', in I. Moxon, J. D. Smart and A. J. Woodman (eds), *Past Perspectives: Studies in Greek and Roman Historical Writing*, Cambridge, 101–19 (= E. Rawson, *Roman Culture and Society: Collected papers*, Oxford, 1991, 488–507).
Reddé, M. (1986), *Mare Nostrum: les infrastructures, le dispositif et l'histoire de la marine militaire sous l'empire romain*, Roma.
Reinhold, M. (1933), *Marcus Agrippa: A biography*, Geneva, NY.
Rich, J. (2018), 'Warlords and the Roman Republic', in T. Ñaco del Hoyo and F. López Sánchez (eds), *War, Warlords and Interstate Relations in the Ancient Mediterranean*, 266–94, Leiden.
Richardson J. S. (1986), *Hispaniae: Spain and the development of Roman imperialism 218–82 BC*, Cambridge.
Ridley R. T. (1980–1), 'The economics of civil war', *Helikon* 20–1: 27–41.
Ridley, R. T. (2005), 'The absent pontifex maximus', *Historia* 54(3): 275–300
Riggsby, A. M. (2006), *Caesar in Gaul and Rome: War in Words*, Austin, TX.
Ritter, H. W. (1969), 'Caesars erstes Zusammentreffen mit Deiotarus', *Historia* 18: 255–6.
Robb, M. A. (2010), *Beyond* Populares *and* Optimates: *Political Language in the Late Republic*, Stuttgart.
Roddaz, J.-M. (1984), *Marcus Agrippa* (BEFAR, 253), Roma.
Roesch, S. (2004), 'La politesse dans la correspondance de Cicéron', in L. Nadjo and É. Gavoille (eds), *Epistulae Antiquae III: Actes du IIIe Colloque International 'L'Épistolaire Antique et ses Prolongements Européens'*, 139–52, Louvain.
Rohr Vio, F. (2020), 'Children for the family: Children for the state: Attitudes towards and the handling of offspring during the Triumvirate', in F. Pina Polo (ed.), *The Triumviral Period: Civil War, Political Crisis and Socioeconomic Transformations*, 171–92, Zaragoza, Servilla.
Roller, D. W. (1998), *The Building Program of Herod the Great*, Berkeley.
Roller, D.W. (2003), *The World of Juba II and Kleopatra Selene: Royal Scholarship on Rome's African Frontier*, London.
Roller, M. B. (2001), *Constructing Autocracy: Aristocrats and Emperors in Julio-Claudian Rome*, Princeton.
Roller, M. B. (2019), 'Losing to Cicero: Asinius Pollio and the Emergence of New Arenas of Competitive Eloquence under Augustus', in: K.-J. Hölkeskamp and H. Beck (eds), *Verlierer und Aussteiger in der, Konkurrenz und Anwesenden'. Agonalität in der politischen Kultur des antiken Rom*, 189–205, Stuttgart.
Romito, F. and D. Sangiovanni (2008), 'Tombe "a grotticella" peligne di età ellenistica', in G. Tagliamonte (ed.), *Ricerche di archeologia medio-adriatica. 1: Le necropoli: Contesti e materiali: Atti dell'incontro di studio, Cavallino-Lecce, 27–28 maggio 2005*, 195–230, Galatina.
Rosenblitt, J. A. (2011), 'The *Devotio* of Sallust's Cotta', *AJPh* 132: 397–427.
Rosenblitt, J. A. (2019), *Rome After Sulla*, London.
Rosenstein, N. S. (1990), *Imperatores victi: Military Defeat and Aristocratic Competition in the Middle and Late Republic*, Berkeley.
Rosenstein, N. S. (2016), '*Bellum se ipsum alet*? Financing mid-Republican imperialism', in H. Beck, M. Jehne and J. Serrati (eds), *Money and Power in the Roman Republic*, 114–30, Brussels.
Rosenstein, N. S. (2018), 'Why No Warlords in Republican Rome?' in T. Ñaco del Hoyo and F. López Sánchez (eds), *War, Warlords, and Interstate Relations in the Ancient Mediterranean*, Leiden, 295–307.
Rosillo-López, C. (2020), 'Public opinion in Rome and the popularity of Sextus Pompeius', in L. Kersten and C. Wendt (eds), *Rector maris: Sextus Pompeius und das Meer*, 187–207, Bonn.
Rossi, A. (2000), 'The camp of Pompey: Strategy of representation in Caesar's *Bellum Ciuile*', *CJ* 95(3): 239–56.

Bibliography

Rowan, C. (2018), *From Caesar to Augustus (c. 49 BC–AD 14): Using Coins as Sources*, Cambridge.
Rowe, G. O. (1967), 'Dramatic structures in Caesar's *Bellum Civile*', *TAPhA* 98: 399–414.
Rüpke, J. (1990), Domi militiae: *Die religiöse Konstruktion des Krieges in Rom*, Stuttgart.
Russell, A. (2016), *The Politics of Public Space in Republican Rome*, Cambridge.
Sacco, L. (2004), 'Devotio', *StudRom* 52(3–4): 312–52.
Saller, R. P. (1982), *Personal Patronage Under the Early Empire*, Cambridge.
Santangelo, F. (2007), *Sulla, the Elites and the Empire*, Leiden.
Santangelo, F. (2016), 'Performing passions, negotiating survival: Italian cities in the late Republican civil wars', in H. Börm, M. Mattheis and J. Wienand (eds), *Civil War in Ancient Greece and Rome: Contexts of Disintegration and Reintegration*, 127–48, Stuttgart.
Santangelo, F. (2020), 'La monotonia delle parole d'ordine: Catchwords e politica nella tarda Repubblica romana', *Futuro Classico* 6: 43–63.
Sanz, A.-M. (2015), 'La *deditio*: un acte diplomatique au coeur de la conquête romaine (fin du IIIe-fin du IIe siècle avant J.C.)', in B. Grass, G. Stouder, J.-L. Ferrary, S. Pittia and P. Sánchez (eds), *La diplomatie romaine sous la République: réflexions sur une pratique. Actes des recontres de Paris (21–22 juin 2013) et Genève (31 octobre-1er novembre 2013)*, 87–105, Besançon.
Sapere, A. V. (2014), '*Ne quid res publica detrimenti capiat*: análisis del discurso de Filipo en el Senado (Salustio, *Historiae*, 1.77 Reynolds)', *Cuadernos de Filología Clásica: Estudios Latinos* 34: 225–39.
Saunders, C. (1923), 'The political sympathies of Servius Sulpicius Rufus', *CR* 37(5–6): 110–13.
Scanlon, T. S. (1998), 'Reflexivity and irony in the proem of Sallust's *Historiae*', in C. Deroux (ed.), *Studies in Latin Literature and Roman History 9* (Collection Latomus, 244), 186–224, Brussels.
Scevola, R. (2020), '*Senatus consultum ultimum*: Orientamenti interpretativi e questioni aperte', in P. Buongiorno (ed.), *Senatus consultum ultimum e stato di eccezione: Fenomeni in prospettiva*, 11–66, Stuttgart.
Schäfer, T. (2017), 'Das Tropaeum Augusti von Lugdunum Convenarum: Skylla, Sex. Pompeius und Octavian', in M. Flecker, S. Krmincek, J. Lipps and R. Posamentir (eds), *Augustus ist tot – Lang lebe der Kaiser! Internationales Kolloquium anlässlich des 2000. Todesjahres des römischen Kaisers vom 20–22 November 2014 in Tübingen*, 337–65, Rahden.
Schede, M. (1919), 'Aus dem Heraion von Samos', *MDAI(A)* 44: 1–46.
Scheidel, W. (1996), 'Finances, Figures and Fiction', *CQ* 46: 222–38.
Scheidel, W. (2007), 'A model of real income growth in Roman Italy', *Historia* 56(3): 322–46.
Scheidel, W. (2008), 'Roman population size: The logic of the debate' in L. de Ligt, and S. J. Northwood (eds), *People, Land and Politics: Demographic Developments and the Transformation of Roman Italy, 300 BC–AD 14*, 17–70, Leiden.
Schettino, M. T. (2020), 'Riflessioni in forma di bilancio sul *senatus consultum servandae rei publicae causa*', in P. Buongiorno (ed.), *Senatus consultum ultimum e stato di eccezione: Fenomeni in prospettiva*, 161–82, Stuttgart.
Schiassi, F. (1820), *Del ritrovamento di medaglie consolare e di familie fatto a Cadriano nel Bolognese l'anno MDCCCXI*, Bologna.
Schmitthenner, W. (1973), *Oktavian und das Testament Cäsars: Eine Untersuchung zu den politischen Anfängen des Augustus*, 2nd edn, München.
Schuller, W. (1995), 'Soldaten und Befehlshaber in Caesars *Bellum civile*', in I. Malkin and W. Z. Rubinsohn (eds), *Leaders and Masses in the Roman World*, 189–99, Leiden.
Schulz, M.-W. (2010), *Caesar und Labienus: Geschichte einer tödlichen Kameradschaft: Caesars Karriere als Feldherr im Spiegel der Kommentarien sowie bei Cassius Dio, Appianus und Lucanus*, Hildesheim.
Schulz, R. (2015), 'Helfer auf Abruf? Fremde Könige im Kontext der römischen Provinzialverwaltung in der Zeit der späten Republik', in E. Baltrusch and J. Wilker (eds), *Amici – socii – clientes? Abhängige Herrschaft im Imperium Romanum*, 37–50, Berlin.
Schulze, W. (1904), *Zur Geschichte lateinischer Eigennamen*, Berlin.

Bibliography

Schwabe, L. (1900), 'Cornelius 395', *RE* IV,1: 1566-90.
Scuderi R. (1979), 'Problemi fiscali a Roma in età Triumvirale', *Clio* 15: 341-68.
Sear, D. R. (1998), *The History and Coinage of the Roman Imperators, 49-27 BC*, London.
Seager, R. (2005), 'Sextus Pompeius: A Rehabilitation', *CR*, 55(2): 620-1.
Shackleton Bailey, D. R. (1960a), 'The credentials of L. Caesar and L. Roscius', *JRS* 50: 80-3.
Shackleton Bailey D. R. (1960b), 'The Roman nobility in the Second Civil War', *CQ* 10: 253-67.
Shackleton Bailey, D. R. (ed.) (1968), *Cicero's Letters to Atticus vol. 4, 49 B.C., 133-210 (Books VII.10-X)*, Cambridge.
Shackleton Bailey, D. R. (1977), *Cicero: Epistulae ad Familares*, Cambridge.
Shackleton Bailey, D. R. (ed.) (1980), *Cicero: Epistulae ad Quintum fratrem et M. Brutum*, Cambridge.
Shackleton Bailey, D. R. (1999), *Cicero: Letters to Atticus, Volume III*, Loeb Classical Library 491, Cambridge, MA.
Shackleton Bailey, D. R. (2004), *Statius: Thebaid, Volume I: Thebaid: Books 1-7*, Loeb Classical Library 207, Cambridge, MA.
Shatzman I. (1975), *Senatorial Wealth and Roman Politics*, Bruxelles.
Shaw, E. (2021), *Sallust and the Fall of the Republic,* Leiden.
Shay, J. (1994), *Achilles in Vietnam: Combat Trauma and the Undoing of Character*, New York.
Shay, J. (2002), *Odysseus in America: Combat Trauma and the Trials of Homecoming*, New York.
Sheffield, G. D. and G. Till (2003), *The challenges of high command: The British experience*, Basingstoke.
Sheppard, S. (2006), *Pharsalus 48 BC: Caesar and Pompey – Clash of the Titans*, Oxford.
Siani-Davies, M. (1997), 'Ptolemy XII Auletes and the Romans', *Historia* 46(3): 306-40.
Sigmund, C. (2014), *'Königtum' in der politischen Kultur des spätrepublikanischen Rom*, Berlin.
Simonetta, B. (1977), *The Coins of the Cappadocian Kings*, Fribourg.
Simpson, C. (2006), 'M. Aemilius Lepidus: Brief speculations on his appointment and continued tenure as *pontifex maximus*, 44-13 B.C.', *Latomus* 65(3): 628-33.
Skard, E. (1956), *Sallust und seine Vorgänger* (Symbolae Osloenses Fasc. Supplet. 15), Oslo.
Skocpol, T. (1979), *States and Social Revolutions: A Comparative Analysis of France, Russia and China*, Cambridge.
Skocpol, T. (1985), *États et révolutions sociales: la révolution en France, en Russie et en Chine*, tr. Noëlle Burgi, Paris.
Smelser, N. J. (2004), 'Psychological trauma and cultural trauma', in J. Alexander, R. Eyerman, B. Giesen, N. J. Smelser and P. Sztompka (eds), *Cultural Trauma and Collective Identity*, 31-59, Berkeley.
Smith, R. E. (1958), *Service in the Post-Marian Roman Army*, Manchester.
Smith, R. R. R. (1988), *Hellenistic Royal Portraits*, Oxford.
Snowdon, M. (2015), 'Beyond *clientela*: the instrumentality of *amicitia* in the Greek East', in M. Jehne and F. Pina Polo (eds), *Foreign Clientelae in the Roman Empire: A Reconsideration*, 209-24, Stuttgart.
Soeters, J., D. J. Winslow and A. Weibull (2006), 'Military culture', in G. Caforio (ed.), *Handbook of the Sociology of the Military*, 237-54, New York.
Somma, M. C. (2015), 'Da Corfinio a Valva: lo sviluppo urbano di un municipio romano tra Tardantichità e alto Medioevo', in P. Arthur and M. L. Imperiale (eds), *VII Congresso nazionale di archeologia medievale: Palazzo Turrisi, Lecce, 9-12 settembre 2015*, 282-6, Firenze.
Somma, M. C., A. Antonelli and V. La Salvia (2018), 'Paesaggi e insediamenti in un'area montana: il caso del territorio valvense tra persistenze e trasformazioni', in G. Volpe (ed.), *Storia e archeologia globale dei paesaggi rurali in Italia fra tardoantico e medioevo*, 463-504, Bari.
Soricelli, G. (2011), 'Assegnazioni graccane e Libri Coloniarum: il caso di Corfinium e Sulmo', in G. Firpo (ed.), *Fides amicorum: Studi in onore di Carla Fayer*, 481-508, Pescara.

Bibliography

Spannagel, M. (1999), *Exemplaria principis: Untersuchungen zur Entstehung und Ausstattung des Augustusforums*, Heidelberg.

Speidel, M. A. (1992), 'Roman army pay scales', *JRS* 82: 87–106.

Speidel, M. A. (2016), 'Actium, allies, and the Augustan *auxilia*: Reconsidering the transformation of military structures and foreign relations in the reign of Augustus', in C. Wolff, P. Faure (eds), *Les auxiliaires de l'armée romaine: Des alliés aux fédérés*, 79–95, Lyon.

Spencer, D. (2019), *Language and Authority in* De Lingua Latina: *Varro's Guide to Being Roman*, Madison, WI.

Spielberg, L. (2023), 'Caesar's talkative centurions: Anecdotal speech, soldierly *fides*, and contemporary history', A. G. Scott (ed.), *Studies in Contemporary Historiography* (*Histos* suppl. 15), 65–106.

Starr, C. G. (1960), *The Roman Imperial Navy: 31 B.C.–A.D. 324*, Chicago.

Steed, K. (2017), 'The speeches of Sallust's *Histories* and the legacy of Sulla', *Historia* 66(4): 401–41.

Steel, C. (2012), 'The *Lex Pompeia de Provinciis* of 52 B.C.: A reconsideration', *Historia* 61(1): 83–93.

Steel, C. (2013), *The End of the Roman Republic 146 to 44 BC: Conquest and Crisis*, Edinburgh.

Steinby, E. M. (ed.) (1993–2000), *Lexicon topographicum urbis Romae*, 6 vols, Roma.

Steinby, E. M. (1993), 'Basilica Porcia', in E. M. Steinby (ed.), *Lexicon topographicum urbis Romae*, vol. 1, 187.

Stem, R. (2005), 'The first eloquent Stoic: Cicero on Cato the Younger', *CJ* 101: 37–49.

Stevenson, T. (2015), 'Appian on the Pharsalus Campaign: Civil Wars 2.48-91,' in K. Welch (ed.), *Appian's Roman History: Empire and Civil War*, 257–75, Swansea.

Stier, H. E. (1969), 'Der Mithridatesbrief aus Sallusts *Historien* als Geschichtsquelle', in R. Stiehl and H. E. Stier (eds), *Beiträge zur alten Geschichte und deren Nachleben: Festschrift für Franz Altheim zum 6.10.1968*, 441–51, Berlin.

Stoffel, E. G. H. C. (1887), *Histoire de Jules César, Guerre Civile*, 2 vols, Paris.

Sullivan, R. D. (1978), 'Priesthoods of the Eastern dynastic aristocracy', in S. Şahin, E. Schwertheim and J. Wagner (eds), *Studien zur Religion und Kultur Kleinasiens: Festschrift für Friedrich Karl Dörner zum 65. Geburtstag am 28. Februar 1976*, 2.914-939, Leiden.

Sumner, G. V. (1971), 'The *Lex Annalis* under Caesar', *Phoenix* 25: 246–71, 357–71.

Sumner, G. V. (1973), *The Orators in Cicero's Brutus: Prosopography and Chronology*, Toronto.

Suspène, A. (2009), 'Les rois amis et alliés face au principat: rapports personnels, représentations du pouvoir et nouvelles stratégies diplomatiques dans l'Orient méditerranéen', in M. Christol and D. Darde (eds), *L'expression du pouvoir au début de l'Empire: Autour de la Maison Carrée à Nîmes: Actes du colloque organisé à l'initiative de la ville de Nîmes et du Musée archéologique (Nîmes, Carré d'Art, 20–22 Octobre 2005)*, 45–51, Paris.

Svoronos, J. N. (1904), *Ta nomismata tou kratous tōn Ptolemaiōn*, 4 vols, Athens.

Syme, R. (1937), 'Pollio, Saloninus and Salonae', *CQ* 31: 39–48 (= R. Syme, *Roman Papers*, Oxford, 1979, 1.18-30).

Syme, R. (1939), *The Roman Revolution*, Oxford.

Syme, R. (1958), 'Imperator Caesar: A study in nomenclature', *Historia* 7(2): 172–88.

Syme, R. (1964), *Sallust*, Berkeley.

Syme, R. (1986), *The Augustan Aristocracy*, Oxford.

Syme, R. (1995), *Anatolica: Studies in Strabo*, ed. Anthony R. Birley, Oxford.

Talbert, R. J. A. (1984), *The Senate of Imperial Rome*, Princeton.

Tan, J. (2017), *Power and Public Finance at Rome, 264–49 BCE*, Oxford.

Tannenbaum, R. F. (2005), 'What Caesar said: Rhetoric and history in Sallust's *Coniuratio Catilinae* 51', in K. Welch and T.W. Hillard (eds), *Roman Crossings: Theory and Practice in the Roman Republic*, 209–24, Swansea.

Tansey, P. (2013), 'Marcia Catonis and the *fulmen clarum*', *CQ* 63: 423–6.

Tansey, P. (2016), *A Selective Prosopographical Study of Marriage in the Roman Elite in the Second and First Centuries B.C.: Revisiting the Evidence*, PhD thesis, Macquarie University.

Tatum, W. J. (2017), 'Intermediaries in political communication: *Adlegatio* and its uses', in C. Rosillo-López (ed.), *Political Communication in the Roman World*, 55–80, Leiden.
Tatum, W. J. (2018), *Quintus Cicero: A Brief Handbook on Canvassing for Office. Translated with Introduction and Commentary*, Oxford.
Taylor, L. R. (1931), *The Divinity of the Roman Emperor*, Middletown, CT.
Taylor, M. J. (2017), 'State finance in the middle Roman Republic: A reevaluation', *AJPh* 138: 143–80.
Taylor, M. J. (2020), 'The evolution of the manipular legion in the early republic', *Historia* 69(1): 38–56.
Thein, A. (2014), 'Reflecting on Sulla's clemency', *Historia* 63(2): 166–86.
Thomas, J.-F. (2007), *Déshonneur et honte en latin: étude sémantique*, Louvain.
Thome, G. (2000), *Zentrale Wertvorstellungen der Römer*, 2 vols, Bamberg.
Thomsen, R. (1973), 'The pay of the Roman soldier and the property qualifications of the Servian classes', in O. S. Due, H. F. Johansen and B. D. Larsen (eds), *Classica et Mediaevalia: Dissertationes 9: Festschrift für F. Blatt*, 194–208, København.
Tiersch, C. (2015), 'Von personaler Anbindung zu territorialer Organisation? Dynamiken römischer Reichsbildung und die Provinzialisierung Zyperns (58 v. Chr.)', in M. Jehne and F. Pina Polo (eds), *Foreign Clientelae in the Roman Empire: A Reconsideration*, 239–60, Stuttgart.
Toher, M. (2017), *Nicolaus of Damascus: The Life of Augustus and the Autobiography*, Cambridge.
Tondo, S. (1963), 'Il *sacramentum militiae* nell'ambiente culturale romano-italico', *SDHI* 29:1–25.
Tordeur, P. H. (2013), 'Le quinaire de Jules César du type Crawford 452/3 (48 av. J.-C.)', *BCEN* 50 (2): 153–9.
Traina, G. (2023) *La guerre mondiale des romains: de l'assassinat de César à la mort d'Antoine et Cléopâtre (44–30 av. J.-C.)*, Paris.
Treggiari, S. (2015), 'The Education of the Ciceros', in W. Martin Bloomer (ed.), *A Companion to Ancient Education*, 240–51, Chichester.
Treggiari, S. (2019), *Servilia and her Family*, Oxford.
Trunk, M. (2008), 'Studien zur Ikonographie des Pompeius Magnus: Die numismatischen und glyptischen Quellen', *JDAI* 123: 101–70.
Tschiedel, H. J. (1981), *Caesars 'Anticato': Eine Untersuchung der Testimonien und Fragmente*, Darmstadt.
Turner, A. J. (2019), 'The lost historians of late Republican civil war', in C. H. Carsten and F. J. Vervaet (eds), *The Historiography of Late Republican Civil War* (Historiography of Rome and Its Empire, 5), 29–53, Leiden.
Valpy, A. (ed.) (1828), *M. Manilii Astronomicon*, vol. 1, London.
Van Minnen, P. (2000), 'An official act of Cleopatra (with a subscription in her own hand)', *AncSoc* 30: 29–34.
Van Wijlick, H. (2015), 'Attitudes of Eastern kings and princes towards Rome in the age of civil war, 49–31 BC', in E. Baltrusch and J. Wilker (eds), *Amici - socii - clientes? Abhängige Herrschaft im Imperium Romanum*, 51–66, Berlin.
Van Wijlick, H. A. M. (2020), *Rome and the Near Eastern Kingdoms and Principalities, 44–31 BC*, Leiden.
Van Wonterghem, F. (1984), *Superaequum, Corfinium, Sulmo*, Firenze.
Vendrand-Voyer, J. (1983), *Normes civiques et métier militaire à Rome sous le Principat*, Clermont-Ferrand.
Verboven, K. (2002), *The Economy of Friends: Economic Aspects of Amicitia and Patronage in the Late Republic*, Brussels.
Versnel, H. S. (1976), 'Two types of Roman *devotio*', *Mnemosyne*, 29(4): 365–410.
Vervaet F. J. (2006), 'The official position of Cn. Pompeius in 49 and 48 BCE', *Latomus* 65(4): 928–53.
Vervaet, F. J. (2014), *The High Command in the Roman Republic: The Principle of the Summum Imperium Auspiciumque from 509 to 19 BCE*, Stuttgart.

Bibliography

Vervaet, F. J. (2020), 'The Triumvirate *rei publicae constituendae*: political and constitutional aspects', in F. Pina Polo (ed.), *The Triumviral Period: Civil War, Political Crisis and Socioeconomic Transformations*, 23–48, Zaragoza, Sevilla.

Von Albrecht, M. (1997), *A History of Roman Literature: From Livius Andronicus to Boethius; With Special Regard to Its Influence on World Literature*. Revised by G. Schmeling and author. Translated with the assistance of Frances and Kevin Newman, Leiden.

Von Domaszewski, A. (1894), 'Die Heere der Bürgerkriege in den Jahren 49 bis 42 vor Christus', *NHJ* 4: 157–88.

Wallmann, P. (1989), *Rei Publicae Constituendae: Untersuchungen zur politischen Propaganda im Zweiten Triumvirat (43–30 v. Chr.)*, Frankfurt am Mainz.

Wardle, D. (ed.) (2014), *Suetonius: Life of Augustus*, Oxford.

Watson, G. R. (1969), *The Roman Soldier*, Ithaca, NY.

Weigel, R. D. (1992), *Lepidus: The Tarnished Triumvir*, London.

Weinstock, S. (1971), *Divus Julius*, Oxford.

Welch, K. (1990), 'The *praefectura urbis* of 45 B.C. and the ambitions of L. Cornelius Balbus', *Antichthon* 24: 53–69.

Welch, K. (2002a), 'Both sides of the coin: Sextus Pompeius and the so-called *Pompeiani*', in A. Powell and K. Welch (eds), *Sextus Pompeius*, 1–30, Swansea.

Welch, K. (2002b), 'Sextus Pompeius and the *res publica* in 42–39 BC', in A. Powell and K. Welch (eds), *Sextus Pompeius*, 31–63, Swansea.

Welch, K. (2006–7), '*Maiestas regia* and the donations of Alexandria', *MedArch* 19/20: 181–92.

Welch, K. (2012), *Magnus Pius: Sextus Pompeius and the Transformation of the Roman Republic*, Swansea.

Welch, K. (ed.) (2015), *Appian's Roman History: Empire and Civil War*, Swansea.

Welch, K. (2019), 'History wars: Who avenged Caesar and why does it matter?' in I. Gildenhard, U. Gotter, and W. Havener (eds), *Augustus and the Destruction of History*, 59–78, Cambridge.

Wendt, C. (2015), '*More clientum*: Roms Perspektive auf befreundete Fürsten', in E. Baltrusch and J. Wilker (eds), *Amici – socii – clientes? Abhängige Herrschaft im Imperium Romanum*, 19–35, Berlin.

Wendt, C. (2020), '*Animus inquies*: Sextus Pompeius als Figur der *stasis*', in L. Kersten and C. Wendt (eds), *Rector maris: Sextus Pompeius und das Meer*, 235–85, Bonn.

Westall, R. W. (1996), 'The Forum Iulium as Representation of Imperator Caesar', *MDAI(R)* 103: 83–118.

Westall, R. W. (2013), 'The Relationship of Appian to Pollio', *ARID* 38: 95–123.

Westall, R. W. (2015a), '"Moving through town": Foreign dignitaries in Rome in the middle and late Republic', in I. Östenberg, S. Malmberg and J. Bjørnebye (eds), *The Moving City: Processions, Passages and Promenades in Ancient Rome*, 23–36, London.

Westall, R. W. (2015b), 'The sources for the civil wars of Appian of Alexandria', in K. Welch (ed.), *Appian's Roman History: Empire and Civil War*, 125–67, Swansea.

Westall, R. W. (2016), 'The sources of Cassius Dio for the Roman civil wars of 49–30 BC', in C. H. Lange and J. M. Madsen (eds), *Cassius Dio: Greek Intellectual and Roman Politician*, 51–75, Leiden.

Westall, R. W. (2017), *Caesar's Civil War: Historical Reality and Fabrication*, Leiden.

Westall, R. W. (2019), 'Fragmentary historians and the Roman civil wars', in C. H. Lange and F. J. Vervaet (eds), *The Historiography of Late Republican Civil War* (Historiography of Rome and Its Empire, 5), 54–86, Leiden.

White, P. (2010), *Cicero in Letters: Epistolary Relations of the Late Republic*, Oxford.

Whittaker, C. R. (2004), *Rome and its Frontiers: The Dynamics of Empire*, London.

Wickham, C. (1982), *Studi sulla società degli Appennini nell'Alto Medioevo: contadini, signori e insediamento nel territorio di Valva (Sulmona)*, Bologna.

Wiedemann, T. (1996), 'Single combat and being Roman', *AncSoc* 27: 91–103.

Bibliography

Will, W. (1996a), 'Aemilius [I 12]', *DNP I*, 178–9, Stuttgart.
Will, W. (1996b), 'Antonius [I 9]', *DNP I*, 810–13, Stuttgart.
Williams, C. A. (2012), *Reading Roman Friendship*, Cambridge.
Williams, G. (1995), '*Libertino patre natus*: True or false?' in S. J. Harrison (ed.), *Homage to Horace: A Bimillenary Celebration*, 296–313, Oxford.
Williams, K. F. (2000), 'Manlius' *mandata*: Sallust *Bellum Catilinae* 33', *CPh* 95(2): 160–71.
Winterling, A. (2008), 'Freundschaft und Klientel im kaiserzeitlichen Rom', *Historia* 57(3): 298–316.
Wirszubski, C. (1950), *Libertas as a Political Idea at Rome During the Late Republic and Early Principate*, Cambridge.
Wiseman, T. P. (1964), 'Some Republican senators and their tribes', *CQ* 14: 122–33.
Wiseman, T. P. (1971), *New Men in Roman Senate, 139 B.C.–A.D. 14*, London.
Wiseman, T. P. (1974), 'Legendary genealogies in late-Republican Rome', *G&R* 21(2): 153–64.
Wiseman, T. P. (1998a), *Roman Drama and Roman History*, Exeter.
Wiseman, T. P. (1998b), 'The publication of *De Bello Gallico*', in K. Welch and A. Powell (eds), *Julius Caesar as Artful Reporter: The War Commentaries as Political Instruments*, 1–10, Swansea.
Wiseman, T. P. (2015), *The Roman Audience: Classical Literature as Social History*, Oxford.
Woodman, A. J. (ed.) (1983), *Velleius Paterculus: The Caesarian and the Augustan Narrative (2.41–93): Edited with a Commentary*, Cambridge.
Woodman, A. J. (2003), 'Poems to historians: Catullus 1 and Horace, *Odes* 2.1', in D. Braund and C. Gill (eds), *Myth, History and Culture in Republican Rome. Studies in Honour of T.P. Wiseman*, 191–216, Exeter.
Woodman, A. J. (ed. and trans.) (2007), *Sallust: Catiline's War, The Jugurthine War, Histories*, London.
Woodman, A. J. (2012), *From Poetry to History: Selected Papers*, Oxford.
Woods, D. (2010), 'On Caesar's coinage in 48 BC', *Latomus* 69: 38–42.
Woytek, B. (1995), 'MAG PIVS IMP ITER: Die Datierung der sizilischen Münzprägung des Sextus Pompeius', *JNG* 45: 79–94.
Woytek, B. (2003), *Arma et nummi: Forschungen zur römischen Finanzgeschichte und Münzprägung der Jahre 49 bis 42 v. Chr.*, Wien.
Wright, F. A. (1937), *Marcus Agrippa: Organizer of Victory*, London.
Wright, N. L. (2008), 'Anazarbos and the Tarkondimotid kings of Cilicia', *AS* 58: 115–25.
Wright, N. L. (2009), 'Tarkondimotid responses to Roman domestic politics: From Antony to Actium', *Journal of the Numismatic Association of Australia* 20: 73–81.
Wright, N. L. (2012), 'The house of Tarkondimotos: A late Hellenistic dynasty between Rome and the East', *AS* 62: 69–88.
Yakobson, A. (1999), *Elections and Electioneering in Rome: A Study in the Political System of the Late Republic*, Stuttgart.
Yates, D. C. (2010), 'The role of Cato the Younger in Caesar's *Bellum Civile*' *CW*, 104(2): 161–74.
Zack, A. (2018), 'C. Iulius Caesar und Hyrkanus II. Überlegungen zur chronologischen Abfolge der Dokumente bei Flavius Josephus *ant*. 14, 10, 2–10 (190–222) und *ant*. 14, 8, 5 (145–8)', *Electrum* 25: 147–85.
Zajko, V. and O'Gorman, E. (eds) (2013), *Classical Myth and Psychoanalysis: Ancient and Modern Stories of the Self. Classical Presences*, Oxford.
Zanker, P. (1988), *The Power of Images in the Age of Augustus*, trans. Alan Shapiro, Ann Arbor.
Zanker, P. ([1987] 2009), *Augustus und die Macht der Bilder*, 5th edn, München.
Zarecki, J. (2014), *Cicero's Ideal Statesman in Theory and Practice*, London.
Zarrow, E. M. (2003), 'Sicily and the coinage of Octavian and Sextus Pompey: Aeneas or the Catanean Brothers?' *NC* 163: 123–35.
Zecchini, G. (1982), 'Asinio Pollione: Dall'attività politica alla riflessione storiografica', *ANRW* 2.30.2: 1265–96.

Bibliography

Zucchetti, E. (2021a), *Discordia, Hegemony, and Popular Subjectivities: Towards a Model for the Analysis of Social Conflict in Ancient Rome*, PhD thesis, Newcastle University.

Zucchetti, E. (2021b), 'Introduction: The Reception of Gramsci's Thought in Historical and Classical Scholarship', in E. Zucchetti and A. M. Cimino (eds), *Antonio Gramsci and the Ancient World*, 1–43, London.

Zucchetti, E. (2021c), 'Hegemony, ideology, and ancient history: Notes towards a development of an intersectional framework', in E. Zucchetti and A. M. Cimino (eds), *Antonio Gramsci and the Ancient World*, 352–64, London.

Zucchetti, E. (2022), 'Performance, legal pronouncements, and political communication in the first Roman civil war: *Iudicare hostes* after Sulla's first march on Rome (88 BCE)', *Hermes* 150: 54–81.

Zumpt, A. W. (1874), *De dictatoris Caesaris die et anno natali*, Berlin.

INDEX

Adriatic Sea 71 n.33, 129
Aemilius Lepidus, M. (*cos.* 78) 27 n.27, 168
Aemilius Lepidus, M. (*cos.* 46) 9, 19, 22, 27 n.31, 64, 75, 84, 85, 92 n.81, 93 n.92, 105, 145, 159, 168, 171, 176
Aeneid 81, 85, 88 n.15, 90 n.47
aerarium 7, 60, 153
Afranius, L. (*cos.* 60) 14, 16, 19, 29 n.51, 43, 44, 183, 184
Africa 21, 59, 60, 66, 71 n.49, 82, 95, 100, 110, 111, 117, 121, 143, 147, 182, 190, 199 n.65
Alexandria 35, 42, 63, 102, 107, 162 n.20
allied rulers
    dynastic legitimacy 6, 104–6, 109
    grants of territory 101–6, 110, 114 n.75
    personal relationships 95–102, 104, 106–11
    Roman recognition 95, 97, 98, 101–6, 108, 110
Allienus, A. (*procos.* Sicily 48–46) 61
Allobroges 100, 144
amicitia 6, 14, 16, 18–21, 23, 29 n.53, 46, 96–102, 110, 111, 118, 126 n.37
    interstate 6, 106, 110
    personal 6, 7, 23, 25, 96, 97, 99, 100, 101, 104, 106, 107, 108, 109, 110, 111, 118
Annius Milo, T. (*pr.* 55) 34
Antiochus I of Commagene 97, 98, 112 n.18
Antiochus XIII 97, 102, 174
Antonius, Iullus (*cos.* 10) 93 n.86
Antonius Creticus, M. (*cos.* 74) 119, 168
Antonius Hybrida, C. (*cos.* 63) 149 n.33
Antonius, L. (*cos.* 41) 146
Antonius, M. (*cos.* 44)
    and allies 101, 103–6, 107–11, 114 n.75
    armies
        finances of 7, 153–66 passim
        leadership of 143–6
    and Asinius Pollio 181, 188, 191–4
    clementia 27 n.31
    coinage 68, 84, 108
    consul (44 BCE) 84, 85, 92 n.85
    dynastic ambitions 9, 93 n.86, 114 n.82
    hostis 15, 86, 177, 199 n.71
    negotiations 19, 22, 29 n.60, 81
    tribune of *plebs* (49 BCE) 42, 44
    Triumvir 75–6, 84
Apollodorus (rhetor) 122
Apollonia 29 n. 50, 68, 71 n.33, 82, 117

Appian 1, 2, 8, 30 n.74, 33, 34, 42, 50 n.25, n.27, 57, 65, 66, 69, 72 n.53, 77, 78, 81, 84, 88 n.10, 89 n.21, n.26, n.29, 90 n.34, 91 n.55, 93 n.87, 101, 107, 114 n.75, 144, 155, 157, 163 n.23, 184, 187, 194, 195, 196, 199 n.76, 200 n.100
Ariminum 36, 46, 54 n.112, 123, 156, 188
Ariobarzanes I (king of Cappadocia) 108, 113 n.48
Ariobarzanes III (king of Cappadocia) 97, 98, 154
armies, *see also* fleets
    auxiliaries 34, 73 n.73, 139 n.30, 153, 155–6, 161, 163 n.23
    financing 7, 154, 155, 159, 161
        extortion from allies via envoys 157
        stipendium (pay) 67–9, 73 n.73, n.86, 100, 153–7, 159, 161, 162 n.1, 163 n.29
        taxes 7, 153, 157–8 with Table 9.3, 160 with Table 9.4, 161, 164 n.41
    legions 9, 22, 34, 44, 49 n.8, 88 n.2, 99, 117, 120, 121, 132, 133, 136, 137, 142, 143, 146, 154, 155, 156, 157,
        162 n.1, n.13, n.18, n.20,
        163 n.29, n.30
        dilectus (levy) 141, 148
        legio IV 146
        legio IX 144
        legio Martia 146
        legionaries 7, 44, 68, 69, 73 n.73, n.86, 156
    morale and discipline
        auctoritas (authority) 6, 142–3,
            149 n.27, n.31
        decimatio (punishment) 144
        deditio (surrender) 17, 27 n.29
        disciplina militaris (obedience) 143
        fas (divine law)
        fas disciplinae (military law) 141, 148
        fortitudo (physical courage) 143
        ius (civil law) 141
        levitas (bonhomie) 141, 148
        missio ignominiosa (dishonourable discharge) 147–8
        sacramentum 141, 148
        virtus (manliness) 6, 36, 96, 139 n.29, 142, 143, 144, 149 n.31
    officers, *see also* prefects
        centurion 27 n.17, 35, 43, 50 n.25, 139 n.29, 142, 143, 144, 146, 147, 188

Index

legatus (lieutenant) 25, 100, 144, 149 n.33
tribunus militum (tribune of soldiers) 134, 144, 146, 147
political life
colloquium (parley) 14, 17, 25, 28 n.42
contio (gathering) 19, 144–7, 150 n.60
recruitment 82, 88 n.2, 154, 155, 162 n.20
rewards
doubled pay 73 n.73
land and money 100, 146, 147,
oak-wreath 61, 62, 71 n.38
Asia Minor 95, 103, 107, 114 n.75, 159–60
Asinius Pollio, C. (*cos.* 40)
and Antonius 181, 188, 191–4
and Caesar 181–2, 185–6, 192
and Cicero 188, 199 n.72
and Octavian (Caesar the Younger) 193–4, 195
Atrium Libertatis, patron of 189–90, 194, 198 n.57, 199 n.61
consul 194, 197 n.35
education of son 195, 200 n.98
homo novus 182, 189, 195, 200 n.98
Peace of Brundisium 189, 193, 194, 196 n.5
tribune of the *plebs* 192
triumph over Parthini 194
writings:
Historiae 181–200 passim
extent 186, 187, 193–4
focalisation 182, 198 n.53
model for Syme 181–2
model for Tacitus 196, 197 n.35
speeches 197 n.34
tragedies 182–2
Atia Maior 119, 122, 123
Atius Balbus, M. (*pr.* 60) 119
Atticus, *see* Caecilius Atticus, Q.
Augustus, *see* Octavian (*cos. suff.* 43)
Avienus, C. (*tr. mil.*) 147

Balventius, T. (centurion) 143
Bellum Alexandrinum 1, 100, 103, 107, 142
Bononia 22, 156, 193
Brundisium 10, 11, 16, 17, 19, 20, 22, 68, 143, 146, 193–4
Brunt, P.A. 34, 46

Caecilius Atticus, Q. (before adoption T. Pomponius Atticus)
correspondent of Cicero 42, 98, 112 n.18, 132, 136
daughter married to Agrippa 199 n.71
neutrality in civil war 27, 30 n.67
publication of letters of Cicero 7, 24
Caecilius Metellus Nepos, Q. (*cos.* 57) 22

Caecilius Metellus Pius Scipio Nasica, Q. (*cos.* 52) 7, 20, 21, 26 n.4, 59, 60, 61, 190, 199 n.66
Caecilius Metellus, Q. (*cos.* 60) 183–5
Caesar (the Elder), *see* Julius Caesar, C. (*cos.* 59)
Caesar (the Younger), *see* Octavian (*cos. suff.* 43)
Calpurnius Piso, L. (*cos.* 58) 31 n.81
Calvisius Sabinus, C. (*cos.* 39) 77
Campania 144, 197 n.35
Caninius Rebilus (*cos. suff.* 45) 20, 22
Capua 24, 156
Carthago Nova 117
Cassius Dio 2, 77, 78, 81, 84, 89 n.21, n.29, 90 n.34, 118, 144–6, 151 n.66, 197 n.32
Cassius Longinus, C. (*pr.* 44)
armies
financing 5, 7, 155–6, 157–8
recruiting 88 n.2, 154–5
allied support 101, 107
death 109, 188
legitimacy 75, 88 n.2
prosecuted by Agrippa 125 n.4
Catanean brothers 80
charisma 5, 142, 143, 149 n.28
Chilo 122
Cicero, *see* Tullius Cicero, M. (*cos.* 63)
Cilicia 30 n.73, 97, 98, 102, 103, 104, 105, 106, 107, 108, 114 n.75, 142
Cimbri 66, 67
Cinna, *see* Cornelius Cinna, L. (*cos.* 87)
Claudius Marcellus, C. (*cos.* 50) 17, 118
Claudius Marcellus, C. (*cos.* 49) 118
Claudius Marcellus, M. (*cos.* 51) 17
Claudius Pulcher, Ap. (*cos.* 54) 21, 97
clementia 14, 15, 16, 17, 18, 27 n.27, n.31, n.32, 28 n.38; *see also* Rome
Cleopatra VII 6, 42, 95, 107, 108, 111, 177, 193
Cleopatra Selene 107, 111
clients
individuals 20, 29 n.62, 69, 85, 100, 112 n.32, 120, 146
monarchs and kingdoms 5, 96, 97, 111, 112
Clodius, A. 20
Clodius Pulcher, P. (*tr. pl.* 58) 34, 102
coalition 4, 36, 41–2, 48, 52 n.66, 188
coins
control marks 55, 62, 67, 70 n.4
denominations 55, 61, 66, 69
dies 55, 57, 58, 70 n.23
hoards 57, 59 Table 3.1, 60, 61, 70 n.21, 79, 91 n.53
legends 46, 55, 60, 62, 64, 65, 68, 71 n.41, 73 n.75, 80, 83, 92 n.73, 108, 115 n.98
mint 58, 60, 61, 71 n.33, 90 n.39, 92 n.78
source of gold for Caesar's 60, 71 n.33

types 55, 61, 62, 72 n.63, 78, 81, 90 n.36
IIIviri monetales 4, 58, 61
Commius (Celtic chief) 44
communication
    mandata 16, 19, 20, 22, 23, 24, 27 n.19,
        31 n.81, n.84, n.88
    oral 17, 18, 21, 23, 31 n.84
    sermo 23
    written 13, 18, 23, 24, 31 n.84
conference (*colloquium*) 14, 17, 19, 21, 25, 28 n.42
consilium 22, 30 n.75, 143
contio 19, 24, 39, 42, 50 n.22, 144, 145, 147, 150 n.60
Cordius Rufus, Man. (*IIIvir mon.* 46) 61
Corfinium 6, 15, 18, 27 n.15, n.17, n.19, 28 n.35,
    29 n.50, 30 n.66, 42, 45, 127–40
    passim, 188
Cornelius Balbus, L., the Elder (*cos. suff.* 40) 13, 15,
    16, 18, 19, 21, 22, 24, 27 n.24, 45, 46,
    187
Cornelius Balbus, L., the Younger (*q.* 44) 9, 16,
    9, 100, 180 n.43, 187, 197 n.24
Cornelius Cinna, L. (*cos.* 87) 17, 27 n.34
Cornelius Lentulus Crus, L. (*cos.* 49) 16, 19, 26 n.4, 53 n.90
Cornelius Lentulus Spinther, P. (*cos.* 57) 29 n.51, 139 n.29, 188
Cornelius Sulla (Felix), L. (*cos.* 88)
    allies 99
    armies, financing of 7, 153, 160, 161
    clementia vs *crudelitas* 16–17, 27 n.34,
        28 n.36, n.37, 45, 137; *see also*
        Sullanum regnum
    coinage 60, 63
    constitution 67
    death 167–8
    destruction of Sulmo 135
    dictatorship 54 n.107, 57
    dynast 9
    divine patronage 76, 88 n.10
    iudicare hostes 26 n.3, n.12, 44
    march (first) on Rome 33, 44–5, 168
    model 53 n.90 (Lentulus), 139 n.32
    Proscriptions 7, 45, 170–1
Cornificius, L. (Caesarian general) 125 n.4, 144
Crastinus (centurion) 35–6, 46, 50 n.27, 51 n.29, 188
crudelitas 14, 15–18, 27 n.28, n.31, n.34, 28 n.36, 54 n.103
Curio, *see* Scribonius Curio, C. (*tr. pl.* 50)

Deiotarus (king of Galatia) 95, 98, 99, 100, 102, 104,
    105, 109, 162 n.20
Demochares (admiral of Sex. Pompeius) 144

dignitas
    of Caesar 47, 139 n.29
        linked to LIBERTAS 28, 36, 45, 46, 50 n.217
    of Pompeius 20
diplomacy 4, 6, 14–15, 18, 25, 26 n.11, 29 n.47, n.61
discourse 3, 4, 5, 9, 14, 18, 38–40, 45–7, 49 n.7,
    51 n.39, n.48, 96–7, 100, 110
divine ancestry or filiation 5, 76, 78, 81, 84, 85, 86,
    87, 94 n.109, n.111; 75–94 passim
    ancestry or lineage
        divine genealogy of Antonii 76, 88 n.9, 118
        divine genealogy of Iulii 76, 85, 88 n.11
    lack of
        gens Cornelia 88 n.10
    syncretism of father with deity
        gens Pompeia 81
Domitius Ahenobarbus, L. (*cos.* 54) 6, 22, 30 n.73,
    99, 119, 132, 137, 138 n.18,
    139 n.29, n.31, 140 n.35, 187
Domitius Calvinus, Cn. (*cos.* 53) 34, 194
Dyrrachium 9, 68, 69, 155, 180 n.43

education 111, 122, 195, 200 n.98
Egus (Celtic noble) 100, 109, 144
Egypt 66, 95, 102, 107, 108, 171
elephant 58, 61, 62
embassies 19, 23, 29 n.50, 98
    envoys 13, 18, 19, 20, 22, 23, 24, 29 n.61, 31 n.81,
        140 n.35
    legatus 13, 157
    praefectus fabrum 22
    sons/younger relatives as 19, 23 29 n.61
Epirus 22, 60, 66, 109

false Marius 85
family ties 19, 23, 25
fleets (ships, navy)
    Ahenobarbus 99
    Antonius and Octavian 155–6
    Caesar 17
    Cassius and Brutus 155–6, 158 Table 9.3,
        163 n.24
    numismatic depictions (*denarii* of Q. Nasidius)
        naval battle 78 Fig. 4.1
        ship with a star 79 Fig. 4.2
    Octavian 77–8, 81, 89 n.31
    Sex. Pompeius 77
Fonteius, A. (*tr. mil.*) 147
friendship 6, 16, 19, 20, 22, 29 n.57, 30 n.68, 45, 96,
    97, 101, 110, 117, 118, 119, 122, 123,
    143
    private relations
        amicus 16, 126 n.37
        familaris 20, 21, 29 n.62
        necessarius 20
        necessitudo 19, 29 n.57

Index

rulers
    amicus et socius populi Romani 97, 100, 108
    socius et amicus rex 102
Fulvia (daughter of Bambalio, wife of Clodius, Curio, and Antonius) 93 n.86, 146

Gaul 4, 42, 55, 56, 60, 62, 64, 65, 66, 67, 71 n.38, 72 n.67, 84, 95, 99, 100, 132, 144, 146, 154, 155, 163 n.23, 183, 192
gens (clan) 117, 119; see also divine ancestry/filiation
Gramsci, Antonio 37–8, 40, 51 n.36, n.37, n.39, n.52

Hannibal 17, 22, 168, 170–1
hegemony 5, 36, 37, 38, 39, 40, 41, 47, 51 n.36, 95–115
Herod ('the Great') 6, 9, 11 n.6, 103, 104, 108, 109, 110
Hirtius, A. (*cos*. 43) 21, 35
Hispania Ulterior 19, 187, 188
Hölkeskamp, Karl-Joachim 46, 54 n.106, 88 n.13
homo
    homo militaris 149 n.33
    homo novus 8, 10, 125 n.10, 182, 189, 195, 196, 200 n.98
Horace (Q. Horatius Flaccus) 8, 174, 178 n.16, 182–6, 190–5, 196 n.5, 197 n.16
Hortensius Hortalus, Q. (*cos*. 69) 123, 124, 126 n.37, n.41, n.42, n.46
hostages 14, 101
    obses (pledge) 14, 19, 29 n.60
Hostilius Saserna, L. (*IIIvir mon*. 48) 58, 61, 62
hostis 13, 15, 26 n.3, n.10, n.12, 44, 48, 52 n.79, 53 n.91, 192

ideology 37, 38, 39, 40, 93 n.94
Ilerda 14, 16, 19, 27 n.17, 53 n.82
Illyria 60, 146, 154, 155, 163 n.23
imperator 4, 7, 36, 62, 63, 95, 101, 110, 119, 141, 142, 144, 145, 146, 147, 148
imperatorial acclamations 62, 63, 71 n.43
imperium 13, 42, 75, 84, 88 n.15, 89 n.26, 92 n.75, 96
inimici 13, 16, 17, 21, 43, 47, 52 n.79
inimicitia 6, 100, 101
Italy 4, 6, 128, 136, 138 n.18, 147, 153, 154, 159, 160, 161, 168, 173, 178 n.6, n.16
    allegiance to Octavian (32 BCE) 192–93
    Caesar's invasion (49 BCE) 13, 19, 22, 47, 64, 186
    Cicero's return (57 BCE) 68
    coin hoards 57–8, 70 n.2
    defence of (42–36 BCE) 77, 82, 85
    shield of Aeneas 86
    troops from (49 BCE) 199 n.65
iuventa 120

Juba I (king of Numidia) 63, 66, 95, 100, 105, 110
Juba II (king of Mauretania) 105, 110, 111
Julia (sister of the Dictator) 119, 120, 121
Julius Caesar, C. (*cos*. 59)
    birthday celebration 56–7, 68–9, 73 n.75, n.79, no. 80, n.86
    coinage 4, 55–73 passim
    consulships 62, 67, 68
    date of birth 56–7, 69, 70 n.9
    dictatorship 60
    legionaries of 35–6, 68–9, 141–51 passim, 154–5, 163 n.29
    victories 62–3, 65–6 (with Table 3.2), 72 n.53
    writings
        De bello civili 4, 13–14, 15–17, 18, 19, 21, 26 n.6, 27 n.28, 29 n.48, 33, 35–6, 42–3, 45, 46, 47, 50 n.18, 52 n.72, 53 n.87, 54 n.107, 132, 188
        De bello Gallico 35, 42–3, 66, 171
Junius Brutus, M. (*pr*. 44)
    affairs in the East 97
    allies in the East 101, 109
    armies and finances 5, 7, 154–8 with Tables 9.1, 9.2, 9.3
    extortion via envoys 157
    death 159, 188
    imperium 75, 88 n.2
    prosecuted 125 n.4

Kalyvas, Stathis 1, 33, 49 n.7

Labienus, T. (*pr*. by 59) 25, 52 n.72, 139 n.29, 142, 143, 191
Laclau, Ernesto 4, 36–41, 47
Lavino river 145
laws, legislation
    leges de provocatione 141
    lex agraria Rulli 102
    lex annalis 55, 67, 69
    lex Antonia 70 n.9
    lex Clodia 112
    lex Cornelia de maiestate 64, 67
    lex Gabinia 77, 168
    lex Pedia 75
    lex Titia 75, 105
legitimacy
    allied rulers 104, 105, 106
    contested: Caesar vs Pompeius 4, 5, 6, 35 36, 42, 47
    diplomatic manoeuvres 13–20, 23, 25, 26 n.10
    contested: Sextus vs Octavian 88 n.3, 92 n.74, 94 n.109
    divine-dynastic 75, 76, 81–2, 84–7, 94 n.109, n.111
    officers 141, 143

Index

lenitas 16, 18, 28 n.38, 46
letters, *see also* speeches
    letter-writing 3, 4, 14, 18, 18, 19, 21, 22, 24, 28 n.44, 31 n.89
    in real-time
        letters of Balbus 27 n.24
        letters of Caesar 13, 15, 16, 17, 18, 20, 21, 22, 24, 42, 45–7, 50 n.22, 53 n.96
        letters of Cicero 14, 20, 24, 42, 96, 97, 98, 112 n.15, n.18, 132, 135, 136, 142
        letters of Pollio 188
    in historiography 168, 171, 172, 177 n.5, 178 n.21, 179 n.39
        letter of Mithridates 168, 171–4, 176, 180 n.44
        letter of Pompey 8, 24, 168, 172, 173
libertas/LIBERTAS 4, 35, 36, 39, 44, 45, 46, 50 n.23, n.27, 51 n.48, 53 n.93, 168, 188, 189, 191, 198 n.53, 199 n.61
Licinius Crassus, M. (*cos.* 70) 21, 22, 30 n.72, 102, 162 n.14
Luca 21, 30 n.73, n.74, 156
Luceria 17, 28 n.36
ludi (games, i.e. festivities or spectacles)
    ludi Apollinares 57
    ludi Victoriae Caesaris 83, 85, 94 n.106
Lutatius Catulus, Q. (*cos.* 102) 67

Macedonia 20, 29 n.50, 69 n.2, 88 n.2, 100, 117, 119, 154, 162 n.18, 173, 189, 194, 198 n.54
magister equitum 84, 92 n.78, 192
Magius, n. (*praefectus fabrum*) 16, 22, 27 n.19
mandata (verbal instructions or orders) 16, 19, 20, 22, 23, 24, 27 n.19, 31 n.81, n.84, n.88
Manilius, the *Astronomica* of 120, 121
Marcia 123, 124, 126 n.37, n.41, n.42, n.46
Marcius Philippus, L. (*cos.* 91) 168, 178 n.5
Marcius Philippus, L. (*cos.* 56) 6, 122, 123, 124, 126 n.42, 168
Marius, Gaius (*cos.* 107) 9, 55, 66, 67, 143, 163 n.36; *see also* false Marius
Mark Anthony, *see* Antonius, M. (*cos.* 44)
Mars 85, 86, 94 n.104, n.106, 121
Massalia 99, 101
Messina, Strait of 77, 78, 81, 90 n.47
Metellus, *see* Caecilius Metellus, Q. (*cos.* 60)
military expenditure, *see* armies
military recruitment, *see* armies
Misenum, Treaty of 81, 91 n.56
Mithridates the Great (king of Pontus) 8, 102, 103, 105, 113 n.48, 153, 167–80 passim
Mithridates of Pergamum 102, 103, 106, 107
Morstein-Marx, Robert 3, 11 n.7, 26 n.1, 35, 39, 40, 45, 50 n.24
Mouffe, Chantal 36, 38, 39, 40, 41, 51 n.39

Munda (battle) 54 n.107, 57, 63, 91 n.50, 162 n.15
Mutina (battle) 69, 75, 84, 91 n.66, 155, 159, 160

names
    nomen 119
    praenomen 118
Nasidius, Q. (*praef. class.* 44) 78 fig. 4.1, 79 fig. 4.2, 90 n.39
Naulochus (battle) 146
naumachia 77
negotiation 3, 4, 13–32 passim, 43, 44, 99, 107
    face-to-face 4, 22, 30 n.77
Neptune 76–82, 87, 88 n.15, 89 n.17, 90 n.34, n.42, 91 n.51, n.56
    offerings to 76, 88 n.14
nodal points 39, 45, 47
normative inversion 8, 167, 169–71, 176; *see also* 'Other'/'Othering'
novus homo, *see* homo novus

Octavian (*cos. suff.* 43)
    and allies 95, 103–4, 105–6, 110–11
    armies, finances of 155–61
    armies, leadership of 146–7
    clementia vs *crudelitas* 27 n.31
    coinage 82–3, 85, 92 n.70, n.73
    destruction of Perusia 186
    dynastic ambitions / divine filiation 5, 82–7, 92 n.70, n.76, n.81, 93 n.95, 94 n.104, n.106
    evolution of name 92 n.76, 93 n.89, 94 n.110
    Forum of Augustus 93 n.94, n.103
    march on Rome 168, 171
    parallels with Sextus Pompeius 75–94 passim
    political relations
        and Agrippa 6, 117–26 passim
        and M. Antonius 84–5, 101, 103, 104, 105, 106, 109, 146, 192–4
        and Asinius Pollio 192–3, 195
        and Caesar 82, 117, cf. 69
        and Cicero 75, 93 n.89, 199 n.71
        and Lepidus 84, 92 n.81, 93 n.92
        and Sextus Pompeius 77–8, 82, 87, 93 n.92, 94 n.110
    proscriptions 10, 157, 159, 160, 170, 192
    triumphs / victories 176
    Triumvir 75, 91 n.66, 145, 176
    writings
        autobiography 194
        Deeds of the Divine Augustus 188
Octavius, C. (*pr.* 61) 119
Ofilius 146, 147
Oppius, C. 13, 15, 18, 19, 22, 24, 45
ordo equester 15, 147
Oricum 22, 25, 27 n.17, 30 n.80, 42
Otacilius (Pompeian naval commander) 17, 25

Index

'Other'/'Othering' 4, 14 ,15, 18, 167, 172; *see also* normative inversion

Paeligni 119, 129
patron-client relationship
    allied monarchs and communities 97, 99, 105, 193
    celebration of patron's birthday 69
    freedmen 119
    patronatus vs 'patronage' 96, 170
    ritual of *salutatio* 97, 146
    similar category among Celts 112 n.32
peace 2, 4, 13, 14, 19, 20, 22, 23, 24, 25, 26 n.6, 29 n.59, 31 n.88, 42, 43, 81, 136, 189, 193, 194, 196 n.5
Perusia 8, 10, 168, 186, 196, 197 n.35
Petreius, M. (*pr.* by 63) 14, 17, 25, 29 n.51, 31 n.94, 43, 44, 149 n.33
Phalaris (tyrant of Akragas) 17
Pharnaces (king of Pontus) 5, 63, 102, 103, 105
Pharsalus (battle) 16, 33, 35, 46, 50 n.27, 68, 69 n.2, 84, 101, 102, 107, 109, 144, 150 n.53, 154, 155, 162 n.15, 188, 192
Philippi (battle) 7, 10, 27 n.31, 86, 94 n.103, 101, 104, 109, 145, 147, 150 n.47, 154–5, 156, 157, 159, 161, 162 n.15, 193, 198 n.47
pietas/Pietas 62, 80, 90 n.43, n. 44, 91 n.50, 168
Pistoia (battle) 49 n.3
Placentia (mutiny) 144
Plutarch (L. Mestrius Plutarchus) 8, 9, 11 n.6, 29 n.61, 30 n.74, 34, 50 n.25, n.27, 57, 65, 66, 69, 72 n.53, 89 n.26, 108, 123, 126 n.37, 126 n.46, 144, 154, 157, 159, 162 n.14, 164 n.41, 175, 184, 186, 187, 195, 196, 197 n.26, 198 n.48
Pompeius Magnus, Cn. (*cos.* 70)
    and allies 97–102, 105, 107, 109
    armies 153, 154, 157, 164 n.41
    coinage 58 Table 3.1, 60, 71 n.25, n.33
    crudelitas 17, 28 n.36
    death 195
    house 114 n.82
    and Mithridates VI 167–80 passim
    negotiations in 49–48 BCE 15–17, 19, 20, 21, 22–4, 25,
    and *populus Romanus* 34–5, 42, 43, 44, 45, 46, 47
    and sea 77–81, 89 n.25, n.26
    and sons, *see* Pompeius Magnus, Cn. (son) and Pompeius, Sex.
    third triumph 65, 68, 89 n.26
Pompeius Magnus, Cn. (elder son of preceding)
Pompeius Magnus Pius, Sex. (*cos. des.* 35)
    coinage 78–81, 90 n.39
    in imperial narratives 76–7 (Florus), 77 (Cassius Dio), 77–8 (Appian), 89 n.16 (Florus), n.17, 90 n.34, 91 n.56
    modern reappraisals 1, 78, 82, 91 n. 51, n.58, 177
    name, evolution of 90 n.43, 94 n.110
    paternity 5, 75–82 passim, figs. 4.1, 4.2
        divine 76–82
        human 75–6, 78–81
    parallels with Octavian 82, 87
    praefectus classis et orae maritimae 75, 77, 81, figs. 4.3, 4.4
    sacrifice to Neptune 76, 90 n.34
    victory in 42 BCE 77
    victory in 38 BCE 77–8
pontifex maximus 63, 84, 92 n.73, n.81
Pontus 66, 102, 103, 105, 162 n.20
populus 24, 34, 35, 42, 43, 45, 46, 47, 48, 52 n.75, n.78, 98, 99, 135
Porcius Cato, M., the Elder (*cos.* 195) 189, 195, 198 n.60, 200 n.98
Porcius Cato, M., the Younger (*pr.* 54) 123–4, 126 n.37, n.46, 142, 162 n.14, 190–1, 199 n.69, n.70
prefects
    praefectus equitum 144
    praefectus fabrum 22
    praefectus orae maritimae 5, 75, 77, 81
    praefectus urbi 82
privatus 21, 30 n.71
Proscriptions 7, 10, 17, 28 n.36, 44, 45, 89 n.19, 137, 153, 157, 159, 160, 164 n.59, 170, 192
Ptolemy XI 102
Ptolemy XII Auletes 42, 97, 102
Ptolemy XIII 42, 107, 199 n.64
Ptolemy XIV 107
Ptolemy XV Caesarion 115 n.98
Ptolemy of Cyprus 102
Pupius, L. (centurion) 27 n.17

Raaflaub, Kurt A. 4, 35, 36, 41, 42, 46, 48, 52 n.66, 54 n.113, 68
Ravenna 21, 30 n.73
reconciliation 4, 11 n.4, 13, 15, 16, 24, 26 n.6, 30 n.75, 44, 48
res publica 15, 17, 22, 26 n.2, 34, 42, 43, 46, 52 n.76, 98, 99, 101, 168, 177
Rome
    Atrium Libertatis 189–90, 194, 198 n.57, 199 n.61
    Fora
        Forum Iulium 1, 93 n.94, 189
        Forum of Augustus 85, 86, 93 n.94
        Forum Romanum 84, 192
    houses
        of Antonius 114 n.82, 146

Index

of Curio 35
of Octavia 110
of Philippus 123–4
Temples
    Clementia, Temple of 28 n.39
    Mars Ultor, Temple of 86, 94 n.103
    Salus, Temple of 69
Romulus 85, 86, 87, 94 n.104, n.106
Roscius Fabatus, L. (*pr.* 49) 23–4, 31 n.81
Roucillus (Celtic noble) 100, 144
Rubicon 60, 145, 186, 187

sacrificial tools 62, 71 n.38
Sallust (C. Sallustius Crispus (*pr.* 46)) 7, 8, 10, 28, 167–80 passim
  career as Caesarian 171, 182
  novus homo 8, 10, 182
  writings:
    Catiline 39, 49 n.3, 149 n.33, 191
    Histories 8, 27 n.27, 167–77 passim, 182
      category confusion 176
      death of Spartacus 175
      letter of Mithridates to Arsaces 168, 171–6
      letter of Pompeius to Senate 168, 172–3
      meta-historical critique 173, 175–6
      use of Mithridates as *alter ego* 172
      vindication, idea of 174–5
    Jugurtha 49 n.3, 139 n.29
Salvidienus Rufus, Q. (Caesarian general) 77, 89 n.21, 90 n.45, 117
Sardinia 21, 91 n.54
Scipio, *see* Caecilius Metellus Pius Scipio Nasica, Q. (*cos.* 52)
Scribonius Curio, C. (*tr. pl.* 50) 17, 27 n.32, 35, 44, 54 n.112, 100, 190, 199 n.65
Scribonius Libo, L. (*cos.* 34) 20, 22, 23, 29 n.51
Scylla 80, 81, 90 n.47, n.48
Scyllaeum, *see* Messina, Strait of
sea, control of 76–81, 87, 88 n.14, 89 n.17, n. 26, 90 n.45, n.48
Second Triumvirate, *see* Triumvirate
senatus consultum ultimum (*SCU*) 3, 13, 14, 15, 19, 23, 26 n.2, n.10, 53 n.91
Sertorius, Q. (*pr.* 85?) 153, 168, 172, 175, 179 n.30
Servilia (mother of Brutus) 1, 22, 30 n.75
Sestius (*tr. pl.* 57) 24, 31 n.87
Sicily 61, 77, 78, 80, 81, 89 n.19, n.29, n.31, 90 n.39, n. 43, 91 n.54, 161, 199 n.65
sidus Iulium 83, 85, 86, 93 n.101
Spain 22, 27 n.17, n.19, 43, 60, 63, 65, 66, 69 n.2, 72 n.67, 82, 99, 101, 111, 113 n.42, 117, 153, 154, 168, 172, 179 n.30, 187, 190, 198 n.46

Spartacus 8, 172, 175
speeches, *see also* letters 3, 4, 7, 39, 50 n.25, 52 n.69, 54 n.107, 168, 177 n.5, 178 n.21, 179 n.32, n.33
speech of Philippus 16, 178 n.5
Sulla, *see* Cornelius Sulla, L. (*cos.* 88)
Sullanum regnum 17, 28 n.36
Sulpicius Rufus, Ser. (*cos.* 51) 19, 20, 25, 29 n.59, 30 n.67
supplicatio 63, 71 n.43
Syme, Ronald (Sir) 39, 40, 91 n.58, 93 n.87, 94 n.110, 114 n.75, 177 n.5, 181–2

Tacitus (P. Cornelius Tacitus (*cos. suff.* 97 CE)) 178 n.8, 180 n.45, 182, 183, 184, 196, 197 n.19, n.35
Tarcondimotus 98, 103, 105, 108, 110
taxes 7, 157, 158, 160, 161, 164 n.41
Terentius Varro, M. (*pr.* ca. 75) 19, 20, 187, 190, 199 n.62, n.63, 29 n.54, n.55
Teutons 56, 66, 67
Thapsus (battle) 147, 162 n.15
'The People' 33–54 passim, esp. 36, 37, 41, 45, 48
Thessaly 60, 66, 154, 159
Torquatus, L. (*pr.* by 49) 27 n.17
trauma 167–80 passim
  cultural 167, 169, 170, 178 n.15
  experiences
    atrocities (Triumviral) 170–1, 173
    cannibalism at Alesia 171
    theft of territory in the East 175
    torture 175
  healing process
    normative inversion 167, 176
    literature as therapy 169
  theory 3, 169, 177 n.1
    Alexander, Jeffrey 169
    Assmann, Jan 170
    Caruth, Cathy 169
    Eckert, Alexandra 170–1
    Erickson, Kai 170
    Freud, Sigmund 169, 178 n.9
tribe
  ethnic-political group
    Gauls 65 with Table 3.2, 66, 72 n.53, 112 n.32
    Romans 119
    Spanish 179 n.30
  metaphorical (grammarians) 174
triumph 63, 65, 66, 68, 69 n.2, 82, 89 n.26, 110, 118, 143, 177, 179 n.30, 193, 194, 199 n.66, n.69
Triumvirate (M. Aemilius Lepidus, M. Antonius, Octavian)

Index

Triumviral period 2, 19, 28 n.44, 29 n.61, 30 n.77, 31 n.92, 109, 135, 167, 168, 169, 170, 173, 176, 177 n.1, 178 n.7
Triumvirate 92 n.74, 155, 168, 183
Triumvirs 8, 75, 81, 88 n.9, 91 n.66, 155, 156, 157, 159, 161, 167, 171, 172, 175, 176, 177, 190, 194
Trojan ancestry/genealogy 76, 86, 88 n.8, 94 n.107
trophy 55, 65, 66, 69 n.2, 71 n.38, 72 n.63, 90 n.48
Tullius Cicero, M. (*cos.* 63)
   and Asinius Pollio 188–9, 191–2, 196
   and Caesar 16, 27 n.33, n.34, 178 n.19
   and D. Brutus 69
   and M. Antonius 92 n.85
   and Octavian 75, 93 n.89
   and Pompeius 20, 24, 28 n.36, 135, 138 n.18
   death 191–2, 196
   family
      daughter Tullia 69
      son Marcus (*cos. suff.* 30) 150 n.53, 199 n.71, 200 n.98
   governor of Cilicia 97–8, 112 n.18, 142, 154
   historical memory 174
   language of
      barbarorum adventus 27 n.33
      clementia 28 n.39
      crudelitas 27 n.34, 28 n.36, 46
      hostis 15
      virtus 149 n.31
   negotiations in 49 BCE 20, 23–4, 25, 29 n.59, 31 n.87, n.88, 46
   writings
      letters 27 n.24, 30 n.78, 42, 112 n.18, 135, 138 n.18, 140 n.34, 158, 188–9
      speeches 96, 99–100, 102
      treatises 7, 96–7, 200 n.98
Tullius Cicero, Q. (*pr.* 62) 183

Valerius Maximus 170–1, 187
Valerius Messalla Corvinus, M. (*cos.* 31) 68
Valerius Messalla Rufus, M. (*cos.* 53) 34, 123
Vatinius, P. (*cos.* 47) 25
Velitrae 119
Venetia 119
Ventidius Bassus, P. (*cos. suff.* 43) 115 n.92
Venus 55, 61, 71 n.38, 76, 83, 85, 86, 87, 88 n.10, n.11, 93 n.94, 94 n.104, n.105
Vergil (P. Vergilius Maro) 81, 86, 93 n.95, 178 n.8, 183, 195
Vesta 55, 71 n.38, 92 n.81
Vibullius Rufus, L. (*praef. fabr.*) 27 n.17, n.19
victoria 16, 18, 28 n.43
Vipsanius Agrippa, M. (*cos.* 37) 5, 6, 101, 110, 117–26 passim, 199 n.71
   accompanies Octavian in Spain (45 BCE) 117–18
   divided family loyalties 5, 6, 122–4
   early acquaintance with Octavian 120–2
   and Eastern allies 101, 110
   existence of older brother 118–19
   married to Caecilia Attica 199 n.71
   moderation 118
   origins 119–20
   prosecutor of C. Cassius (43) 125 n.4
Vipsanius, L. (father of Agrippa) 118
Vipsanius, L. (?) (brother of Agrippa) 5, 6, 117–26 passim
   Lucius likely *praenomen* 5, 6, 118
voluntas 45, 46, 47, 54 n.100
Volusenus Quadratus, C. (*tr. mil.*) 144, 150 n.52
Vulteius Capito, C. (*tr. mil.*) 144

war economy 7, 153, 157, 160, 161, 165 n.77
Wiseman, T. Peter 28 n.41, 29 n.61, 42, 43, 88 n.13, 119, 120